The Influence of Sea Power upon History
1660-1805

Alfred Thayer Mahan
The Influence of Sea Power upon History
1660-1805

Prentice–Hall Inc.,
Englewood Cliffs, N.J.
A Bison Book

First US Edition published by
Prentice-Hall, Inc.,
Englewood Cliffs
New Jersey 07632

Produced by Bison Books Limited
4 Cromwell Place London SW7

Library of Congress Catalog
Card Number: 79-89594

ISBN 0 13 464537 5

Printed in Hong Kong

Captions writer: Antony Preston
Cartographer: Richard Natkiel
Designer: Mike Wade
Editor: Stephanie Lindsay
Indexer: Don Slater

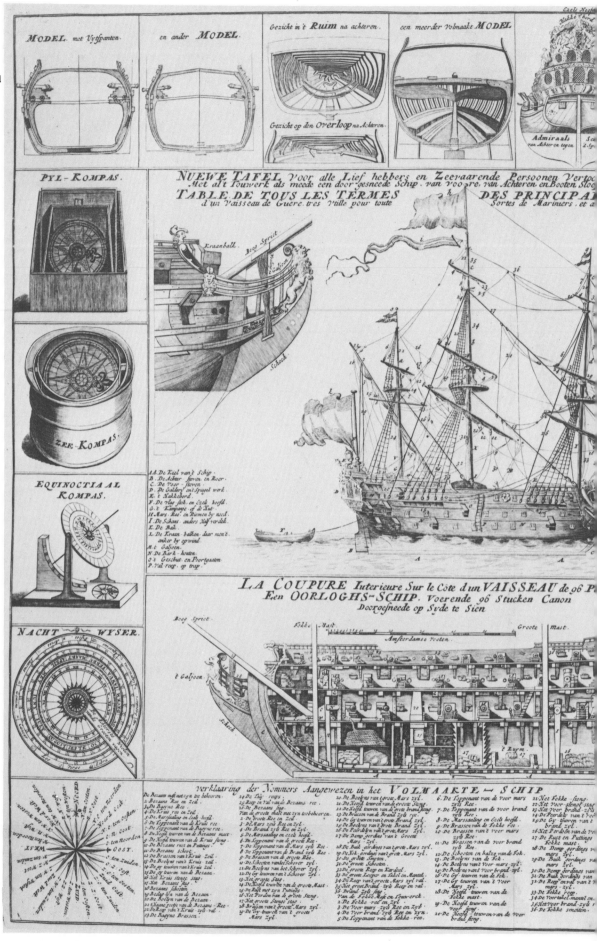

p 1: *A captain, by T Rowlandson, c 1800.*

p 2-3: *Lord Rodney's victory over the French fleet off Dominica 1782, by Robert Dodd.*

p 4-5: *Engraving of a 96-gun warship, by Pieter Schenk, c 1680.*

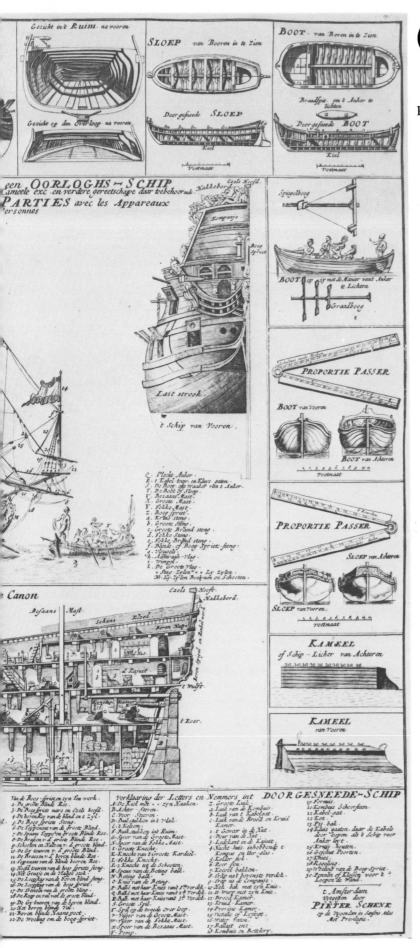

Contents

Introduction

by Antony Preston

Alfred Thayer Mahan suffered more than his fair share of adulation, which was followed by discrediting, debunking and oblivion, the normal progression for most literary authorities. Why this shy naval officer-turned historian and lecturer should have run the whole gamut of public fickleness is in itself a question worth asking. In his day Mahan has even been blamed for starting the First World War, while his defenders claim that he was some sort of Delphic oracle, whose writings contain all the clues to the future.

To understand the impact of Mahan and his work one must understand both the state of the world in the last decades of the nineteenth century and the state of military historical writing. As John Keegan has shown in his penetrating analysis *The Face of Battle*, the art of military history only developed as a serious academic study in the second half of the nineteenth century. If the historians of land warfare took so long to marshal their thoughts it can be imagined that the much smaller numbers of naval historians were even slower to make themselves heard. Naval history has always been a minority interest. Even Great Britain, a country steeped in maritime affairs, has no chair of naval history in its universities, and with the exception of the United States, other countries show even less concern to advance this highly complex academic discipline.

The reason lay partly in the nineteenth century obsession with the 'decisive' nature of battles first advanced by Sir Edward Creasy in 1851. If the great naval battles of the eighteenth century had decided anything at all it was that the Royal Navy had triumphed over all its adversaries and had thereby guaranteed Great Britain an apparently unassailable position in the world. Did this phenomenon really warrant any analysis? Secure in their belief that God was an English gentleman, English historians were content to chronicle the battles and wrangle over the finer points of tactics, while the French remained almost mute on the subject as they had so many humiliations to forget.

The attitude inside the naval profession was even worse. Captain Roskill reminds us that when in 1873 the Royal Navy set up its first naval college in Greenwich, J K Laughton had to ask permission to have history added to the curriculum, as it had never been taught previously. The apotheosis of the British tradition was Trafalgar, but if naval officers learned anything from studying the battle it was no more than Nelson's rousing slogan, 'Engage the enemy more closely.'

There was an endeavor to work out tactics suited to the new age of breech-loading guns and steam propulsion, but this was understandably hindered by the lack of concrete examples. We who have lived in this violent century cannot imagine what it was like to live in the 1880s, when people who talked of the Great War meant the 20-year conflict between Great Britain and France. Naval actions between 1815 and 1890 could be counted on the fingers of one hand and none of them could be called decisive. Navarino had been a yardarm-to-yardarm affair like Trafalgar, Sinope had been nothing but a massacre of a small Turkish squadron by a much larger Russian force, and Lissa, 1866, was as much the result of Italian ineptitude as any tactical skill on the Austrian side. The small actions produced even more bizarre results, such as the Battle of Yucatan, in which two Texan wooden sailing brigs defeated a Mexican squadron, not only steam-powered but armed with the same sort of shell-guns which destroyed the Turks at Sinope. Small wonder that the would-be naval analyst was baffled.

If tactical and strategic analysis was in the doldrums the same could not be said for technical progress. Before the Napoleonic Wars were over the British and the Americans were experimenting with steam engines, and Robert Fulton had built his submarine *Nautilus*. Submarines had to wait another 80 years before they became a workable proposition but the Royal Navy took the plunge in 1821, when it ordered its first class of small paddle-warships. Despite a grinding parsimony and public apathy, important research was done in Britain into screw propellers and iron hulls, with the result that the first propeller-driven ship of the line went to sea in 1846. Progress was rapid in other fields too, with iron hulls and many varieties of steam engines not only proposed but built for the Royal Navy.

The major bugbear of this early period was the shell-gun. Not a new invention, it had been adapted by the Frenchman Paixhans from the older mortar, and by combining an exploding hollow canister with the comparative accuracy and penetration of the long smooth-bore gun it gave ships much greater destructive power. By 1853 it was claimed that wooden ships of the line were nothing but 'eggshells armed with hammers' and it was confidently predicted that a future fleet action like Trafalgar would last less than half an hour because of the colossal destruction by shells bursting in wooden hulls. Although the Russians took several hours to finish off a puny Turkish squadron at Sinope and the Texans fought the modern Mexican squadron to a standstill the theorists were unanimous in their opinions.

The Crimean War did little to enlighten them. True, the British and French showed that iron armor was the answer to the menace of the shell, but there was nothing more exciting than a few bombardments to provide evidence or any new doctrines. For years there was great enthusiasm for shallow-draughted ships of every description, and this was sustained by the essentially river and coastal operations of the Civil War (in which Mahan served first as lieutenant and then as lieutenant commander). The highlight of the naval war was the fight between the *Monitor* and *Merrimack* at Hampton Roads, but for all its novelty it was as inconclusive as the others. The Battle of Lissa in 1866 fulfilled all the criteria for a decisive battle, with the Italian fleet routed by the smaller but more determined Austrian fleet, but its only influence on tactics was to set theorists on a new craze for ramming, an obsession which took 30 years to subside.

Lissa was to be the last battle in the Western Hemisphere for 32 years, a period in which naval technology began to accelerate at increasing speed. Although officers like Colomb in England tried to grapple with the bewildering implications of higher speed, greater maneuverability, all-round arcs of fire, bigger guns and finally the torpedo, there was a growing feeling that science and technical advance had made history irrelevant. Also as so often happens, convincing reasons were conjured up to justify this skepticism. To cite one very important example: the need to protect commerce by convoying shipping, demonstrated vividly in the Napoleonic Wars, was rapidly abandoned because it had not been used in the American Civil War, and the lack of endurance of warships was then cited as a reason for not convoying. With touching naïveté the Great Powers had abolished privateering (in other words, private enterprise commerce-raiding), and this was assumed to provide a guarantee against indiscriminate destruction of shipping.

All the while, the expanding heavy industries of Europe, Great Britain and the United States were able to feed the world's navies with bigger ships and more effective armaments. By the end of the 1880s the conflicting arguments about future trends in ship-design had resolved themselves and the outlines of the modern battleship, cruiser and destroyer were broadly determined. Thereafter the acceleration took the form of bigger ships, better armor and more powerful guns, but above all the increasing production of steel made it possible to build fleets. Countries which lacked the heavy industry had no difficulty in buying ships from the major industrial nations, so that the last two decades of the nineteenth century saw an enormous expansion of naval strength throughout the world. To complicate matters these big ships made a powerful impression on a public which was more aware of them than any previous generation, thanks to newspapers and growing literacy. Increasingly, battle fleets came to be identified, in the eyes of the public, with national prestige and power, and relative strengths were calculated in numbers of battleships. It was an age of strident chauvinism: 'We've got the ships, we've got the men, we've got the money too,' was the cry. The spirit of Jingoism was rampant in England, but it was matched in other countries, a reflection of the tensions which underlay that seemingly tranquil century.

People at all levels, in both civilian and military life, were thus acutely aware of the potential of naval power, and ready to hear the authentic voice of prophecy. This is the reason for the astounding impact of Mahan's ideas when they got into print. His lucidly argued theses were exactly the explanation and justification needed for the events of the previous decades. It was a period of colonial expansion by the European Powers, and by definition overseas possessions meant sea communications. This in turn meant vulnerability to attack by sea, a constant worry to the British in particular.

The influence of history upon Mahan was hardly accidental. His father, Professor Dennis Mahan, was a noted authority on field fortifications and siege warfare, and it is obvious that his son was reared in an atmosphere of erudition and methodical study. Even so, the first opportunity came by accident. In 1876 the 36-year old Commander Mahan was put on furlough pay (the traditional half-pay dreaded by eighteenth-century naval officers) as part of a general rundown of the US Navy's strength. Like others before him Mahan took his family to France, where the cost of living was a lighter burden on his purse. For the

first time he had an urge to write, although this first took the form of a dilettante interest in the architecture of cathedrals, and was unsuccessful.

A year later he returned to the United States to take over the Ordnance Department at the Naval Academy, and it is hardly surprising that the atmosphere of Annapolis stirred him to write on naval matters. In 1878 his essay on 'Naval Education for Officers and Men' won third prize in the Naval Institute's annual essay prize competition. Its honorable mention was well deserved, for it contained two perceptive observations. The first was that the age of intake should be low in order to get boys of good native ability whose formal education was possibly inferior to boys from more privileged backgrounds. The second was that too much academic study and theoretical

Above: *Captain Alfred Thayer Mahan USN (1840–1914) at the height of his reputation.*

work would make sea-officers cautious, trusting in formulae rather than personal judgments.

Mahan's tenure of the Ordnance Department seems to have been happy, for he was free from financial worries and was surrounded by all the inspiration he could want, as well as the sources. In 1880 he was transferred to run the Navigation Department of New York Navy Yard, a device to avoid going on half-pay once again, but it had no noticeable effect on his growing interest in historical analysis. His scholarly reputation in the Navy was sufficiently established for Scribner's to approach him in 1881 to write the *Gulf and Inland Waters* volume in their naval history of the Civil War.

A short period of sea-duty followed as commanding officer of the *Wachusett*, but in the summer of 1884 he received an invitation from Captain Stephen B Luce to become a lecturer in history and tactics at the Naval War College. Luce's influence on Mahan cannot be over-estimated, for he prepared the ground by his sympathetic attitude; in addition to founding the Naval War College he had himself realized that a systematic study of naval history must precede any attempt to formulate doctrines for the future. His letters and essays on the subject show how broad his outlook was, but above all he deserves credit for identifying the spark of genius in his former executive officer. When Luce left to command the North Atlantic Squadron in 1886 he was able to ensure that the post of President went to Mahan, giving him the prestige needed to give maximum effect to his teachings.

The Influence of Sea Power upon History 1660–1783 was based on Mahan's lectures at the War College, and if contemporary accounts are to be believed, their impact was dramatic. Luce is said to have been searching for a 'naval Jomini' to give form to the rising tide of intellectual curiosity, and at the end of the session the Commodore rose to his feet, exclaiming that his Jomini had been found, and that his name was Mahan. Given the sterility and poverty of ideas that had gone before, the enthusiasm is easily understood. Mahan started his lectures by giving a comprehensive idea of the factors which affected the maritime strength of a nation and then went on to show how naval warfare was subject to principles of warfare, just like land warfare. After chaos and uncertainty, law and order is always refreshing.

One of the most appealing attributes of Mahan as a lecturer was his ability to elucidate the problem with brilliant analogies drawn from events. His method was to work from the narrative to the deduction, rather than the other way round, and this, combined with a superb grasp of the telling phrase and the elegant epigram, made his work uniquely exciting. He was the first to grasp the concept of Sea Power, that amorphous benefit which flows from Command of the Sea. Mahan showed how Sea Power was able to interact with apparently unrelated events on land, and how it could even exert a decisive influence over those events. The promise of his first book was more than justified by its sequel, *The Influence of Sea Power upon the French Revolution and Empire 1793–1812*, which appeared two years later, in 1892. By switching from the broad but varied canvas of the seventeenth and eighteenth centuries to the clash between the Royal Navy at its most brilliant and the forces of the Revolution and Napoleon, Mahan could demonstrate his arguments with much greater force.

It was the second book which contained that inspired phrase, which enshrined everything that Mahan had to say: 'Those far-distant storm-beaten ships upon which the Grand Army never looked, stood between it and the dominion of the world.' The British had not been unduly ecstatic about his first volume but this masterly dissection of how their hero Nelson and his band of brothers had accomplished the downfall of France caused an extraordinary upsurge of enthusiasm.

Professor Laughton reviewed the book enthusiastically and the well-known navalist Thomas Gibson Bowles wrote to Mahan begging to be considered as a personal disciple and friend. As we have already seen the moment was propitious, with the influential and vociferous already converted to the cause of naval expansion. The Kaiser ordered Mahan's books to be bought for ship's and training schools' libraries, while even

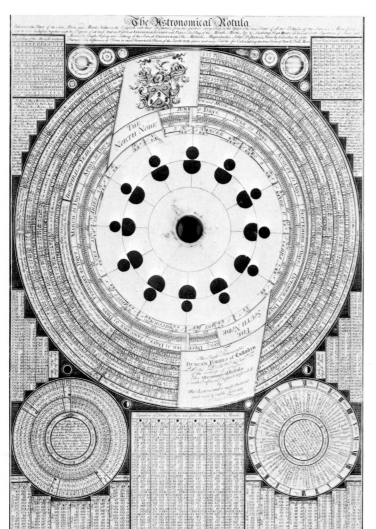

Above: *A celestial planisphere.*

Left: *An astronomical rotula. The eighteenth century was the Golden Age of sail because of the enormous improvement in timekeeping and navigation as much as any technical innovations in ship design. Old navigational aids such as the astronomical rotula and celestial planisphere were replaced by the sextant and the accurate chart.*

Right: *Theodore Roosevelt, the most influential supporter of Mahan's ideas.*

the landward-looking German General Staff was heard quoting his ideas. In the words of Baron von Lüttwitz, 'We must be so strong at sea, that no nation which feels itself safe from our military power, may dare to overlook us in partition negotiations, and there is no time to be lost.' Sentiments like this, uttered in England and Germany in great profusion, accounted for the blame heaped on Mahan for encouraging the great naval race between Germany and Great Britain. The charge does not stand up to close investigation. Anglo-German rivalry had much deeper roots than that, and the loss of stability in international affairs which became so noticeable in the 1890s cannot be blamed on two works of naval history. Mahan's popularity was a symptom rather than a cause, but it is fair to say that his arguments helped to convince key figures such as the Kaiser, and gave form and respectability to their arguments.

The great impact of Mahan's ideas in the United States was undoubtedly helped by his personal friendship with Theodore Roosevelt. The two men met five years after Roosevelt had written his polemic on the War of 1812, when he lectured at the War College on the same subject. When the Cleveland administration tried to abolish the War College in 1893 it was Roosevelt and his friends who fought the battle for Mahan and Luce outside the Navy. Again it was Roosevelt who helped Mahan when in 1894 his flag-officer submitted an unfavorable fitness report. Thanks to Roosevelt's political connections, a squalid affair inspired by professional jealousy was stamped on before it could affect Mahan's naval career adversely.

When Roosevelt became Assistant Secretary of the Navy in 1897 he confided freely in Mahan in return for advice on strategic matters, and this continued when be became Vice-President in 1900 and then President on McKinley's death. Mahan was thus uniquely placed to influence the US Navy's transition from an antiquated coastal-defense force to a major fleet capable of meeting any other navy on an equal footing. It is no coincidence that within two years of his death the United States began its first building program intended to achieve a navy 'second to none.' That dream was not fulfilled but the Two-Ocean Navy planned in 1940 was just as much a part of the legacy of Mahan's advice to his political friends.

The United States clearly listened to Mahan's advice, but to a later generation of students it seems that some of Mahan's most ardent disciples elsewhere hardly bothered to read his books, or had certainly not understood very clearly what he was trying to say. This was partly a result of his seductive style, with its rhetoric and vivid allusions. As Herbert Rosinski pointed out, Mahan regarded theory as entirely subordinate to history. Although he developed the concept of Sea Power and defined its principles he was less willing to try to analyze the whole structure of naval warfare. In other words, what he did not say was as important as anything that he did say. This was not a reflection on Mahan's scholarship but a result of being so far ahead of contemporary thought. He appears to have been groping toward some sort of analysis in his later work, but it is wholly unsystematic.

In a very perceptive essay published in *Brassey's Annual* in 1941 Herbert Rosinski drew attention to the problems inherent in taking Mahan's work too literally. What Mahan meant by Sea Power was something slightly different—*Superior* Sea Power—for he was talking about the Royal Navy with its great preponderance over the French and Dutch. Sea warfare differs fundamentally from land warfare in that the inferior belligerent is utterly helpless, no matter how many minor actions his navy can win. This was a lesson first learned, ironically, by the Americans. Twice they fought successfully against the British but each time the last battle went to their opponents. De Grasse won the Battle of the Virginia Capes but his defeat at the Battle of the Saints in 1782 deprived the Americans of Canada; the brilliant frigate actions of the War of 1812 were followed by the destruction of American seaborne trade and the burning of Washington.

A major problem of Sea Power is the indivisibility of the sea, which means that there cannot be partial control of it; it has no frontier to be defended and no natural features to strengthen the defense. Mahan grasped this when he said that it must be a fundamental principle to assure defense by means of offense. This was not as trite as it sounds, for command of the sea can only be guaranteed by destroying or neutralizing hostile forces in that sea. Once that command of the sea is established the weaker side is totally excluded from it, and although sporadic raids can be mounted against the superior power they can never be more than pinpricks.

Mahan's critics maintain that he overreached himself by claiming too much for Sea Power, and by confusing commercial domination of the sea with military control of it. There is some truth in this accusation, although it lies more in the uncritical and even unscrupulous use made of his ideas by his disciples. 'Mahanism' became a valuable propaganda tool in the hands of navalists in many countries, and Mahan himself was not above pontificating on contemporary power politics to some extent. He gave his blessing to the acquisition of colonies and espoused the building of a strong American battle fleet, but these were the status symbols of a world power in the late nineteenth century, and one feels now that this may have been Mahan the patriotic naval officer speaking rather than Mahan the historian. Such was his prestige that even the most insignificant utterance was pounced on as a pearl of wisdom.

The Germans showed the worst tendency, out of all the naval powers, to misinterpret and misunderstand Mahan, despite paying such lip-service. Tirpitz was obsessed with Mahan's dictum that commercial dominance had to be backed by military superiority, and believed that Great Britain would use her Navy to crush German trade rivalry. Whereas a modest increase in naval strength would have been sufficient to give security from France and Russia, an undeniable necessity in purely military terms, he felt that a huge fleet would be necessary to guard Germany's commercial interests; the overseas trade and colonial possessions which she had so recently gained. This resulted in the hideous dilemma of having to outbuild the world's biggest shipbuilding nation and to outstrip the most successful navy, which happened to sit astride Germany's overseas communications. The original confusion in the mind of Tirpitz may have been implanted by Mahan, but it was more than compensated for by his trenchant phrase which was apparently lost on the Germans:

'The dilemma of Great Britain is that she cannot help commanding the approaches to Germany by the mere possession of the very means essential to her own existence. . . .'

Thus Germany's leaders sought to ward off a danger which was largely imaginary by posing a challenge to the British which they could never hope to substantiate.

Another criticism of Mahan is that by emphasizing the power of offense and by belittling *guerre de course* he failed to predict the reality of the two World Wars, in which the Germans maintained a 'fleet in being' to tie down the superior British Fleet and turned to their U-Boats to destroy commerce. This is partly true in that Mahan did not spell out the concept of a fleet in being, but the failure to foresee a war on commerce was the result of a perversion of his doctrines by such strategic amateurs as Fisher. Mahan had steadfastly praised the value of convoying and other measures of commerce-protection, and would have been horrified to hear that in 1916 most British officers regarded

convoy as a defensive (and therefore useless) measure. The Germans were, however, equally confounded by the British, who by failing to keep to the close blockade which everyone assumed they would, kept their own Grand Fleet 'in being' at Scapa Flow. By refusing to allow their strength to be whittled down by hit-and-run attacks from torpedo-boats and U-Boats the British made nonsense of the work so assiduously carried out by Tirpitz during the previous 20 years.

The great might-have-been is what Mahan would have made of the events of 1914–18, for he would undoubtedly have modified and extended his doctrines in the light of experience. He died in December 1914, and did not see the fulfilment of his prophecy that Sea Power would in the end grind Germany down, no matter what victories her armies won on land. It is fanciful to think of the elderly admiral (he would have been 78 in 1918) influencing naval thought in the 1920s and 1930s. The shocking carnage of the Western Front had changed basic attitudes, and instead of the highly romanticized ideas of imperialism and colonial adventure there was a new idealism. There was henceforth to be a new world order, guaranteed by the League of Nations rather than any single country's good will. What was seen as the disastrous and financially ruinous naval race which had led up to 1914 was replaced by international treaties of limitation such as the Washington Treaty of 1922. This was the nadir of 'Mahanism,' for his assumptions had been made under completely different conditions, and until at least 1930 the science of naval strategy and tactics lay in the doldrums once more.

Inevitably the rising threat of the dictatorships led to the revival of serious thought about the future of naval warfare. Slowly naval officers came to realize that the fundamental concepts of Sea Power and Command of the Sea would have to be studied, reassessed and modified to cope with the enormous changes brought about by the new Air Power. For the traditional right of navies to exist was now seriously challenged by the most extreme advocates of Air Power such as Mitchell, Trenchard and Douhet. Air Power, they claimed, was not subject to any long-established principles of warfare, and in effect the rulebook could be discarded.

Enlightenment did not come quickly to either side in this argument, but in the event the new 'Modified Mahanism' was amply vindicated. Germany showed once again that she could not offset Great Britain's winning combination of a large fleet and a perfect strategic position. Japan, on the other hand, after apparently using Mahan's doctrines with deadly effect in her war against Russia in 1904, showed that her admirals had understood as little as Tirpitz or Dönitz about what they really implied. By a doctrinaire adherence to offensive ideas at the expense of defensive measures her admirals condemned themselves to an overwhelming defeat in the Pacific, with the destruction of the mercantile marine by submarines, mines and air attack. Great Britain, in contrast, grasped from the start that the Battle of the Atlantic was the most crucial of all, and with the help of her Allies inflicted an even more massive defeat on the U-Boats than that which they had suffered in 1917–18.

Air Power lived up to its promise, but only when used within a framework of proper military principles. One of the most surprising discoveries was that the much-vaunted strategic bombing of Germany could only succeed if the old naval concept of Command of the Sea was adapted. Only when bombers were escorted through hostile air space by fighters could they win local command and reduce their losses. On the other hand Sea Power proved no better than Air Power at influencing the outcome on land. The final outcome of the war in Europe was settled by the Russian armies in the East and the

Left: *A quadrant.*

Above: *A Galilean telescope.*

Allied invasion in the West.

Since 1945 the underlying assumptions of Western strategy have been a continuation of the evolution of Mahan's doctrines. The United States and her allies make no secret of their intention to use their command of the sea to offset the overwhelming land strength of the Soviet Union. Leaving aside the strategic nuclear weapons (which are in any case in equilibrium) and accepting the very important modifications brought about by Air Power, the United States still has to use the sea to reinforce Europe or any other part of the world in which its allies need help. Spectacular air-lifts of goods can be achieved for a short while, but when it comes to feeding a country or supplying it with oil-fuel and raw materials there is no alternative to merchant shipping. It is no coincidence that the Soviet Union's expansion of her navy has been matched by an equally impressive build-up of her merchant fleet, and each in its way represents a threat to the West's command of the sea.

In retrospect the major flaw in Mahan's thesis was not so much a fundamental error as an over-extension based on insufficient data. Having enunciated the concept of Sea Power and having proved conclusively that it was the only reason why Great Britain had vanquished all her rivals and had not been beaten by Napoleon, he was then tempted to claim that Sea Power was markedly superior to Land Power by its inherent quality. This was demonstrably true of British Sea Power in 1793-1815 and earlier, but it was only true for the British while they fought opponents who drew their strength from overseas possessions. Against even a small land power like the American colonies, the Royal Navy was unable to bring its massive strength to bear for long enough to influence the outcome. It is significant that the land campaign was decided by a relatively minor naval action which prevented the British from raising the siege of Yorktown, whereas they were able to administer a humiliating defeat on the French in the West Indies and bring the war to a close on more favorable terms than they had hoped.

The French were, like the American colonists, a land power,

but to finance their enormous military effort in Europe and their overseas adventures they had to develop overseas trade. The need could be even more basic, as in 1794 when the collapse of the French Revolution was averted by the arrival of the grain convoy which eluded Howe after the Glorious 1st of June. It could work equally well in reverse, as in the Revolutionary War, when France wished to ship arms and troops to the colonists. Once France abandoned her conquests and fell back on her own resources it took the threat of a massive invasion by the land forces of Russia, Prussia, Austria and Britain to bring an end to the war; what made Waterloo decisive was above all the fact that Wellington and Blücher's armies were only the vanguard of six million troops.

The two World Wars showed even more clearly that too much had been claimed for Sea Power. It had worked unaided in the eighteenth century because international rivalry was expressed in terms of overseas trade, but it could never have brought about a British conquest of Europe. Despite this obvious limitation Mahan's more rabid disciples continued to make such claims up to 1914, and they must bear much of the blame for the discrediting of his doctrines. The reputations of great men have to be protected from their friends.

Today Sea Power is better understood, but we might have waited much longer for that understanding if Mahan had not devoted his formidable intellect to the subject. After a lapse of 90 years his foresight seems all the more remarkable. If we discard the aberrations in detail and retain the fundamentals we are still left with an original exposition of naval strategy which is without equal. Furthermore after a period of declining influence and oblivion Mahan's basic views have been vindicated, and are now seen as the foundation of naval strategy. It is the true measure of his greatness that we can still learn so much from his writing.

ANTONY PRESTON
October 1979

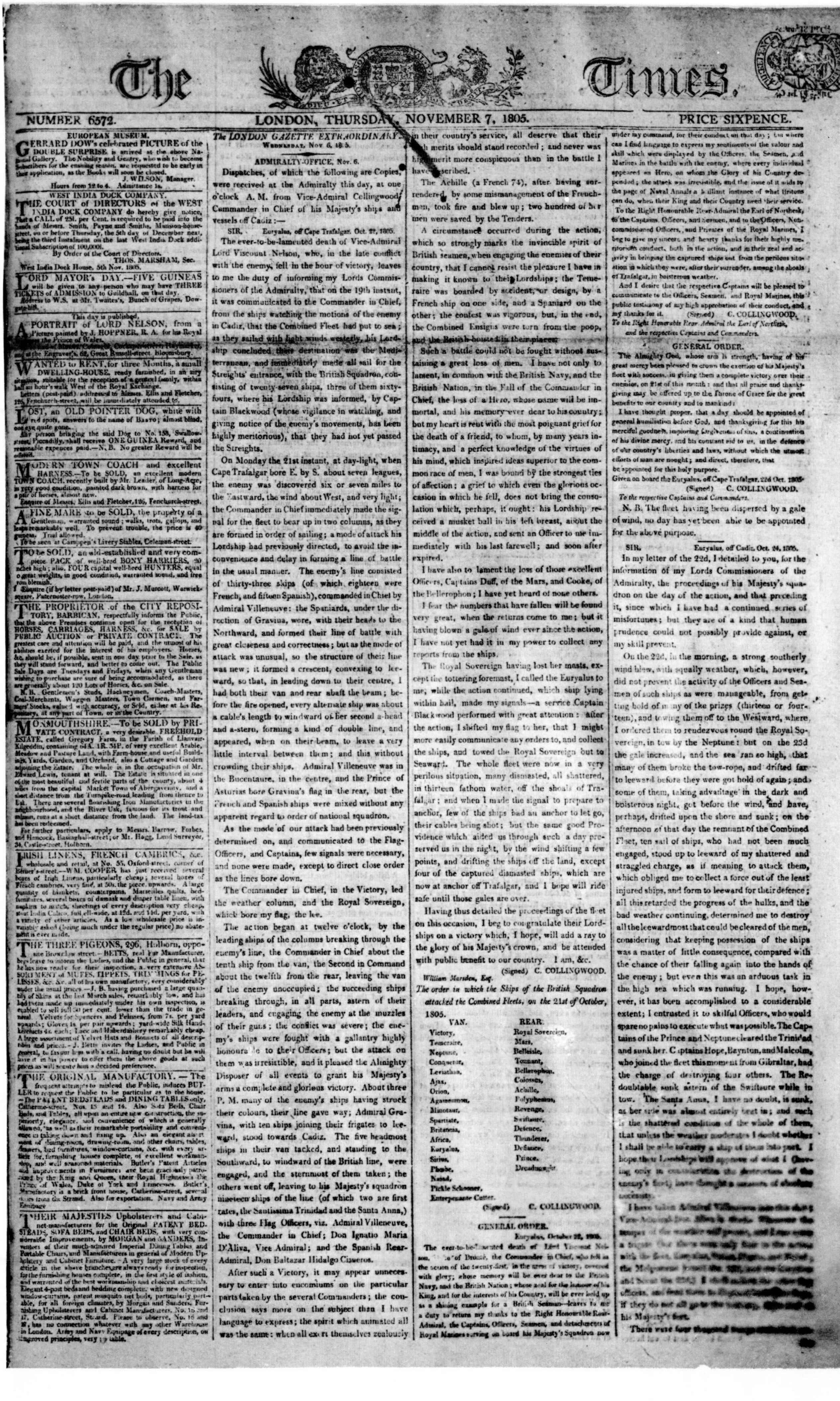

The  Times.

NUMBER 6572.   **LONDON, THURSDAY, NOVEMBER 7, 1805.**   **PRICE SIXPENCE.**

The LONDON GAZETTE EXTRAORDINARY.
WEDNESDAY, Nov. 6, 1805.

ADMIRALTY-OFFICE, Nov. 6.

Dispatches, of which the following are Copies, were received at the Admiralty this day, at one o'clock A.M. from Vice-Admiral Collingwood, Commander in Chief of his Majesty's ships and vessels off Cadiz:—

SIR,   Euryalus, off Cape Trafalgar, Oct. 22, 1805.

The ever-to-be-lamented death of Vice-Admiral Lord Viscount Nelson, who, in the late conflict with the enemy, fell in the hour of victory, leaves to me the duty of informing my Lords Commissioners of the Admiralty, that on the 19th instant, it was communicated to the Commander in Chief, from the ships watching the motions of the enemy in Cadiz, that the Combined Fleet had put to sea; as they sailed with light winds westerly, his Lordship concluded their destination was the Mediterranean, and immediately made all sail for the Streights' entrance, with the British Squadron, consisting of twenty-seven ships, three of them sixty-fours, where his Lordship was informed, by Captain Blackwood (whose vigilance in watching, and giving notice of the enemy's movements, has been highly meritorious), that they had not yet passed the Streights.

On Monday the 21st instant, at day-light, when Cape Trafalgar bore E. by S. about seven leagues, the enemy was discovered six or seven miles to the Eastward, the wind about West, and very light; the Commander in Chief immediately made the signal for the fleet to bear up in two columns, as they are formed in order of sailing; a mode of attack his Lordship had previously directed, to avoid the inconvenience and delay in forming a line of battle in the usual manner. The enemy's line consisted of thirty-three ships (of which eighteen were French and fifteen Spanish), commanded in Chief by Admiral Villeneuve: the Spaniards, under the direction of Gravina, were, with their heads to the Northward, and formed their line of battle with great closeness and correctness; but as the mode of attack was unusual, so the structure of their line was new; it formed a crescent, convexing to leeward, so that, in leading down to their centre, I had both their van and rear abaft the beam; before the fire opened, every alternate ship was about a cable's length to windward of her second a-head and a-stern, forming a kind of double line, and appeared, when on their beam, to leave a very little interval between them; and this without crowding their ships. Admiral Villeneuve was in the Bucentaure, in the centre, and the Prince of Asturias bore Gravina's flag in the rear, but the French and Spanish ships were mixed without any apparent regard to order of national squadron.

As the mode of our attack had been previously determined on, and communicated to the Flag-Officers, and Captains, few signals were necessary, and none were made, except to direct close order as the lines bore down.

The Commander in Chief, in the Victory, led the weather column, and the Royal Sovereign, which bore my flag, the lee.

The action began at twelve o'clock, by the leading ships of the columns breaking through the enemy's line, the Commander in Chief about the tenth ship from the van, the Second in Command about the twelfth from the rear, leaving the van of the enemy unoccupied; the succeeding ships breaking through, in all parts, astern of their leaders, and engaging the enemy at the muzzles of their guns; the conflict was severe; the enemy's ships were fought with a gallantry highly honourable to their Officers; but the attack on them was irresistible, and it pleased the Almighty Disposer of all events to grant his Majesty's arms a complete and glorious victory. About three P.M. many of the enemy's ships having struck their colours, their line gave way; Admiral Gravina, with ten ships joining their frigates to leeward, stood towards Cadiz. The five headmost ships in their van tacked, and standing to the Southward, to windward of the British line, were engaged, and the sternmost of them taken; the others went off, leaving to his Majesty's squadron nineteen ships of the line (of which two are first rates, the Santissima Trinidad and the Santa Anna,) with three Flag Officers, viz. Admiral Villeneuve, the Commander in Chief; Don Ignatio Maria D'Aliva, Vice Admiral; and the Spanish Rear-Admiral, Don Baltazar Hidalgo Cisneros.

After such a Victory, it may appear unnecessary to enter into encomiums on the particular parts taken by the several Commanders; the conclusion says more on the subject than I have language to express; the spirit which animated all was the same: when all exert themselves zealously in their country's service, all deserve that their merits should stand recorded; and never was high merit more conspicuous than in the battle I have described.

The Achille (a French 74), after having surrendered, by some mismanagement of the Frenchmen, took fire and blew up; two hundred of her men were saved by the Tenders.

A circumstance occurred during the action, which so strongly marks the invincible spirit of British seamen, when engaging the enemies of their country, that I cannot resist the pleasure I have in making it known to their Lordships; the Temeraire was boarded by accident, or design, by a French ship on one side, and a Spaniard on the other; the contest was vigorous, but, in the end, the Combined Ensigns were torn from the poop, and the British hoisted in their places.

Such a battle could not be fought without sustaining a great loss of men. I have not only to lament, in common with the British Navy, and the British Nation, in the Fall of the Commander in Chief, the loss of a Hero, whose name will be immortal, and his memory ever dear to his country; but my heart is rent with the most poignant grief for the death of a friend, to whom, by many years intimacy, and a perfect knowledge of the virtues of his mind, which inspired ideas superior to the common race of men, I was bound by the strongest ties of affection; a grief to which even the glorious occasion in which he fell, does not bring the consolation which, perhaps, it ought: his Lordship received a musket ball in his left breast, about the middle of the action, and sent an Officer to me immediately with his last farewell; and soon after expired.

I have also to lament the loss of those excellent Officers, Captains Duff, of the Mars, and Cooke, of the Bellerophon; I have yet heard of none others.

I fear the numbers that have fallen will be found very great, when the returns come to me; but it having blown a gale of wind ever since the action, I have not yet had it in my power to collect any reports from the ships.

The Royal Sovereign having lost her masts, except the tottering foremast, I called the Euryalus to me, while the action continued, which ship lying within hail, made my signals—a service Captain Blackwood performed with great attention: after the action, I shifted my flag to her, that I might more easily communicate my orders to, and collect the ships, and towed the Royal Sovereign out to Seaward. The whole fleet were now in a very perilous situation, many dismasted, all shattered, in thirteen fathom water, off the shoals of Trafalgar; and when I made the signal to prepare to anchor, few of the ships had an anchor to let go, their cables being shot; but the same good Providence which aided us through such a day preserved us in the night, by the wind shifting a few points, and drifting the ships off the land, except four of the captured dismasted ships, which are now at anchor off Trafalgar, and I hope will ride safe until those gales are over.

Having thus detailed the proceedings of the fleet on this occasion, I beg to congratulate their Lordships on a victory which, I hope, will add a ray to the glory of his Majesty's crown, and be attended with public benefit to our country.   I am, &c.
(Signed) C. COLLINGWOOD.

William Marsden, Esq.

The order in which the Ships of the British Squadron attacked the Combined Fleets, on the 21st of October, 1805.

VAN.	REAR.
Victory,	Royal Sovereign,
Temeraire,	Mars,
Neptune,	Belleisle,
Conqueror,	Tonnant,
Leviathan,	Bellerophon,
Ajax,	Colossus,
Orion,	Achille,
Agamemnon,	Polyphemus,
Minotaur,	Revenge,
Spartiate,	Swiftsure,
Britannia,	Defence,
Africa,	Thunderer,
Euryalus,	Defiance,
Sirius,	Prince,
Phœbe,	Dreadnought,
Naiad,	
Pickle Schooner,	
Entreprenante Cutter.	

(Signed) C. COLLINGWOOD.

GENERAL ORDER.

Euryalus, October 22, 1805.

The ever-to-be-lamented death of Lord Viscount Nelson, Duke of Bronté, the Commander in Chief, who fell in the action of the twenty-first, in the arms of victory, covered with glory; whose memory will be ever dear to the British Navy, and for the interest of his Country, will be ever held up as a shining example for a British Seaman—leaves to me a duty to return my thanks to the Right Honourable Rear-Admiral, the Captains, Officers, Seamen, and detachments of Royal Marines serving on board his Majesty's Squadron now under my command, for their conduct on that day; for where can I find language to express my sentiments of the valour and skill which were displayed by the Officers, the Seamen, and Marines, in the battle with the enemy, where every individual appeared an Hero, on whom the Glory of his Country depended; the attack was irresistible, and the issue of it adds to the page of Naval Annals a brilliant instance of what Britons can do, when their King and their Country need their service.

To the Right Honourable Rear-Admiral the Earl of Northesk, to the Captains, Officers, and Seamen, and to the Officers, Non-commissioned Officers, and Privates of the Royal Marines, I beg to give my sincere and hearty thanks for their highly meritorious conduct, both in the action, and in their zeal and activity in bringing the captured ships out from the perilous situation in which they were, after their surrender, among the shoals of Trafalgar, in boisterous weather.

And I desire that the respective Captains will be pleased to communicate to the Officers, Seamen, and Royal Marines, this public testimony of my high approbation of their conduct, and my thanks for it.   (Signed)   C. COLLINGWOOD.

To the Right Honourable Rear-Admiral the Earl of Northesk, and the respective Captains and Commanders.

GENERAL ORDER.

The Almighty God, whose arm is strength, having of his great mercy been pleased to crown the exertion of his Majesty's fleet with success, in giving them a complete victory over their enemies, on 21st of this month; and that all praise and thanksgiving may be offered up to the Throne of Grace for the great benefits to our country and to mankind;

I have thought proper, that a day should be appointed of general humiliation before God, and thanksgiving for this his merciful goodness, imploring forgiveness of sins, a continuation of his divine mercy, and his constant aid to us, in the defence of our country's liberties and laws, without which the utmost efforts of man are nought; and direct, therefore, that it be appointed for this holy purpose.

Given on board the Euryalus, off Cape Trafalgar, 22d Oct. 1805.
(Signed) C. COLLINGWOOD.

To the respective Captains and Commanders.

N. B. The fleet having been dispersed by a gale of wind, no day has yet been able to be appointed for the above purpose.

SIR,   Euryalus, off Cadiz, Oct. 24, 1805.

In my letter of the 22d, I detailed to you, for the information of my Lords Commissioners of the Admiralty, the proceedings of his Majesty's squadron on the day of the action, and that preceding it, since which I have had a continued series of misfortunes; but they are of a kind that human prudence could not possibly provide against, or my skill prevent.

On the 22d, in the morning, a strong southerly wind blew, with squally weather, which, however, did not prevent the activity of the Officers and Seamen of such ships as were manageable, from getting hold of many of the prizes (thirteen or fourteen), and towing them off to the Westward, where I ordered them to rendezvous round the Royal Sovereign, in tow by the Neptune; but on the 23d the gale increased, and the sea ran so high, that many of them broke the tow-rope, and drifted far to leeward before they were got hold of again; and some of them, taking advantage in the dark and boisterous night, got before the wind, and have, perhaps, drifted upon the shore and sunk; on the afternoon of that day the remnant of the Combined Fleet, ten sail of ships, who had not been much engaged, stood up to leeward of my shattered and straggled charge, as if meaning to attack them, which obliged me to collect a force out of the least injured ships, and form to leeward for their defence; all this retarded the progress of the hulks, and the bad weather continuing, determined me to destroy all the leewardmost that could be cleared of the men, considering that keeping possession of the ships was a matter of little consequence, compared with the chance of their falling again into the hands of the enemy; but even this was an arduous task in the high sea which was running. I hope, however, it has been accomplished to a considerable extent; I entrusted it to skilful Officers, who would spare no pains to execute what was possible. The Captains of the Prince and Neptune cleared the Trinidad and sunk her. Captains Hope, Baynton, and Malcolm, who joined the fleet this moment from Gibraltar, had the charge of destroying four others. The Redoubtable sunk astern of the Swiftsure while in tow. The Santa Anna, I have no doubt, is sunk, as her side was almost entirely beat in; and such is the shattered condition of the whole of them, that unless the weather moderates I doubt whether I shall be able to carry a ship of them into port. I hope their Lordships will approve of what I (having only in consideration the destruction of the enemy's fleet) have thought a measure of absolute necessity.

I have taken Admiral Villeneuve into this ship, Vice-Admiral Don Aliva is dead. Whenever the temper of the weather will permit, and I can spare a frigate (for there were only four in the action with the fleet, Euryalus, Sirius, Phoebe, and Naiad; the Melpomene joined the 22d, and the Eurydice and Scout the 23d) I shall collect the other Flag Officers, and send them to England with their Flags (if they do not all go to the bottom), to be laid at his Majesty's feet.

There were four thousand troops ...

Preface

The definite object proposed in this work is an examination of the general history of Europe and America with particular reference to the effect of sea power upon the course of that history. Historians generally have been unfamiliar with the conditions of the sea, having as to it neither special interest nor special knowledge; and the profound determining influence of maritime strength upon great issues has consequently been overlooked. This is even more true of particular occasions than of the general tendency of sea power. It is easy to say in a general way, that the use and control of the sea is and has been a great factor in the history of the world; it is more troublesome to seek out and show its exact bearing at a particular juncture. Yet, unless this be done, the acknowledgment of general importance remains vague and insubstantial; not resting, as it should, upon a collection of special instances in which the precise effect has been made clear, by an analysis of the conditions at the given moments.

A curious exemplification of this tendency to slight the bearing of maritime power upon events may be drawn from two writers of that English nation which more than any other has owed its greatness to the sea. 'Twice,' says Arnold in his History of Rome, 'Has there been witnessed the struggle of the highest individual genius against the resources and institutions of a great nation, and in both cases the nation was victorious. For seventeen years Hannibal strove against Rome, for sixteen years Napoleon strove against England; the efforts of the first ended in Zama, those of the second in Waterloo.' Sir Edward Creasy, quoting this, adds: 'One point, however, of the similitude between the two wars has scarcely been adequately dwelt on; that is, the remarkable parallel between the Roman general who finally defeated the great Carthaginian, and the English general who gave the last deadly overthrow to the French emperor. Scipio and Wellington both held for many years commands of high importance, but distant from the main theatres of warfare. The same country was the scene of the principal military career of each. It was in Spain that Scipio, like Wellington, successively encountered and overthrew nearly all the subordinate generals of the enemy before being opposed to the chief champion and conqueror himself. Both Scipio and Wellington restored their countrymen's confidence in arms when shaken by a series of reverses, and each of them closed a long and perilous war by a complete and overwhelming defeat of the chosen leader and the chosen veterans of the foe.'

Neither of these Englishmen mentions the yet more striking coincidence, that in both cases the mastery of the sea rested with the victor. The Roman control of the water forced Hannibal to that long, perilous march through Gaul in which more than half his veteran troops wasted away; it enabled the elder Scipio, while sending his army from the Rhône on to Spain, to intercept Hannibal's communications, to return in person and face the invader at the Trebia. Throughout the war the legions passed by water, unmolested and unwearied, between Spain, which was Hannibal's base, and Italy; while the issue of the decisive battle of the Metaurus, hinging as it did upon the interior position of the Roman armies with reference to the forces of Hasdrubal and Hannibal, was ultimately due to the fact that the younger brother could not bring his succoring reinforcements by sea, but only by the land route through Gaul. Hence at the critical moment the two Carthaginian armies were separated by the length of Italy, and one was destroyed by the combined action of the Roman generals.

On the other hand, naval historians have troubled themselves little about the connection between general history and their own particular topic, limiting themselves generally to the duty of simple chroniclers of naval occurrences. This is less true of the French than of the English; the genius and training of the former people leading them to more careful inquiry into the causes of particular results and the mutual relation of events.

There is not, however, within the knowledge of the author any work that professes the particular object here sought; namely, an estimate of the effect of sea power upon the course of history and the prosperity of nations. As other histories deal with the wars, politics, social and economical conditions of countries, touching upon maritime matters only incidentally and generally unsympathetically, so the present work aims at putting maritime interests in the foreground, without divorcing them, however, from their surroundings of cause and effect in general history, but seeking to show how they modified the latter, and were modified by them.

The period embraced is from 1660, when the sailing-ship era, with its distinctive features, had fairly begun, to 1783, the end of the American Revolution. While the thread of general history upon which the successive maritime events is strung is intentionally slight, the effort has been to present a clear as well as accurate outline. Writing as a naval officer in full sympathy with his profession, the author has not hesitated to digress freely on questions of naval policy, strategy, and tactics; but as technical language has been avoided, it is hoped that these matters, simply presented, will be found of interest to the unprofessional reader.

A. T. MAHAN.

December, 1889.

Introductory

Steam versus sail

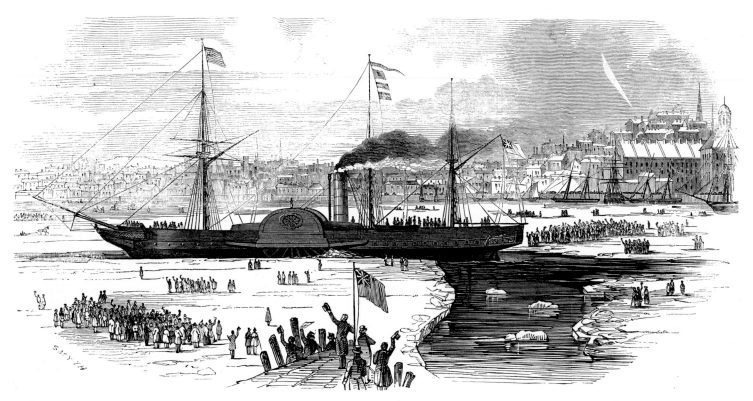

The history of Sea Power is largely, though by no means solely, a narrative of contests between nations, of mutual rivalries, of violence frequently culminating in war. The profound influence of sea commerce upon the wealth and strength of countries was clearly seen long before the true principles which governed its growth and prosperity were detected. To secure to one's own people a disproportionate share of such benefits, every effort was made to exclude others, either by the peaceful legislative methods of monopoly or prohibitory regulations, or, when these failed, by direct violence. The clash of interests, the angry feelings roused by conflicting attempts thus to appropriate the larger share, if not the whole, of the advantages of commerce, and of distant unsettled commercial regions, led to wars. On the other hand, wars arising from other causes have been greatly modified in their conduct and issue by the control of the sea. Therefore the history of sea power, while embracing in its broad sweep all that tends to make a people great upon the sea or by the sea, is largely a military history; and it is in this aspect that it will be mainly, though not exclusively, regarded in the following pages.

A study of the military history of the past, such as this, is enjoined by great military leaders as essential to correct ideas and to the skilful conduct of war in the future. Napoleon names among the campaigns to be studied by the aspiring soldier, those of Alexander, Hannibal, and Caesar, to whom gunpowder was unknown; and there is a substantial agreement among professional writers that, while many of the conditions of war vary from age to age with the progress of weapons, there are certain teachings in the school of history which remain constant, and being, therefore, of universal application, can be elevated to the rank of general principles. For the same reason the study of the sea history of the past will be found instructive, by its illustration of the general principles of maritime war, notwithstanding the great changes that have been brought about in naval weapons by the scientific advances of the past half century, and by the introduction of steam as the motive power.

It is doubly necessary thus to study critically the history and experience of naval warfare in the days of sailing-ships, because while these will be found to afford lessons of present application and value, steam navies have as yet made no history which can be quoted as decisive in its teaching. Of the one we have much experimental knowledge; of the other, practically none. Hence theories about the naval warfare of the future are almost wholly presumptive; and although the attempt has been made to give them a more solid basis by dwelling upon the resemblance between fleets of steamships and fleets of galleys moved by oars, which have a long and well-known history, it will be well not to be carried away by this analogy until it has been thoroughly tested. The resemblance is indeed far from superficial. The feature which the steamer and the galley have in common is the

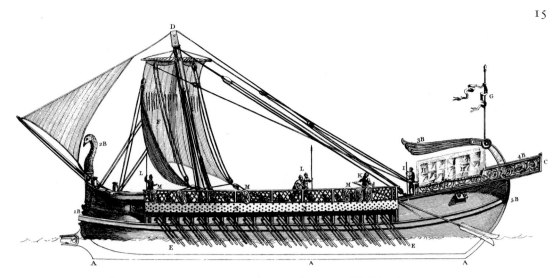

ability to move in any direction independent of the wind. Such a power makes a radical distinction between those classes of vessels and the sailing-ship; for the latter can follow only, a limited number of courses when the wind blows, and must remain motionless when it fails. But while it is wise to observe things that are alike, it is also wise to look for things that differ; for when the imagination is carried away by the detection of points of resemblance—one of the most pleasing of mental pursuits—it is apt to be impatient of any divergence in its new-found parallels, and so may overlook or refuse to recognize such. Thus the galley and the steamship have in common, though unequally developed, the important characteristic mentioned, but in at least two points they differ; and in an appeal to the history of the galley for lessons as to fighting steamships, the differences as well as the likeness must be kept steadily in view, or false deductions may be made. The motive power of the galley when in use necessarily and rapidly declined, because human strength could not long maintain such exhausting efforts, and consequently tactical movements could continue but for a limited time; and again, during the galley period offensive weapons were not only of short range, but were almost wholly confined to hand-to-hand encounter. These two conditions led almost necessarily to a rush upon each other, not, however, without some dexterous attempts to turn or double on the enemy, followed by a hand-to-hand *mêlée*. In such a rush

and such a *mêlée* a great consensus of respectable, even eminent naval opinion of the present day finds the necessary outcome of modern naval weapons—a kind of Donnybrook Fair, in which, as the history of *mêlées* shows, it will be hard to know friend from foe. Whatever may prove to be the worth of this opinion, it cannot claim an historical basis in the sole fact that galley and steamship can move at any moment directly upon the enemy, and carry a beak upon their prow, regardless of the points in which galley and steamship differ. As yet this opinion is only a presumption, upon which final judgment may well be deferred until the trial of battle has given further light. Until that time there is room for the opposite view—that a *mêlée* between numerically equal fleets, in which skill is reduced to a minimum, is not the best that can be done with the elaborate and mighty weapons of this age. The surer of himself an admiral is, the finer the tactical development of his fleet, the better his captains, the more reluctant must he necessarily be to enter into a *mêlée* with equal forces, in which all these advantages will be thrown away, chance reign supreme, and his fleet be placed on terms of equality with an assemblage of ships which have never before acted together. History has lessons as to when *mêlées* are, or are not, in order.

The galley, then, has one striking resemblance to the steamer, but differs in other important features which are not so immediately apparent and are therefore less accounted of. In the

Above: *A small sixteenth-century merchant ship drawn by Holbein. Although the scale is exaggerated, sailing ships were remarkably crowded because of the number of men needed to work the rigging.*

sailing-ship, on the contrary, the striking feature is the difference between it and the more modern vessel; the points of resemblance, though existing and easy to find, are not so obvious, and therefore are less heeded. This impression is enhanced by the sense of utter weakness in the sailing-ship as compared with the steamer, owing to its dependence upon the wind; forgetting that, as the former fought with its equals, the tactical lessons are valid. The galley was never reduced to impotence by a calm, and hence receives more respect in our day than the sailing-ship; yet the latter displaced it and remained supreme until the utilization of steam. The powers to injure an enemy from a great distance, to manoeuvre for an unlimited length of time without wearing out the men, to devote the greater part of the crew to the offensive weapons instead of to the oar, are common to the sailing vessel and the steamer, and are at least as important, tactically considered, as the power of the galley to move in a calm or against the wind.

In tracing resemblances there is a tendency not only to overlook points of difference, but to exaggerate points of likeness—to be fanciful. It may be so considered to point out that as the sailing-ship had guns of long range, with comparatively great penetrative power, and carronades, which were of shorter range but great smashing effect, so the modern steamer has its batteries of long-range guns and of torpedoes, the latter being effective only within a limited distance and then injuring by smashing, while the gun, as of old, aims at penetration. Yet these are distinctly tactical considerations, which must affect the plans of admirals and captains; and the analogy is real, not forced. So also both the sailing-ship and the steamer contemplate direct contact with an enemy's vessel—the former to carry her by boarding, the latter to sink her by ramming; and to both this is the most difficult of their tasks, for to effect it the ship must be carried to a single point of the field of action, whereas projectile weapons may be used from many points of a wide area.

The relative positions of two sailing-ships, or fleets, with reference to the direction of the wind involved most important tactical questions, and were perhaps the chief care of the seamen of that age. To a superficial glance it may appear that since this has become a matter of such indifference to the steamer, no analogies to it are to be found in present conditions, and the

lessons of history in this respect are valueless. A more careful consideration of the distinguishing characteristics of the lee and the weather 'gage,' directed to their essential features and disregarding secondary details, will show that this is a mistake. (A ship was said to have the weather-gage, or 'the advantage of the wind,' or 'to be to windward,' when the wind allowed her to steer for her opponent, and did not let the latter head straight for her. The extreme case was when the wind blew direct from one to the other; but there was a large space on either side of this line to which the term 'weather-gage' applied. If the lee ship be taken as the centre of a circle, there were nearly three eighths of its area in which the other might be and still keep the advantage of the wind to a greater or less degree. Lee is the opposite of weather.) The distinguishing feature of the weather-gage was that it conferred the power of giving or refusing battle at will, which in turn carries the usual advantage of an offensive attitude in the choice of the method of attack. This advantage was accompanied by certain drawbacks, such as irregularity introduced into the order, exposure to raking or enfilading cannonade, and the sacrifice of part or all of the artillery-fire of the assailant—all of which were incurred in approaching the enemy. The ship, or fleet with the lee-gage could not attack; if it did not wish to retreat, its action was confined to the defensive, and to receiving battle on the enemy's terms. This disadvantage was compensated by the comparative ease of maintaining the order of battle undisturbed, and by a sustained artillery-fire to which the enemy for a time was unable to reply. Historically, these favorable and unfavorable characteristics have their counterpart and analogy in the offensive and defensive operations of all ages. The offence undertakes certain risks and disadvantages in order to reach and destroy the enemy; the defence, so long as it remains such, refuses the risks of advance, holds on to a careful, well-ordered position, and avails itself of the exposure to which the assailant submits himself. These radical differences between the weather- and lee-gage were so clearly recognized, through the cloud of lesser details accompanying them, that the former was ordinarily chosen by the English, because their steady policy was to assail and destroy their enemy; whereas the French sought the lee-gage, because by so doing they were usually able

Right: *A modern model based on careful study of a late fifteenth century merchantman, probably Flemish, and identified as a 'kraeck.'*

Below: *A Dutch man-o'-war of the sixteenth century. A new tradition of ship design was being created in Northern Europe, marking a complete break with the Mediterranean traditions.*

to cripple the enemy as he approached, and thus evade decisive encounters and preserve their ships. The French, with rare exceptions, subordinated the action of the navy to other military considerations, grudged the money spent upon it, and therefore sought to economize their fleet by assuming a defensive position and limiting its efforts to the repelling of assaults. For this course the lee-gage, skilfully used, was admirably adapted so long as an enemy displayed more courage than conduct; but when Rodney showed an intention to use the advantage of the wind, not merely to attack, but to make a formidable concentration on a part of the enemy's line, his wary opponent, De Guichen, changed his tactics. In the first of their three actions the Frenchman took the lee-gage; but after recognizing Rodney's purpose he manoeuvred for the advantage of the wind, not to attack, but to refuse action except on his own terms. The power to assume the offensive, or to refuse battle, rests no longer with the wind, but with the party which has the greater speed; which in a fleet will depend not only upon the speed of the individual ships, but also upon their tactical uniformity of action. Henceforth the ships which have the greatest speed will have the weather-gage.

failures, the same from age to age. Conditions and weapons change; but to cope with the one or successfully wield the others, respect must be had to these constant teachings of history in the tactics of the battlefield, or in those wider operations of war which are comprised under the name of strategy.

It is however in these wider operations, which embrace a whole theatre of war, and in a maritime contest may cover a large portion of the globe, that the teachings of history have a more evident and permanent value, because the conditions remain more permanent. The theatre of war may be larger or smaller, its difficulties more or less pronounced, the contending armies more or less great, the necessary movements more or less easy, but these are simply differences of scale, of degree, not of kind. As a wilderness gives place to civilization, as means of communication multiply, as roads are opened, rivers bridged, food-resources increased, the operations of war become easier, more rapid, more extensive; but the principles to which they must be conformed remain the same. When the march on foot was replaced by carrying troops in coaches, when the latter in turn gave place to railroads, the scale of distances was increased,

Left: *A modern model of an Elizabethan galleon based on drawings thought to represent the* Elizabeth Jonas. *Much of what we know about Elizabethan designs is based on this single set of data, although written descriptions of a variety of types survive.*

Far right: *Model of a herring buss c 1584, a typical sturdy craft engaged in the vital business of fishing, which incidentally provided the best training for naval seamen.*

Right: *Contemporary model of an English man-o'-war dated 1580-1600.*

It is not therefore a vain expectation, as many think, to look for useful lessons in the history of sailing-ships as well as in that of galleys. Both have their points of resemblance to the modern ship; both have also points of essential difference, which make it impossible to cite their experiences or modes of action as tactical *precedents* to be followed. But a precedent is different from and less valuable than a principle. The former may be originally faulty, or may cease to apply through change of circumstances; the latter has its roots in the essential nature of things, and, however various its application as conditions change, remains a standard to which action must conform to attain success. War has such principles; their existence is detected by the study of the past, which reveals them in successes and in

or, if you will, the scale of time diminished; but the principles which dictated the point at which the army should be concentrated, the direction in which it should move, the part of the enemy's position which it should assail, the protection of communications, were not altered. So, on the sea, the advance from the galley timidly creeping from port to port to the sailing-ship launching out boldly to the ends of the earth, and from the latter to the steamship of our own time, has increased the scope and the rapidity of naval operations without necessarily changing the principles which should direct them; and the speech of Hermocrates twenty-three hundred years ago, before quoted, contained a correct strategic plan, which is as applicable in its principles now as it was then. Before hostile armies or fleets are

Left: *Model of a Portuguese caravel of 1536.*

are strategic questions, and upon all these history has a great deal to say. There has been of late a valuable discussion in English naval circles as to the comparative merits of the policies of two great English admirals, Lord Howe and Lord St Vincent, in the disposition of the English navy when at war with France. The question is purely strategic, and is not of mere historical interest; it is of vital importance now, and the principles upon which its decision rests are the same now as then. St Vincent's policy saved England from invasion, and in the hands of Nelson and his brother admirals led straight up to Trafalgar.

brought into con*tact* (a word which perhaps better than any other indicates the dividing line between tactics and strategy), there are a number of questions to be decided, covering the whole plan of operations throughout the theatre of war. Among these are the proper function of the navy in the war; its true objective; the point or points upon which it should be concentrated; the establishment of depots of coal and supplies; the maintenance of communications between these depots and the home base; the military value of commerce-destroying as a decisive or a secondary operation of war; the system upon which commerce-destroying can be most efficiently conducted, whether by scattered cruisers or by holding in force some vital centre through which commercial shipping must pass. All these

It is then particularly in the field of naval strategy that the teachings of the past have a value which is in no degree lessened. They are there useful not only as illustrative of principles, but also as precedents, owing to the comparative permanence of the conditions. This is less obviously true as to tactics, when the fleets come into collision at the point to which strategic considerations have brought them. The unresting progress of mankind causes continual change in the weapons; and with that must come a continual change in the manner of fighting—in the handling and disposition of troops or ships on the battlefield. Hence arises a tendency on the part of many connected with maritime matters to think that no advantage is to be gained from the study of former experiences; that time so used is wasted.

This view, though natural, not only leaves wholly out of sight those broad strategic considerations which lead nations to put fleets afloat, which direct the sphere of their action, and so have modified and will continue to modify the history of the world, but is one-sided and narrow even as to tactics. The battles of the past succeeded or failed according as they were fought in conformity with the principles of war; and the seaman who carefully studies the causes of success or failure will not only detect and gradually assimilate these principles, but will also acquire increased aptitude in applying them to the tactical use of the ships and weapons of his own day. He will observe also that changes of tactics have not only taken place *after* changes in weapons, which necessarily is the case, but that the interval between such changes has been unduly long. This doubtless arises from the fact that an improvement of weapons is due to the energy of one or two men, while changes in tactics have to overcome the inertia of a conservative class; but it is a great evil. It can be remedied only by a candid recognition of each change, by careful study of the powers and limitations of the new ship or weapon, and by a consequent adaptation of the method of using it to the qualities it possesses, which will constitute its tactics. History shows that it is vain to hope that military men generally will be at the pains to do this, but that the one who does will go into battle with a great advantage—a lesson in itself of no mean value.

We may therefore accept now the words of a French tactician, Morogues, who wrote a century and a quarter ago: 'Naval tactics are based upon conditions the chief causes of which, namely the arms, may change; which in turn causes necessarily a change in the construction of ships, in the manner of handling them, and so finally in the disposition and handling of fleets.' His further statement, that 'it is not a science founded upon principles absolutely invariable,' is more open to criticism. It would be more correct to say that the application of its principles varies as the weapons change. The application of the principles doubtless varies also in strategy from time to time, but the variation is far less; and hence the recognition of the underlying principle is easier. This statement is of sufficient importance to our subject to receive some illustrations from historical events.

The battle of the Nile, in 1798, was not only an overwhelming victory for the English over the French fleet, but had also the decisive effect of destroying the communications between France and Napoleon's army in Egypt. In the battle itself the English admiral, Nelson, gave a most brilliant example of grand tactics, if that be, as has been defined, 'the art of making good combinations preliminary to battles as well as during their progress.' The particular tactical combination depended upon a condition now passed away, which was the inability of the lee ships of a fleet at anchor to come to the help of the weather ones before the latter were destroyed; but the principles which

underlay the combination, namely, to choose that part of the enemy's order which can least easily be helped, and to attack it with superior forces, has not passed away. The action of Admiral Jervis at Cape St Vincent, when with fifteen ships he won a victory over twenty-seven, was dictated by the same principle, though in this case the enemy was not at anchor, but under way. Yet men's minds are so constituted that they seem more impressed by the transiency of the conditions than by the undying principle which coped with them. In the strategic effect of Nelson's victory upon the course of the war, on the contrary, the principle involved is not only more easily recognized, but it is at once seen to be applicable to our own day. The issue of the enterprise in Egypt depended upon keeping open the communications with France. The victory of the Nile destroyed the naval force, by which alone the communications could be assured, and determined the final failure; and it is at once seen, not only that the blow was struck in accordance with the principle of striking at the enemy's line of communication, but also that the same principle is valid now, and would be equally so in the days of the galley as of the sailing-ship or steamer.

Nevertheless, a vague feeling of contempt for the past, supposed to be obsolete, combines with natural indolence to blind men even to those permanent strategic lessons which lie close to the surface of naval history. For instance, how many look upon the battle of Trafalgar, the crown of Nelson's glory and the seal of his genius, as other than an isolated event of exceptional grandeur? How many ask themselves the strategic question, 'How did the ships come to be just there?' How many realize it to be the final act in a great strategic drama, extending over a year or more, in which two of the greatest leaders that ever lived, Napoleon and Nelson, were pitted against each other? At Trafalgar it ·was not Villeneuve that failed, but Napoleon that was vanquished; not Nelson that won, but England that was saved; and why? Because Napoleon's combinations failed, and Nelson's intuitions and activity kept the English fleet ever on the track of the enemy, and brought it up in time at the decisive moment. The tactics at Trafalgar, while open to criticism in detail, were in their main features conformable to the principles of war, and their audacity was justified as well by the urgency of the case as by the results; but the great lessons of efficiency in preparation, of activity and energy in execution, and of thought and insight on the part of the English leader during the previous months, are strategic lessons, and as such they still remain good.

In these two cases events were worked out to their natural and decisive end. A third may be cited, in which, as no such definite end was reached, an opinion as to what should have been done may be open to dispute. In the war of the American Revolution, France and Spain became allies against England in 1779. The united fleets thrice appeared in the English Channel,

Left: *A merchantman and a yacht off Dover c 1759, by Brooking.*

Above: *A stormy day at sea c 1664 by Julius Porcellis.*

Above: *As the eighteenth century progressed theoretical naval architecture developed and the subject became less of a black art.*

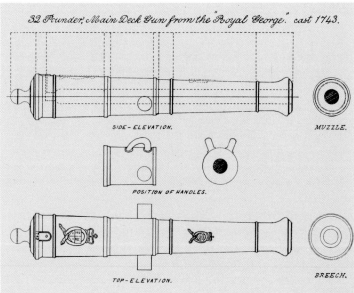

Above: *Metallurgy improved as well, allowing the standard of gun manufacture to improve.*

once to the number of sixty-six sail of the line, driving the English fleet to seek refuge in its ports because far inferior in numbers. Now, the great aim of Spain was to recover Gibraltar and Jamaica; and to the former end immense efforts both by land and sea were put forth by the allies against that nearly impregnable fortress. They were fruitless. The question suggested—and it is purely one of naval strategy—is this: Would not Gibraltar have been more surely recovered by controlling the English Channel, attacking the British fleet even in its harbors, and threatening England with annihilation of commerce and invasion at home, than by far greater efforts directed against a distant and very strong outpost of her empire? The English people, from long immunity, were particularly sensitive to fears of invasion, and their great confidence in their fleets, if rudely shaken, would have left them proportionately disheartened. However decided, the question as a point of strategy is fair; and it is proposed in another form by a French officer of the period, who favored directing the great effort on a West India island which might be exchanged against Gibraltar. It is not, however, likely that England would have given up the key of the Mediterranean for any other foreign possession, though she might have yielded it to save her firesides and her capital.

Napoleon once said that he would reconquer Pondicherry on the banks of the Vistula. Could he have controlled the English Channel, as the allied fleet did for a moment in 1779, can it be doubted that he would have conquered Gibraltar on the shores of England?

To impress more strongly the truth that history both suggests strategic study and illustrates the principles of war by the facts which it transmits, two more instances will be taken, which are more remote in time than the period specially considered in this work. How did it happen that, in two great contests between the powers of the East and of the West in the Mediterranean, in one of which the empire of the known world was at stake, the opposing fleets met on spots so near each other as Actium and Lepanto? Was this a mere coincidence, or was it due to conditions that recurred, and may recur again? If the latter, it is worth while to study out the reason; for it there should again arise a great eastern power of the sea like that of Antony or of Turkey, the strategic questions would be similar. At present, indeed, it seems that the centre of sea power, resting mainly with England and France, is overwhelmingly in the West; but should any chance add to the control of the Black Sea basin, which Russia now has, the possession of the entrance to the Mediterranean,

Below: *A small mid-eighteenth-century man-o'-war firing a salute.*

Below: *The Battle of Cape St Vincent in February 1797 first brought Nelson to the public's attention for his brilliance and bravery.*

Left: *At the Battle of the Nile in 1798 Nelson showed that it was possible to gain truly decisive victory by annihilating the enemy. It was at the Nile that he broke new ground by a double envelopment of the French, despite the fact that they were anchored close inshore.*

Below: *The moment of decision at the Nile, as the French flag-ship l'Orient blew up (left). Although the French fought gallantly they were overwhelmed by the concentration of fire from Nelson's 74-gun ships.*

the existing strategic conditions affecting sea power would all be modified. Now, were the West arrayed against the East, England and France would go at once unopposed to the Levant, as they did in 1854, and as England alone went in 1878; in case of the change suggested, the East, as twice before, would meet the West half-way.

At a very conspicuous and momentous period of the world's history, Sea Power had a strategic bearing and weight which has received scant recognition. There cannot now be had the full knowledge necessary for tracing in detail its influence upon the issue of the Second Punic War; but the indications which remain are sufficient to warrant the assertion that it was a determining factor. An accurate judgment upon this point cannot be formed by mastering only such facts of the particular contest as have been clearly transmitted, for as usual the naval transactions have been slightingly passed over; there is needed also familiarity with the details of general naval history in order to draw, from slight indications, correct inferences based upon a knowledge of what has been possible at periods whose history is well known. The control of the sea, however real, does not imply that an enemy's single ships or small squadrons cannot steal out of port, cannot cross more or less frequented tracts of

ocean, make harassing descents upon unprotected points of a long coastline, enter blockaded harbors. On the contrary, history has shown that such evasions are always possible, to some extent, to the weaker party, however great the inequality of naval strength. It is not therefore inconsistent with the general control of the sea, or of a decisive part of it, by the Roman fleets, that the Carthaginian admiral Bomilcar in the fourth year of the war, after the stunning defeat of Cannae, landed four thousand men and a body of elephants in south Italy; nor that in the seventh year, flying from the Roman fleet off Syracuse, he again appeared at Tarentum, then in Hannibal's hands; nor that Hannibal sent despatch vessels to Carthage; nor even that, at last, he withdrew in safety to Africa with his wasted army. None of these things prove that the government in Carthage could, if it wished, have sent Hannibal the constant support which, as a matter of fact, he did not receive; but they do tend to create a natural impression that such help could have been given. Therefore the statement, that the Roman preponderance at sea had a decisive effect upon the course of the war, needs to be made good by an examination of ascertained facts. Thus the kind and degree of its influence may be fairly estimated.

At the beginning of the war, Mommsen says, Rome controlled the seas. To whatever cause, or combination of causes, it be attributed, this essentially non-maritime state had in the First Punic War established over its sea-faring rival a naval supremacy, which still lasted. In the second war there was no naval battle of importance—a circumstance which in itself, and still more in connection with other well-ascertained facts, indicates a superiority analogous to that which at other epochs has been marked by the same feature.

As Hannibal left no memoirs, the motives are unknown which determined him to the perilous and almost ruinous march through Gaul and across the Alps. It is certain, however, that his fleet on the coast of Spain was not strong enough to contend with that of Rome. Had it been, he might still have followed the

Above: *The fortress of Gibraltar guarded access to the Mediterranean but until the end of the nineteenth century it was very difficult to base a fleet there during the winter months. It was also too far from Toulon, the main French base.*

Right: *A coin bearing the likeness of Scipio Africanus, conqueror of Hannibal. The Second Punic War was an outstanding example of a land power, Rome, turning itself into a maritime power in order to strike at Carthage. Despite the loss of an entire fleet the Romans mastered the new element and went on to make their own innovations in the art of sea warfare.*

Left: *A Dutch print celebrating the joint capture of Gibraltar with suitable allegorical references and a highly fanciful picture of the Rock itself.*

road he actually did, for reasons that weighed with him; but had he gone by the sea, he would not have lost thirty-three thousand out of the sixty thousand veteran soldiers with whom he started.

While Hannibal was making this dangerous march, the Romans were sending to Spain, under the two elder Scipios, one part of their fleet, carrying a consular army. This made the voyage without serious loss, and the army established itself successfully north of the Ebro, on Hannibal's line of communications. At the same time another squadron, with an army commanded by the other consul, was sent to Sicily. The two

together numbered two hundred and twenty ships. On its station each met and defeated a Carthaginian squadron with an ease which may be inferred from the slight mention made of the actions, and which indicates the actual superiority of the Roman fleet.

After the second year the war assumed the following shape: Hannibal, having entered Italy by the north, after a series of successes had passed southward around Rome and fixed himself in southern Italy, living off the country—a condition which tended to alienate the people, and was especially precarious when in contact with the mighty political and military system

of control which Rome had there established. It was therefore from the first urgently necessary that he should establish, between himself and some reliable base, that stream of supplies and reinforcements which in terms of modern war is called 'communications.' There were three friendly regions which might, each or all, serve as such a base—Carthage itself, Macedonia, and Spain. With the first two, communication could be had only by sea. From Spain, where his firmest support was found, he could be reached by both land and sea, unless an enemy barred the passage; but the sea route was the shorter and easier.

In the first years of the war, Rome, by her sea power, controlled absolutely the basin between Italy, Sicily, and Spain, known as the Tyrrhenian and Sardinian Seas. The sea-coast from Ebro to the Tiber was mostly friendly to her. In the fourth year, after the battle of Cannae, Syracuse forsook the Roman alliance, the revolt spread through Sicily, and Macedonia also entered into an offensive league with Hannibal. These changes extended the necessary operations of the Roman fleet, and taxed its strength. What disposition was made of it, and how did it thereafter influence the struggle?

The indications are clear that Rome at no time ceased to

control the Tyrrhenian Sea, for her squadrons passed unmolested from Italy to Spain. On the Spanish coast also she had full sway till the younger Scipio saw fit to lay up the fleet. In the Adriatic, a squadron and naval station were established at Brindisi to check Macedonia, which performed their task so well that not a soldier of the phalanxes ever set foot in Italy. 'The want of a war fleet,' says Mommsen, 'paralyzed Philip in all his movements.' Here the effect of Sea Power is not even a matter of inference.

In Sicily, the struggle centred about Syracuse. The fleets of Carthage and Rome met there, but the superiority evidently lay with the latter; for though the Carthaginians at times succeeded in throwing supplies into the city, they avoided meeting the Roman fleet in battle. With Lilybaeum, Palermo, and Messina in its hands, the latter was well based in the north coast of the island. Access by the south was left open to the Carthaginians, and they were thus able to maintain the insurrection.

Putting these facts together, it is a reasonable inference, and supported by the whole tenor of the history, that the Roman sea power controlled the sea north of a line drawn from Tarragona in Spain to Lilybaeum (the modern Marsala), at the west end of Sicily, thence round by the north side of the island through the straits of Messina down to Syracuse, and from there to Brindisi in the Adriatic. This control lasted, unshaken, throughout the

loyalty and devotion which he had no reason to hope from the faction-cursed mother-city in Africa.

At the time of his starting, the Carthaginian power in Spain was secured from Cadiz to the river Ebro. The region between this river and the Pyrenees was inhabited by tribes friendly to the Romans, but unable, in the absence of the latter, to oppose a successful resistance to Hannibal. He put them down, leaving eleven thousand soldiers under Hanno to keep military possession of the country, lest the Romans should establish themselves there, and thus disturb his communications with his base.

Cnaeus Scipio, however, arrived on the spot by sea the same year with twenty thousand men, defeated Hanno, and occupied both the coast and interior north of the Ebro. The Romans thus held ground by which they entirely closed the road between Hannibal and reinforcements from Hasdrubal, and whence they could attack the Carthaginian power in Spain; while their own communications with Italy, being by water, were secured by their naval supremacy. They made a naval base at Tarragona, confronting that of Hasdrubal at Cartagena, and then invaded the Carthaginian dominions. The war in Spain went on under the elder Scipios, seemingly a side issue, with varying fortune for seven years; at the end of which time Hasdrubal inflicted upon them a crushing defeat, the two brothers were killed, and

war. It did not exclude maritime raids, large or small, such as have been spoken of; but it did forbid the sustained and secure communications of which Hannibal was in deadly need.

On the other hand, it seems equally plain that for the first ten years of the war the Roman fleet was not strong enough for sustained operations in the sea between Sicily and Carthage, nor indeed much to the south of the line indicated. When Hannibal started, he assigned such ships as he had to maintaining the communications between Spain and Africa, which the Romans did not then attempt to disturb.

The Roman sea power, therefore, threw Macedonia wholly out of the war. It did not keep Carthage from maintaining a useful and most harassing diversion in Sicily; but it did prevent her sending troops, when they would have been most useful, to her great general in Italy. How was it as to Spain?

Spain was the region upon which the father of Hannibal and Hannibal himself had based their intended invasion of Italy. For eighteen years before this began they had occupied the country, extending and consolidating their power, both political and military, with rare sagacity. They had raised, and trained in local wars, a large and now veteran army. Upon his own departure, Hannibal intrusted the government to his younger brother, Hasdrubal, who preserved toward him to the end a

the Carthagians nearly succeeded in breaking through to the Pyrenees with reinforcements for Hannibal. The attempt, however, was checked for the moment; and before it could be renewed, the fall of Capua released twelve thousand veteran Romans, who were sent to Spain under Claudius Nero, a man of exceptional ability, to whom was due later the most decisive military movement made by any Roman general during the Second Punic War. This seasonable reinforcement, which again assured the shaken grip on Hasdrubal's line of march, came by sea—a way which, though most rapid and easy, was closed to the Carthaginians by the Roman navy.

Two years later the younger Publius Scipio, celebrated afterward as Africanus, received the command in Spain, and captured Cartagena by a combined military and naval attack; after which he took the most extraordinary step of breaking up his fleet and transferring the seamen to the army. Not contented to act merely as the 'containing' force against Hasdrubal by closing the passes of the Pyrenees, Scipio pushed forward into southern Spain, and fought a severe but indecisive battle on the Guadalquivir; after which Hasdrubal slipped away from him, hurried north, crossed the Pyrenees at their extreme west, and pressed on to Italy, where Hannibal's position was daily growing weaker, the natural waste of his army not being replaced.

The war had lasted ten years, when Hasdrubal, having met little loss on the way, entered Italy at the north. The troops he brought, could they be safely united with those under the command of the unrivalled Hannibal, might give a decisive turn to the war, for Rome herself was nearly exhausted; the iron links which bound her own colonies and the allied States to her were strained to the utmost, and some had already snapped. But the military position of the two brothers was also perilous in the extreme. One being at the river Metaurus, the other in Apulia, two hundred miles apart, each was confronted by a superior enemy, and both these Roman armies were between their separated opponents. This false situation, as well as the long delay of Hasdrubal's coming, was due to the Roman control of the sea, which throughout the war limited the mutual support of the Carthaginian brothers to the route through Gaul. At the very time that Hasdrubal was making his long and dangerous circuit by land, Scipio had sent eleven thousand men from Spain by sea to reinforce the army opposed to him. The upshot was that messengers from Hasdrubal to Hannibal, having to pass over so wide a belt of hostile country, fell into the hands of Claudius Nero, commanding the southern Roman army, who thus learned the route which Hannibal intended to take. Nero correctly appreciated the situation, and, escaping the

never achieved. There were two lines possible—the one direct by sea, the other circuitous through Gaul. The first was blocked by the Roman sea power, the second imperilled and finally intercepted through the occupation of northern Spain by the Roman army. This occupation was made possible through the control of the sea, which the Carthaginians never endangered. With respect to Hannibal and his base, therefore, Rome occupied two central positions, Rome itself and northern Spain, joined by an easy interior line of communications, the sea; by which mutual support was continually given.

Had the Mediterranean been a level desert of land, in which the Romans held strong mountain ranges in Corsica and Sardinia, fortified posts at Tarragona, Lilybaeum, and Messina, the Italian coastline nearly to Genoa, and allied fortresses in Marseilles and other points; had they also possessed an armed force capable by its character of traversing that desert at will, but in which their opponents were very inferior and therefore compelled to a great circuit in order to concentrate their troops, the military situation would have been at once recognized, and no words would have been too strong to express the value and effect of that peculiar force. It would have been perceived, also, that the enemy's force of the same kind might, however inferior in strength, make an inroad, or raid, upon the territory thus

Above right and left: Galley warfare was chaotic but simple, with ramming followed by boarding. The great Roman innovation was the corvus *or crow, a boarding bridge which enabled the heavily armed Roman soldiers to get aboard the Carthaginian ships more easily. Once aboard they were superior to the more lightly armed enemy.*

vigilance of Hannibal, made a rapid march with eight thousand of his best troops to join the forces in the north. The junction being effected, the two consuls fell upon Hasdrubal in overwhelming numbers and destroyed his army; the Carthaginian leader himself falling in the battle. Hannibal's first news of the disaster was by the head of his brother being thrown into his camp. He is said to have exclaimed that Rome would now be mistress of the world; and the battle of Metaurus is generally accepted as decisive of the struggle between the two States.

The military situation which finally resulted in the battle of the Metaurus and the triumph of Rome may be summed up as follows: To overthrow Rome it was necessary to attack her in Italy at the heart of her power, and shatter the strongly linked confederacy of which she was the head. This was the objective. To reach it, the Carthaginians needed a solid base of operations and a secure line of communications. The former was established in Spain by the genius of the great Barca family; the latter was

held, might burn a village or waste a few miles of borderland, might even cut off a convoy at times, without, in a military sense, endangering the communications. Such predatory operations have been carried on in all ages by the weaker maritime belligerent, but they by no means warrant the inference, irreconcilable with the known facts, 'that neither Rome nor Carthage could be said to have undisputed mastery of the sea,' because 'Roman fleets sometimes visited the coasts of Africa, and Carthaginian fleets in the same way appeared off the coast of Italy.' In the case under consideration, the navy played the part of such a force upon the supposed desert; but as it acts on an element strange to most writers, as its members have been from time immemorial a strange race apart, without prophets of their own, neither themselves nor their calling understood, its immense determining influence upon the history of that era, and consequently upon the history of the world, has been overlooked. If the preceding argument is sound, it is as defective to omit sea power from the list of principal factors in the result, as it would be absurd to claim for it an exclusive influence.

Instances such as have been cited, drawn from widely separated periods of time, both before and after that specially treated in this work, serve to illustrate the intrinsic interest of the subject, and the character of the lessons which history has to

teach. As before observed, these come more often under the head of strategy than of tactics; they bear rather upon the conduct of campaigns than of battles, and hence are fraught with more lasting value. To quote a great authority in this connection, Jomini says: 'Happening to be in Paris near the end of 1851, a distinguished person did me the honor to ask my opinion as to whether recent improvements in fire-arms would cause any great modifications in the way of making war. I replied that they would probably have an influence upon the details of tactics, but that in great strategic operations and the grand combinations of battles, victory would, now as ever, result from the application of the principles which had led to the success of great generals in all ages; of Alexander and Caesar, as well as of Frederick and Napoleon.' This study has become more than ever important now to navies, because of the great and steady power of movement possessed by the modern steamer. The best-planned schemes might fail through stress of weather in the days of the galley and the sailing-ship; but this difficulty has almost disappeared. The principles which should direct great naval combinations have been applicable to all ages, and are deducible from history; but the power to carry them out with little regard to the weather is a recent gain.

The definitions usually given of the word 'strategy' confine it to military combinations embracing one or more fields of operations, either wholly distinct or mutually dependent, but always regarded as actual or immediate scenes of war. However this may be on shore, a recent French author is quite right in pointing out that such a definition is too narrow for naval strategy. 'This,' he says, 'differs from military strategy in that it is as necessary in peace as in war. Indeed, in peace it may gain its most decisive victories by occupying in a country, either by purchase or treaty, excellent positions which would perhaps hardly be got by war. It learns to profit by all opportunities of settling on some chosen point of a coast, and to render definitive an occupation which at first was only transient.' A generation that has seen England within ten years occupy successively Cyprus and Egypt, under terms and conditions on their face transient, but which have not yet led to the abandonment of the positions taken, can readily agree with this remark; which indeed receives constant illustration from the quiet persistency with which all the great sea powers are seeking position after position, less noted and less noteworthy than Cyprus and Egypt, in the different seas to which their people and their ships penetrate. 'Naval strategy has indeed for its end to found, support, and increase, as well in peace as in war, the sea power of a country;' and therefore its study has an interest and value for all citizens of a free country, but especially for those who are charged with its foreign and military relations.

The general conditions that either are essential to or powerfully affect the greatness of a nation upon the sea will now be examined; after which a more particular consideration of the various maritime nations of Europe at the middle of the seventeenth century, where the historical survey begins, will serve at once to illustrate and give precision to the conclusions upon the general subject.

Left: *A Roman bireme (below), a merchantman (above) and a smaller craft, as depicted in a mosaic. The projecting rostrum or beak for ramming can be seen on the warship's bow: the rostra was a public platform in Rome decorated with bronze beakheads from captured ships.*

Chapter 1

The Elements of Sea Power

The first and most obvious light in which the sea presents itself from the political and social point of view is that of a great highway; or better, perhaps, of a wide common, over which men may pass in all directions, but on which some well-worn paths show that controlling reasons have led them to choose certain lines of travel rather than others. These lines of travel are called trade routes; and the reasons which have determined them are to be sought in the history of the world.

Notwithstanding all the familiar and unfamiliar dangers of the sea, both travel and traffic by water have always been easier and cheaper than by land. The commercial greatness of Holland was due not only to her shipping at sea, but also to the numerous tranquil water-ways which gave such cheap and easy access to her own interior and to that of Germany. This advantage of carriage by water over that by land was yet more marked in a period when roads were few and very bad, wars frequent and society unsettled, as was the case two hundred years ago. Sea traffic then went in peril of robbers, but was nevertheless safer and quicker than that by land. A Dutch writer of that time, estimating the chances of his country in a war with England, notices among other things that the water-ways of England failed to penetrate the country sufficiently; therefore, the roads being bad, goods from one part of the kingdom to the other must go by sea, and be exposed to capture by the way. As regards purely internal trade, this danger has generally disappeared at the present day. In most civilized countries, now, the destruction or disappearance of the coasting trade would only be an inconvenience, although water transit is still the cheaper. Nevertheless, as late as the wars of the French Republic and the First Empire, those who are familiar with the history of the period, and the light naval literature that has grown up around it, know how constant is the mention of convoys stealing from point to point along the French coast, although the sea swarmed with English cruisers and there were good inland roads.

Under modern conditions, however, home trade is but a part of the business of a country bordering on the sea. Foreign necessaries of luxuries must be brought to its ports, either in its own or in foreign ships, which will return, bearing in exchange the products of the country, whether they be the fruits of the earth or the works of men's hands; and it is the wish of every nation that this shipping business should be done by its own vessels. The ships that thus sail to and fro must have secure ports to which to return, and must, as far as possible, be followed by the protection of their country throughout the voyage.

This protection in time of war must be extended by armed shipping. The necessity of a navy, in the restricted sense of the word, springs, therefore, from the existence of a peaceful shipping, and disappears with it, except in the case of a nation which has aggressive tendencies, and keeps up a navy merely as a branch of the military establishment. As the United States has at present no aggressive purposes, and as its merchant service has disappeared, the dwindling of the armed fleet and general lack of interest in it are strictly logical consequences. When for any reason sea trade is again found to pay, a large enough shipping interest will reappear to compel the revival of the war fleet. It is possible that when a canal route through the Central American Isthmus is seen to be a near certainty, the aggressive impulse may be strong enough to lead to the same result. This is doubtful, however, because a peaceful, gain-loving nation is not far-sighted, and far-sightedness is needed for adequate military preparation, especially in these days.

As a nation, with its unarmed and armed shipping, launches forth from its own shores, the need is soon felt of points upon which the ships can rely for peaceful trading, for refuge and supplies. In the present day friendly, though foreign, ports are to be found all over the world; and their shelter is enough while peace prevails. It was not always so, nor does peace always endure, though the United States have been favored by so long a continuance of it. In earlier times the merchant seaman, seeking for trade in new and unexplored regions, made his gains at risk of life and liberty from suspicious or hostile nations, and was under great delays in collecting a full and profitable freight. He therefore intuitively sought at the far end of his trade route one or more stations, to be given to him by force or favor, where he could fix himself or his agents in reasonable security, where his ships could lie in safety, and where the merchantable products of the land could be continually collecting, awaiting the arrival of

Left: *Amsterdam in the seventeenth century, a thriving center of maritime commerce.*

Right: *A grisaille by Van de Velde of Dutch warships anchoring close inshore, c 1693.*

the home fleet, which should carry them to the mother-country. As there was immense gain, as well as much risk, in these early voyages, such establishments naturally multiplied and grew until they became colonies; whose ultimate development and success depended upon the genius and policy of the nation from which they sprang, and form a very great part of the history, and particularly of the sea history, of the world. All colonies had not the simple and natural birth and growth above described. Many were more formal, and purely political, in their conception and founding, the act of the rulers of the people rather than of private individuals; but the trading-station with its after expansion, the work simply of the adventurer seeking gain, was in its reasons and essence the same as the elaborately organized and chartered colony. In both cases the mother-country had won a foothold in a foreign land, seeking a new outlet for what it had to sell, a new sphere for its shipping, more employment for its people, more comfort and wealth for itself.

The needs of commerce, however, were not all provided for when safety had been secured at the far end of the road. The voyages were long and dangerous, the seas often beset with enemies. In the most active days of colonizing there prevailed on the sea a lawlessness the very memory of which is now almost lost, and the days of settled peace between maritime nations were few and far between. Thus arose the demand for

stations along the road, like the Cape of Good Hope, St Helena, and Mauritius, not primarily for trade, but for defence and war; the demand for the possession of posts like Gibraltar, Malta, Louisburg, at the entrance of the Gulf of St Lawrence—posts whose value was chiefly strategic, though not necessarily wholly so. Colonies and colonial posts were sometimes commercial, sometimes military in their character; and it was exceptional that the same position was equally important in both points of view, as New York was.

In these three things—production, with the necessity of exchanging products, shipping, whereby the exchange is carried on, and colonies, which facilitate and enlarge the operations of shipping and tend to protect it by multiplying points of safety— is to be found the key to much of the history, as well as of the policy, of nations bordering upon the sea. The policy has varied both with the spirit of the age and with the character and clear-sightedness of the rulers; but the history of the seaboard nations has been less determined by the shrewdness and foresight of governments than by conditions of position, extent, configuration, number and character of their people—by what are called, in a word, natural conditions. It must however be admitted, and will be seen, that the wise or unwise action of individual men has at certain periods had a great modifying influence upon the growth of sea power in the broad sense, which includes not only

Above: *The English pirate John Avery, alias Long Ben, who captured the Mocha Fleet along with the daughter of the Great Mogul and her dowry.*

Left: *Dutch merchantmen preparing for sea by Hendrik Dubbels, 1676.*

Above: *The French buccaneer Francis Lolonois. The* boucaniers *took their name from* boucan, *or grilled meat, a delicacy of the Caribbean, but they liked to be thought of as the 'Brethren of the Coast.'*

the military strength afloat, that rules the sea or any part of it by force of arms, but also the peaceful commerce and shipping from which alone a military fleet naturally and healthfully springs, and on which it securely rests.

The principal conditions affecting the sea power of nations may be enumerated as follows: I Geographical Position. II Physical Conformation, including, as connected therewith, natural productions and climate. III Extent of Territory. IV Number of Population. V Character of the People. VI Character of the Government, including therein the national institutions.

I GEOGRAPHICAL POSITION

It may be pointed out, in the first place, that if a nation be so situated that it is neither forced to defend itself by land nor induced to seek extension of its territory by way of the land, it has, by the very unity of its aim directed upon the sea, an advantage as compared with a people one of whose boundaries is continental. This has been a great advantage to England over both France and Holland as a sea power. The strength of the latter was early exhausted by the necessity of keeping up a large army and carrying on expensive wars to preserve her independence; while the policy of France was constantly diverted, sometimes wisely and sometimes most foolishly, from the sea

to projects of continental extension. These military efforts expended wealth; whereas a wiser and consistent use of her geographical position would have added to it.

The geographical position may be such as of itself to promote a concentration, or to necessitate a dispersion, of the naval forces. Here again the British Islands have an advantage over France. The position of the latter, touching the Mediterranean as well as the ocean, while it has its advantages, is on the whole a source of military weakness at sea. The eastern and western French fleets have only been able to unite after passing through the Straits of Gibraltar, in attempting which they have often risked and sometimes suffered loss. The position of the United States upon the two oceans would be either a source of great weakness or a cause of enormous expense, had it a large sea commerce on both coasts.

England, by her immense colonial empire, has sacrificed much of this advantage of concentration of force around her own shores; but the sacrifice was wisely made, for the gain was greater than the loss, as the event proved. With the growth of her colonial system her war fleets also grew, but her merchant shipping and wealth grew yet faster. Still, in the wars of the American Revolution, and of the French Republic and Empire, to use the strong expression of a French author, 'England, despite the immense development of her navy, seemed ever, in the

Right: *The Arsenal at Brest. Unfortunately for the French this magnificent harbor was too far to the west to be of use in blockading the English Channel. To make matters worse the prevailing winds blew from the west, tending to pen a sailing fleet in harbor and helping English blockaders to remain on station.*

Below: *An Indiaman in a light breeze. These large merchantmen were often as well armed as a warship and were doughty antagonists for privateers.*

midst of riches, to feel all the embarrassment of poverty.' The might of England was sufficient to keep alive the heart and the members; whereas the equally extensive colonial empire of Spain, through her maritime weakness, but offered so many points for insult and injury.

The geographical position of a country may not only favor the concentration of its forces, but give the further strategic advantage of a central position and a good base for hostile operations against its probable enemies. This again is the case with England; on the one hand she faces Holland and the northern powers, on the other France and the Atlantic. When threatened with a coalition between France and the naval powers of the North Sea and the Baltic, as she at times was, her fleets in the Downs and in the Channel, and even that off Brest, occupied interior positions, and thus were readily able to interpose their united force against either one of the enemies which should seek to pass through the Channel to effect a junction with its ally. On

either side, also, Nature gave her better ports and a safer coast to approach. Formerly this was a very serious element in the passage through the Channel; but of late, steam and the improvement of her harbors have lessened the disadvantage under which France once labored. In the days of sailing-ships, the English fleet operated against Brest making its base at Torbay and Plymouth. The plan was simply this: in easterly or moderate weather the blockading fleet kept its position without difficulty; but in westerly gales, when too severe, they bore up for English ports, knowing that the French fleet could not get out till the wind shifted, which equally served to bring them back to their station.

The advantage of geographical nearness to an enemy, or to the object of attack, is nowhere more apparent than in that form of warfare which has lately received the name of commerce-destroying, which the French call *guerre de course*. This operation of war, being directed against peaceful merchant vessels which are usually defenceless, calls for ships of small military force. Such ships, having little power to defend themselves, need a refuge or point of support near at hand; which will be found either in certain parts of the sea controlled by the fighting ships of their country, or in friendly harbors. The latter give the strongest support, because they are always in the same place, and the approaches to them are more familiar to the commerce-destroyer than to his enemy. The nearness of France to England has thus greatly facilitated her *guerre de course* directed against the latter. Having ports on the North Sea, on the Channel, and on the Atlantic, her cruisers started from points near the focus of English trade, both coming and going. The distance of these ports from each other, disadvantageous for regular military combinations, is an advantage for this irregular secondary operation; for the essence of the one is concentration of effort, whereas for commerce-destroying diffusion of effort is the rule. Commerce-destroyers scatter, that they may see and

seize more prey. These truths receive illustration from the history of the great French privateers, whose bases and scenes of action were largely on the Channel and North Sea, or else were found in distant colonial regions, where islands like Guadaloupe and Martinique afforded similar near refuge. The necessity of renewing coal makes the cruiser of the present day even more dependent than of old on his port. Public opinion in the United States has great faith in war directed against an enemy's commerce; but it must be remembered that the Republic has no ports very near the great centres of trade abroad. Her geographical position is therefore singularly disadvantageous for carrying on successful commerce-destroying, unless she find bases in the ports of an ally.

If, in addition to facility for offence, Nature has so placed a country that it has easy access to the high sea itself, while at the same time it controls one of the great thoroughfares of the world's traffic, it is evident that the strategic value of its position

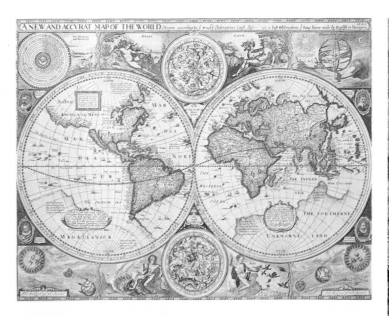

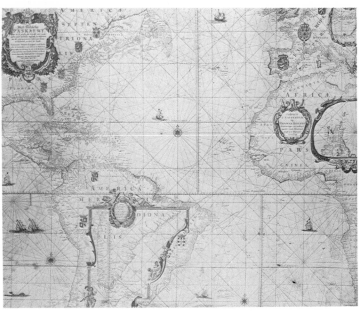

Above: *The growth of trade encouraged the growth of cartography, and this was helped by the rapid improvements in astronomy and navigation.*

Top: *The original Portuguese, Spanish and Dutch traders kept their charts secret to avoid competition.*

Right above: *The Cape of Good Hope was also feared by sailors as the 'Cape of Storms.' It became a port of call in 1652.*

is very high. Such again is, and to a greater degree was, the position of England. The trade of Holland, Sweden, Russia, Denmark, and that which went up the great rivers to the interior of Germany, had to pass through the Channel close by her doors; for sailing-ships hugged the English coast. This northern trade had, moreover, a peculiar bearing upon sea power; for naval stores, as they are commonly called, were mainly drawn from the Baltic countries.

But for the loss of Gibraltar, the position of Spain would have been closely analogous to that of England. Looking at once upon the Atlantic and the Mediterranean, with Cadiz on the one side and Cartagena on the other, the trade to the Levant must have passed under her hands, and that round the Cape of Good Hope not far from her doors. But Gibraltar not only deprived her of the control of the Straits, it also imposed an obstacle to the easy junction of the two divisions of her fleet.

At the present day, looking only at the geographical position

of Italy, and not at the other conditions affecting her sea power, it would seem that with her extensive sea-coast and good ports she is very well placed for exerting a decisive influence on the trade route to the Levant and by the Isthmus of Suez. This is true in a degree, and would be much more so did Italy now hold all the islands naturally Italian; but with Malta in the hands of England, and Corsica in those of France, the advantages of her geographical position are largely neutralized. From race affinities and situation those two islands are as legitimately objects of desire to Italy as Gibraltar is to Spain. If the Adriatic were a great highway of commerce, Italy's position would be still more influential. These defects in her geographical completeness, combined with other causes injurious to a full and secure development of sea power, make it more than doubtful whether Italy can for some time be in the front rank among the sea nations.

As the aim here is not an exhaustive discussion, but merely an attempt to show, by illustration, how vitally the situation of a country may affect its career upon the sea, this division of the subject may be dismissed for the present; the more so as instances which will further bring out its importance will continually recur in the historical treatment. Two remarks, however, are here appropriate.

Circumstances have caused the Mediterranean Sea to play a greater part in the history of the world, both in a commercial and a military point of view, than any other sheet of water of the same size. Nation after nation has striven to control it, and the strife still goes on. Therefore a study of the conditions upon which preponderance in its water has rested, and now rests, and of the relative military values of different points upon its coasts, will be more instructive than the same amount of effort expended in another field. Furthermore, it has at the present time a very marked analogy in many respects to the Caribbean Sea— an analogy which will be still closer if a Panama canal-route ever be completed. A study of the strategic conditions of the Mediterranean, which have received ample illustration, will be an excellent prelude to a similar study of the Caribbean, which has comparatively little history.

The second remark bears upon the geographical position of the United States relatively to a Central-American canal. If one be made, and fulfil the hopes of its builders, the Caribbean will be changed from a terminus, and place of local traffic, or at best a broken and imperfect line of travel, as it now is, into one of the great highways of the world. Along this path a great commerce will travel, bringing the interests of the other great nations, the European nations, close along our shores, as they have never been before. With this it will not be so easy as heretofore to stand aloof from international complications. The position of the United States with reference to this route will resemble that of England to the Channel, and of the Mediterranean countries to

the Suez route. As regards influence and control over it, depending upon geographical position, it is of course plain that the centre of the national power, the permanent base, is much nearer than that of other great nations. The positions now or hereafter occupied by them on island or mainland, however strong, will be but outposts of their power; while in all the raw materials of military strength no nation is superior to the United States. She is, however, weak in a confessed unpreparedness for war; and her geographical nearness to the point of contention loses some of its value by the character of the Gulf coast, which is deficient in ports combining security from an enemy with facility for repairing war-ships of the first class, without which ships no country can pretend to control any part of the sea. In case of a contest for supremacy in the Caribbean, it seems evident from the depth of the South Pass of the Mississippi, the nearness of New Orleans, and the advantages of the Mississippi Valley for water transit, that the main effort of the country must pour down that valley, and its permanent base of operations be found there. The defence of the entrance to the Mississippi, however, presents peculiar difficulties; while the only two rival ports, Key West and Pensacola, have too little depth of water, and are much less advantageously placed with reference to the resources of the country. To get the full benefit of superior geographical position, these defects must be overcome. Furthermore, as her distance from the Isthmus, though relatively less, is still considerable, the United States will have to obtain in the Caribbean stations fit for contingent, or secondary, bases of operations; which by their natural advantages, susceptibility of defence, and nearness to the central strategic issue, will enable her fleets to remain as near the scene as any opponent. With ingress and egress from the Mississippi sufficiently protected, with such outposts in her hands, and with the communications between them and the home base secured, in short, with proper military preparation, for which she has all necessary means, the preponderance of the United States on this field follows, from her geographical position and her power, with mathematical certainty.

II PHYSICAL CONFORMATION

The peculiar features of the Gulf coast, just alluded to, come properly under the head of Physical Conformation of a country, which is placed second for discussion among the conditions which affect the development of sea power.

The seaboard of a country is one of its frontiers; and the easier the access offered by the frontier to the region beyond, in this case the sea, the greater will be the tendency of a people toward intercourse with the rest of the world by it. If a country be imagined having a long seaboard, but entirely without a harbor, such a country can have no sea trade of its own, no shipping, no navy. This was practically the case with Belgium when it was a Spanish and an Austrian province. The Dutch, in 1648, as a condition of peace after a successful war, exacted that the Scheldt should be closed to sea commerce. This closed the harbor of Antwerp and transferred the sea trade of Belgium to Holland. The Spanish Netherlands ceased to be a sea power.

Numerous and deep harbors are a source of strength and wealth, and doubly so if they are the outlets of navigable streams, which facilitate the concentration in them of a country's internal trade; but by their very accessibility they become a source of weakness in war, if not properly defended. The Dutch in 1667 found little difficulty in ascending the Thames and burning a large fraction of the English navy within sight of London; whereas a few years later the combined fleets of England and France, when attempting a landing in Holland, were foiled by the difficulties of the coast as much as by the valor of the Dutch fleet. In 1778 the harbor of New York, and with it undisputed control of the Hudson River, would have been lost to the English, who were caught at disadvantage, but for the hesitancy of the French admiral. With that control, New England would have been restored to close and safe communication with New York, New Jersey, and Pennsylvania; and this blow, following so closely on Burgoyne's disaster of the year before, would probably have led the English to make an earlier peace. The Mississippi is a mighty source of wealth and strength to the United States; but the feeble defences of its mouth and the number of its subsidiary streams penetrating the country made it a weakness and source of disaster to the Southern Confederacy. And lastly, in 1814, the occupation of the Chesapeake and the destruction of Washington gave a sharp lesson of the dangers incurred through the noblest water-ways, if their approaches be undefended; a lesson recent enough to be easily recalled, but which, from the present appearance of the coast defences, seems to be yet more easily forgotten. Nor should it be thought that conditions have changed; circumstances and details of offence and defence have been modified, in these days as before, but the great conditions remain the same.

Before and during the great Napoleonic wars, France had no port for ships-of-the-line east of Brest. How great the advantage to England, which in the same stretch has two great arsenals, at Plymouth and at Portsmouth, besides other harbors of refuge and supply. This defect of conformation has since been remedied by the works at Cherbourg.

Besides the contour of the coast, involving easy access to the sea, there are other physical conditions which lead people to the sea or turn them from it. Although France was deficient in military ports on the Channel, she had both there and on the ocean, as well as in the Mediterranean, excellent harbors, favorably situated for trade abroad, and at the outlet of large rivers, which would foster internal traffic. But when Richelieu had put an end to civil war, Frenchmen did not take to the sea with the eagerness and success of the English and Dutch. A principal reason for this has been plausibly found in the physical conditions which have made France a pleasant land, with a delightful climate, producing within itself more than its people needed. England, on the other hand, received from Nature but little, and, until her manufactures were developed, had little to export. Their many wants, combined with their restless activity and other conditions that favored maritime enterprise, led her people abroad; and they there found lands more pleasant and richer than their own. Their needs and genius made them merchants and colonists, then manufacturers and producers; and between products and colonies shipping is the inevitable link. So their sea power grew. But if England was drawn to the sea, Holland was driven to it; without the sea England languished, but Holland died. In the height of her greatness, when she was

Left: The East Side of New York in 1746, already a busy commercial port.

Below center: A Dutch fluyt, this time taking up her moorings.

Below bottom: Dutch frigates, like the 1st to 5th Rates, emphasized shallow draft because of the numerous shoals and sandbanks off the Dutch coast.

Below: Another fluyt being careened. Shipwrights are burning off weed and barnacles before recoating the timbers. From an engraving by Zeeman c 1650.

one of the chief factors in European politics, a competent native authority estimated that the soil of Holland could not support more than one eighth of her inhabitants. The manufactures of the country were then numerous and important, but they had been much later in their growth than the shipping interest. The poverty of the soil and the exposed nature of the coast drove the Dutch first to fishing. Then the discovery of the process of curing the fish gave them material for export as well as home consumption, and so laid the corner-stone of their wealth. Thus they had become traders at the time that the Italian republics, under the pressure of Turkish power and the discovery of the passage round the Cape of Good Hope, were beginning to decline, and they fell heirs to the great Italian trade of the Levant. Further favored by their geographical position, intermediate between the Baltic, France, and the Mediterranean, and at the mouth of the German rivers, they quickly absorbed nearly all the carrying-trade of Europe. The wheat and naval stores of the Baltic, the trade of Spain with her colonies in the New World, the wines of France, and the French coasting-trade were, little more than two hundred years ago, transported in Dutch shipping. Much of the carrying-trade of England, even, was then done in Dutch bottoms. It will not be pretended that all this prosperity proceeded only from the poverty of Holland's natural resources. Something does not grow from nothing. What is true, is, that by the necessitous condition of her people they were driven to the sea, and were, from their mastery of the shipping business and the size of their fleets, in a position to profit by the sudden expansion of commerce and the spirit of exploration which followed on the discovery of America and of the passage round the Cape. Other causes concurred, but their whole prosperity stood on the sea power to which their poverty gave birth. Their food, their clothing, the raw material for their manufactures, the very timber and hemp with which they built and rigged their ships (and they built nearly as many as all Europe besides), were imported; and when a disastrous war with England in 1653 and 1654 had lasted eighteen months, and their shipping business was stopped, it is said 'the sources of revenue which had always maintained the riches of the State, such as fisheries and commerce, were almost dry. Workshops were closed, work was suspended. The Zuyder Zee became a forest of masts; the country was full of beggars; grass grew in the streets, and in Amsterdam fifteen hundred houses were untenanted.' A humiliating peace alone saved them from ruin.

This sorrowful result shows the weakness of a country depending wholly upon sources external to itself for the part it is playing in the world. With large deductions, owing to differences of conditions which need not here be spoken of, the case of Holland then has strong points of resemblance to that of Great Britain now; and they are true prophets, though they seem to be having small honor in their own country, who warn her that the continuance of her prosperity at home depends primarily upon maintaining her power abroad. Men may be discontented at the lack of political privilege; they will be yet more uneasy if they come to lack bread. It is of more interest to Americans to note that the result to France, regarded as a power of the sea, caused by the extent, delightfulness, and richness of the land, has been reproduced in the United States. In the beginning, their forefathers held a narrow strip of land upon the sea, fertile in parts though little developed, abounding in harbors and near rich fishing-grounds. These physical conditions combined with an inborn love of the sea, the pulse of that English blood which still beat in their veins, to keep alive all those tendencies and pursuits upon which a healthy sea power depends. Almost every one of the original colonies was on the sea or on one of its great tributaries. All export and import

tended toward one coast. Interest in the sea and an intelligent appreciation of the part it played in the public welfare were easily and widely spread; and a motive more influential than care for the public interest was also active, for the abundance of ship-building materials and a relative fewness of other investments made shipping a profitable private interest. How changed the present condition is, all know. The centre of power is no longer on the seaboard. Books and newspapers vie with one another in describing the wonderful growth, and the still undeveloped riches, of the interior. Capital there finds its best investments, labor its largest opportunities. The frontiers are neglected and politically weak; the Gulf and Pacific coasts actually so, the Atlantic coast relatively to the central Mississippi Valley. When the day comes that shipping again pays, when the three sea frontiers find that they are not only militarily weak, but poorer for lack of national shipping, their united efforts may avail to lay again the foundations of our sea power. Till then, those who follow the limitations which lack of sea power placed upon the career of France may mourn that their own country is being led, by a like redundancy of home wealth, into the same neglect of that great instrument.

Among modifying physical conditions may be noted a form like that of Italy—a long peninsula, with a central range of mountains dividing it into two narrow strips, along which the roads connecting the different ports necessarily run. Only an absolute control of the sea can wholly secure such communications, since it is impossible to know at what point an enemy coming from beyond the visible horizon may strike; but still, with an adequate naval force centrally posted, there will be good hope of attacking his fleet, which is at once his base and line of communications, before serious damage has been done. The long, narrow peninsula of Florida, with Key West at its extremity, though flat and thinly populated, presents at first sight conditions like those of Italy. The resemblance may be only superficial, but it seems probable that if the chief scene of a naval war were the Gulf of Mexico, the communications by land to the end of the peninsula might be a matter of consequence, and open to attack.

When the sea not only borders, or surrounds, but also separates a country into two or more parts, the control of it becomes not only desirable, but vitally necessary. Such a physical condition either gives birth and strength to sea power, or makes the country powerless. Such is the condition of the present kingdom of Italy, with its islands of Sardinia and Sicily; and hence in its youth and still existing financial weakness it is seen to put forth such vigorous and intelligent efforts to create a military navy. It has even been argued that, with a navy decidedly superior to her enemy's, Italy could better base her power upon her islands than upon her mainland; for the insecurity of the lines of communication in the peninsula, already pointed out, would most seriously embarrass an invading army surrounded by a hostile people and threatened from the sea.

The Irish Sea, separating the British Islands, rather resembles an estuary than an actual division; but the history has shown the danger from it to the United Kingdom. In the days of Louis XIV, when the French navy nearly equalled the combined English and Dutch, the gravest complications existed in Ireland, which passed almost wholly under the control of the natives and the French. Nevertheless, the Irish Sea was rather a danger to the English—a weak point in their communications—than an advantage to the French. The latter did not venture their ships-of-the-line in its narrow waters, and expeditions intending to land were directed upon the ocean ports in the south and west. At the supreme moment the great French fleet was sent upon the south coast of England, where it decisively defeated the

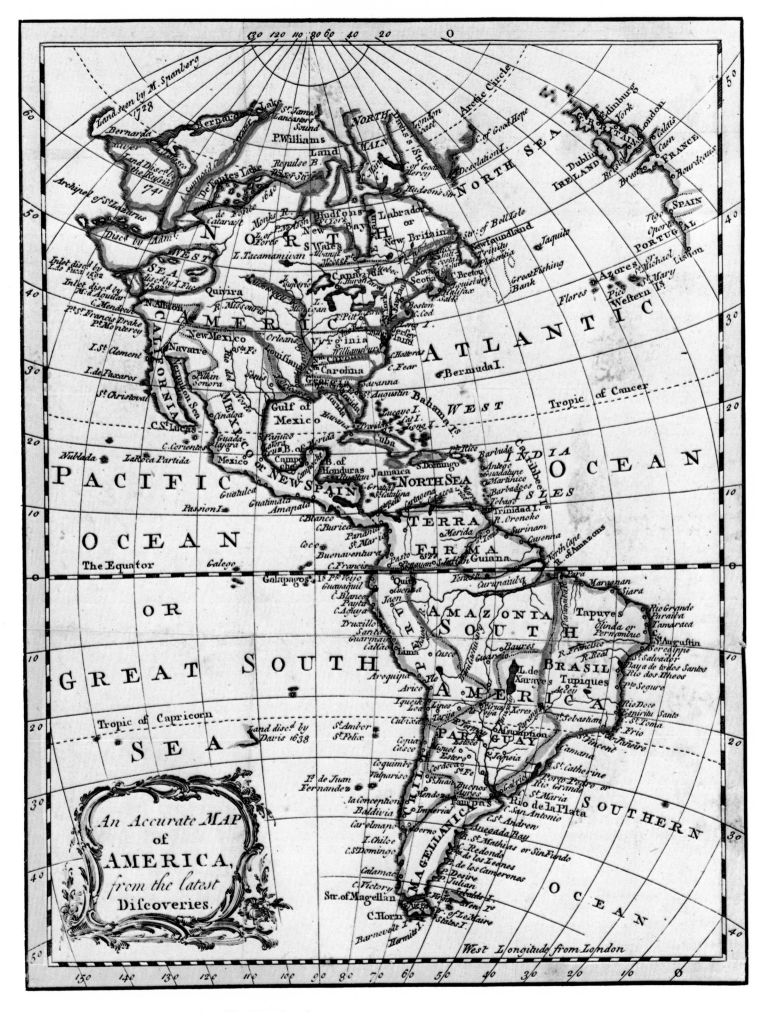

Above: *The New World as it was in the middle of the eighteenth century;
Canada had passed under British control and the 13 colonies were not yet
independent.*

allies, and at the same time twenty-five frigates were sent to St George's Channel, against the English communications. In the midst of a hostile people, the English army in Ireland was seriously imperilled, but was saved by the battle of the Boyne and the flight of James II. This movement against the enemy's communications was strictly strategic, and would be just as dangerous to England now as in 1690.

Spain, in the same century, afforded an impressive lesson of the weakness caused by such separation when the parts are not knit together by a strong sea power. She then still retained, as remnants of her past greatness, the Netherlands (now Belgium), Sicily, and other Italian possessions, not to speak of her vast colonies in the New World. Yet so low had the Spanish sea power fallen, that a well-informed and sober-minded Hollander of the day could claim that 'in Spain all the coast is navigated by a few Dutch ships; and since the peace of 1648 their ships and seamen are so few that they have publicly begun to hire our ships to sail to the Indies, whereas they were formerly careful to exclude all foreigners from there. . . . It is manifest,' he goes on, 'that the West Indies, being as the stomach to Spain (for from it nearly all the revenue is drawn), must be joined to the Spanish head by a sea force; and that Naples and the Netherlands, being like two arms, they cannot lay out their strength for Spain, nor receive anything thence but by shipping—all which may easily be done by our shipping in peace, and by it obstructed in war.' Half a century before, Sully, the great minister of Henry IV, had characterized Spain 'as one of those States whose legs and arms are strong and powerful, but the heart infinitely weak and feeble.' Since his day the Spanish navy had suffered not only disaster, but annihilation; not only humiliation, but degradation. The consequences briefly were that shipping was destroyed; manufactures perished with it. The government depended for its support, not upon a widespread healthy commerce and industry that could survive many a staggering blow, but upon a narrow stream of silver trickling through a few treasure-ships from America, easily and frequently intercepted by an enemy's cruisers. The loss of half a dozen galleons more than once paralyzed its movements for a year. While the war in the Netherlands lasted, the Dutch control of the sea forced Spain to send her troops by a long and costly journey overland instead of by sea; and the same cause reduced her to such straits for necessaries that, by a mutual arrangement which seems very odd to modern ideas, her wants were supplied by Dutch ships, which thus maintained the enemies of their country, but received in return specie which was welcome in the Amsterdam exchange. In America, the Spanish protected themselves as best they might behind masonry, unaided from home; while in the Mediterranean they escaped insult and injury mainly

through the indifference of the Dutch, for the French and English had not yet begun to contend for mastery there. In the course of history the Netherlands, Naples, Sicily, Minorca, Havana, Manila, and Jamaica were wrenched away, at one time or another, from this empire without a shipping. In short, while Spain's maritime impotence may have been primarily a symptom of her general decay, it became a marked factor in precipitating her into the abyss from which she has not yet wholly emerged.

Except Alaska, the United States has no outlying possession—no foot of ground inaccessible by land. Its contour is such as to present few points specially weak from their saliency, and all important parts of the frontiers can be readily attained—cheaply by water, rapidly by rail. The weakest frontier, the Pacific, is far removed from the most dangerous of possible enemies. The internal resources are boundless as compared with present needs; we can live off ourselves indefinitely in 'our little corner,' to use the expression of a French officer to the author. Yet should that little corner be invaded by a new commercial route through the Isthmus, the United States in her turn may have the rude awakening of those who have abandoned their share in the common birthright of all people, the sea.

III EXTENT OF TERRITORY

The last of the conditions affecting the development of a nation as a sea power, and touching the country itself as distinguished from the people who dwell there, is Extent of Territory. This may be dismissed with comparatively few words.

As regards the development of sea power, it is not the total number of square miles which a country contains, but the length of its coast-line and the character of its harbors that are to be considered. As to these it is to be said that, the geographical and physical conditions being the same, extent of sea-coast is a source of strength or weakness according as the population is large or small. A country is in this like a fortress; the garrison must be proportioned to the *enceinte*. A recent familiar instance is found in the American War of Secession. Had the South had a people as numerous as it was warlike, and a navy commensurate to its other resources as a sea power, the great extent of its sea-coast and its numerous inlets would have been elements of great strength. The people of the United States and the Government of that day justly prided themselves on the effectiveness of the blockade of the whole Southern coast. It was a great feat, a very great feat; but it would have been an impossible feat had the Southerners been more numerous, and a nation of seamen. What was there shown was not, as has been said, how such a blockade can be maintained, but that such a blockade is possible in the face of a population not only unused to the sea, but also scanty in numbers. Those who recall how the blockade was maintained, and the class of ships that blockaded during great part of the war, know that the plan, correct under the circumstances, could not have been carried out in the face of a real navy. Scattered unsupported along the coast, the United States ships kept their places, singly or in small detachments, in face of an extensive network of inland water communications which favored secret concentration of the enemy. Behind the first line of water communications were long estuaries, and here and there strong fortresses, upon either of which the enemy's ships could always fall back to elude pursuit or to receive protection. Had there been a Southern navy to profit by such advantages, or by the scattered condition of the United States ships, the latter could not have been distributed as they were; and being forced to concentrate for mutual support, many small but useful approaches would have been left open to commerce. But as the Southern coast, from its extent and many inlets, might have been a source of strength, so, from those very characteristics, it became a fruitful source of injury. The great story of the opening of the Mississippi is but the most striking illustration of an action that was going on incessantly all over the South. At every breach of the sea frontier, war-ships were entering. The streams that had carried the wealth and supported the trade of the seceding States turned against them, and admitted their enemies to their hearts. Dismay, insecurity, paralysis prevailed in regions that might, under happier auspices, have kept a nation alive through the most exhausting war. Never did sea power play a greater or a more decisive part than in the contest which determined that the course of the world's history would be modified by the existence of one great nation, instead of several rival States, in the North American continent. But while just pride is felt in the well-earned glory of those days, and the greatness of the results due to naval preponderance is

admitted, Americans who understand the facts should never fail to remind the over-confidence of their countrymen that the South not only had no navy, not only was not a seafaring people, but that also its population was not proportioned to the extent of the sea-coast which it had to defend.

IV NUMBER OF POPULATION

After the consideration of the natural conditions of a country should follow an examination of the characteristics of its population as affecting the development of sea power; and first among these will be taken, because of its relations to the extent of the territory, which has just been discussed, the number of the people who live in it. It has been said that in respect of dimensions it is not merely the number of square miles, but the extent and character of the sea-coast that is to be considered with reference to sea power; and so, in point of population, it is not only the

Opposite: The Spanish 3rd Rate (74 guns) Glorioso *which was captured by HMS* Russell *(80 guns) 8 October 1747. The warships of almost all navies were classified into divisions, or Rates, according to the number of guns they carried. Admiral Lord Anson introduced this system of classification in the early 1750s, but its terms are often applied to earlier vessels for easy reference.*

Right: Stephen Decatur, one of the first American naval officers to rise to distinction. He fought the Barbary pirates in 1803–04 and during the War of 1812 captured HMS Macedonian.

Above: *Sir Edward Pellew, later Lord Exmouth, was one of the originals for Captain Hornblower. He had a highly successful career as a frigate captain and destroyed the 74-gun Droits de l'Homme in 1797 by forcing her ashore.*

grand total, but the number following the sea, or at least readily available for employment on ship-board and for the creation of naval material, that must be counted.

For example, formerly and up to the end of the great wars following the French Revolution, the population of France was much greater than that of England; but in respect of sea power in general, peaceful commerce as well as military efficiency, France was much inferior to England. In the matter of military efficiency this fact is the more remarkable because at times, in point of military preparation at the outbreak of war, France had the advantage; but she was not able to keep it. Thus in 1778, when war broke out, France, through her maritime inscription, was able to man at once fifty ships-of-the-line. England, on the contrary, by reason of the dispersal over the globe of that very shipping on which her naval strength so securely rested, had much trouble in manning forty at home; but in 1782 she had one hundred and twenty in commission or ready for commission, while France had never been able to exceed seventy-one. Again, as late as 1840, when the two nations were on the verge of war in the Levant, a most accomplished French officer of the day, while extolling the high state of efficiency of the French fleet and the eminent qualities of its admiral, and expressing confidence in the results of an encounter with an equal enemy goes on to say: 'Behind the squadron of twenty-one ships-of-the-line which we could then assemble, there was no reserve; not another ship could have been commissioned within six months.' And this was due not only to lack of ships and of

Right: *The destruction of the* Droits de l'Homme *by the frigates* Indefatigable *and* Amazon, *14 January 1797. The French 3rd Rate was caught on a lee shore and ran aground, but the* Amazon *could not get clear either.*

Below: *The great Battle of Lepanto, 7 October 1571, stemmed the advance of Islam in the Mediterranean. Although often described as a mêlée of galleys, modern research shows that Don Juan fought a carefully planned battle, making use of his strongest ships to provide local superiority and firepower.*

paring of naval material, or following other callings more or less closely connected with the water and with craft of all kinds. Such kindred callings give an undoubted aptitude for the sea from the outset. There is an anecdote showing curious insight into this matter on the part of one of England's distinguished seamen, Sir Edward Pellew. When the war broke out in 1793, the usual scarceness of seamen was met. Eager to get to sea and to fill his complement otherwise than with landsmen, he instructed his officers to seek for Cornish miners; reasoning from the conditions and dangers of their calling, of which he had personal knowledge, that they would quickly fit into the demands of sea life. The result showed his sagacity, for, thus escaping an otherwise unavoidable delay, he was fortunate enough to capture the first frigate taken in the war in single combat; and what is especially instructive is, that although but a few weeks in commission, while his opponent had been over a year, the losses, heavy on both sides, were nearly equal.

It may be urged that such reserve strength has now nearly lost the importance it once had, because modern ships and weapons take so long to make, and because modern States aim at developing the whole power of their armed force, on the outbreak of war, with such rapidity as to strike a disabling blow before the enemy can organize an equal effort. To use a familiar phrase, there will not be time for the whole resistance of the national fabric to come into play; the blow will fall on the organized military fleet, and if that yield, the solidity of the rest of the structure will avail nothing. To a certain extent this is

proper equipments, though both were wanting. 'Our maritime inscription,' he continues, 'was so exhausted by what we had done [in manning twenty-one ships], that the permanent levy established in all quarters did not supply reliefs for the men, who were already more than three years on cruise.'

A contrast such as this shows a difference in what is called staying power, or reserve force, which is even greater than appears on the surface; for a great shipping afloat necessarily employs, besides the crews, a large number of people engaged in the various handicrafts which facilitate the making and retrue; but then it has always been true, though to a less extent formerly than now. Granted the meeting of two fleets which represent practically the whole present strength of their two nations, if one of them be destroyed, while the other remains fit for action, there will be much less hope now than formerly that the vanquished can restore his navy for that war; and the result will be disastrous just in proportion to the dependence of the nation upon her sea power. A Trafalgar would have been a much more fatal blow to England than it was to France, had the English fleet then represented, as the allied fleet did, the bulk of the nation's power. Trafalgar in such a case would have been to England what Austerlitz was to Austria, and Jena to Prussia; an empire would have been laid prostrate by the destruction or disorganization of its military forces, which, it is said, were the favorite objective of Napoleon.

But does the consideration of such exceptional disasters in the past justify the putting a low value upon that reserve strength, based upon the number of inhabitants fitted for a certain kind of military life, which is here being considered? The blows just mentioned were dealt by men of exceptional genius, at the head of armed bodies of exceptional training, *esprit-de-corps*, and prestige, and were, besides, inflicted upon opponents more or less demoralized by conscious inferiority and previous defeat. Austerlitz had been closely preceded by Ulm, where thirty thousand Austrians laid down their arms without a battle; and the history of the previous years had been one long record of Austrian reverse and French success. Trafalgar followed closely upon a cruise, justly called a campaign, of almost constant failure; and farther back, but still recent, were the memories of St Vincent for the Spaniards, and of the Nile for the French, in the allied fleet. Except the case of Jena, these crushing overthrows were not single disasters, but final blows; and in the Jena campaign there was a disparity in numbers, equipment, and general preparation for war, which makes it less applicable in considering what may result from a single victory.

England is at the present time the greatest maritime nation in the world; in steam and iron she has kept the superiority she had in the days of sail and wood. France and England are the two powers that have the largest military navies; and it is so far an open question which of the two is the more powerful, that they may be regarded as practically of equal strength in material for a sea war. In the case of a collision can there be assumed such a difference of personnel, or of preparation, as to make it probable that a decisive inequality will result from one battle or one campaign? If not, the reserve strength will begin to tell; organized reserve first, then reserve of seafaring population, reserve of mechanical skill, reserve of wealth. It seems to have been somewhat forgotten that England's leadership in mechanical arts gives her a reserve of mechanics, who can easily familiarize themselves with the appliances of modern iron-clads; and as her commerce and industries feel the burden of the war, the surplus of seamen and mechanics will go to the armed shipping.

The whole question of the value of a reserve, developed or undeveloped, amounts now to this: Have modern conditions of warfare made it probable that, of two nearly equal adversaries, one will be so prostrated in a single campaign that a decisive result will be reached in that time? Sea warfare has given no answer. The crushing successes of Prussia against Austria, and of Germany against France, appear to have been those of a stronger over a much weaker nation, whether the weakness were due to natural causes, or to official incompetency. How would a delay like that of Plevna have affected the fortune of war, had Turkey had any reserve of national power upon which to call?

Right: Spanish galleons and carracks c 1561.

If time be, as is everywhere admitted, a supreme factor in war, it behooves countries whose genius is essentially not military, whose people, like all free people, object to pay for large military establishments, to see to it that they are at least strong enough to gain the time necessary to turn the spirit and capacity of their subjects into the new activities which war calls for. If the existing force by land or sea is strong enough so to hold out, even though at a disadvantage, the country may rely upon its natural resources and strength coming into play for whatever they are worth—its numbers, its wealth, its capacities of every kind. If, on the other hand, what force it has can be overthrown and crushed quickly, the most magnificent possibilities of natural power will not save it from humiliating conditions, nor, if its foe be wise, from guarantees which will postpone revenge to a distant future. The story is constantly repeated on the smaller fields of war: 'If so-and-so can hold out a little longer, this can be saved or that can be done'; as in sickness it is often said: 'If the patient can only hold out so long, the strength of his constitution may pull him through.'

England to some extent is now such a country. Holland was such a country; she would not pay, and if she escaped, it was but by the skin of her teeth. 'Never in time of peace and from fear of a rupture,' wrote their great statesman, De Witt, 'will they take resolutions strong enough to lead them to pecuniary sacrifices beforehand. The character of the Dutch is such that, unless danger stares them in the face, they are indisposed to lay out money for their own defence. I have to do with a people

who, liberal to profusion where they ought to economize, are often sparing to avarice where they ought to spend.'

That our own country is open to the same reproach, is patent to all the world. The United States has not that shield of defensive power behind which time can be gained to develop its reserve of strength. As for a seafaring population adequate to her possible needs, where is it? Such a resource, proportionate to her coast-line and population, is to be found only in a national merchant shipping and its related industries, which at present scarcely exist. It will matter little whether the crews of such ships are native or foreign born, provided they are attached to the flag, and her power at sea is sufficient to enable the most of them to get back in case of war. When foreigners by thousands are admitted to the ballot, it is of little moment that they are given fighting-room on board ship.

Though the treatment of the subject has been somewhat discursive, it may be admitted that a great population following callings related to the sea is, now as formerly, a great element of sea power; that the United States is deficient in that element; and that its foundations can be laid only in a large commerce under her own flag.

V NATIONAL CHARACTER

The effect of national character and aptitudes upon the development of sea power will next be considered.

If sea power be really based upon a peaceful and extensive commerce, aptitude for commercial pursuits must be a dis-

tinguishing feature of the nations that have at one time or another been great upon the sea. History almost without exception affirms that this is true. Save the Romans, there is no marked instance to the contrary.

All men seek gain and, more or less, love money; but the way in which gain is sought will have a marked effect upon the commercial fortunes and the history of the people inhabiting a country.

If history may be believed, the way in which the Spaniards and their kindred nation, the Portuguese, sought wealth, not only brought a blot upon the national character, but was also fatal to the growth of a healthy commerce; and so to the industries upon which commerce lives, and ultimately to that national wealth which was sought by mistaken paths. The desire for gain rose in them to fierce avarice; so they sought in the new-found worlds which gave such an impetus to the commercial and maritime development of the countries of Europe, not new fields of industry, not even the healthy excitement of exploration and adventure, but gold and silver. They had many great qualities; they were bold, enterprising, temperate, patient of suffering, enthusiastic, and gifted with intense national feeling. When to these qualities are added the advantages of Spain's position and well-situated ports, the fact that she was first to occupy large and rich portions of the new worlds and long remained without a competitor, and that for a hundred years after the discovery of America she was the leading State in Europe, she might have been expected to take the foremost place among the sea powers. Exactly the contrary was the result, as all know. Since the battle of Lepanto in 1571, though engaged in many wars, no sea victory of any consequence shines on the pages of Spanish history; and the decay of her commerce sufficiently accounts for the painful and sometimes ludicrous inaptness shown on the decks of her ships of war. Doubtless such a result is not to be attributed to one cause only. Doubtless the government of Spain was in many ways such as to cramp and blight a free and healthy development of private enterprise; but the character of a great people breaks through or shapes the character of its government, and it can hardly be doubted that had the bent of the people been toward trade, the action of government would have been drawn into the same current. The great field of the colonies, also, was remote from the centre of that despotism which blighted the growth of old Spain. As it was, thousand of Spaniards, of the working as well as the upper classes, left Spain; and the occupations in which they engaged abroad sent home little but specie, or merchandise of small bulk, requiring but small tonnage. The mother-country herself produced little but wool, fruit, and iron; her manufactures were naught; her industries suffered; her population steadily decreased. Both she and her colonies depended upon the Dutch for so many of the necessaries of life, that the products of their scanty industries could not suffice to pay for them. 'So that Holland merchants,' writes a contemporary, 'who carry money to most parts of the world to buy commodities, must out of this single country of Europe carry home money, which they receive in payment of their goods.' Thus their eagerly sought emblem of wealth passed quickly from their hands. It has already been pointed out how weak, from a military point of view, Spain was from this decay of her shipping. Her wealth being in small bulk on a few ships, following more or less regular routes, was easily seized by an enemy, and the sinews of war paralyzed; whereas the wealth of England and Holland, scattered over thousands of ships in all parts of the world, received many bitter blows in many exhausting wars, without checking a growth which, though painful, was steady. The fortunes of Portugal, united to Spain during a most critical period of her history, followed the same downward path; although foremost in the beginning of the race for development by sea, she fell utterly behind. 'The mines of Brazil were the ruin of Portugal, as those of Mexico and Peru had been of Spain; all manufactures fell into insane contempt; ere long the English supplied the Portuguese not only with clothes, but with all merchandise, all commodities, even to salt-fish and grain. After their gold, the Portuguese abandoned their very soil; the vineyards of Oporto were finally bought by the English with Brazilian gold, which had only passed through Portugal to be spread throughout England.' We are assured that in fifty years, five hundred millions of dollars were extracted from 'the mines of Brazil, and that at the end of the time Portugal had but twenty-five millions in specie'—a striking example of the difference between real and fictitious wealth.

The English and Dutch were no less desirous of gain than the southern nations. Each in turn has been called 'a nation of shopkeepers,' but the jeer, in so far as it is just, is to the credit of their wisdom and uprightness. They were no less bold, no less enterprising, no less patient. Indeed, they were more patient, in that they sought riches not by the sword but by labor, which is the reproach meant to be implied by the epithet; for thus they took the longest, instead of what seemed the shortest, road to wealth. But these two peoples, radically of the same race, had other qualities, no less important than those just named, which combined with their surroundings to favor their development by sea. They were by nature business-men, traders, producers, negotiators. Therefore both in their native country and abroad, whether settled in the ports of civilized nations, or of barbarous eastern rulers, or in colonies of their own foundation, they everywhere strove to draw out all the resources of the land, to develop and increase them. The quick instinct of the born trader, shopkeeper if you will, sought continually new articles to exchange; and this search, combined with the industrious

character evolved through generations of labor, made them necessarily producers. At home they became great as manufacturers; abroad, where they controlled, the land grew richer continually, products multiplied, and the necessary exchange between home and the settlements called for more ships. Their shipping therefore increased with these demands of trade, and nations with less aptitude for maritime enterprise, even France herself, great as she has been, called for their products and for the service of their ships. Thus in many ways they advanced to power at sea. This natural tendency and growth were indeed modified and seriously checked at times by the interference of other governments, jealous of a prosperity which their own people could invade only by the aid of artificial support—a support which will be considered under the head of governmental action as affecting sea power.

The tendency to trade, involving of necessity the production of something to trade with, is the national characteristic most important to the development of sea power. Granting it and a good seaboard, it is not likely that the dangers of the sea, or any aversion to it, will deter a people from seeking wealth by the paths of ocean commerce. Where wealth is sought by other means, it may be found; but it will not necessarily lead to sea power. Take France. France has a fine country, an industrious people, an admirable position. The French navy has known periods of great glory, and in its lowest estate has never dishonored the military reputation so dear to the nation. Yet as a maritime State, securely resting upon a broad basis of sea commerce, France, as compared with other historical sea-peoples, has never held more than a respectable position. The chief reason for this, so far as national character goes, is the way

Below: *The port of Dieppe as seen in 1765 by Joseph Vernet. Although ideal for privateering, the harbors on the French side of the English Channel were mostly too small to accommodate a big fleet.*

Above: *Vernet's view of Marseilles in 1754. Although a great commercial port since Roman times, it never developed as a naval base because of the proximity of Toulon.*

Below: *Rochefort, by Vernet in 1762. This small dockyard on the Atlantic coast has now fallen into disuse, but remained important to the end of the nineteenth century.*

in which wealth is sought. As Spain and Portugal sought it by digging gold out of the ground, the temper of the French people leads them to seek it by thrift, economy, hoarding. It is said to be harder to keep than to make a fortune. Possibly—but the adventurous temper, which risks what it has to gain more, has much in common with the adventurous spirit that conquers worlds for commerce. The tendency to save and put aside, to venture timidly and on a small scale, may lead to a general diffusion of wealth on a like small scale, but not to the risks and development of external trade and shipping interests. To illustrate—and the incident is given only for what it is worth—a French officer, speaking to the author about the Panama Canal, said: 'I have two shares in it. In France we don't do as you, where a few people take a great many shares each. With us a large number of people take one share or a very few. When these were in the market my wife said to me, "You take two shares, one for you and one for me."' As regards the stability of a man's personal fortunes this kind of prudence is doubtless wise; but when excessive prudence or financial timidity becomes a national trait, it must tend to hamper the expansion of commerce and of the nation's shipping. The same caution in money matters, appearing in another relation of life, has checked the production of children, and keeps the population of France nearly stationary.

people and the fruitfulness of the soil saved commerce from total decay, it was pursued under a sense of humiliation which caused its best representatives to escape from it as soon as they could. Louis XIV, under the influence of Colbert, put forth an ordinance 'authorizing all noblemen to take an interest in merchant ships, goods and merchandise, without being considered as having derogated from nobility, provided they did not sell at retail,' and the reason given for this action was, 'that it imports the good of our subjects and our own satisfaction, to efface the relic of a public opinion, universally prevalent, that maritime commerce is incompatible with nobility.' But a

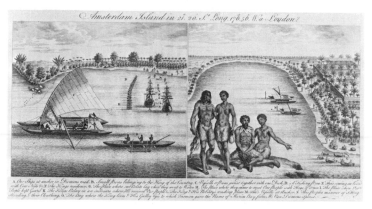

Above: *King Charles II turned the English Navy into the Royal Navy and in his reign the Admiralty began to assume its final form as the central administration. In other respects, however, the Merry Monarch's foreign policy and his extravagance did the Navy great harm.*

The noble classes of Europe inherited from the Middle Ages a supercilious contempt for peaceful trade, which has exercised a modifying influence upon its growth, according to the national character of different countries. The pride of the Spaniards fell easily in with this spirit of contempt, and co-operated with that disastrous unwillingness to work and wait for wealth which turned them away from commerce. In France, the vanity which is conceded even by Frenchmen to be a national trait led in the same direction. The numbers and brilliancy of the nobility, and the consideration enjoyed by them, set a seal of inferiority upon an occupation which they despised. Rich merchants and manufacturers sighed for the honors of nobility, and upon obtaining them, abandoned their lucrative professions. Therefore, while the industry of the

prejudice involving conscious and open superiority is not readily effaced by ordinances, especially when vanity is a conspicuous trait in national character; and many years later Montesquieu taught that it is contrary to the spirit of monarchy that the nobility should engage in trade.

In Holland there was a nobility; but the State was republican in name, allowed large scope to personal freedom and enterprise, and the centres of power were in the great cities. The foundation of the national greatness was money—or rather wealth. Wealth, as a source of civic distinction, carried with it also power in the State; and with power there went social position and consideration. In England the same result obtained. The nobility were proud; but in a representative government the power of wealth could be neither put down nor overshadowed. It was patent to the eyes of all, it was honored by all; and in England as well as Holland, the occupations which were the source of wealth shared in the honor given to wealth itself. Thus, in all the countries named, social sentiment, the outcome of national characteristics, had a marked influence upon the national attitude toward trade.

In yet another way does the national genius affect the growth of sea power in its broadest sense; and that is in so far as it possesses the capacity for planting healthy colonies. Of colonization, as of all other growths, it is true that it is most healthy when it is most natural. Therefore colonies that spring from the felt wants and natural impulses of a whole people will have the most solid foundations; and their subsequent growth will be surest when they are least trammelled from home, if the people have the genius for independent action. Men of the past three centuries have keenly felt the value to the mother-country of colonies as outlets for the home products and as a nursery for commerce and shipping; but efforts at colonization have not had the same general origin, nor have different systems all had the same success. The efforts of statesmen, however far-seeing and careful, have not been able to supply the lack of strong natural impulse; nor can the most minute regulation from home produce as good results as a happier neglect, when the germ of self-development is found in the national character. There has been no greater

selfish. However founded, as soon as it was recognized to be of consequence, the colony became to the home country a cow to be milked; to be cared for, of course, but chiefly as a piece of property valued for the returns it gave. Legislation was directed toward a monopoly of its external trade; the places in its government afforded posts of value for occupants from the mother-country; and the colony was looked upon, as the sea still so often is, as a fit place for those who were ungovernable or useless at home. The military administration, however, so long as it remains a colony, is the proper and necessary attribute of the home government.

The fact of England's unique and wonderful success as a great colonizing nation is too evident to be dwelt upon; and the reason for it appears to lie chiefly in two traits of the national character. The English colonist naturally and readily settles down in his new country, identifies his interest with it, and though keeping an affectionate remembrance of the home from which he came, has no restless eagerness to return. In the second place, the Englishman at once and instinctively seeks to develop the resources of the new country in the broadest sense. In the former particular he differs from the French, who were ever longingly looking back to the delights of their pleasant land; in the latter, from the Spaniards, whose range of interest and ambition was too narrow for the full evolution of the possi-

Left above: *The Dutch sailor Anthony van Diemen explored the East Indies in 1636, and for many years Tasmania was known as Van Diemen's Land.*

Left below: *Landing through the surf at Madras, one of the East India Company's most prosperous trading posts in India.*

Right: *Another view by J B East of the means of embarking and disembarking at Madras at the beginning of the nineteenth century.*

display of wisdom in the national administration of successful colonies than in that of unsuccessful. Perhaps there has been even less. If elaborate system and supervision, careful adaptation of means to ends, diligent nursing, could avail for colonial growth, the genius of England has less of this systematizing faculty than the genius of France; but England, not France, has been the great colonizer of the world. Successful colonization, with its consequent effect upon commerce and sea power, depends essentially upon national character; because colonies grow best when they grow of themselves, naturally. The character of the colonist, not the care of the home government, is the principle of the colony's growth.

This truth stands out the clearer because the general attitude of all the home governments toward their colonies was entirely

bilities of a new country.

The character and the necessities of the Dutch led them naturally to plant colonies, and by the year 1650 they had in the East Indies, in Africa, and in America a large number, only to name which would be tedious. They were then far ahead of England in this matter. But though the origin of these colonies, purely commercial in its character, was natural, there seems to have been lacking to them a principle of growth. 'In planting them they never sought an extension of empire, but merely an acquisition of trade and commerce. They attempted conquest only when forced by the pressure of circumstances. Generally they were content to trade under the protection of the sovereign of the country.' This placid satisfaction with gain alone, unaccompanied by political ambition, tended, like the despotism of

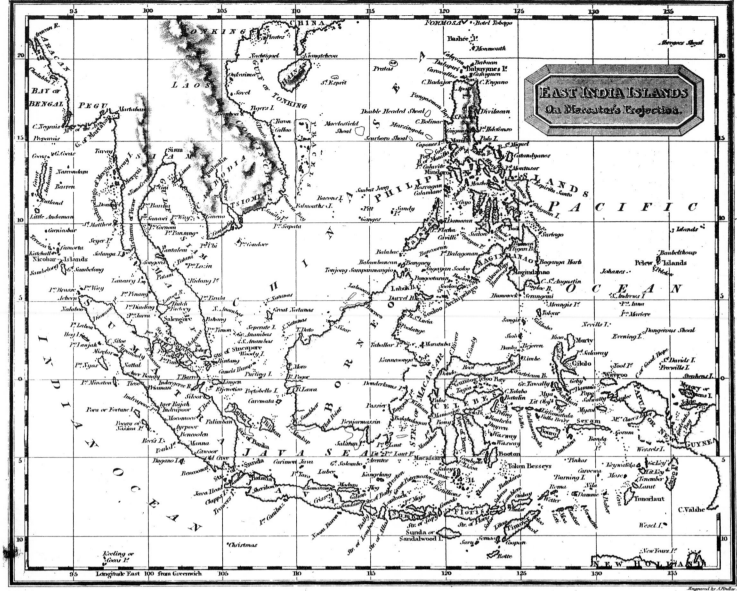

France and Spain, to keep the colonies mere commercial dependencies upon the mother-country, and so killed the natural principle of growth.

Before quitting this head of the inquiry, it is well to ask how far the national character of Americans is fitted to develop a great sea power, should other circumstances become favorable.

It seems scarcely necessary, however, to do more than appeal to a not very distant past to prove that, if legislative hindrances be removed, and more remunerative fields of enterprise filled up, the sea power will not long delay its appearance. The instinct for commerce, bold enterprise in the pursuit of gain, and a keen scent for the trails that lead to it, all exist; and if there be in the future any fields calling for colonization, it cannot be doubted that Americans will carry to them all their inherited aptitude for self-government and independent growth.

VI CHARACTER OF THE GOVERNMENT

In discussing the effects upon the development of a nation's sea power exerted by its government and institutions, it will be necessary to avoid a tendency to over-philosophizing, to confine attention to obvious and immediate causes and their plain results, without prying too far beneath the surface for remote and ultimate influences.

Nevertheless, it must be noted that particular forms of government with their accompanying institutions, and the character of rulers at one time or another, have exercised a very marked influence upon the development of sea power. The

Above: An 1817 map of the East Indies, the prized Spice Islands which drove first the Portuguese and then the Dutch and English to develop their overseas trade.

various traits of a country and its people which have so far been considered constitute the natural characteristics with which a nation, like a man, begins its career; the conduct of the government in turn corresponds to the exercise of the intelligent will-power, which, according as it is wise, energetic and persevering, or the reverse, causes success or failure in a man's life or a nation's history.

It would seem probable that a government in full accord with the natural bias of its people would most successfully advance its growth in every respect; and, in the matter of sea power, the most brilliant successes have followed where there has been intelligent direction by a government fully imbued with the spirit of the people and conscious of its true general bent. Such a government is most certainly secured when the will of the people, or of their best natural exponents, has some large share in making it; but such free governments have sometimes fallen short, while on the other hand despotic power, wielded with judgment and consistency, has created at times a great sea commerce and a brilliant navy with greater directness than can be reached by the slower processes of a free people. The difficulty in the latter case is to insure perseverance after the death of a particular despot.

England having undoubtedly reached the greatest height of sea power of any modern nation, the action of her government first claims attention. In general direction this action has been consistent, though often far from praiseworthy. It has aimed steadily at the control of the sea. One of its most arrogant expressions dates back as far as the reign of James I, when she had scarce any possessions outside her own islands; before Virginia or Massachusetts was settled. Here is Richelieu's account of it:—

'The Duke of Sully, minister of Henry IV [one of the most chivalrous princes that ever lived], having embarked at Calais in a French ship wearing the French flag at the main, was no sooner in the Channel than, meeting an English despatch-boat which was there to receive him, the commander of the latter ordered the French ship to lower her flag. The Duke, considering that his quality freed him from such an affront, boldly refused; but this refusal was followed by three cannon-shot, which, piercing his ship, pierced the heart likewise of all good Frenchmen. Might forced him to yield what right forbade, and for all the complaints he made he could get no better reply from the English captain than this: "That just as his duty obliged him to honor the ambassador's rank, it also obliged him to exact the honor due to the flag of his master as sovereign of the sea." If the words of King James himself were more polite, they nevertheless had no other effect than to compel the Duke to take counsel of his prudence, feigning to be satisfied, while his wound was all the time smarting and incurable. Henry the Great had to practise moderation on this occasion; but with the resolve another time to sustain the rights of his crown by the force that, with the aid of time, he should be able to put upon the sea.'

Below: *Louis XIV of France. He improved France's military power and prestige but at a tremendous cost in life and money, and set up the bureaucracy which finally strangled the* Ancien Regime.

This act of unpardonable insolence, according to modern ideas, was not so much out of accord with the spirit of nations in that day. It is chiefly noteworthy as the most striking, as well as one of the earliest indications of the purpose of England to assert herself at all risks upon the sea; and the insult was offered under one of her most timid kings to an ambassador immediately representing the bravest and ablest of French sovereigns. This empty honor of the flag, a claim insignificant except as the outward manifestation of the purpose of a government, was as rigidly exacted under Cromwell as under the kings. It was one of the conditions of peace yielded by the Dutch after their disastrous war of 1654. Cromwell, a despot in everything but name, was keenly alive to all that concerned England's honor and strength, and did not stop at barren salutes to promote them. Hardly yet possessed of power, the English navy sprang rapidly into a new life and vigor under his stern rule. England's rights, or reparation for her wrongs, were demanded by her fleets throughout the world—in the Baltic, in the Mediterranean, against the Barbary States, in the West Indies; and under him the conquest of Jamaica began that extension of her empire, by force of arms, which has gone on to our own days. Nor were equally strong peaceful measures for the growth of English trade and shipping forgotten. Cromwell's celebrated Navigation Act declared that all imports into England or her colonies must be conveyed exclusively in vessels belonging to England herself, or to the country in which the products carried were grown or manufactured. This decree, aimed specially at the

Below: *The young exiled king, Charles II, dancing at the Hague 1660.*

Dutch, the common carriers of Europe, was resented throughout the commercial world; but the benefit to England, in those days of national strife and animosity was so apparent that it lasted long under the monarchy. A century and a quarter later we find Nelson, before his famous career had begun, showing his zeel for the welfare of England's shipping by enforcing this same act in the West Indies against American merchant-ships.

When Cromwell was dead, and Charles II sat on the throne of his father, this king, false to the English people, was yet true to England's greatness and to the traditional policy of her government on the sea. In his treacherous intrigues with Louis XIV, by which he aimed to make himself independent of Parliament and people, he wrote to Louis: 'There are two impediments to a perfect union. The first is the great care France is now taking to create a commerce and to be an imposing maritime power. This is so great a cause of suspicion with us, who can possess importance only by our commerce and our naval force, that every step which France takes in this direction will perpetuate the jealousy between the two nations.' In the midst of the negotiations which preceded the detestable attack of the two kings upon the Dutch republic, a warm dispute arose as to who should command the united fleets of France and England. Charles was inflexible on this point. 'It is the custom of the English,' said he, 'to command at sea;' and he told the French ambassador plainly that, were he to yield, his subjects would not obey him. In the projected partition of the United Provinces he reserved for England the maritime plunder in positions that controlled the mouths of the rivers Scheldt and Meuse. The navy under Charles preserved for some time the spirit and discipline impressed on it by Cromwell's iron rule; though later it shared in the general decay of *morale* which marked this evil reign. Monk, having by a great strategic blunder sent off a fourth of his fleet, found himself in 1666 in presence of a greatly superior Dutch force. Disregarding the odds, he attacked without hesitation, and for three days maintained the fight with honor, though with loss. Such conduct is not war; but in the single eye that looked to England's naval prestige and dictated his action, common as it was to England's people as well as to her government, has lain the secret of final success following many blunders through the centuries. Charles's successor, James II, was himself a seamen, and had commanded in two great sea-fights. When William III came to the throne, the

Below: *The landing of William of Orange at Torbay in 1688.*

Above: *HMS* Ipswich, *a 70-gun 3rd Rate. Although technically a second rebuilding of a 1694 ship this 1730 model indicates that a new ship was built at Portsmouth in that year. She was hulked at Gibraltar in 1757 and broken up about seven years later.*

governments of England and Holland were under one hand, and continued united in one purpose against Louis XIV until the Peace of Utrecht in 1713; that is, for a quarter of a century. The English government more and more steadily, and with conscious purpose, pushed on the extension of her sea dominion and fostered the growth of her sea power. While as an open enemy she struck at France upon the sea, so as an artful friend, many at least believed, she sapped the power of Holland afloat.

The treaty between the two countries provided that of the sea forces Holland should furnish three eighths, England five

eighths, or nearly double. Such a provision, coupled with a further one which made Holland keep up an army of 102,000 against England's 40,000, virtually threw the land war on one and the sea war on the other. The tendency, whether designed or not, is evident; and at the peace, while Holland received compensation by land, England obtained, besides commercial privileges in France, Spain, and the Spanish West Indies, the important maritime concessions of Gibraltar and Port Mahon in the Mediterranean; of Newfoundland, Nova Scotia, and Hudson's Bay in North America. The naval power of France and Spain had disappeared; that of Holland thenceforth steadily declined. Posted thus in America, the West Indies, and the Mediterranean, the English government thenceforth moved firmly forward on the path which made of the English kingdom the British Empire. For the twenty-five years following the Peace of Utrecht, peace was the chief aim of the ministers who directed the policy of the two great seaboard nations, France and England; but amid all the fluctuations of continental politics in a most unsettled period, abounding in petty wars and shifty treaties, the eye of England was steadily fixed on the maintenance of her sea power. In the Baltic, her fleets checked the attempts of Peter the Great upon Sweden, and so maintained a balance of power in that sea, from which she drew not only a great trade but the chief part of her naval stores, and which the Czar aimed to make a Russian lake. Denmark endeavored to establish an East India company aided by foreign capital; England and Holland not only forbade their subjects to join it; but threatened Denmark, and thus stopped an enterprise they thought adverse to their sea interests. In the Netherlands, which by the Utrecht Treaty had passed to Austria, a similar East India company, having Ostend for its port, was formed, with the emperor's sanction. This step, meant to restore to the Low Countries the trade lost to them through their natural outlet of the Scheldt, was opposed by the sea powers England and Holland; and their greediness for the monopoly of trade, helped in this instance by France, stifled this company also after a few years of struggling life. In the Mediterranean, the Utrecht settlement was disturbed by the emperor of Austria, England's natural ally in the then existing state of European politics.

Backed by England, he, having already Naples, claimed also Sicily in exchange for Sardinia. Spain resisted; and her navy, just beginning to revive under a vigorous minister, Alberoni, was crushed and annihilated by the English fleet off Cape Passaro in 1718; while the following year a French army, at the bidding of England, crossed the Pyrenees and completed the work by destroying the Spanish dock-yards. Thus England, in addition to Gibraltar and Mahon in her own hands, saw Naples and Sicily in those of a friend, while an enemy was struck down.

In Spanish America, the limited privileges to English trade, wrung from the necessities of Spain, were abused by an extensive and scarcely disguised smuggling system; and when the exasperated Spanish government gave way to excesses in the mode of suppression, both the minister who counselled peace and the opposition which urged war defended their opinions by alleging the effects of either upon England's sea power and honor. While England's policy thus steadily aimed at widening and strengthening the bases of her sway upon the ocean, the other governments of Europe seemed blind to the dangers to be feared from her sea growth. The miseries resulting from the overweening power of Spain in days long gone by seemed to be forgotten; forgotten also the more recent lesson of the bloody and costly wars provoked by the ambition and exaggerated power of Louis XIV. Under the eyes of the statesmen of Europe there was steadily and visibly being built up a third overwhelming power, destined to be used as selfishly, as aggressively, though not as cruelly, and much more successfully than any that had preceded it. This was the power of the sea, whose workings, because more silent than the clash of arms, are less often noted, though lying clearly enough on the surface. It can scarcely be denied that England's uncontrolled dominion of the seas, during almost the whole period chosen for our subject, was by long odds the chief among the military factors that determined the final issue. So far, however, was this influence from being foreseen after Utrecht, that France for twelve years, moved by personal exigencies of her rulers, sided with England against Spain; and when Fleuri came into power in 1726, though this policy was reserved, the navy of France received no attention, and the only blow at England was the establishment of a Bourbon prince, a natural enemy to her, upon the throne of the two Sicilies in 1736. When war broke out with Spain in 1739, the navy of England was in numbers more than equal to the combined navies of Spain and France; and during the quarter of a century of nearly uninterrupted war that followed, this numerical disproportion increased. In these wars England, at first instinctively, afterward with conscious

Below: *Rigging plan and inboard section of a 1st Rate 1752.*

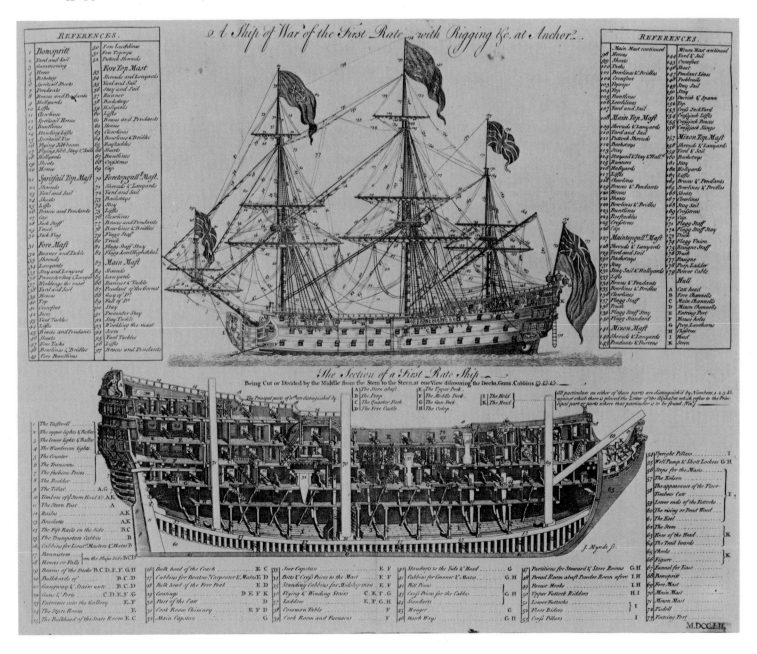

purpose under a government that recognized her opportunity and the possibilities of her great sea power, rapidly built up that mighty colonial empire whose foundations were already securely laid in the characteristics of her colonists and the strength of her fleets. In strictly European affairs her wealth, the outcome of her sea power, made her play a conspicuous part during the same period. The system of subsidies, which began half a century before in the wars of Marlborough and received its most extensive development half a century later in the Napoleonic wars, maintained the efforts of her allies, which would have been crippled, if not paralyzed, without them.

Who can deny that the government which with one hand strengthened its fainting allies on the continent with the life-blood of money, and with the other drove its own enemies off the sea and out of their chief possessions, Canada, Martinique, Guadeloupe, Havana, Manila, gave to its country the foremost rôle in European politics; and who can fail to see that the power which dwelt in that government, with a land narrow in extent and poor in resources, sprang directly from the sea? The policy in which the English government carried on the war is shown by a speech of Pitt, the master-spirit during its course, though he lost office before bringing it to an end. Condemning the Peace of 1763, made by his political opponent, he said: 'France is chiefly, if not exclusively, formidable to us as a maritime and commercial power. What we gain in this respect is valuable to us, above all, through the injury to her which results from it. You have left to France the possibility of reviving her navy.'

Yet England's gains were enormous; her rule in India was assured, and all North America east of the Mississippi in her hands. By this time the onward path of her government was clearly marked out, had assumed the force of a tradition, and was consistently followed. The war of the American Revolution

Right: *An eighteenth-century depiction of a sailor and his wife.*

Bottom: *The Rake's Progress applied to the six stage's of a sailor's life.*

Below: *Cruikshank's view of the 'Honest Tars and Marines of the Argonaut' contributing their pennies to a fund to drive England's enemies into the sea. The arrears of pay and cheating by pursers revealed during the Spithead Mutiny in 1797 make such a scene doubtful, to say the least.*

Entering as Landsman

Carousing on board

In Irons for getting drunk

Boarding a French brig

Promoted to Boatswain & exercising his Authority

Laid up a Greenwich pensioner — relating his adventures

The SAILORS PROGRESS — sic transit gloria mundi

was, it is true, a great mistake, looked at from the point of view of sea power; but the government was led into it insensibly by a series of natural blunders. Putting aside political and constitutional considerations, and looking at the question as purely military or naval, the case was this: the American colonies were large and growing communities at a great distance from England. So long as they remained attached to the mother-country, as they then were enthusiastically, they formed a solid base for her sea power in that part of the world; but their extent and population were too great, when coupled with the distance from England, to afford any hope of holding them by force, *if* any powerful nations were willing to help them. This 'if,' however, involved a notorious probability; the humiliation of France and Spain was so bitter and so recent that they were sure to seek revenge, and it was well known that France in particular had been carefully and rapidly building up her navy. Had the colonies been thirteen islands, the sea power of England would quickly have settled the question; but instead of such a physical barrier they were separated only by local jealousies which a common danger sufficiently overcame. To enter deliberately on such a contest, to try to hold by force so extensive a territory, with a large hostile population, so far from home, was to renew the Seven Years' War with France and Spain, and with the Americans, against, instead of for, England. The Seven Years' War had been so heavy a burden that a wise government would have known that the added weight could not be borne, and have seen it was necessary to conciliate the colonists. The government of the day was not wise, and a large element of England's sea power was sacrificed; but by mistake, not wilfully; through arrogance, not through weakness.

This steady keeping to a general line of policy was doubtless made specially easy for successive English governments by the

Above: *Rowlandson's view of the officers' life afloat. Apart from the freer access to wine, officers had to eat the same weevily biscuit and salt pork as the men.*

clear indications of the country's conditions. Singleness of purpose was to some extent imposed. The firm maintenance of her sea power, the haughty determination to make it felt, the wise state of preparation in which its military element was kept, were yet more due to that feature of her political institutions which practically gave the government, during the period in question, into the hands of a class—a landed aristocracy. Such a class, whatever its defects otherwise, readily takes up and carries on a sound political tradition, is naturally proud of its country's glory, and comparatively insensible to the sufferings of the community by which that glory is maintained. It readily lays on the pecuniary burden necessary for preparation and for endurance of war. Being as a body rich, it feels those burdens less. Not being commercial, the sources of its own wealth are not so immediately endangered, and it does not share that political timidity which characterizes those whose property is exposed and business threatened—the proverbial timidity of capital. Yet in England this class was not insensible to anything that touched her trade for good or ill. Both houses of Parliament vied in careful watchfulness over its extension and protection, and to the frequency of their inquiries a naval historian attributes the increased efficiency of the executive power in its management of the navy. Such a class also naturally imbibes and keeps up a spirit of military honor, which is of the first importance in ages when military institutions have not yet provided the sufficient substitute in what is called *esprit-de-corps*. But although full of class feeling and class prejudice, which made themselves felt in the navy as well as elsewhere, their practical sense left open the way of promotion to its highest honors to the more humbly born; and every age saw admirals who had sprung from the lowest of the people. In this the temper of the English upper class differed markedly from that of the French. As late as 1789, at the outbreak of the Revolution, the French Navy List still bore the name of an official whose duty was to verify the proofs of noble birth on the part of those intending to enter the naval school.

Since 1815, and especially in our own day, the government of England has passed very much more into the hands of the people at large. Whether her sea power will suffer therefrom remains to be seen. Its broad basis still remains in a great trade, large mechanical industries, and an extensive colonial system. Whether a democratic government will have the foresight, the keen sensitiveness to national position and credit, the willingness to insure its prosperity by adequate outpouring of money in times of peace, all which are necessary for military preparation, is yet an open question. Popular governments are not generally favorable to military expenditure, however necessary, and there are signs that England tends to drop behind.

It has already been seen that the Dutch Republic, even more than the English nation, drew its prosperity and its very life from the sea. The character and policy of its government were far less favorable to a consistent support of sea power. Composed cf seven provinces, with the political name of the United Provinces, the actual distribution of power may be roughly described to Americans as an exaggerated example of States Rights. Each of the maritime provinces had its own fleet and its own admiralty, with consequent jealousies. This disorganizing tendency was partly counteracted by the great preponderance of the Province of Holland, which alone contributed five sixths of the fleet and fifty-eight per cent of the taxes, and consequently had a proportionate share in directing the national policy. Although intensely patriotic, and capable of making the last sacrifices for freedom, the commercial spirit of the people penetrated the government, which indeed might be called a commercial aristocracy, and made it averse to war, and to the

expenditures which are necessary in preparing for war. As has before been said, it was not until danger stared them in the face that the burgomasters were willing to pay for their defences. While the republican government lasted, however, this economy was practised least of all upon the fleet; and until the death of John de Witt in 1672, and the peace with England in 1674, the Dutch navy was in point of numbers and equipment able to make a fair show against the combined navies of England and France. Its efficiency at this time undoubtedly saved the country from the destruction planned by the two kings. With De Witt's death the republic passed away, and was followed by the practically monarchical government of William of Orange. The life-long policy of this prince, then only eighteen, was resistance to Louis XIV and to the extension of French power. This resistance took shape upon the land rather than the sea—a tendency promoted by England's withdrawal from the war. As early as 1676, Admiral De Ruyter found the force given him unequal to cope with the French alone. With the eyes of the government fixed on the land frontier, the navy rapidly declined. In 1688, when William of Orange needed a fleet to convoy him to England, the burgomasters of Amsterdam objected that the navy was incalculably decreased in strength, as well as deprived of its ablest commanders. When king of England, William still kept his position as stadtholder, and with it his general European policy. He found in England the sea power he needed, and used the resources of Holland for the land war. This Dutch prince consented that in the allied fleets, in councils of war, the Dutch admirals should sit below the junior English captain; and Dutch interests at sea were sacrificed as readily as Dutch pride to the demands of England. When William died, his policy was still followed by the government which succeeded him. Its aims were wholly centred upon the land, and at the Peace of Utrecht, which closed a series of wars extending over forty years, Holland, having established no sea claim, gained nothing in the way of sea resources, of colonial extension, or of commerce.

Of the last of these wars an English historian says: 'The economy of the Dutch greatly hurt their reputation and their trade. Their men-of-war in the Mediterranean were always victualled short, and their convoys were so weak and ill-provided that for one ship that we lost, they lost five, which begat a general notion that we were the safer carriers, which certainly had a good effect. Hence it was that our trade rather increased than diminished in this war.'

From that time Holland ceased to have a great sea power, and rapidly lost the leading position among the nations which that power had built up. It is only just to say that no policy could have saved from decline this small, though determined nation,

Left: *Action in the Dutch wars c 1667.*

left what he called his political will, in which he pointed out the opportunities of France for achieving sea power, based upon her position and resources; and French writers consider him the virtual founder of the navy, not merely because he equipped ships, but from the breadth of his views and his measures to insure sound institutions and steady growth. After his death, Mazarin inherited his views and general policy, but not his lofty and martial spirit, and during his rule the newly formed navy disappeared. When Louis XIV took the government into his own hands, in 1661, there were but thirty ships of war, of which only three had as many as sixty guns. Then began a most astonishing manifestation of the work which can be done by absolute government ably and systematically wielded. That part of the administration which dealt with trade, manufactures, shipping, and colonies, was given to a man of great practical genius, Colbert, who had served with Richelieu and had drunk

Below: *This picture by Rembrandt of a ship surveyor and his wife shows the extent to which the Dutch acknowledged the importance of the technical arts.*

Above: *Cardinal Richelieu was one of the great architects of French sea power. He laid down a coherent policy which paid attention to the substance of maritime strength as much as to the outward form.*

in face of the persistent enmity of Louis XIV. The friendship of France, insuring peace on her landward frontier, would have enabled her, at least for a longer time, to dispute with England the dominion of the seas; and as allies the navies of the two continental States might have checked the growth of the enormous sea power which has just been considered. Sea peace between England and Holland was only possible by the virtual subjection of one or the other, for both aimed at the same object. Between France and Holland it was otherwise; and the fall of Holland proceeded, not necessarily from her inferior size and numbers, but from faulty policy on the part of the two governments. It does not concern us to decide which was the more to blame.

France, admirably situated for the possession of sea power, received a definite policy for the guidance of her government from two great rulers, Henry IV and Richelieu. With certain well-defined projects of extension eastward upon the land were combined a steady resistance to the House of Austria, which then ruled in both Austria and Spain, and an equal purpose of resistance to England upon the sea. To further this latter end, as well as for other reasons, Holland was to be courted as an ally. Commerce and fisheries as the basis of sea power were to be encouraged, and a military navy was to be built up. Richelieu

in fully his ideas and policy. He pursued his aims in a spirit thoroughly French. Everything was to be organized, the spring of everything was in the minister's cabinet. 'To organize producers and merchants as a powerful army, subjected to an active and intelligent guidance, so as to secure an industrial victory for France by order and unity of efforts, and to obtain the best products by imposing on all workmen the processes recognized as best by competent men. . . . To organize seamen and distant commerce in large bodies like the manufactures and internal commerce, and to give as a support to the commercial power of France a navy established on a firm basis and of dimensions hitherto unknown,'—such, we are told, were the aims of Colbert as regards two of the three links in the chain of sea power. For the third, the colonies at the far end of the line, the same governmental direction and organization were evidently purposed; for the government began by buying back Canada, Newfoundland, Nova Scotia, and the French West India Islands from the parties who then owned them. Here, then, is seen pure, absolute, uncontrolled power gathering up into its hands all the reins for the guidance of a nation's course, and proposing so to direct it as to make, among other things, a great sea power.

To enter into the details of Colbert's action is beyond our

Left: French and English ships in action at the beginning of the eighteenth century.

Opposite: This lurid version of the Battle of La Hougue attempts to give an impression of the desperate hand-to-hand fighting. All manner of weapons were used by boarding parties, including tomahawks and blunderbusses.

purpose. It is enough to note the chief part played by the government in building up the sea power of the State, and that this very great man looked not to any one of the bases on which it rests to the exclusion of the others, but embraced them all in his wise and provident administration. Agriculture, which increases the products of the earth, and manufactures, which multiply the products of man's industry; internal trade routes and regulations, by which the exchange of products from the interior to the exterior is made easier; shipping and customs regulations tending to throw the carrying-trade into French hands, and so to encourage the building of French shipping, by which the home and colonial products should be carried back and forth; colonial administration and development, by which a far-off market might be continually growing up to be monopolized by the home trade; treaties with foreign States favoring French trade, and taxes on foreign ships and products tending to break down that of rival nations—all these means, embracing countless details, were employed to build up for France (1) Production; (2) Shipping; (3) Colonies and Markets—in a word, sea power. The study of such a work is simpler and easier when thus done by one man, sketched out by a kind of logical process, than when slowly wrought by conflicting interests in a more complex government. In the few years of Colbert's administration is seen the whole theory of sea power put into practice in the systematic, centralizing French way; while the illustration of the same theory in English and Dutch history is spread over generations. Such growth, however, was forced, and depended upon the endurance of the absolute power which watched over it; and as Colbert was not king, his control lasted only till he lost the king's favor. It is, however, most interesting to note the results of his labors in the proper field for governmental action— in the navy. It has been said that in 1661, when he took office, there were but thirty armed ships, of which three only had over sixty guns. In 1666 there were seventy, of which fifty were ships of the line and twenty were fire-ships; in 1671, from seventy the number had increased to one hundred and ninety-six. In 1683 there were one hundred and seven ships of from twenty-four to one hundred and twenty guns, twelve of which carried over seventy-six guns, besides many smaller vessels. The order and system introduced into the dock-yards made them vastly more efficient than the English. An English captain, a prisoner in France while the effect of Colbert's work still lasted in the hands of his son, writes:

'When I was first brought prisoner thither, I lay four months in a hospital at Brest for care of my wounds. While there I was astonished at the expedition used in manning and fitting out their ships, which till then I thought could be done nowhere sooner than in England, where we have ten times the shipping, and consequently ten times the seamen, they have in France; but there I saw twenty sail of ships, of about sixty guns each, got ready in twenty days' time; they were brought in and the men were discharged; and upon an order from Paris they were careened, keeled up, rigged, victualled, manned, and out again in the said time with the greatest ease imaginable. I likewise saw a ship of one hundred guns that had all her guns taken out in four or five hours' time; which I never saw done in England in twenty-four hours, and this with the greatest ease and less hazard than at home. This I saw under my hospital window.'

A French naval historian cites certain performances which are simply incredible, such as that the keel of a galley was laid at four o'clock, and that at nine she left port, fully armed. These traditions may be accepted as pointing, with the more serious statements of the English officer, to a remarkable degree of system and order, and abundant facilities for work.

Yet all this wonderful growth, forced by the action of the government, withered away like Jonah's gourd when the government's favor was withdrawn. Time was not allowed for its roots to strike down deep into the life of the nation. Colbert's work was in the direct line of Richelieu's policy, and for a time it seemed there would continue the course of action which would make France great upon the sea as well as predominant upon the land. For reasons which it is not yet necessary to give, Louis came to have feelings of bitter enmity against Holland; and as these feelings were shared by Charles II, the two kings determined on the destruction of the United Provinces. This war, which broke out in 1672, though more contrary to natural feeling on the part of England, was less of a political mistake for her than for France, and especially as regards sea power. France was helping to destroy a probable, and certainly an indispensable ally; England was assisting in the ruin of her greatest rival on the sea, at this time, indeed, still her commercial superior. France, staggering under debt and utter confusion in her finances when Louis mounted the throne, was just seeing her way clear in 1672, under Colbert's reforms and their happy results. The war, lasting six years, undid the greater part of his work. The agricultural classes, manufactures, commerce, and the colonies, all were smitten by it; the establishments of Colbert languished, and the order he had established in the finances was overthrown. Thus the action of Louis—and he alone was the directing government of France—struck at the roots of her sea power, and alienated her best sea ally. The territory and the military power of France were increased, but the springs of commerce and of a peaceful shipping had been exhausted in the process; and although the military navy was for some years kept up with splendor and efficiency, it soon began to dwindle, and by the end of the reign had practically disappeared. The same false policy, as regards the sea, marked the rest of this reign of fifty-four years. Louis steadily turned his back upon the sea interests of France, except the fighting-ships, and either could not or would not see that the latter were of little use and uncertain life, if the peaceful shipping and the industries, by which they were supported, perished. His policy, aiming at supreme power in Europe by military strength and territorial extension, forced England and Holland into an alliance, which, as has before been said, directly drove France off the sea, and indirectly swamped Holland's power thereon. Colbert's navy perished, and for the last ten years of Louis' life no great French fleet put to sea, though there was constant war. The simplicity of form in an absolute monarchy thus brought out strongly how great the influence of government can be upon both the growth and the decay of sea power.

The latter part of Louis' life thus witnessed that power failing by the weakening of its foundations, of commerce, and of the wealth that commerce brings. The government that followed, likewise absolute, of set purpose and at the demand of England, gave up all pretence of maintaining an effective navy. The reason for this was that the new king was a minor; and the regent, being bitterly at enmity with the king of Spain, to injure him and preserve his own power, entered into alliance with England. He aided her to establish Austria, the hereditary enemy of France, in Naples and Sicily to the detriment of Spain, and in union with her destroyed the Spanish navy and dock-yards. Here again is found a personal ruler disregarding the sea interests of France, ruining a natural ally, and directly aiding, as Louis XIV indirectly and unintentionally aided, the growth of a mistress of the seas. This transient phase of policy passed away with the death of the regent in 1726; but from that time until 1760 the government of France continued to disregard her maritime interests. It is said, indeed, that owing to some wise modifications of her fiscal regulations, mainly in the direction of free trade (and due to Law, a minister of Scotch birth), commerce with the East and West Indies wonderfully increased, and that the islands of Guadeloupe and Martinique became very rich and thriving; but both commerce and colonies lay at the mercy of England when war came, for the navy fell into decay. In 1756, when things were no longer at their worst, France had but forty-five ships-of-the-line, England nearly one hundred and thirty; and when the forty-five were to be armed and equipped, there was found to be neither material nor rigging nor supplies; not even enough artillery.

A false policy of continental extension swallowed up the resources of the country, and was doubly injurious because, by leaving defenceless its colonies and commerce, it exposed the greatest source of wealth to be cut off, as in fact happened. The small squadrons that got to sea were destroyed by vastly superior

force; the merchant shipping was swept away, and the colonies, Canada, Martinique, Guadeloupe, India, fell into England's hands. If it did not take too much space, interesting extracts might be made, showing the woful misery of France, the country that had abandoned the sea, and the growing wealth of England amid all her sacrifices and exertions. A contemporary writer has thus expressed his view of the policy of France at this period:

'France, by engaging so heartily as she has done in the German war, has drawn away so much of her attention and her revenue from her navy that it enabled us to give such a blow to her maritime strength as possibly she may never be able to recover. Her engagement in the German war has likewise drawn her from the defence of her colonies, by which means we have conquered some of the most considerable she possessed. It has withdrawn her from the protection of her trade, by which it is entirely destroyed, while that of England has never, in the profoundest peace, been in so flourishing a condition. So that, by embarking in this German war, France has suffered herself to be undone, so far as regards her particular and immediate quarrel with England.'

In the Seven Years' War France lost thirty-seven ships-of-the-line and fifty-six frigates—a force three times as numerous as the whole navy of the United States at any time in the days of sailing-ships. 'For the first time since the Middle Ages,' says a French historian, speaking of the same war, 'England had conquered France single-handed, almost without allies, France having powerful auxiliaries. She had conquered solely by the superiority of her government.' Yes; but it was by the superiority of her government using the tremendous weapon of her sea power—the reward of a consistent policy perseveringly directed to one aim.

The profound humiliation of France, which reached its depths between 1760 and 1763, at which latter date she made peace, has an instructive lesson for the United States in this our period of commercial and naval decadence. We have been spared her humiliation; let us hope to profit by her subsequent example. Between the same years (1760 and 1763) the French people rose, as afterward in 1793, and declared they would have a navy. 'Popular feeling, skilfully directed by the government, took up the cry from one end of France to the other, "The navy must be restored." Gifts of ships were made by cities, by corporations, and by private subscriptions. A prodigious activity sprang up in the lately silent ports; everywhere ships were building or repairing.' This activity was sustained; the arsenals were replenished, the material of every kind was put on a satisfactory footing, the artillery reorganized, and ten thousand trained gunners drilled and maintained.

The tone and action of the naval officers of the day instantly felt the popular impulse, for which indeed some loftier spirits among them had been not only waiting but working. At no time was greater mental and professional activity found among French naval officers than just then, when their ships had been suffered to rot away by governmental inaction. Thus a prominent French officer of our own day writes:

'The sad condition of the navy in the reign of Louis XV, by closing to officers the brillant career of bold enterprises and successful battles, forced them to fall back upon themselves. They drew from study the knowledge they were to put to the proof some years later, thus putting into practice that fine saying of Montesquieu, "Adversity is our mother, Prosperity our step-mother. . . ." By the year 1769 was seen in all its splendor that brilliant galaxy of officers whose activity stretched to the ends of the earth, and who embraced in their works and in their investigations all the branches of human knowledge. The Académie de Marine, founded in 1752, was reorganized.'

The Académie's first director, a post-captain named Bigot de Morogues, wrote an elaborate treatise on naval tactics, the first original work on the subject since Paul Hoste's, which it was designed to supersede. Morogues must have been studying and formulating his problems in tactics in days when France had no fleet, and was unable to much as to raise her head at sea under the blows of her enemy. At the same time England had no similar book; and an English lieutenant, in 1762, was just translating a part of Hoste's great work, omitting by far the larger part. It was not until nearly twenty years later that Clerk, a Scotch private gentleman, published an ingenious study of naval tactics, in which he pointed out to English admirals the system by which the French had thwarted their thoughtless and ill-combined attacks. 'The researches of the Académie de Marine, and the energetic impulse which it gave to the labors of officers, were not, as we hope to show later, without influence upon the relatively prosperous condition in which the navy was at the beginning of the American war.'

It has already been pointed out that the American War of Independence involved a departure from England's traditional and true policy, by committing her to a distant land war, while powerful enemies were waiting for an opportunity to attack her at sea. Like France in the then recent German wars, like Napoleon later in the Spanish war, England, through undue self-confidence, was about to turn a friend into an enemy, and so expose the real basis of her power to a rude proof. The French government, on the other hand, avoided the snare into which it had so often fallen. Turning her back on the European continent, having the probability of neutrality there, and the certainty of alliance with Spain by her side, France advanced to the contest with a fine navy and a brilliant, though perhaps relatively inexperienced, body of officers. On the other side of the Atlantic she had the support of a friendly people, and of her own or allied ports, both in the West Indies and on the continent. The wisdom

of this policy, the happy influence of this action of the government upon her sea power, is evident; but the details of the war do not belong to this part of the subject. To Americans, the chief interest of that war is found upon the land; but to naval officers upon the sea, for it was essentially a sea war. The intelligent and systematic efforts of twenty years bore their due fruit; for though the warfare afloat ended with a great disaster, the combined efforts of the French and Spanish fleets undoubtedly bore down England's strength and robbed her of her colonies. In the various naval undertakings and battles the honor of France was upon the whole maintained; though it is difficult, upon consideration of the general subject, to avoid the conclusion that the inexperience of French seamen as compared with English, the narrow spirit of jealousy shown by the noble corps of officers toward those of different antecedents, and above all, the miserable traditions of three quarters of a century already alluded to, the miserable policy of a government which taught them first to save their ships, to economize the material, prevented French admirals from reaping, not the mere glory, but the positive advantages that more than once were within their grasp. When Monk said the nation that would rule upon the sea must always attack, he set the key-note to England's naval policy; and had the instructions of the French government consistently breathed the same spirit, the war of 1778 might have ended sooner and better than it did. It seems ungracious to criticise the conduct of a service to which, under God, our nation owes that its birth was not a miscarriage; but writers of its own country abundantly reflect the spirit of the remark. A French officer who served afloat during this war, in a work of calm and judicial tone, says:

'What must the young officers have thought who were at Sandy Hook with D'Estaing, at St Christopher with De Grasse, even those who arrived at Rhode Island with De Ternay, when they saw that these officers were not tried at their return?'

Within ten years of the peace of 1783 came the French Revolution; but that great upheaval which shook the foundations of States, loosed the ties of social order, and drove out of the navy nearly all the trained officers of the monarchy who were attached to the old state of things, did not free the French navy from a false system. It was easier to overturn the form of government than to uproot a deep-seated tradition. Hear again a third French officer, of the highest rank and literary accomplishments, speaking of the inaction of Villeneuve, the admiral who commanded the French rear at the battle of the Nile, and who did not leave his anchors while the head of the column was being destroyed:

'A day was to come [Trafalgar] in which Villeneuve in his turn, like De Grasse before him, and like Duchayla, would complain of being abandoned by part of his fleet. We have come to suspect some secret reason for this fatal coincidence. It is not natural that among so many honorable men there should so often be found admirals and captains incurring such a reproach. If the name of some of them is to this very day sadly associated with the memory of our disasters, we may be sure the fault is not wholly their own. We must rather blame the nature of the operations in which they were engaged, and that system of defensive war prescribed by the French government, which Pitt, in the English Parliament, proclaimed to be the forerunner of certain ruin. That system, when we wished to renounce it, had already penetrated our habits; it had, so to say, weakened our arms and paralyzed our self-reliance. Too often did our squadrons leave port with a special mission to fulfil, and with the intention of avoiding the enemy; to fall in with him was at once a piece of bad luck. It was thus that our ships went into action; they submitted to it instead of forcing it. . . . Fortune would have hesitated longer between the two fleets, and not have borne in the end so heavily against ours, if Brueys, meeting Nelson half way, could have gone out to fight him. This fettered and timid war, which Villaret and Martin had carried on, had lasted long, thanks to the circumspection of some English admirals and the traditions of the old tactics. It was with these traditions that the battle of the Nile had broken; the hour for decisive action had come.'

Above: A French 80-gun 2nd Rate c 1800. The two-decker 74s and 80s were more popular than the three-deckers because they were cheaper to build, more maneuverable and faster. Nelson's fleet at the Nile in 1798, for example, was made up largely of 74-gun ships.

Left: A French 120-gun ship c 1790. Although 100 guns was the normal maximum for a 1st Rate there were a few giant ships-of-the-line such as the French l'Orient and the Spanish Santisima Trinidad.

Above: The American sloop Ranger, commanded by John Paul Jones, engaging the English 14-gun sloop Drake off Belfast on 24 April 1778. The cruise of the Ranger demonstrated just how much damage a solitary raider could achieve against the enemy's commerce.

Below: *The first operation of the Continental Navy under Commander Esek Hopkins, 3 March 1776. Although John Paul Jones and other captains showed great initiative the new navy authorized by Congress achieved very little, and it declined from 27 ships in 1776 to three in 1781.*

Some years later came Trafalgar, and again the government of France took up a new policy with the navy. The author last quoted speaks again:

'The emperor, whose eagle glance traced plans of campaign for his fleets as for his armies, was wearied by these unexpected reverses. He turned his eyes from the one field of battle in which fortune was faithless to him, and decided to pursue England elsewhere than upon the seas; he undertook to rebuild his navy, but without giving it any part in the struggle which became more furious than ever. . . . Nevertheless, far from slackening, the activity of our dock-yards redoubled. Every year ships-of-the-line were either laid down or added to the fleet. Venice and Genoa, under his control, saw their old splendors rise again, and from the shores of the Elbe to the head of the Adriatic all the ports of the continent emulously seconded the creative thought of the emperor. Numerous squadrons were assembled in the Scheldt, in Brest Roads, and in Toulon. . . . But to the end the emperor refused to give this navy, full of ardor and self-reliance, an opportunity to measure its strength with the enemy. . . . Cast down by constant reverses, he had kept up our armed ships only to oblige our enemies to blockades whose cost must end by exhausting their finances.'

When the empire fell, France had one hundred and three ships-of-the-line and fifty-five frigates.

To turn now from the particular lessons drawn from the history of the past to the general question of the influence of government upon the sea career of its people, it is seen that that influence can work in two distinct but closely related ways.

First, in peace: The government by its policy can favor the natural growth of a people's industries and its tendencies to seek adventure and gain by way of the sea; or it can try to develop such industries and such sea-going bent, when they do not naturally exist; or, on the other hand, the government may by mistaken action check and fetter the progress which the people left to themselves would make. In any one of these ways the influence of the government will be felt, making or marring the sea power of the country in the matter of peaceful commerce; upon which alone, it cannot be too often insisted, a thoroughly strong navy can be based.

Secondly, for war: The influence of the government will be felt in its most legitimate manner in maintaining an armed navy, of a size commensurate with the growth of its shipping and the importance of the interests connected with it. More important even than the size of the navy is the question of its institutions, favoring a healthful spirit and activity, and providing for rapid development in time of war by an adequate reserve of men and of ships and by measures for drawing out that general reserve power which has before been pointed to, when considering the character and pursuits of the people. Undoubtedly under this second head of war-like preparation must come the mainten-ance of suitable naval stations, in those distant parts of the world to which the armed shipping must follow the peaceful vessels of commerce. The protection of such stations must depend either upon direct military force, as do Gibraltar and Malta, or upon a surrounding friendly population, such as the American colo-nists once were to England, and, it may be presumed, the Australian colonists now are. Such friendly surroundings and backing, joined to a reasonable military provision, are the best of defences, and when combined with decided preponderance at sea, make a scattered and extensive empire, like that of England, secure; for while it is true that an unexpected attack may cause disaster in some one quarter, the actual superiority of naval power prevents such disaster from being general or irremediable. History has sufficiently proved this. England's naval bases have been in all parts of the world; and her fleets have at once protected them, kept open the communications between them, and relied upon them for shelter.

Colonies attached to the mother-country afford, therefore, the surest means of supporting abroad the sea power of a country. In peace, the influence of the government should be felt in promoting by all means a warmth of attachment and a unity of interest which will make the welfare of one the welfare of all, and the quarrel of one the quarrel of all; and in war, or rather for war, by inducing such measures of organization and defence as shall be felt by all to be fair distribution of a burden of which each reaps the benefit.

Such colonies the United States has not and is not likely to have. As regards purely military naval stations, the feeling of her people was probably accurately expressed by an historian of the English navy a hundred years ago, speaking then of Gibraltar and Port Mahon. 'Military governments,' said he, 'agree so little with the industry of a trading people, and are in themselves so repugnant to the genius of the British people, that I do not wonder that men of good sense and of all parties have inclined to give up these, as Tangiers was given up.' Having therefore no foreign establishments, either colonial or military, the ships of war of the United States, in war, will be like land birds, unable to fly far from their own shores. To provide resting-places for them, where they can coal and repair, would be one of the first duties of a government proposing to itself the development of the power of the nation at sea.

As the practical object of this inquiry is to draw from the lessons of history inferences applicable to one's own country and service, it is proper now to ask how far the conditions of the United States involve serious danger, and call for action on the part of the government, in order to build again her sea power. It will not be too much to say that the action of the government since the Civil War, and up to this day, has been effectively directed solely to what has been called the first link in the chain which makes sea power. Internal development, great produc-tion, with the accompanying aim and boast of self-sufficingness, such has been the object, such to some extent the result. In this the government has faithfully reflected the bent of the control-ling elements of the country, though it is not always easy to feel that such controlling elements are truly representative, even in a free country. However that may be, there is no doubt that, besides having no colonies, the intermediate link of a peaceful shipping, and the interests involved in it, are now likewise lacking. In short, the United States has only one link of the three.

The circumstances of naval war have changed so much within the last hundred years, that it may be doubted whether such disastrous effects on the one hand, or such brilliant prosperity on the other, as were seen in the wars between England and France, could now recur. In her secure and haughty sway of the seas England imposed a yoke on neutrals which will never again be borne; and the principle that the flag covers the goods is forever secured. The commerce of a belligerent can therefore now be safely carried on in neutral ships, except when contra-band of war or to blockaded ports; and as regards the latter, it is also certain that there will be no more paper blockades. Putting aside therefore the question of defending her seaports from capture or contribution, as to which there is practical unanimity in theory and entire indifference in practice, what need has the United States of sea power? Her commerce is even now carried on by others; why should her people desire that which, if possessed, must be defended at great cost? So far as this question is economical, it is outside the scope of this work; but conditions which may entail suffering and loss on the country by war are directly pertinent to it. Granting therefore that the foreign trade of the United States, going and coming, is on board ships which an enemy cannot touch except when bound to a block-aded port, what will constitute an efficient blockade? The

present definition is, that it is such as to constitute a manifest danger to a vessel seeking to enter or leave the port. This is evidently very elastic. Many can remember that during the Civil War, after a night attack on the United States fleet off Charleston, the Confederates next morning sent out a steamer with some foreign consuls on board, who so far satisfied themselves that no blockading vessel was in sight that they issued a declaration to that effect. On the strength of this declaration some Southern authorities claimed that the blockade was technically broken, and could not be technically re-established without a new notification. Is it necessary, to constitute a real danger to blockade-runners, that the blockading fleet should be in sight? Half a dozen fast steamers, cruising twenty miles off-shore between the New Jersey and Long Island coast, would be a very real danger to ships seeking to go in or out by the principal entrance to New York; and similar positions might effec-

tively blockade Boston, the Delaware, and the Chesapeake. The main body of the blockading fleet, prepared not only to capture merchant-ships but to resist military attempts to break the blockade, need not be within sight, nor in a position known to the shore. The bulk of Nelson's fleet was fifty miles from Cadiz two days before Trafalgar, with a small detachment watching close to the harbor. The allied fleet began to get under way at 7 a.m., and Nelson, even under the conditions of those days, knew it by 9.30. The English fleet at that distance was a very real danger to its enemy. It seems possible, in these days of submarine telegraphs, that the blockading forces in-shore and off-shore, and from one port to another, might be in telegraphic communication with one another along the whole coast of the United States, readily giving mutual support; and if, by some fortunate military combination, one detachment were attacked in force, it could warn the others and retreat upon them.

Granting that such a blockade off one port were broken on one day, by fairly driving away the ships maintaining it, the notification of its being re-established could be cabled all over the world the next. To avoid such blockades there must be a military force afloat that will at all times so endanger a blockading fleet that it can by no means keep its place. Then neutral ships, except those laden with contraband of war, can come and go freely, and maintain the commercial relations of the country with the world outside.

It may be urged that, with the extensive sea-coast of the United States, a blockade of the whole line cannot be effectively kept up. No one will more readily concede this than officers who remember how the blockade of the Southern coast alone was maintained. But in the present condition of the navy, and, it may be added, with any additions not exceeding those so far proposed by the government, the attempt to blockade Boston, New York, the Delaware, the Chesapeake, and the Mississippi, in other words, the great centres of export and import, would not entail upon one of the large maritime nations efforts

a navy which, if not capable of reaching distant countries, shall at least be able to keep clear the chief approaches to its own. The eyes of the country have for a quarter of a century been turned from the sea; the results of such a policy and of its opposite will be shown in the instance of France and of England. Without asserting a narrow parallelism between the case of the United States and either of these, it may safely be said that it is essential to the welfare of the whole country that the conditions of trade and commerce should remain, as far as possible, unaffected by an external war. In order to do this, the enemy must be kept not only out of our ports, but far away from our coasts.

Can this navy be had without restoring the merchant shipping? It is doubtful. History has proved that such a purely military sea power can be built up by a despot, as was done by Louis XIV; but though so fair seeming, experience showed that his navy was like a growth which having no root soon withers away. But in a representative government any military expenditure must have a strongly represented interest behind it, convinced of its necessity. Such an interest in sea power does

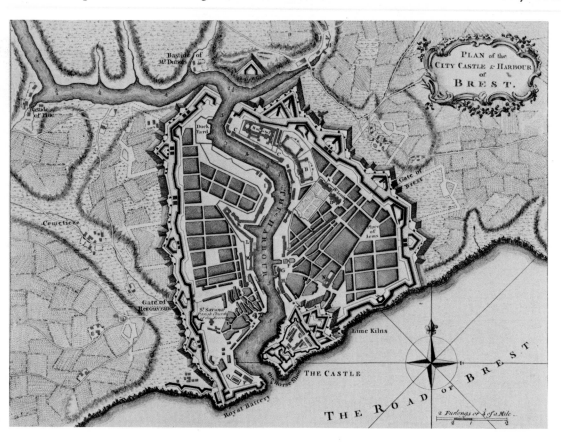

Left: *The great arsenal of Brest in Brittany, the main Atlantic base of the French fleet. Its main drawback was its remoteness from the English Channel, being too far to the west. Conversely it required a great effort to maintain a close blockade of Brest, but this was achieved by Cornwallis during the Revolutionary and Napoleonic Wars.*

greater than have been made before. England has at the same time blockaded Brest, and Biscay coast, Toulon, and Cadiz, when there were powerful squadrons lying within the harbors. It is true that commerce in neutral ships can then enter other ports of the United States than those named; but what a dislocation of the carrying traffic of the country, what failure of supplies at times, what inadequate means of transport by rail or water, of dockage, of lighterage, of warehousing, will be involved in such an enforced change of the ports of entry! Will there be no money loss, no suffering, consequent upon this? And when with much pain and expense these evils have been partially remedied, the enemy may be led to stop the new inlets as he did the old. The people of the United States will certainly not starve, but they may suffer grievously. As for supplies which are contraband of war, is there not reason to fear that the United States is not now able to go alone if an emergency should arise?

The question is eminently one in which the influence of the government should make itself felt, to build up for the nation

not exist, cannot exist here without action by the government. How such a merchant shipping should be built up, whether by subsidies or by free trade, by constant administration of tonics or by free movement in the open air, is not a military but an economical question. Even had the United States a great national shipping, it may be doubted whether a sufficient navy would follow; the distance which separates her from other great powers, in one way a protection, is also a snare. The motive, if any there be, which will give the United States a navy, is probably now quickening in the Central American Isthmus. Let us hope it will not come to the birth too late.

Here concludes the general discussion of the principal elements which affect, favorably or unfavorably, the growth of sea power in nations. The aim has been, first to consider those elements in their natural tendency for or against, and then to illustrate by particular examples and by the experience of the past. Such discussions, while undoubtedly embracing a wider field, yet fall mainly within the province of strategy, as dis-

Left: *English men-o'-war engaging the Barbary pirates. The first serious effort to deal with these pests was made by Blake in 1655, and they were not exterminated until the French conquest of Algeria in 1830.*

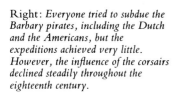

Right: *Everyone tried to subdue the Barbary pirates, including the Dutch and the Americans, but the expeditions achieved very little. However, the influence of the corsairs declined steadily throughout the eighteenth century.*

tinguished from tactics. The considerations and principles which enter into them belong to the unchangeable, or unchanging, order of things, remaining the same, in cause and effect, from age to age. They belong, as it were, to the Order of Nature, of whose stability so much is heard in our day; whereas tactics, using as its instruments the weapons made by man, shares in the change and progress of the race from generation to generation. From time to time the superstructure of tactics has to be altered or wholly torn down; but the old foundations of strategy so far remain, as though laid upon a rock. There will next be examined the general history of Europe and America, with particular reference to the effect exercised upon that history, and upon the welfare of the people, by sea power in its broad sense. From time to time, as occasion offers, the aim will be to recall and reinforce the general teaching, already elicited, by particular illustrations. The general tenor of the study will therefore be strategical, in that broad definition of naval strategy which has before been quoted and accepted: 'Naval strategy has for its end to found, support, and increase, as well in peace as in war, the sea power of a country.' In the matter of particular battles, while freely admitting that the change of details has made obsolete much of their teaching, the attempt will be made to point out where the application or neglect of true general principles has produced decisive effects; and, other things being equal, those actions will be preferred which, from their association with the names of the most distinguished officers, may be presumed to show how far just tactical ideas obtained in a particular age or a particular service. It will also be desirable, where analogies between ancient and modern weapons appear on the surface, to derive such probable lessons as they offer, without laying undue stress upon the points of resemblance. Finally, it must be remembered that, among all changes, the nature of man remains much the same; the personal equation, though uncertain in quantity and quality in the particular instance, is sure always to be found.

Chapter 2

The Second Anglo-Dutch War

Above: *Apart from his other pursuits, Charles II brought back the pastime of yachting from his exile in Holland.*

The period at which our historical survey is to begin has been loosely stated as the middle of the seventeenth century. The year 1660 will now be taken as the definite date at which to open. In May of that year Charles II was restored to the English throne amid the general rejoicing of the people. In March of the following year, upon the death of Cardinal Mazarin, Louis XIV assembled his ministers and said to them: 'I have summoned you to tell you that it has pleased me hitherto to permit my affairs to be governed by the late cardinal; I shall in future be my own prime minister. I direct that no decree be sealed except by my orders, and I order the secretaries of State and the superintendent of the finances to sign nothing without my command.' The personal government thus assumed was maintained, in fact as well as in name, for over half a century.

Within one twelvemonth then are seen, setting forward upon a new stage of national life, after a period of confusion more or less prolonged, the two States which, amid whatever inequalities have had the first places in the sea history of modern Europe and America, indeed, of the world at large. Sea history, however, is but one factor in that general advance and decay of nations which is called their history; and if sight be lost of the other factors to which it is so closely related, a distorted view, either exaggerated or the reverse, of its importance will be formed. It is with the belief that that importance is vastly underrated, if not practically lost sight of, by people unconnected with the sea, and particularly by the people of the United States in our own day, that this study has been undertaken.

We must first look at the general condition of European States at the time from which the narrative starts. In the struggles, extending over nearly a century, whose end is marked by the Peace of Westphalia, the royal family known as the House of Austria had been the great overwhelming power which all others feared. During the long reign of the Emperor Charles V, who abdicated a century before, the head of that house had united in his own person the two crowns of Austria and Spain, which carried with them, among other possessions, the countries we now know as Holland and Belgium, together with a preponderating influence in Italy. After his abdication the two great monarchies of Austria and Spain were separated; but though ruled by different persons, they were still in the same family, and tended toward that unity of aim and sympathy which marked dynastic connections in that and the following century. To this bond of union was added that of a common religion.

Placed between Spain and the German States, among which Austria stood foremost without a rival, internal union and checks upon the power of the House of Austria were necessities of French political existence. Happily, Providence raised up to her in close succession two great rulers, Henry IV and Richelieu

—men in whom religion fell short of bigotry, and who, when forced to recognize it in the sphere of politics, did so as masters and not as slaves. Under them French statesmanship received a guidance, which Richelieu formulated as a tradition, and which moved on the following general lines; (1) Internal union of the kingdom, appeasing or putting down religious strife and centralizing authority in the king; (2) Resistance to the power of the House of Austria, which actually and necessarily carried with it alliance with Protestant German States and with Holland; (3) Extension of the boundaries of France to the eastward, at the expense mainly of Spain, which then possessed not only the present Belgium, but other provinces long since incorporated with France; and (4) The creation and development of a great sea power, adding to the wealth of the kingdom, and intended

than a century before, was now long in decay and scarcely formidable; the central weakness had spread to all parts of the administration. In extent of territory, however, she was still great. The Spanish Netherlands still belonged to her; she held Naples, Sicily, and Sardinia; Gibraltar had not yet fallen into English hands; her vast possessions in America—with the exception of Jamaica, conquered by England a few years before —were still untouched. The condition of her sea power, both for peace and war, has been already alluded to. The navy of Spain was then in full decay, and its weakness did not escape the piercing eye of the cardinal. An encounter which took place between the Spanish and Dutch fleets in 1639 shows most plainly the state of degradation into which this once proud navy had fallen.

specially to make head against France's hereditary enemy, England; for which end again the alliance with Holland was to be kept in view. It may be noted that of these four elements necessary to the greatness of France, sea power was one; and as the second and third were practically one in the means employed, it may be said that sea power was one of the two great means by which France's *external* greatness was to be maintained. England on the sea, Austria on the land, indicated the direction that French effort was to take.

As regards the condition of France in 1660, and her readiness to move onward in the road marked by Richelieu, it may be said that internal peace was secured, the power of the nobles wholly broken, religious discords at rest; the tolerant edict of Nantes was still in force, while the remaining Protestant discontent had been put down by the armed hand. All power was absolutely centred in the throne. In other respects, though the kingdom was at peace, the condition was less satisfactory. There was practically no navy; commerce, internal and external, was not prosperous; the finances were in disorder; the army small. Spain, the nation before which all others had trembled less

'Her navy at this time,' says the narrative quoted, 'met one of those shocks, a succession of which during this war degraded her from her high station of mistress of the seas in both hemispheres, to a contemptible rank among maritime powers. The king was fitting out a powerful fleet to carry the war to the coasts of Sweden, and for its equipment had commanded a reinforcement of men and provisions to be sent from Dunkirk. A fleet accordingly set sail, but were attacked by Von Tromp, some captured, the remainder forced to retire within the harbor again. Soon after, Tromp seized three English [neutral] ships carrying 1070 Spanish soldiers from Cadiz to Dunkirk; he took the

Above: *Louis XIV meets Philip IV of Spain at l'Ile des Faisans in 1660, from a tapestry after Lebrun.*

troops out, but let the ships go free. Leaving seventeen vessels to blockade Dunkirk, Tromp with the remaining twelve advanced to meet the enemy's fleet on its arrival. It was soon seen entering the Straits of Dover to the number of sixty-seven sail, and having two thousand troops. Being joined by De Witt with four more ships, Tromp with his small force made a resolute attack upon the enemy. The fight lasted till four p.m., when the Spanish admiral took refuge in the Downs. Tromp determined to engage if they should come out; but Oquendo with his powerful fleet, many of which carried from sixty to a hundred guns, suffered himself to be blockaded; and the English admiral told Tromp he was ordered to join the Spaniards if hostilities began. Tromp sent home for instructions, and the action of England only served to call out the vast maritime powers of the Dutch. Tromp was rapidly reinforced to ninety-six sail and twelve fire-ships, and ordered to attack. Leaving a detached squadron to observe the English, and to attack them if they helped the Spaniards, he began the fight embarrassed by a thick fog, under cover of which the Spaniards cut their cables to escape. Many running too close to shore went aground, and most of the remainder attempting to retreat were sunk, captured, or driven on the French coast. Never was victory more complete.'

When a navy submits to such a line of action, all tone and pride must have departed; but the navy only shared in the general decline which made Spain henceforward have an ever lessening weight in the policy of Europe.

That part of the Spanish dominions which was then known as the Low Countries, or the Roman Catholic Netherlands (our modern Belgium), was about to be a fruitful source of variance between France and her natural ally, the Dutch Republic. This State, whose political name was the United Provinces, had now reached the summit of its influence and power—a power based, as has already been explained, wholly upon the sea, and upon the use of that element made by the great maritime and commercial genius of the Dutch people. A recent French author thus describes the commercial and colonial conditions, at the accession of Louis XIV, of this people, which beyond any other in modern times, save only England, has shown how the harvest of the sea can lift up to wealth and power a country intrinsically weak and without resources:

'Holland had become the Phoenicia of modern times. Mistresses of the Scheldt, the United Provinces closed the outlets of Antwerp to the sea, and inherited the commercial power of that rich city, which an ambassador of Venice in the fifteenth century had compared to Venice herself. They received besides in their principal cities the workingmen of the Low Countries who fled from Spanish tyranny of conscience. The manufacturers of clothes, linen stuffs, etc., which employed six hundred thousand souls, opened new sources of gain to a people previously content with the trade in cheese and fish.

The naval and commercial power of the republic developed rapidly. The merchant fleet of Holland alone numbered 10,000 sail, 168,000 seamen, and supported 260,000 inhabitants. She had taken possession of the greater part of the European carrying-trade, and had added thereto, since the peace, all the carriage of merchandise between America and Spain, did the same service for the French ports. The north countries, Brandenburg, Denmark, Sweden, Muscovy, Poland, access to which was opened by the Baltic to the Provinces, were for them an inexhaustible market of exchange. They fed it by the produce they sold there, and by purchase of the products of the North—wheat, timber, copper, hemp, and furs. The total value of merchandise yearly shipped in Dutch bottoms, in all seas, exceeded a thousand million francs. The Dutch had made themselves, to use a contemporary phrase, the wagoners of all seas.'

It was through its colonies that the republic had been able thus to develop its sea trade. It had the monopoly of all the products of the East. The powerful East India Company, founded in 1602, had built up in Asia an empire, with possessions

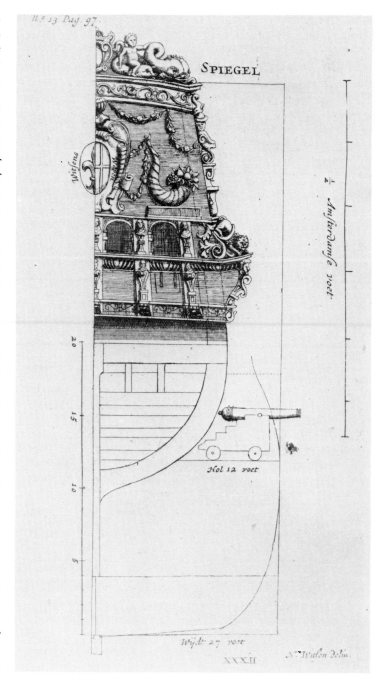

Above: *A typical Dutch man-o'-war's stern, from a technical illustration. By the last quarter of the seventeenth century the art of projecting a three-dimensional image of a ship on paper was far advanced, resulting in detailed construction plans.*

taken from the Portuguese. Mistress in 1650 of the Cape of Good Hope, which guaranteed it a stopping-place for its ships, it reigned as a sovereign in Ceylon, and upon the coasts of Malabar and Coromandel. It had made Batavia its seat of government, and extended its traffic to China and Japan. Meanwhile the West India Company, of more rapid rise, but less durable, had manned eight hundred ships of war and trade. It had used them to seize the remnants of Portuguese power upon the shores of Guinea, as well as in Brazil.

Right: *A small Dutch man-o'-war lying off Gibraltar.*

The United Provinces had thus become the warehouse wherein were collected the products of all nations.

The colonies of the Dutch at this time were scattered throughout the eastern seas, in India, in Malacca, in Java, the Moluccas, and various parts of the vast archipelago lying to the northward of Australia. They had possessions on the west coast of Africa, and as yet the colony of New Amsterdam remained in their hands. In South America the Dutch West India Company had owned nearly three hundred leagues of coast from Bahia in Brazil northward; but much had recently escaped from their hands.

The United Provinces owed their consideration and power to their wealth and their fleets. The sea, which beats like an inveterate enemy against their shores, had been subdued and made a useful servant; the land was to prove their destruction. A long and fierce strife had been maintained with an enemy more cruel than the sea—the Spanish kingdom; the successful ending, with its delusive promise of rest and peace, but sounded the knell of the Dutch Republic. So long as the power of Spain remained unimpaired, or at least great enough to keep up the terror that she had long inspired, it was to the interest of England and of France, both sufferers from Spanish menace and intrigue, that the United Provinces should be strong and independent. When Spain fell, and repeated humiliations showed that her weakness was real and not seeming, other motives took the place of fear. England coveted Holland's trade and sea dominion; France desired the Spanish Netherlands. The United Provinces had reason to oppose the latter as well as the former.

Under the combined assaults of the two rival nations, the intrinsic weakness of the United Provinces was soon to be felt and seen. Open to attack by the land, few in numbers, and with a government ill adapted to put forth the united strength of a people, above all unfitted to keep up adequate preparation for war, the decline of the republic and the nation was to be more striking and rapid than the rise. As yet, however, in 1660, no indications of the coming fall were remarked. The superiority of their fleet, the valor of their troops, the skill and firmness of their diplomacy, had caused the prestige of their government to be recognized. Weakened and humiliated by the last English war, they had replaced themselves in the rank of great powers.

The general character of the government has been before mentioned, and need here only be recalled. It was a loosely knit confederacy, administered by what may not inaccurately be called a commercial aristocracy, with all the political timidity of that class, which has so much to risk in war. The effect of these two factors, sectional jealousy and commercial spirit, upon the military navy was disastrous. It was not kept up properly in peace, there were necessarily rivalries in a fleet which was rather a maritime coalition than a united navy, and there was too little of a true military spirit among the officers. A more heroic people than the Dutch never existed; the annals of Dutch sea-fights give instances of desperate enterprise and endurance certainly not excelled, perhaps never equalled, elsewhere; but they also exhibit instances of defection and misconduct which show a lack of military spirit, due evidently to lack of professional pride and training. This professional training scarcely existed in any navy of that day, but its place was largely supplied in monarchical countries by the feeling of a military caste. It remains to be noted that the government, weak enough from the causes named, was yet weaker from the division of the people into two great factions bitterly hating each other. The one, which was the party of the merchants (burgomasters), and

Left: *Peter the Great inspecting Dutch ships in 1670. Russia's 'Technocraft Czar' learned the art of shipbuilding in Holland and England before starting to build a navy of his own.*

Right: *Van de Velde's drawings of the bow and stern carvings of the 90-gun 2nd Rate* St Michael *of 1669.*

Below: *Phineas Pett sharing the canvas with his great masterpiece the* Sovereign of the Seas. *This magnificently decorated 100-gun 1st Rate was launched in 1637 and rebuilt in 1660 under the new name* Royal Sovereign.

now in power, favored the confederate republic as described; the other desired a monarchical government under the House of Orange. The Republican party wished for a French alliance, if possible, and a strong navy; the Orange party favored England to whose royal house the Prince of Orange was closely related, and a powerful army. Under these conditions of government, and weak in numbers, the United Provinces in 1660, with their vast wealth and external activities, resembled a man kept up by stimulants. Factitious strength cannot endure indefinitely; but it is wonderful to see this small State, weaker by far in numbers than either England or France, endure the onslaught of either singly, and for two years of both in alliance, not only without being destroyed, but without losing her place in Europe. She owed this astonishing result partly to the skill of one or two men, but mainly to her sea power.

The conditions of England, with reference to her fitness to

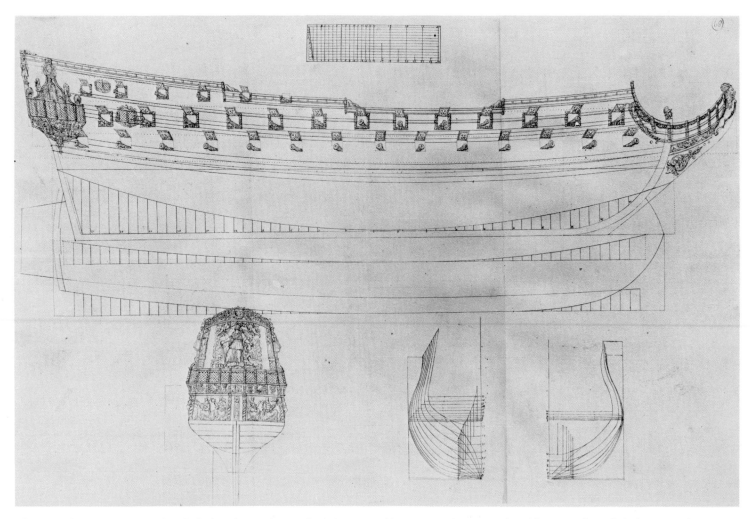

Above: *Anthony Deane's 1670 sheer draft of a 3rd Rate, showing the sophistication of late seventeenth-century technical drawing. The method of projecting the hull-form on paper was to remain unchanged for another 150 years.*

enter upon the impending strife, differed from those of both Holland and France. Although monarchical in government. and with much real power in the king's hands, the latter was not able to direct the policy of the kingdom wholly at his will. He had to reckon, as Louis had not, with the temper and wishes of his people. When danger became imminent, the king gave way before the feeling of the English nation. Charles himself hated Holland; he hated it as republic; he hated the existing government because opposed in internal affairs to his connections, the House of Orange; and he hated it yet more because in the days of his exile, the republic, as one of the conditions of peace with Cromwell, had driven him from her borders. He was drawn to France by the political sympathy of a would-be absolute ruler, possibly by his Roman Catholic bias, and very largely by the money paid him by Louis, which partially freed him from the control of Parliament. The English, of the same race as the Dutch, and with similar conditions of situation, were declared rivals for the control of the sea and of commerce; and as the Dutch were now leading in the race, the English were the more eager and bitter. At the first, therefore, popular rivalry and enmity seconded the king's wishes; the more so as France had not for some years been formidable on the continent. As soon, however, as the aggressive policy of Louis XIV was generally recognized, the English people, both nobles and commons, felt the great danger to be there, as a century before it had been in Spain. The transfer of the Spanish Netherlands (Belgium) to France would tend toward the subjection of Europe, and especially would be a blow to the sea power both of the Dutch and English; for it was not to be supposed that Louis would allow the Scheldt and port of Antwerp to remain closed, as they then were, under a treaty wrung by the Dutch from the

weakness of Spain. The reopening to commerce of that great city would be a blow alike to Amsterdam and to London. With the revival of inherited opposition to France the ties of kindred began to tell; the memory of past alliance against the tyranny of Spain was recalled; and similarity of religious faith, still a powerful motive, drew the two together. At the same time the great and systematic efforts of Colbert to build up the commerce and the navy of France excited the jealousy of both the sea powers; rivals themselves, they instinctively turned against a third party intruding upon their domain. Charles was unable to resist the pressure of his people under all these motives; wars between England and Holland ceased, and were followed, after Charles's death, by close alliance.

Although her commerce was less extensive, the navy of England in 1660 was superior to that of Holland, particularly in organization and efficiency. The stern, enthusiastic religious government of Cromwell, grounded on military strength, had made its mark both on the fleet and army. The names of several of the superior officers under the Protector, among which that of Monk stands foremost, appear in the narrative of the first of the Dutch wars under Charles. This superiority in tone and discipline gradually disappeared under the corrupting influence of court favor in a licentious government; and Holland, which upon the whole was worsted by England alone upon the sea in 1665, successfully resisted the combined navies of England and France in 1672. As regards the material of the three fleets, we are told that the French ships had greater displacement than the English relatively to the weight of artillery and stores; hence they could keep, when fully loaded, a greater height of battery. Their hulls also had better lines. These advantages would naturally follow from the thoughtful and systematic way in which the French navy at that time was restored from a state of decay. The Dutch ships, from the character of their coast, were flatter-bottomed and of less draught, and thus were able, when pressed, to find a refuge among the shoals; but they were in consequence less weatherly and generally of lighter scantling than those of either of the other nations.

The general state of Europe being as described, the spring that was to set the various wheels in motion was in the hands of Louis XIV. The weakness of his immediate neighbors, the great resources of his kingdom, only waiting for development, the unity of direction resulting from his absolute power, his own practical talent and untiring industry, aided during the first half of his reign by a combination of ministers of singular ability, all united to make every government in Europe hang more or less upon his action, and be determined by, if not follow, his lead. The greatness of France was his object, and he had the choice of advancing it by either of two roads, by the land or by the sea; not that the one wholly forbade the other, but that France, overwhelmingly strong as she then was, had not power to move with equal steps on both paths.

Louis chose extension by land. He had married the eldest daughter of Philip IV, the then reigning king of Spain; and though by the treaty of marriage she had renounced all claim to her father's inheritance, it was not difficult to find reasons for disregarding this stipulation. Technical grounds were found for setting it aside as regarded certain portions of the Netherlands and Franche Comté, and negotiations were entered into with the court of Spain to annul it altogether. The matter was the more important because the male heir to the throne was so feeble that it was evident that the Austrian line of Spanish kings would end in him. The desire to put a French prince on the Spanish throne—either himself, thus uniting the two crowns, or else one of his family, thus putting the House of Bourbon in authority on both sides of the Pyrenees—was the false light which led Louis astray during the rest of his reign, to the final destruction of the sea power of France and the impoverishment

and misery of his people. Louis failed to understand that he had to reckon with all Europe. The direct project on the Spanish throne had to wait for a vacancy; but he got ready at once to move upon the Spanish possessions to the east of France.

In order to do this more effectually, he cut off from Spain every possibly ally by skilful diplomatic intrigues, the study of which would give a useful illustration of strategy in the realm of politics, but he made two serious mistakes to the injury of the sea power of France. Portugal had until twenty years before been united to the crown of Spain, and the claim to it had not been surrendered. Louis considered that were Spain to regain that kingdom she would be too strong for him easily to carry out his aims. Among other means of prevention he promoted a marriage between Charles II and the Infanta of Portugal, in consequence of which Portugal ceded to England, Bombay in India, and Tangiers in the Straits of Gibraltar, which was reputed an excellent port. We see here a French king, in his eagerness for extension by land, inviting England to the Mediterranean, and forwarding her alliance with Portugal. Portugal became a dependent and outpost of England, by which she readily landed in the Peninsula down to the days of Napoleon. Indeed, if independent of Spain, she is too weak not to be under the control of the power that rules the sea and so has readiest access to her. Louis continued to support her against Spain, and secured her independence.

On the other hand, Louis obtained from Charles II the cession of Dunkirk on the Channel, which had been seized and used by Cromwell. This surrender was made for money, and was inexcusable from the maritime point of view. Dunkirk was for the English a bridge-head into France. To France it became a haven for privateers, the bane of England's commerce in the Channel and the North Sea. As the French sea power waned, England in treaty after treaty exacted the dismantling of the works of Dunkirk, which it may be said in passing was the home port of the celebrated Jean Bart and other great French privateersmen.

Right: The bloody Battle of Scheveningen on 29–31 July 1653, in which Marten Harpertszoon Tromp was killed. By a strange coincidence the Battle of Camperdown was fought in the same locality in 1797 and was also distinguished by its ferocity.

Meanwhile the greatest and wisest of Louis' ministers, Colbert, was diligently building up that system of administration, which, by increasing and solidly basing the wealth of the State, should bring a surer greatness and prosperity than the king's more showy enterprises. Upon the sea a policy of skilful aggression upon the shipping and commerce of the Dutch and English quickly began, and was instantly resented. Great trading companies were formed, directing French enterprise to the Baltic, to the Levant, to the East and West Indies; customs regulations were amended to encourage French manufactures, and to allow goods to be stored in bond in the great ports, by which means it was hoped to make France take Holland's place as the great warehouse for Europe, a function for which her geographical position eminently fitted her; while tonnage duties on foreign shipping, direct premiums on homebuilt ships, and careful, rigorous colonial decrees giving French vessels the monopoly of trade to and from the colonies, combined to encourage the growth of her mercantile marine. England

retaliated at once; the Dutch, more seriously threatened because their carrying-trade was greater and their home resources smaller, only remonstrated for a time; but after three years they also made reprisals. Colbert, relying on the great superiority of France as an actual, and still more as a possible producer, feared not to move steadily on the grasping path marked out; which, in building up a great merchant shipping, would lay the broad base for the military shipping, which was being yet more rapidly forced on by the measures of the State. Prosperity grew apace. At the end of twelve years everything was flourishing, everything rich in the State, which was in utter confusion when he took charge of the finances and marine.

Leibnitz, one of the world's great men, pointed out to Louis that to turn the arms of France against Egypt would give her, in the dominion of the Mediterranean and the control of Eastern trade, a victory over Holland greater than the most successful campaign on land; and while insuring a much needed peace within his kingdom, would build up a power on the sea that

Above: *English ships becalmed, 1693.*

would insure preponderance in Europe. This memorial called Louis from the pursuit of glory on the land to seek the durable grandeur of France in the possession of a great sea power, the elements of which, thanks to the genius of Colbert, he had in his hands. This project of Leibnitz will be more fully referred to when the narrative reaches the momentous date at which it was broached; when Louis with his kingdom and navy in the highest pitch of efficiency, stood at the point where the roads parted, and then took the one which settled that France should not be the

Above: *HMS* Resolution *in a gale, 1667.*

power of the sea. This decision, which killed Colbert and ruined the prosperity of France, was felt in its consequences from generation to generation afterward, as the great navy of England, in war after war, swept the seas, insured the growing wealth of the island kingdom through exhausting strifes, while drying up the external resources of French trade and inflicting consequent misery. The false line of policy that began with Louis XIV also turned France away from a promising career in India, in the days of his successor.

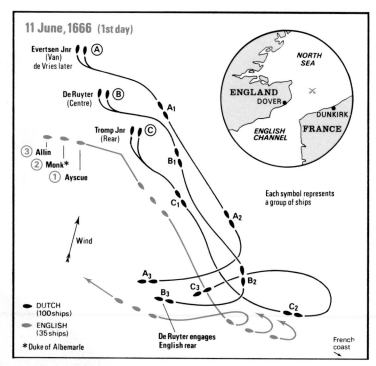

11 June, 1666 (1st day)

Evertsen Jnr
(Van)
de Vries later

De Ruyter
(Centre)

Tromp Jnr
(Rear)

③ Allin
② Monk*
① Ayscue

Wind

Each symbol represents
a group of ships

● DUTCH
(100 ships)
● ENGLISH
(35 ships)

*Duke of Albemarle

De Ruyter engages
English rear

French
coast

NORTH
SEA

ENGLAND
DOVER

ENGLISH
CHANNEL

DUNKIRK
FRANCE

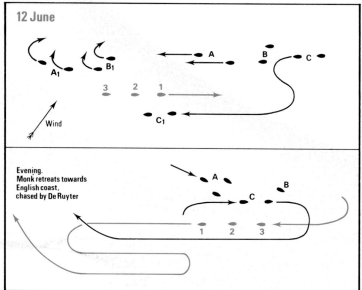

12 June

Wind

Evening.
Monk retreats towards
English coast,
chased by De Ruyter

13 June: Monk continues retreat westward followed by De Ruyter. 'Royal Prince' runs
aground on Galloper Shoal and is taken by Tromp. Rupert's squadron rejoins
English fleet.

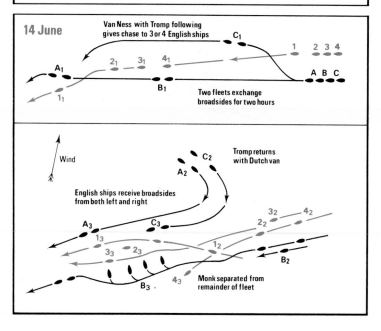

14 June

Van Ness with Tromp following
gives chase to 3 or 4 English ships

Two fleets exchange
broadsides for two hours

Wind

Tromp returns
with Dutch van

English ships receive broadsides
from both left and right

Monk separated from
remainder of fleet

*Left: The Four Days' Battle, 1–4 June 1666. Notice that differences occur
between Mahan's historical dates and those of modern historians, partly as a
result of the use of different sources, especially calendars.*

Meanwhile the two maritime States, England and Holland,
though eying France distrustfully, had greater and growing
grudges against each other, which under the fostering care of
Charles II led to war. The true cause was doubtless commercial
jealousy, and the conflict sprang immediately from collisions
between the trading companies. Hostilities began on the west
coast of Africa; and an English squadron, in 1664, after subduing several Dutch stations there, sailed to New Amsterdam
(now New York), and seized it. All these affairs took place
before the formal declaration of war in February, 1665. The
United Provinces would gladly have avoided the war; the able
man who was at their head saw too clearly the delicate position
in which they stood between England and France. They claimed,
however, the support of the latter in virtue of a defensive treaty
made in 1662. Louis allowed the claim, but unwillingly; and
the still young navy of France gave practically no help.

The war between the two sea States was wholly maritime,
and had the general characteristics of all such wars. Three great
battles were fought—the first off Lowestoft, on the Norfolk
coast, June 13, 1665; the second, known as the Four Days'
Battle in the Straits of Dover, often spoken of by French writers
as that of the Pas de Calais, lasting from the 11th to the 14th of
June, 1666; and the third, off the North Foreland, August 4 of
the same year. In the first and last of these the English had a
decided success; in the second the advantage remained with the
Dutch. This one only will be described at length, because of it
alone has been found such a full, coherent account as will allow a
clear and accurate tactical narrative to be given.

In the first battle off Lowestoft, it appears that the Dutch
commander, Opdam, who was not a seaman but a cavalry
officer, had very positive orders to fight; the discretion proper
to a commander-in-chief on the spot was not intrusted to him.
To interfere thus with the commander in the field or afloat is one
of the most common temptations to the government in the
cabinet, and is generally disastrous. In the Lowestoft fight the
Dutch van gave way; and a little later one of the junior admirals
of the centre, Opdam's own squadron, being killed, the crew
was seized with a panic, took the command of the ship from her
officers, and carried her out of action. This movement was
followed by twelve or thirteen other ships, leaving a great gap
in the Dutch line. The occurrence shows, what has before been
pointed out, that the discipline of the Dutch fleet and the tone of
the officers were not high, despite the fine fighting qualities of
the nation, and although it is probably true that there were
more good seamen among the Dutch than among the English
captains.

Opdam, seeing the battle going against him, seems to have
yielded to a feeling approaching despair. He sought to grapple
the English commander-in-chief, who on this day was the Duke
of York, the king's brother. He failed in this, and in the desperate struggle which followed, his ship blew up. Shortly after,
three, or as one account says four, Dutch ships ran foul of one
another, and this group was burned by one fire-ship; three or
four others singly met the same fate a little later. The Dutch
fleet was now in disorder, and retreated under cover of the
squadron of Van Tromp, son of the famous old admiral who in
the days of the Commonwealth sailed through the Channel
with a broom at his masthead.

Right: *The Four Days' Fight, 1666.*

Fire-ships are seen here to have played a very conspicuous part, more so certainly than in the war of 1653, though at both periods they formed an appendage to the fleet. There is on the surface an evident resemblance between the rôle of the fire-ship and the part assigned in modern warefare to the torpedo-cruiser. The terrible character of the attack, the comparative smallness of the vessel making it, and the large demands upon the nerve of the assailant, are the chief points of resemblance; the great points of difference are the comparative certainty with which the modern vessel can be handled, which is partly met by the same advantage in the iron-clad over the old ship-of-the-line, and the instantaneousness of the injury by torpedo, whose attack fails or succeeds at once, whereas that of the fire-ship required time for effecting the object, which in both cases is total destruction of the hostile ship, instead of crippling or otherwise reducing it.

A French officer, who has been examining the records of the French navy, states that the fire-ship first appears, incorporated as an arm of the fleet, in 1636.

'Whether specially built for the purpose, or whether altered from other purposes to be fitted for their particular end, they received a special equipment. Easily known by grappling-irons which were always fitted to their yards, the fire-ship saw its rôle growing less in the early years of the eighteenth century. It was finally to disappear from the fleets *whose speed it delayed and whose evolutions were by it complicated.* As the ships-of-war grew larger, their action in concert with fire-ships became daily more difficult. On the other hand, there had already been abandoned the idea of combining them with the fighting-ships to form a few *groups, each* provided with all the means of attack and defence. The formation of the close-hauled line-of-battle, by assigning the fire-ships a place in a second line placed half a league on the side farthest from the enemy, made them more and more unfitted to fulfil their office. Finally the use of shells, enabling ships to be set on fire more surely and quickly, and introduced on board at the period of which we are now treating, though the general use did not obtain until much later, was the last blow to the fire-ship.'

Those who are familiar with the theories and discussions of our own day on the subject of fleet tactics and weapons, will recognize in this short notice of a long obsolete type certain ideas which are not obsolete. The fire-ship disappeared from fleets 'whose speed it delayed.' In heavy weather small bulk must always mean comparatively small speed. In moderate sea, we are now told, the speed of the torpedo-boat falls from twenty knots to fifteen or less, and the seventeen to nineteen knot cruiser can either run away from the pursuing boats, or else hold them at a distance under fire of machine and heavy guns. These boats are sea-going, 'and it is thought can keep the sea in all weathers; but to be on board a 110-foot torpedo-boat, when the sea is lively, is said to be far from agreeable. The heat, noise, and rapid vibrations of the engines are intense. Cooking seems to be out of the question, and it is said that if food were well cooked few would be able to appreciate it. To obtain necessary rest under these conditions, added to the rapid motions of the boat, is most difficult.' Larger boats are to be built; but the factor of loss of speed in rough weather will remain, unless the size of the torpedo-cruiser is increased to a point that will certainly lead to fitting them with something more than

torpedoes. Like fire-ships, *small* torpedo-cruisers will delay the speed and complicate the evolutions of the fleet with which they are associated. The disappearance of the fire-ship was also hastened, we are told, by the introduction of shell firing, or incendiary projectiles; and it is not improbable that for deep-sea fighting the transfer of the torpedo to a class of larger ships will put and end to the mere torpedo-cruiser. The fires-ship continued to be used against fleets at anchor down to the days of the American Civil War; and the torpedo-boat will always be useful within an easy distance of its port.

A third phase of naval practice two hundred years ago, mentioned in the extract quoted, involves an idea very familiar to modern discussions; namely, the group formation. 'The idea of combining fire-ships with the fighting-ships to form a few groups, each provided with all the means of attack and defence,' was for a time embraced; for we are told that it was later on abandoned. It may be remarked that in a well-organized fleet there are two degrees of command which are in themselves both natural and necessary, that can be neither done away nor ignored;

Below: *Cornelis Tromp was the second son of Marten Tromp, a much more impetuous leader than his father.*

these are the command of the whole fleet as one unit, and the command of each ship as a unit in itself. When a fleet becomes too large to be handled by one man, it must be subdivided, and in the heat of action become practically two fleets acting to one common end; as Nelson, in his noble order at Trafalgar, said, 'The second in command will, *after* my intentions are made known to him' (mark the force of the 'after,' which so well protects the functions both of the commander-in-chief and the second), 'have the entire direction of his line, to make the attack upon the enemy, and to follow up the blow until they are captured or destroyed.'

Looking simply to the principle underlying the theory, and disregarding the seeming tactical clumsiness of the special groups proposed, the question is: Shall there be introduced between the natural commands of the admiral and of the captains of individual ships a third artificial contrivance, which on the one hand will in effect partly supersede the supreme authority, and on the other will partly fetter the discretion of commanders of ships? A further difficulty springing from the narrow principle

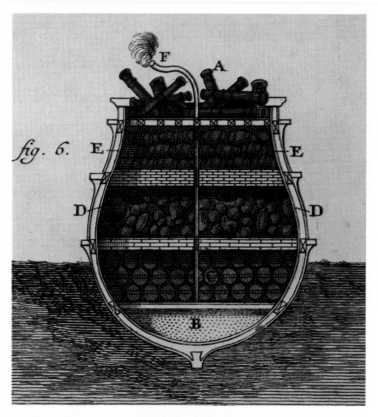

fig. 6.

Above: *A somewhat fanciful cross section of a fire-ship. The fire-ship was generally put together using an old vessel or merchant ship, which was filled with combustibles including tar, pitch and gunpowder. Used more as a psychological weapon than simply a direct threat to the timbers, it was sent off downwind, to draw out the enemy ships from their moorings in order to engage in action.*

of support specially due to particular ships, on which the group system rests, is this: that when signals can no longer be seen, the duty of the captain to his own ship and to the fleet at large will be complicated by his duty to observe certain relations to particular ships; which particular ships must in time come to have undue prominence in his views. The group formation had its day of trial in old times, and disappeared before the test of experience; whether in its restored form it will survive, time will show. It may be said, before quitting the subject, that as an order of sailing, corresponding to the route-step of an army in march, a loose group formation has some advantages; maintaining some order without requiring that rigid exactness of position, to observe which by day and night must be a severe strain on

captain and deck-officers. Such a route-order should not, however, be permitted until a fleet has reached high tactical precision.

To return to the question of fire-ships and torpedo-boats, the rôle of the latter, it is often said, is to be found in that *mêlée* which is always to succeed a couple of headlong passes between the opposing fleets. In the smoke and confusion of that hour is the opportunity of the torpedo-boat. This certainly sounds plausible, and the torpedo vessel certainly has a power of movement not possessed by the fire-ship. A *mêlée* of the two fleets, however, was not the condition most favorable for the fire-ship.

In the midst of the confused *mêlées* of 1652 the fire-ship 'acted, so to speak, alone, seeking by chance an enemy to grapple, running the risk of a mistake, without protection against the guns of the enemy, nearly sure to be sunk by him or else burned uselessly. All now, in 1665, has become different. Its prey is clearly pointed out; it knows it, follows it easily into the relatively fixed position had by it in the enemy's line. On the other hand, the ships of his own division do not lose sight of the fire-ship. They accompany it as far as possible, cover it with their artillery to the end of its course, and disengage it before burning, if the fruitlessness of the attempt is seen soon enough. Evidently under such conditions its action, always uncertain (it cannot be otherwise), nevertheless acquires greater chances of success.' These instructive comments need perhaps the qualifying, or additional, remark that confusion in the enemy's order at the time that your own remains good gives the best opening for a desperate attack. A French officer, traced the disappearance of the fire-ship:

'Here then we see the fire-ship at the point of its highest importance. That importance will decrease, the fire-ship itself will end by disappearing from engagements in *the open sea*, when naval artillery becoming more perfect shall have greater range, be more accurate and more rapid; when ships receiving better forms, greater steering power, more extensive and better balanced sail power, shall be able, thanks to quicker speed and handling, to avoid almost certainly the fire-ships sent against them; when finally, fleets led on principles of tactics as skilful as they were timid, tactics which will predominate a century later during the whole war of American Independence, when these fleets, in order not to jeopardize the perfect regularity of their order of battle, will avoid coming to close quarters, and will leave to the cannon alone to decide the fate of an action.'

In this discussion the writer has in view the leading feature which, while aiding the action of the fire-ship, also gives this war of 1665 its peculiar interest in the history of naval tactics. In it is found for the first time the close-hauled line-of-battle undeniably adopted as the fighting order of the fleets. The credit for this development is generally given to the Duke of York, afterward James II; but the question to whom the improvement is due is of little importance to sea-officers of the present day when compared with the instructive fact that so long a time elapsed between the appearance of the large sailing-ship, with its broadside battery, and the systematic adoption of the order which was best adapted to develop the full power of the fleet for mutual support. Why did it take so long for the capable men of that day to reach this order? The reason—and herein lies the lesson for the officer of today—was doubtless the same that leaves the order of battle so uncertain now; namely, that the necessity of war did not force men to make up their minds, until the Dutch at last met in the English their equals on the sea. The sequence of ideas which resulted in the line-of-battle is clear and logical. Though familiar enough to seamen, it will be here stated in the words of the writer last quoted, because they have a neatness and precision entirely French:

'With the increase of power of the ship-of-war, and with the perfecting of its sea and warlike qualities, there has come an equal progress in the art of utilizing them. . . . As naval evolutions become more skilful, their importance grows from day to day. To these evolutions there is needed a base, a point from which they depart and to which they return. A fleet of war-ships must be always ready to meet an enemy; logically, therefore, this point of departure for naval evolutions must be the order of battle. Now, since the disappearance of galleys, almost all the artillery is found upon the sides of a ship of war. Hence it is the beam that must necessarily and always be turned toward the enemy. On the other hand, it is necessary that the sight of the latter must never be interrupted by a friendly ship. Only one formation allows the ships of the same fleet to satisfy fully these conditions. That formation is the line ahead [column]. This line, therefore, is imposed as the only order of battle, and consequently as the basis of all fleet tactics. In order that this order of battle, this long thin line of guns, may not be injured or broken at some point weaker than the rest, there is at the same time felt the necessity of putting in it only ships which, if not of equal force, have at least equally strong sides. Logically it follows, at the same moment in which the line ahead became definitively the order for battle, there was established the

commanders, brought forth by their respective countries in the seventeenth century. Monk was possibly inferior to Blake in the annals of the English navy; but there is a general agreement that De Ruyter is the foremost figure, not only in the Dutch service, but among all the naval officers of that age. The account about to be given is mainly taken from a recent number of the 'Revue Maritime et Coloniale,' and is there published as a letter, recently discovered, from a Dutch gentleman serving as volunteer on board De Ruyter's ship, to a friend in France.

The numbers of the two fleets were: English about eighty ships, the Dutch about one hundred; but the inequality in numbers was largely compensated by the greater size of many of the English. A great strategic blunder by the government in London immediately preceded the fight. The king was informed that a French squadron was on its way from the Atlantic to join the Dutch. He at once divided his fleet, sending twenty ships under Prince Rupert to the westward to meet the French, while the remainder under Monk were to go east and oppose the Dutch.

distinction between the ships "of the line," alone destined for a place therein, and the lighter ships meant for other uses.'

If to these we add the considerations which led to making the line-of-battle a close-hauled line, we have the problem fully worked out. But the chain of reasoning was as clear two hundred and fifty years ago as it is now; why then was it so long in being worked out? Partly, no doubt, because old traditions—in those days traditions of galley-fighting—had hold of and confused men's minds; chiefly because men are too indolent to seek out the foundation truths of the situation in their day, and develop the true theory of action from its base up.

We come now to the justly celebrated Four Days' Battle of June, 1666, which claims special notice, not only on account of the great number of ships engaged on either side, nor yet only for the extraordinary physical endurance of the men who kept up a hot naval action for so many successive days, but also because the commanders-in-chief on either side, Monk and De Ruyter, were the most distinguished seamen, or rather sea-

Above: An attack by fire-ships on an English fleet. Usually old or damaged ships, these floating incendiary bombs were rightly feared.

A position like that of the English fleet, threatened with an attack from two quarters, presents one of the subtlest temptations to a commander. The impulse is very strong to meet both by dividing his own numbers as Charles did; but unless in possession of overwhelming force it is an error, exposing both divisions to be beaten separately, which, as we are about to see, actually happened in this case. The result of the first two days was disastrous to the larger English division under Monk, which was then obliged to retreat toward Rupert; and probably the opportune return of the latter alone saved the English fleet from a very serious loss, or at the least from being shut up in their own ports. A hundred and forty years later, in the exciting game of strategy that was played in the Bay of Biscay before Trafalgar, the English admiral Cornwallis made precisely the same blunder, dividing his fleet into two equal parts out of supporting distance, which Napoleon at the time characterized as a glaring piece of stupidity. The lesson is the same in all ages.

Below: *The Four Days' Battle, 1666.*

The Dutch had sailed for the English coast with a fair easterly wind, but it changed later to southwest with thick weather, and freshened, so that De Ruyter, to avoid being driven too far, came to anchor between Dunkirk and the Downs (see Map of the Four Days' Battle on page 78). The fleet then rode with its head to the south-southwest and the van on the right; while Tromp, who commanded the rear division in the natural order, was on the left. For some cause this left was most to windward, the centre squadron under Ruyter being to leeward, and the right, or van, to leeward again of the centre (see Map June 11, 1666, A, van; B, centre; C, rear: in this part of the action the Dutch order was inverted, so that the actual van was the proper rear. The great number of ships engaged in the fleet actions of these Anglo-Dutch wars make it impossible to represent each ship and at the same time preserve clearness in the plans. Each figure of a ship therefore represents a group, more or less numerous). This was the position of the Dutch fleet at daylight of June 11, 1666; and although not expressly so stated, it is likely, from the whole tenor of the narratives, that it was not in good order.

The same morning Monk, who was also at anchor, made out the Dutch fleet to leeward, and although so inferior in numbers determined to attack at once, hoping that by keeping the advantage of the wind he would be able to commit himself only so far as might seem best. He therefore stood along the Dutch line on the starboard tack, leaving the right and centre out of cannon-shot, until he came abreast of the left, Tromp's squadron. Monk then had thirty-five ships well in hand; but the rear had opened and was straggling, as is apt to be the case with long columns. With the thirty-five he then put his helm

up and ran down for Tromp, whose squadron cut their cables and made sail on the same tack; the two engaged lines thus standing over toward the French coast, and the breeze heeling the ships so that the English could not use their lower-deck guns (June 11). The Dutch centre and rear also cut (B_2, C_2), and followed the movement, but being so far to leeward, could not for some time come into action. It was during this time that a large Dutch ship, becoming separated from her own fleet, was set on fire and burned, doubtless the ship in which was Count de Guiche.

As they drew near Dunkirk the English went about, probably all together; for in the return to the northward and westward the proper English van fell in with and was roughly handled by the Dutch centre under Ruyter himself (see B_3). This fate would be more likely to befall the rear, and indicates that a simultaneous movement had reversed the order. The engaged ships had naturally lost to leeward, thus enabling Ruyter to fetch up with them. Two English flag-ships were here disabled and cut off; one, the *Swiftsure*, hauled down her colors after the admiral, a young man of only twenty-seven, was killed. 'Highly to be admired,' says a contemporary writer, 'was the resolution of Vice-Admiral Berkeley, who, though cut off from the line, surrounded by enemies, great numbers of his men killed, his ship disabled and boarded on all sides, yet continued fighting almost alone, killed several with his own hand, and would accept no quarter; till at length, being shot in the throat with a musket-ball, he retired into the captain's cabin, where he was found dead, extended at his full length upon a table, and almost covered with his own blood.' Quite as heroic, but more fortunate in its issue, was the conduct of the other English

Above: *Vice-Admiral Sir James Berkeley, who fought his flagship, the 46-gun* Swiftsure, *with great gallantry at the Four Days' Fight. His ship was cut off and surrounded by De Ruyter's center but the 27-year-old Berkeley refused to surrender.*

actual rear, but proper van], which from noon up to that time had not been able to reach the enemy [see A₂] from their leewardly position.' The merit of Monk's attack as a piece of grand tactics is evident, and bears a strong resemblance to that of Nelson at the Nile. Discerning quickly the weakness of the Dutch order, he had attacked a vastly superior force in such a way that only part of it could come into action; and though the English actually lost more heavily, they carried off a brilliant prestige and must have left considerable depression and heart-burning among the Dutch. The eye-witness goes on: 'The affair continued until ten p.m., friends and foes mixed together and as likely to receive injury from one as from the other. It will be remarked that the success of the day and the misfortunes of the English came from their being too much scattered, too extended in their line; but for which we could never have cut off a corner of them, as we did. The mistake of Monk was in not keeping his ships better together;' that is, closed up. The remark is just, the criticism scarcely so; the opening out of the line was almost unavoidable in so long a column of sailing-ships, and was one of the chances taken by Monk when he offered battle.

The English stood off on the port tack to the west or west-northwest, and next day returned to the fight. The Dutch were now on the port tack in natural order, the right leading, and were to windward; but the enemy, being more weatherly and better disciplined, soon gained the advantage of the wind. The English this day had forty-four ships in action, the Dutch about eighty; many of the English, as before said, larger. The two fleets passed on opposite tacks, the English to windward (see Map June 12, A, B, C); but Tromp, in the rear, seeing that

Below: *The Four Days' Fight, 1–4 June 1666 was the biggest sea battle since* Lepanto. *In this slugging match the English lost many more men and ships than the Dutch but their discipline prevented the disaster from being much greater.*

admiral thus cut off; and the incidents of his struggle, though not specially instructive otherwise, are worth quoting, as giving a lively picture of the scenes which passed in the heat of the contests of those days, and afford coloring to otherwise dry details.

'Being in a short time completely disabled, one of the enemy's fire-ships grappled him on the starboard quarter; he was, however, freed by the almost incredible exertions of his lieutenant, who, having in the midst of the flames loosed the grappling-irons, swung back on board his own ship unhurt. The Dutch, bent on the destruction of this unfortunate ship, sent a second which grappled her on the larboard side, and with greater success than the former; for the sails instantly taking fire, the crew were so terrified that nearly fifty of them jumped overboard. The admiral, Sir John Harman, seeing this confusion, ran with his sword drawn among those who remained, and threatened with instant death the first man who should attempt to quit the ship, or should not exert himself to quench the flames. The crew then returned to their duty and got the fire under; but the rigging being a good deal burned, one of the topsail yards fell and broke Sir John's leg. In the midst of this accumulated distress, a third fire-ship prepared to grapple him, but was sunk by the guns before she could effect her purpose. The Dutch vice-admiral, Evertzen, now bore down on him and offered quarter; but Sir John replied, "No, no, it is not come to that yet," and giving him a broadside, killed the Dutch commander; after which the other enemies sheered off.'

It is therefore not surprising that the account we have been following reported two English flag-ships lost, one by a fire-ship. 'The English chief still continued on the port tack, and,' says the writer, 'as night fell we could see him proudly leading his line past the squadron of North Holland and Zealand [the

the Dutch order of battle was badly formed, the ships in two or three lines, overlapping and so masking each other's fire, went about and gained to windward of the enemy's van; which he was able to do from the length of the line, and because the English, running parallel to the Dutch order, were off the wind. 'At this moment two flag-officers of the Dutch van kept broad off, presenting their sterns to the English. Ruyter, greatly astonished, tried to stop them, but in vain, and therefore felt obliged to imitate the manoeuvre in order to keep his squadron together; but he did so with some order, keeping some ships around him, and was joined by one of the van ships, disgusted with the conduct of his immediate superior. Tromp was now in

Left: Jean Bart, the great French corsair. He was born at Dunkerque in 1650 and died in 1702, having inflicted severe damage on English trade in the Channel and foreshadowed the feats of the eighteenth-century privateers.

The third day Monk continued retreating to the westward. He burned, by the English accounts, three disabled ships sent ahead those that were most crippled, and himself brought up the rear with those that were in fighting condition, which are variously stated, again by the English, at twenty-eight and sixteen in number (see June 13). One of the largest and finest of the English fleet, the *Royal Prince*, of ninety guns, ran aground on the Galloper Shoal and was taken by Tromp (June 13); but Monk's retreat was so steady and orderly that he was otherwise unmolested. This shows that the Dutch had suffered very severely. Toward evening Rupert's squadron was seen; and all the ships of the English fleet, except those crippled in action, were at last united.

The next day the wind came out again very fresh from the southwest, giving the Dutch the weather-gage. The English, instead of attempting to pass upon opposite tacks, came up from astern relying upon the speed and handiness of their ships. So doing, the battle engaged all along the line on the port tack, the English to leeward (see Map June 14). The Dutch fire-ships were badly handled and did no harm, whereas the English burned two of their enemies. The two fleets ran on thus, exchanging broadsides for two hours, at the end of which time the bulk of the English fleet had passed through the Dutch line (First picture. This result was probably due simply to the greater weatherliness of the English ships. It would perhaps be more accurate to say that the Dutch had sagged to leeward so that they drifted through the English line). All regularity of order was henceforward lost. 'At this moment,' says the eye-witness, 'the lookout was extraordinary, for all were separated, the English as well as we. But luck would have it that the largest of our fractions surrounding the admiral remained to windward, and the largest fraction of the English, also with their admiral, remained to leeward [June 14, first picture]. This was the cause of our victory and their ruin. Our admiral had with him thirty-five or forty ships of his own and of other squadrons, for the squadrons were scattered and order much lost. The rest of the Dutch ships had left him. The leader of the van, Van Ness, had gone off with fourteen ships in chase of three or four English ships, which under a press of sail had gained to windward of the Dutch van [see C_1]. Van Tromp with the rear squadron had fallen to leeward, and so had to keep on [to leeward of Ruyter and the English main body, see C_1] after Van Ness, in order to rejoin the admiral by passing round the English centre.' De Ruyter and the English main body kept up a sharp action, beating to windward all the time. Tromp, having carried sail, overtook Van Ness, and returned bringing the van back with him (A_2, C_2); but owing to the constant plying to windward of the English main body he came up to leeward of it and could not rejoin Ruyter, who was at this point to windward. Ruyter, seeing this, made signal to the ships around him, and the main body of the Dutch kept away before the wind (B_2, B_3), which was then very strong. 'Thus in less than no time we found ourselves in the midst of the English; who, being attacked on both sides, were thrown into confusion and saw their whole order destroyed, as well by dint of the action, as by the strong wind that was then blowing. This was the hottest of the fight. We saw the high admiral of England separated from his fleet, followed only by one fire-ship. With that he gained to windward, and passing through the North Holland squadron, placed himself again at the head of fifteen or twenty ships that rallied to him.'

great danger, separated [by his own act first and then by the conduct of the van] from his own fleet by the English, and would have been destroyed but for Ruyter, who, seeing the urgency of the case, hauled up for him,' the van and centre thus standing back for the rear on the opposite tack to that on which they entered action. This prevented the English from keeping up the attack on Tromp, lest Ruyter should gain the wind of them, which they could not afford to yield because of their very inferior numbers. Both the action of Tromp and that of the junior flag-officers in the van, though showing very different degrees of warlike ardor, bring out strongly the lack of sub-ordination and of military feeling which has been charged against the Dutch officers as a body; no signs of which appear among the English at this time.

How keenly Ruyter felt the conduct of his lieutenants was manifested when 'Tromp, immediately after this partial action, went on board his flagship. The seamen cheered him; but Ruyter said, "This is no time for rejoicing, but rather for tears.' Indeed, our position was bad, each squadron acting differently, in no line, and all the ships huddled together like a flock of sheep, so packed that the English might have surrounded all of them with their forty ships [see June 12]. The English were in admirable order, but did not push their advantage as they should, whatever the reason.' The reason no doubt was the same that often prevented sailing-ships from pressing an advantage—disability from crippled spars and rigging, added to the inexpediency of such inferior numbers risking a decisive action.

Ruyter was thus able to draw his fleet out into line again, although much maltreated by the English, and the two fleets passed again on opposite tacks, the Dutch to leeward, and Ruyter's ship the last in his column. As he passed the English rear, he lost his maintopmast and mainyard. After another partial encounter the English drew away to the northwest toward their own shores, the Dutch following them; the wind being still from southwest, but light. The English were now fairly in retreat, and the pursuit continued all night, Ruyter's own ship dropping out of sight in the rear in a crippled state.

Thus ended this great sea-fight, the most remarkable, in some of its aspects, that has ever been fought upon the ocean. Amid conflicting reports it is not possible to do more than estimate the results. A fairly impartial account says: 'The States lost in these actions three vice-admirals, two thousand men, and four ships. The loss of the English was five thousand killed and three thousand prisoners; and they lost besides seventeen ships, of which nine remained in the hands of the victors.' There is no doubt that the English had much the worst of it, and that this was owing wholly to the original blunder of weakening the fleet by a great detachment sent in another direction. Great detachments are sometimes necessary evils, but in this case no necessity existed. Granting the approach of the French, the proper course for the English was to fall with their whole fleet upon the Dutch before their allies could come up. This lesson is as applicable today as it ever was. A second lesson, likewise of present application, is the necessity of sound military institutions for implanting correct military feeling, pride, and discipline. Great as was the first blunder of the English, and serious as was the disaster, there can be no doubt that the consequences would have been much worse but for the high spirit and skill with which the plans of Monk were carried out by his subordinates, and the lack of similar support to Ruyter on the part of the Dutch subalterns. In the movements of the English, we hear nothing of two juniors turning tail at a critical moment, nor of a third, with misdirected ardor, getting on the wrong side of the enemy's fleet. Their drill also, their tactical precision, was remarked even then. The Frenchman De Guiche, after witnessing this Four Days' Fight, wrote:

'Nothing equals the beautiful order of the English at sea. Never was a line drawn straighter than that formed by their ships; thus they bring all their fire to bear upon those who draw near them. . . . They fight like a line of cavalry which is handled according to rule, and applies itself solely to force back those who oppose; whereas the Dutch advance like cavalry whose squadrons leave their ranks and come separately to the charge.'

The Dutch government, averse to expense, unmilitary in its tone, and incautious from long and easy victory over the degenerate navy of Spain, had allowed its fleet to sink into a mere assembly of armed merchantmen. Things were at their worst in the days of Cromwell. Taught by the severe lessons of that war, the United Provinces, under an able ruler, had done much to mend matters, but full efficiency had not yet been gained.

Below: *This Dutch print of the Four Days' Fight gives an impression of the confusion inherent in seventeenth-century sea battles, before the introduction of the line of battle. The inset portraits are Michiel de Ruyter (left) and his able lieutenant Cornelis Tromp (right).*

England, as has been said before, still felt the impress of Cromwell's iron hand upon her military institutions; but that impress was growing weaker. Before the next Dutch war Monk was dead, and was poorly replaced by the cavalier Rupert. Court extravagance cut down the equipment of the navy as did the burgomaster's parsimony, and court corruption undermined discipline as surely as commercial indifference. The effect was evident when the fleets of the two countries met again, six years later.

There was one well-known feature of all the military navies of that day which calls for a passing comment; for its correct bearing and value is not always, perhaps not generally, seen. The command of fleets and of single vessels was often given to soldiers, to military men unaccustomed to the sea, and ignorant how to handle the ship, that duty being intrusted to another class of officer. Looking closely into the facts, it is seen that this made a clean division between the direction of the fighting and of the motive power of the ship. The inconvenience and inefficiency of such a system was obvious then as it is now, and the logic of facts gradually threw the two functions into the hands of one corps of officers, the result being the modern naval officer, as that term is generally understood. Unfortunately, in this process of blending, the less important function was allowed to get the upper hand; the naval officer came to feel more proud of his dexterity in managing the motive power of his ship than of his skill in developing his military efficiency. The English naval officer thought more of that which likened him to the merchant captain than of that which made him akin to the soldier. In the French navy this result was less general, owing probably to the more military spirit of the government, and especially of the nobility, to whom the rank of officer was reserved. The English corps of officers was of different origin. There was more than the writer thought in Macaulay's well-known saying: 'There were seamen and there were gentlemen in the navy of Charles II; but the seamen were not gentlemen, and the gentlemen were not seamen.' The trouble was not in the absence or presence of gentlemen as such, but in the fact that under the conditions of that day the gentleman was pre-eminently the military element of society; and that the seaman, after the Dutch wars, gradually edged the gentleman, and with him the military tone and spirit as distinguished from simple courage, out of the service. The studious and systematic side of the French character also inclined the French officer, when not a trifler, to consider and develop tactical questions in a logical manner; to prepare himself to handle fleets, not merely as a seaman but as a military man. The source whence the Dutch mainly drew their officers does not certainly appear. It is likely, from many indications, that they were generally merchant seamen, with little original military feeling; but the severity with which the delinquents were punished both by the State and by popular frenzy, seems to have driven these officers, who were far from lacking the highest personal courage, into a sense of what military loyalty and subordination required. They made a very different record in 1672 from that of 1666.

Before finally leaving the Four Day's Fight, the conclusions of another writer, Chabaud-Arnault, may well be quoted:

'Such was that bloody Battle of the Four Days, or Straits of Calais, the most memorable sea-fight of modern days; not, indeed, by its results, but by the aspect of its different phases; by the fury of the combatants; by the boldness and skill of the leaders; and by the new character which it gave to sea warfare. More than any other this fight marks clearly the passage from former methods to the tactics of the end of the seventeenth century. For the first time we can follow, as though traced upon a plan, the principal movements of the contending fleets. It seems quite clear that to the Dutch as well as to the British have been given a tactical book and a code of signals; or, at the least, written instructions, extensive and precise, to serve instead of such a code. We feel that each admiral now has his squadron in hand, and that even the commander-in-chief disposes at his will, during the fight, of the various subdivisions of his fleet. Compare this action with those of 1652, and one plain fact stares you in the face —that between the two dates naval tactics have undergone a revolution.

'Such were the changes that distinguish the war of 1665 from that of 1652. As in the latter epoch, the admiral still thinks the weathergage an advantage for his fleet; but it is no longer, from the tactical point of view, the principal, we might almost say the sole, preoccupation. Now he wishes above all to keep his fleet in good order and compact as long as possible, so as to keep the power of *combining*, during the action, the movements of the different squadrons.'

This commentary is justified in so far as it points out general aims and tendencies; but the results were not as complete as might be inferred from it.

The English, notwithstanding their heavy loss in the Four Days' Battle, were at sea again within two months, much to the surprise of the Dutch; and on the 4th of August another severe fight was fought off the North Foreland, ending in the complete defeat of the latter, who retired to their own coasts. The English followed, and effected an entrance into one of the Dutch harbors,

where they destroyed a large fleet of merchantmen as well as a town of some importance. Toward the end of 1666 both sides were tired of the war, which was doing great harm to trade, and weakening both navies to the advantage of the growing sea power of France. Negotiations looking toward peace were opened; but Charles II, ill disposed to the United Provinces, confident that the growing pretentions of Louis XIV to the Spanish Netherlands would break up the existing alliance between Holland and France, and relying also upon the severe reverses suffered at sea by the Dutch, was exacting and haughty in his demands. To justify and maintain this line of conduct he should have kept up his fleet, the prestige of which had been so advanced by its victories. Instead of that, poverty, the result of extravagance and of his home policy, led him to permit it to decline; ships in large numbers were laid up; and he readily adopted an opinion which chimed in with his penury, and which, as it has had advocates at all periods of sea history, should be noted and condemned here. This opinion, warmly opposed by Monk, was:

'That as the Dutch were chiefly supported by trade, as the supply of their navy depended upon trade, and, as experience showed, nothing provoked the people so much as injuring their trade, his Majesty should therefore apply himself to this, which would effectually humble them, at the same time that it would less exhaust the English

than fitting out such mighty fleets as had hitherto kept the sea every summer. . . . Upon these motives the king took a fatal resolution of laying up his great ships and keeping only a few frigates on the cruise.'

In consequence of this economical theory of carrying on a war, the Grand Pensionary of Holland, De Witt, who had the year before caused soundings of the Thames to be made, sent into the river, under De Ruyter, a force of sixty or seventy ships-of-the-line, which on the 14th of June, 1667, went up as high as Gravesend, destroying ships at Chatham and in the Medway, and taking possession of Sheerness. The light of the fires could be seen from London, and the Dutch fleet remained in possession of the mouth of the river until the end of the month. Under this blow, following as it did upon the great plague and the great fire of London, Charles consented to peace, which was signed July 31, 1667, and is known as the Peace of Breda.

Before going on again with the general course of the history of the times, it will be well to consider for a moment the theory which worked so disastrously for England in 1667; that, namely, of maintaining a sea-war mainly by preying upon the enemy's commerce. This plan, which involves only the maintenance of a few swift cruisers and can be backed by the spirit of greed in a nation, fitting out privateers without direct expense to the State, possesses the specious attractions which economy always presents. The great injury done to the wealth and prosperity of the enemy is also undeniable; and although to some extent his merchant-ships can shelter themselves ignobly under a foreign flag while the war lasts, this *guerre de course*, as the French call it, this commerce-destroying, to use our own phrase, must, if in itself successful, greatly embarrass the foreign government and distress its people. Such a war, however, cannot

Left: *Despite the defeat at the Four Days' Fight the English recovered quickly and were in a position to dictate terms at the end of the Second Dutch War. All this changed on 14 June 1667, when De Ruyter sailed up the Medway and burned the English fleet at Chatham. Charles II had imprudently ordered the fleet to be laid up before the peace negotiations were over, and this disaster following on the Great Plague and Fire of London forced England to make peace on reasonable terms.*

Top: *It was hardly surprising that the Dutch should see the Peace of Breda on 31 July 1667 as a miraculous deliverance.*

stand alone; it must be *supported*, to use the military phrase; unsubstantial and evanescent in itself, it cannot reach far from its base. That base must be either home ports, or else some solid outpost of the national power, on the shore or the sea; a distant dependency or a powerful fleet. Failing such support, the cruiser can only dash out hurriedly a short distance from home, and its blows, though painful, cannot be fatal. It was not the policy of 1667, but Cromwell's powerful fleets of ships-of-the-line in 1652, that shut the Dutch merchantmen in their ports and caused the grass to grow in the streets of Amsterdam.

Macaulay says of this period: 'During many months of 1693 the English trade with the Mediterranean had been interrupted almost entirely. There was no chance that a merchantman from London or Amsterdam would, if unprotected, reach the Pillars of Hercules without being boarded by a French privateer; and the protection of armed vessels was not easily obtained.' Why? Because the vessels of England's navy were occupied watching the French navy, and this diversion of them from the cruisers and privateers constituted the support which a commerce-destroying war must have. A French historian, Martin, speaking of the same period in England (1696), says: 'The state of the finances was deplorable; money was scarce, maritime insurance thirty per cent, the Navigation Act was virtually suspended, and the English shipping reduced to the necessity of sailing under the Swedish and Danish flags.' Half a century later the French government was again reduced, by long neglect of the navy, to a cruising warfare. With what results? First, the French historian says: 'From June, 1756, to June, 1760, French privateers captured from the English more than twenty-five hundred merchantmen. In 1761, though France had not, so to speak, a single ship-of-the-line at sea, and though the English had taken two hundred and forty of our privateers, their comrades still took eight hundred and twelve vessels. But,' he goes on to say, 'the prodigious growth of the English shipping explains the number of these prizes.' In other words, the suffering involved to England in such numerous captures, which must have caused great individual injury and discontent, did not really prevent the growing prosperity of the State and of the community at large. The English naval historian, speaking of the same period, says: 'While the commerce of France was nearly destroyed, the trading-fleet of England covered the seas. Every year her commerce was increasing; the money which the war carried out was returned by the produce of her industry.' The historian of the French navy, Lapeyrouse-Bonfils, speaking of an earlier phase of the same wars, says: 'The English fleets, having nothing to resist them, swept the seas. Our privateers and single cruisers, having no fleet to keep down the abundance of their enemies, ran short careers. Twenty thousand French seamen lay in English prisons.' When on the other hand, in the War of the American Revolution France resumed the policy of Colbert and of the early reign of Louis XIV, and kept large battle-fleets afloat, the same result again followed as in the days of Tourville.

So far we have been viewing the effect of a purely cruising warfare, not based upon powerful squadrons, only upon that particular part of the enemy's strength against which it is

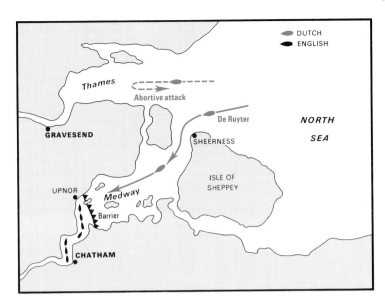

Above: *De Ruyter in the Medway, 14 June 1667.*

theoretically directed—upon his commerce and general wealth; upon the sinews of war. The evidence seems to show that even for its own special ends such a mode of war is inconclusive, worrying but not deadly; it might almost be said that it causes needless suffering.

We may conclude that it is not the taking of individual ships or convoys, be they few or many, that strikes down the money power of a nation; it is the possession of that overbearing power on the sea which drives the enemy's flag from it, or allows it to appear only as a fugitive; and which, by controlling the great common, closes the highways by which commerce moves to and from the enemy's shores. This overbearing power can only be exercised by great navies, and by them (on the broad sea) less efficiently now than in the days when the neutral flag had not its present immunity. It is not unlikely that, in the event of a war between maritime nations, an attempt may be made by the one having a great sea power and wishing to break down its enemy's commerce, to interpret the phrase 'effective blockade' in the manner that best suits its interests at the time; to assert that the speed and disposal of its ships make the blockade effective at much greater distances and with fewer ships than formerly. The determination of such a question will depend, not upon the weaker belligerent, but upon neutral powers; it will raise the issue between belligerent and neutral rights; and if the belligerent have a vastly overpowering navy he may carry his point, just as England, when possessing the mastery of the seas, long refused to admit the doctrine of the neutral flag covering the goods.

Left: *De Ruyter's attack on the Medway was not marred by any large-scale atrocities against civilians but his month-long occupation of Chatham caused great consternation in London and increased pressure on the King and Parliament for a quick settlement.*

Above: *English indignation at De Ruyter's burning of the fleet at Chatham overlooked the fact that it drew its inspiration from a daring raid on Dutch commercial shipping known as 'Holme's Bonfire' in which large numbers of Dutch ships had been destroyed the year before.*

Chapter 3

From Solebay to the Texel

Shortly before the conclusion of the Peace of Breda, Louis XIV made his first step toward seizing parts of the Spanish Netherlands and Franche Comté. Under the leadership of Holland, but with the hearty co-operation of the English minister, an alliance was formed between the two countries and Sweden, hitherto the friend of France, to check Louis' advance before his power became too great. The attack first on the Netherlands in 1667, and then on Franche Comté in 1668, showed the hopeless weakness of Spain to defend her possessions; they fell almost without a blow. Louis was deeply angered at the Triple Alliance, and his wrath was turned mainly upon Holland, in which from the necessities of her position he recognized his most steadfast opponent. He set his mind upon the destruction of the republic. This policy was directly contrary to that laid down by Richelieu, and to the true welfare of France. It was to England's interest, at least just then, that the United Provinces should not be trodden down by France; but it was much more to the interest of France that they should not be subjected to England. England, free from the continent, might stand alone upon the seas contending with France; but France, hampered by her continental politics, could not hope to wrest the control of the seas from England without an ally. This ally Louis proposed to destroy, and he asked England to help him.

Before the royal purpose had passed into action, and while there was still time to turn the energies of France into another channel, a different course was proposed to the king. This was the project of Leibnitz, before spoken of, which has special interest for our subject because, in proposing to reverse the lines which Louis then laid down, to make continental expansion secondary and growth beyond the sea the primary object of France, the tendency avowedly and necessarily was to base the greatness of the country upon the control of the sea and of commerce. The immediate object offered to the France of that day, with the attainment of which, however, she could not have

controlled the trade not only of India and the far East, but also of the Levant; but the enterprise could not have stopped there. The necessity of mastering the Mediterranean and opening the Red Sea, closed to Christian vessels by Mohammedan bigotry, would have compelled the occupation of stations on either side of Egypt; and France would have been led step by step, as England has been led by the possession of India, to the seizure of points like Malta, Cyprus, Aden, in short, to a great sea power. That is clear now; but it will be interesting to hear the arguments by which Leibnitz sought to convince the French king two hundred years ago.

After pointing out the weakness of the Turkish Empire, and the readiness with which it might be further embarrassed by stirring up Austria and Poland, the latter the traditional ally of

Left: The Third Dutch War was forced on Holland by the ambitions of Louis XIV and the implacable hatred of Charles II. Although English commerce was locked in rivalry with the Dutch, the instinctive English suspicion of France and their religious sympathies with the Dutch meant that Charles had to keep the French alliance secret.

Above: The Battle of Solebay was fought in Southwold Bay on the east coast of England 7 June 1672. Tactically it was a draw in that the French failed to support their English allies effectively, but it was a strategic victory for De Ruyter, winning precious time for the beleaguered United Provinces.

stopped short, was the conquest of Egypt; that country which, facing both the Mediterranean and Eastern seas, gave control of the great commercial route which in our own day has been complemented by the Suez Canal. That route had lost much of its value by the discovery of the way round the Cape of Good Hope, and yet more by the unsettled and piratical conditions of the seas through which it lay; but with a really strong naval power occupying the key of the position it might have been largely restored. Such a power posted in Egypt would, in the already decaying condition of the Ottoman Empire, have

France; after showing that France had no armed enemy in the Mediterranean, and that on the other side of Egypt she would meet the Portuguese colonies, longing to obtain protection against the Dutch in India, the memorial proceeds:

'Whoever has Egypt will have all the coasts and islands of the Indian Ocean. It is in Egypt that Holland will be conquered; it is there she will be despoiled of what alone renders her prosperous, the treasures of the East. She will be struck without being able to ward off the blow. Should she wish to oppose the designs of France upon Egypt, she would be overwhelmed with the universal hatred of Christians;

Above: *English ships of the center division at Solebay. Note the Red Ensign, worn by all ship commanded by an Admiral of the Red. The junior White Ensign did not become the Royal Navy's exclusive ensign for another two hundred years.*

properly be called a strategic use of their dangerous coast and shoals, upon which were based their sea operations. To this course they were forced by the desperate odds under which they were fighting; but they did not use their shoals as a mere shelter—the warfare they waged was the defensive-offensive. When the wind was fair for the allies to attack, Ruyter kept under cover of his islands, or at least on ground where the enemy dared not follow; but when the wind served so that he might attack in his own way, he turned and fell upon them. There are also apparent indications of tactical combinations, on his part, of a higher order than have yet been met; though it is possible that the particular acts referred to, consisting in partial attacks amounting to little more than demonstrations against the French contingent, may have sprung from political motives. The action of the French was at times suspicious; it has been alleged that Louis ordered his admiral to economize his fleet, and

Below: *Edward Russell, Lord Orford, who commanded the English squadrons at Solebay. He was misled by De Ruyter's pretended retreat and divided his fleet, allowing the Dutch admiral to engage in overwhelming numbers one portion. Even so it was a hard fight with heavy casualties on both sides.*

attacked at home, on the contrary, not only could she ward off the aggression, but she could avenge herself sustained by universal public opinion, which suspects the views of France of ambition.'

The memorial had no effect. 'All that the efforts of ambition and human prudence could do to lay the foundations for the destruction of a nation, Louis XIV now did. Diplomatic strategy on a vast scale was displayed in order to isolate and hem in Holland.' The Triple Alliance was broken; the King of England, though contrary to the wishes of his people, made an offensive alliance with Louis; and Holland, when the war began, found herself without an ally in Europe, except the worn-out kingdom of Spain and the Elector of Brandenburg, then by no means a first-class State. But in order to obtain the help of Charles II, Louis not only engaged to pay him large sums of money, but also to give to England, from the spoils of Holland and Belgium, Walcheren, Sluys, and Cadsand, and even the islands of Goree and Voorn; the control, that is, of the mouths of the great commercial rivers the Scheldt and the Meuse. It is evident that in his eagerness for the ruin of Holland and his own continental aggrandizement Louis was playing directly into England's hand, as to power on the sea.

During the years preceding the war the Dutch made every diplomatic effort to avert it, but the hatred of Charles and Louis prevented any concession being accepted as final. On the 23rd of March the English, without declaration of war, attacked a fleet of Dutch merchantmen; and on the 29th the king declared war. This was followed, April 6th, by the declaration of Louis XIV; and on the 28th of the same month he set out to take command in person of his army.

The war which now began, including the third and last of the great contests between the English and Dutch upon the ocean was not, like those before it, purely a sea war; and it will be necessary to mention its leading outlines on the land also, not only to give clearness of impression, but also to bring out the desperate straits to which the republic was reduced, and the final deliverance through its sea power in the hands of the great seaman De Ruyter.

The naval war differs from those that preceded it in more than one respect; but its most distinctive feature is that the Dutch, except on one occasion at the very beginning, did not send out their fleet to meet the enemy, but made what may

Right: *The burning of the Royal James (100 guns), flag-ship of the Earl of Sandwich at Solebay. Wooden warships with their tarred rigging were always vulnerable to destruction by fire, and every effort was made to limit the risk; even pipe smoking was controlled.*

there is good reason to believe that toward the end of the two years that England remained in his alliance he did do so.

The authorities of the United Provinces, knowing that the French fleet at Brest was to join the English in the Thames, made great exertions to fit out their squadron so as to attack the latter before the junction was made; but the wretched lack of centralization in their naval administration caused this project to fail. A blow at the English fleet in its own waters, by a superior force, before its ally arrived, was a correct military conception; judging from the after-history of this war, it might well have produced a profound effect upon the whole course of the struggle. Ruyter finally got to sea and fell in with the allied fleets, but though fully intending to fight, fell back before them to his own coast. The allies did not follow him there, but retired, apparently in full security, to Southwold Bay, on the east coast of England, some ninety miles north of the mouth of the Thames. There they anchored in three divisions—two English, the rear and centre of the allied line, to the northward, and the van, composed of French ships, to the southward. Ruyter followed them, and on the early morning of June 7, 1672, the Dutch fleet was signalled by a French lookout frigate in the northward and eastward; standing down before a northeast wind for the allied fleet, from which a large number of boats and men were ashore in watering parties. The Dutch order of battle was in two lines, the advanced one containing eighteen ships with fire-ships. Their total force was ninety-one ships-of-the-line; that of the allies one hundred and one.

The wind was blowing toward the coast, which here trends nearly north and south, and the allies were in an awkward position. They had first to get under way, and they could not fall back to gain time or room to establish their order. Most of the ships cut their cables, and the English made sail on the starboard tack, heading about north-northwest, a course which forced them soon to go about; whereas the French took the other tack. The battle began therefore by the separation of the allied fleet. Ruyter sent one division to attack the French, or rather to contain them; for these opponents exchanged only a distant cannonade, although the Dutch, being to windward, had the choice of closer action if they wished it. He fell furiously upon the two English divisions, and apparently with superior forces; for the English naval historians claim that the Dutch were in the proportion of three to two. If this can be accepted, it gives a marked evidence of Ruyter's high qualities as a general officer, in advance of any other who appears in this century.

The results of the battle, considered simply as an engagement, were indecisive; both sides lost heavily, but the honors and the substantial advantages all belonged to the Dutch, or rather to De Ruyter. He had outgeneralled the allies by his apparent retreat, and then returning had surprised them wholly unprepared. The false move by which the English, two thirds of the whole, stood to the northward and westward, while the other third, the French, went off to the east and south, separated the allied fleet; Ruyter threw his whole force into the gap, showing front to the French with a division probably smaller in numbers, but which, from its position to windward, had the choice of coming to close action or not, while with the remainder he fell in much superior strength upon the English.

In this battle, called indifferently Southwold Bay and Solebay, Ruyter showed a degree of skill combined with vigor which did not appear upon the sea, after his death, until the days of Suffren and Nelson. His battles of the war of 1672 were no 'affairs of circumspection,' though they were fought circumspectly; his aim was no less than the enemy's total overthrow, by joining good combinations to fury of attack. At Solebay he was somewhat, though not greatly, inferior to his enemies; afterward much more so.

Above: *A Victorian rendering of Lord Sandwich refusing to abandon the* Royal James *after she had caught fire during the Battle of Solebay. Although a much overworked theme, the military code of honor required that a captain should be the last to leave his ship.*

The substantial results of Solebay fight were wholly favorable to the Dutch. The allied fleets were to have assisted the operations of the French army by making a descent upon the coast of Zealand. Ruyter's attack had inflicted an amount of damage, and caused an expenditure of ammunition, which postponed the sailing of the fleet for a month; it was a diversion, not only important, but vital in the nearly desperate condition to which the United Provinces were reduced ashore.

The progress of the land campaign must now be briefly described. It was early in May that the French army in several corps moved forward, passing through the outskirts of the Spanish Netherlands, and directing their attack upon Holland from the south and east. Within a month the French were in the heart of the country, having carried all before them, and with no organized force remaining in their front sufficient of itself to stop them. In the fortnight following the battle of Solebay, terror and disorganization spread throughout the republic. On the 15th of June the Grand Pensionary obtained permission of the States-General to send a deputation to Louis XIV, begging him to name the terms on which he would grant them peace; any humiliation to the foreigner was better in the eyes of the politician than to see the opposite party, the House of Orange, come into power on his downfall.

Negotiations ensued. The burgomasters—the party representing wealth and commerce—favored submission; they shrank from the destruction of their property and trade. New advances were made; but while the envoys were still in the camp of Louis, the populace and the Orange party rose, and with them the spirit of resistance. On the 25th of June Amsterdam opened the dykes, and her example was followed by the other cities of Holland; immense loss was entailed, but the flooded country and cities contained therein, standing like islands amid the waters, were safe from attack by land forces until freezing weather. The revolution continued. William of Orange, afterward William III of England, was on the 8th of July made stadtholder, and head of the army and navy; and the two De Witts, the heads of the republican party, were murdered by a mob a few weeks later.

Three naval battles were fought in 1673, all near the coast of the United Provinces; the first two, June 7 and June 14, off Schoneveldt, from which place they have taken their name; the third, known as the battle of the Texel, August 21. In all three Ruyter attacked, choosing his own time, and retiring when it suited him to the protection of his own shores. For the allies to carry out their objects and make any diversion upon the seaboard, or on the other hand to cripple the sea resources of the hard-pressed Provinces, it was necessary first to deal successfully with Ruyter's fleet. The great admiral and his government both felt this, and took the resolution that 'the fleet should be posted in the passage of Schoneveldt, or a little farther south toward Ostend, to observe the enemy, and if attacked, or seeing the enemy's fleet disposed to make a descent upon the shores of the United Provinces, should resist vigorously, by opposing his designs and destroying his ships.' From this position, with good lookouts, any movement of the allies would be known.

The English and French put to sea about the 1st of June, under the command of Prince Rupert, first cousin to the king. The French were under Vice-Admiral d'Estrées, the same who had commanded them at Solebay. A force of six thousand English troops at Yarmouth was ready to embark if De Ruyter was worsted. On the 7th of June the Dutch were made out, riding within the sands at Shoneveldt. A detached squadron was sent to draw them out, but Ruyter needed no invitation; the wind served, and he followed the detached squadron with such impetuosity as to attack before the allied line was fairly formed.

On this occasion the French occupied the centre. The affair was indecisive, if a battle can be called so in which an inferior force attacks a superior, inflicts an equal loss, and frustrates the main object of the enemy. A week later Ruyter again attacked, with results which though indecisive as before as to the particular action, forced the allied fleet to return to the English coast to refit, and for supplies. The Dutch in these encounters had fifty-five ships-of-the-line; their enemies eighty-one, fifty-four of which were English.

The allied fleets did not go to sea again until the latter part of July, and this time they carried with them a body of troops meant for landing. On the 20th of August the Dutch fleet was seen under way between the Texel and the Meuse. Rupert at once got ready to fight; but as the wind was from the northward and westward, giving the allies the weather-gage, and with it the choice of the method of attack, Ruyter availed himself of his local knowledge, keeping so close to the beach that the enemy dared not approach—the more so as it was late in the day. During the night the wind shifted to east-southeast off the land, and at day break, to use the words of a French official narrative, the Dutch 'made all sail and stood down boldly into action.'

The allied fleet was to leeward on the port tack, heading about south—the French in the van, Rupert in the centre, and Sir Edward Spragge commanding the rear. De Ruyter divided his fleet into three squadrons, the leading one of which, of ten or twelve ships only, he sent against the French; while with the rest of his force he attacked the English in the centre and rear (see Map page 98). If we accept the English estimate of the forces, which gives the English sixty ships, the French thirty, and the Dutch seventy, Ruyter's plan of attack, by simply holding the French in check as at Solebay, allowed him to engage the English on equal terms. The battle took on several distinct phases, which it is instructive to follow. M de Martel, commanding the van of the French, and consequently the leading subdivision of the allied fleet, was ordered to stretch ahead, go about and gain to windward of the Dutch van, so as to place it between two fires. This he did (1_1); but as soon as Bankert—the same who had manoeuvred so judiciously at Solebay the year before—saw the danger, he put his helm up and ran through the remaining twenty ships of D'Estrées' squadron with his own twelve (A_1, A_2)—a feat as creditable to him as it was discreditable to the French; and then wearing round stood down to De Ruyter, who was hotly engaged with Rupert (B_1). He was not followed by D'Estrées, who suffered him to carry this important reinforcement to the Dutch main attack undisturbed. This practically ended the French share in the fight.

Rupert, during his action with De Ruyter, kept off continually, with the object of drawing the Dutch farther away from their coast, so that if the wind shifted they might not be able to regain its shelter. De Ruyter followed him, and the consequent separation of the centre from the van (B_2, B_3) was one of the reasons alleged by D'Estrées for his delay. It does not, however, seem to have prevented Bankert from joining his chief.

In the rear an extraordinary action on the part of Sir Edward Spragge increased the confusion in the allied fleet. For some reason this officer considered Tromp, who commanded the Dutch rear, as his personal antagonist, and in order to facilitate the latter's getting into action, he hove-to (stopped) the whole English rear to wait for him. This ill-timed point of honor on Spragge's part seems to have sprung from a promise he had made to the king that he would bring back Tromp alive or dead, or else lose his own life. The stoppage, which recalls the irresponsible and insubordinate action of the junior Dutch flag-officers in the former war, of course separated the rear (3_1, 3_2, 3_3), which also drifted rapidly to leeward, Spragge and Tromp

carrying on a hot private action on their own account. These two junior admirals sought each other personally, and the battle between their flags was so severe that Spragge twice had to shift his own to another ship; on the second occasion the boat in which he was embarked was sunk by shot, and he drowned.

Rupert, thus forsaken by his van and rear, found himself alone with Ruyter (B_3); who, reinforced by his van, had the address further to cut off the rear subdivision of the allied centre, and to surround the remaining twenty ships with probably thirty or forty of his own. It is not creditable to the gunnery of the day that more substantial results did not follow; but it is to be remembered that all Ruyter's skill could secure, except for probably a very short time, was an action on equal terms with the English; his total inferiority in numbers could not be quite overcome. The damage to the English and Dutch may therefore have been great, and was probably nearly equal.

Rupert finally disengaged himself, and seeing that the English rear (3_3) was not replying well to its immediate opponents, ran down toward it, Ruyter following him; the two opposing centres steering parallel courses, and within cannon-shot, but by mutual consent, induced perhaps by ammunition running short, refraining from firing. At four p.m. the centres

Above: *When a big ship like the 1st Rate* Royal James *caught fire in battle it caused enormous confusion, for her consorts tended to sheer away to avoid sparks from the burning rigging and balks of timber blown about by the inevitable explosion of her magazine.*

Top: *The Second Battle of Schoneveldt, fought on 14 June 1673 only a week after the First Battle of Schoneveldt. Although De Ruyter showed his usual verve in taking on heavy odds neither battle achieved any important results.*

and rears united, and toward five a fresh engagement began, which continued till seven, when Ruyter withdrew, probably because of the approach of the French, who, by their own accounts, rejoined Rupert about that time. This ended the battle, which, like all that preceded it in this war, may be called a drawn fight, but as to which the verdict of the English naval historian is doubtless correct: 'The consequences which the Dutch, through the prudence of their admiral, drew from this battle were exceedingly great; for they opened their ports, which were entirely blocked up, and put an end to all thoughts, by removing the possibility, of an invasion.'

The military features of the action have sufficiently appeared in the account that has been given—the skill of De Ruyter; the firmness and promptness of Bankert, first in checking and then in passing through the French division; the apparent disloyalty or, at the best, inefficiency of the latter; the insubordination and military blundering of Spragge; the seeming lack of everything but hard fighting on Rupert's part. The allies indulged in bitter mutual recriminations. The French king ordered an inquiry by the intendant of the navy at Brest, who made a report upon which the account here given has mainly rested, and which leaves little doubt of the dishonor of the French arms in this battle. The intendant at Brest ends an official report: 'It would appear in all these sea-fights Ruyter has never cared to attack the French squadron, and that in this last action he had detached ten

ships of the Zealand squadron to keep it in play.' No stronger testimony is needed to Ruyter's opinion of the inefficiency or faithlessness of that contingent to the allied forces.

Another chapter in the history of maritime coalitions was closed, on the 21st of August, 1673, by the battle of the Texel. In it, as in others, were amply justified the words with which a modern French naval officer has stamped them: 'United by momentary political interests, but at bottom divided to the verge of hatred, never following the same path in counsel or in action, they have never produced good results, or at least results proportioned to the efforts of the powers allied against a common enemy. The navies of France, Spain, and Holland seem, at several distinct times, to have joined only to make more complete the triumph of the British arms.' When to this well-ascertained tendency of coalitions is added the equally well known jealousy of every country over the increasing power of a neighbor, and the consequent unwillingness to see such increase obtained by crushing another member of the family of nations, an approach is made to the measure of naval strength required by a State. It is not necessary to be able to meet all others combined, as some Englishmen have seemed to think; it is necessary only to be able to meet the strongest on favorable terms, sure that the others will not join in destroying a factor in the political equilibrium, even if they hold aloof. England and Spain were allies in Toulon in 1793, when the excesses of

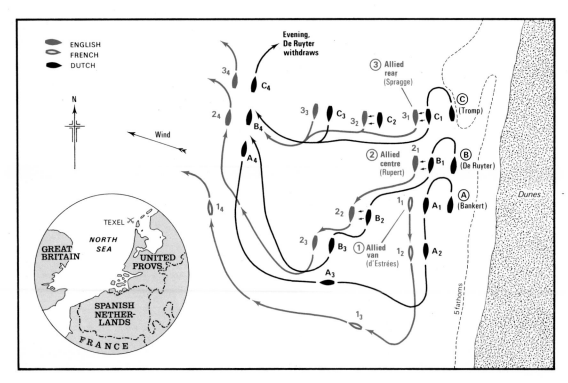

Left: *The Battle of the Texel, 21 August 1673.*

Revolutionary France seemed to threaten the social order of Europe; but the Spanish admiral told the English flatly that the ruin of the French navy, a large part of which was there in their hands, could not fail to be injurious to the interests of Spain, and a part of the French ships was saved by his conduct, which has been justly characterized as not only full of firmness, but also as dictated by the highest political reason.

The battle of the Texel, closing the long series of wars in which the Dutch and English contended on equal terms for the mastery of the seas, saw the Dutch navy in its highest efficiency, and its greatest ornament, De Ruyter, at the summit of his glory. Long since old in years, for he was now sixty-six, he had lost none of his martial vigor; his attack was as furious as eight years before, and his judgment apparently had ripened rapidly through the experience of the last war, for there is far more evidence of plan and military insight than before. To him, under the government of the great Pensionary De Witt, with whom he was in close sympathy, the increase of discipline and sound military tone now apparent in the Dutch navy must have been largely due. He went to this final strife of the two great sea-peoples in the fulness of his own genius, with an admirably tempered instrument in his hands, and with the glorious disadvantage of numbers, to save his country. The mission was fulfilled not by courage alone, but by courage, forethought, and skill. The attack at the Texel was, in its general lines, the same as that at Trafalgar, the enemy's van being neglected to fall on the centre and rear, and as at Trafalgar the van, by failing to do its duty, more than justified the conception; but as the odds against De Ruyter were greater than those against Nelson, so was his success less.

Above left: *The first phase of the Battle of the Texel, fought on 21 August 1673. The Anglo-French fleet is in the foreground with D'Estrées leading the French in the van, Prince Rupert in the center and Sir Edward Spragge at the rear.*

Above right: *The third phase of the Battle of the Texel. Prince Rupert was left alone by Spragge and D'Estrées to face De Ruyter at odds of two-to-one. Only lack of ammunition and the return of the French squadron saved the Prince from a more severe mauling.*

Right: *The stern of Cornelis Tromp's flag-ship* Gouden Leeuw, *which engaged the English* Royal Prince *at the Texel. This detail is taken from Willem Van de Velde the Younger's painting of the battle.*

Nine days after the battle of the Texel, on the 30th of August, 1673, a formal alliance was made between Holland on the one hand, and Spain, Lorraine, and the emperor of Germany on the other, and the French ambassador was dismissed from Vienna. Louis almost immediately offered Holland comparatively moderate terms; but the United Provinces, with their new allies by their sides and with their backs borne firmly upon the sea which had favored and supported them, set their face steadily against him. In England the clamor of the people and Parliament became louder; the Protestant feeling and the old enmity to France were daily growing, as was the national distrust of the king. Charles, though he had himself lost none of his hatred of the republic, had to give way. Louis, seeing the gathering storm, made up his mind, by the counsel of Turenne, to withdraw from his dangerously advanced position by evacuating Holland, and to try to make peace with the Provinces separately while continuing the war with the House of Austria in Spain and Germany. Thus he returned to Richelieu's policy, and Holland was saved. February 19, 1674, peace was signed between England and the Provinces. The latter recognized the absolute supremacy of the English flag from Cape Finisterre in Spain to Norway, and paid a war indemnity.

The withdrawal of England, which remained neutral during the remaining four years of the war, necessarily made it less maritime. The King of France did not think his navy either in numbers or efficiency, able to contend alone with that of Holland; he therefore withdrew it from the ocean and confined his sea enterprises to the Mediterranean, with one or two half-privateering expeditions to the West Indies. The war became more and more continental, and drew in more and more the other powers of Europe. Gradually the German States cast their

Above: *The fight of the* Royal Prince, *surrounded by Dutch ships. She has lost her mainmast and mizzen, robbing her of the means to maneuver and allowing her enemies to rake her from end to end.*

Right: *The three-decker* Royal Prince *was built in 1670, but in 1694 she was rebuilt, a euphemism for building what amounted to a new ship, and was renamed* Royal William.

lot with Austria, and on May 28, 1674, the Diet proclaimed war against France. The great work of French policy in the last generations was undone, Austria had resumed her supremacy in Germany, and Holland had not been destroyed.

Another maritime strife arose in the Mediterranean by the revolt of the Sicilians against the Spanish rule. The help they asked from France was granted as a diversion against Spain, but the Sicilian enterprise never became more than a side issue. Its naval interest springs from bringing Ruyter once more on the scene, and that as the antagonist of Duquesne, the equal, and by some thought even the superior, of Tourville, whose name has always stood far above all others in the French navy of that day.

Left: The final stage of the Texel battle as seen through the eyes of the French artist Eugène Isabey. Jean Bart brings his ship into action to rescue the English center squadron.

Below: In a hard-fought action against the French off Agosta in Sicily 22 April 1676 De Ruyter received a mortal wound. He died a week later at Syracuse, a terrible loss to his country.

Messina revolted in July, 1674, and the French king at once took it under his protection. The Spanish navy throughout seems to have behaved badly, certainly inefficiently; and early in 1675 the French were safely established in the city. During the year their naval power in the Mediterranean was much increased, and Spain, unable to defend the island herself, applied to the United Provinces for a fleet, the expenses of which she would bear. The Provinces, 'fatigued by the war, involved in debt, suffering cruelly in their commerce, exhausted by the necessity of paying the emperor and all the German princes, could no longer fit out the enormous fleets which they had once opposed to France and England.' They however hearkened to Spain and sent De Ruyter, with a squadron of only eighteen ships and four fire-ships. The admiral, who had noted the growth of the French navy, said the force was too small, and departed oppressed in spirit, but with the calm resignation which was habitual to him. He reached Cadiz in September, and in the mean time the French had further strengthened themselves by the capture of Agosta, a port commanding the southeast of Sicily. De Ruyter was again delayed by the Spanish government, and did not reach the north coast of the island until the end of December, when head winds kept him from entering the Straits of Messina. He cruised between Messina and the Lipari Islands in a position to intercept the French fleet convoying troops and supplies, which was expected under Duquesne.

On the 7th of January, 1676, the French came in sight, twenty ships-of-the-line and six fire-ships; the Dutch had but nineteen ships, one of which was a Spaniard, and four fire-ships; and it must be remembered that, although there is no detailed account of the Dutch ships in this action, they were as a rule inferior to those of England, and yet more to those of France. The first day was spent in manoeuvring, the Dutch having the weather-gage; but during that night, which was squally and drove the Spanish

galleys accompanying the Dutch to take refuge under Lipari, the wind shifted, and coming out at west-southwest, gave the French the weather-gage and the power to attack. Duquesne resolved to use it, and sending the convoy ahead, formed his line on the starboard tack standing south; the Dutch did the same, and waited for him.

The two fleets being drawn up in line-of-battle on the starboard tack, heading south, as has been said, De Ruyter awaited the attack which he had refused to make. Being between the French and their port, he felt they must fight. At nine a.m. the French line kept away all together and ran down obliquely upon the Dutch, a manoeuvre difficult to be performed with accuracy, and during which the assailant receives his enemy's fire at disadvantage. In doing this, two ships in the French van were seriously disabled. 'M de la Fayette, in the *Prudente*, began the action; but having rashly thrown himself into the midst of the enemy's van, he was dismantled and forced to haul off.' Confusion ensued in the French line, from the difficult character of the manoeuvre. 'Vice-Admiral de Preulli, commanding the van, in keeping away took too little room, so that in coming to the wind again, the ships, in too close order, lapped and interfered with one another's fire. The absence of M de la Fayette from the line threw the *Parfait* into peril. Attacked by two ships, she lost her maintopmast and had also to haul off for repairs.' Again, the French came into action in succession instead of all together, a usual and almost inevitable result of the manoeuvre in question. 'In the *midst* of a terrible cannonade,' that is, after part of his ships were engaged, 'Duquesne, commanding the centre, took post on the beam of Ruyter's division.' The French rear came into action still later, after the centre. 'Langeron and Bethune, commanding leading ships of the French centre, are crushed by superior forces.' How can this be, seeing the French had the more ships? It was because, as the narrative tells us, 'the French had not yet repaired the disorder of the first movement.' However, all at last got into action, and Duquesne gradually restored order. The Dutch, engaged all along the line, resisted everywhere, and there was not one of their ships which was not closely engaged; more cannot be said for the admiral and captains of the inferior fleet. The remaining part of the fight is not very clearly related. Ruyter is said to have given way continually with his two leading divisions; but whether this was a confession of weakness or a tactical move does not appear. The rear was separated, in permitting which either Ruyter or the immediate commander was at fault; but the attempts made by the French to surround and isolate it failed, probably because of damaged

spars, for one French ship did pass entirely around the separated division. The action ended at 4.30 p.m., except in the rear, and the Spanish galleys shortly after came up and towed the disabled Dutch ships away. Their escape shows how injured the French must have been.

Those who are familiar with Clerk's work on naval tactics, published about 1780, will recognize in this account of the battle of Stromboli all the features to which he called the attention of English seamen in his thesis on the methods of action employed by them and their adversaries in and before his time. Clerk's thesis started from the postulate that English seamen and officers were superior in skill or spirit, or both, to the French, and their ships on the whole as fast; that they were conscious of this superiority and therefore eager to attack, while the French, equally conscious of inferiority, or for other reasons, were averse to decisive engagements. With these dispositions the latter, feeling they could rely on a blindly furious attack by the English, had evolved a crafty plan by which, while seeming to fight, they really avoided doing so, and at the same time did the enemy much harm. This plan was to take the lee-gage; the characteristic of which, as has before been pointed out, is that it is a defensive position, and to await attack. The English error, according to Clerk, upon which the French had learned by experience that they could always count, was in drawing up their line parallel to the enemy, or nearly so, and then keeping away all together to attack, ship for ship, each its opposite in the hostile line. By standing down in this manner the assailant lost the use of most of his artillery, while exposed to the full fire of his opponent, and invariably came up in confusion, because the order of attack was one difficult to maintain at any time, and much more so in the smoke under fire, with torn sails and falling masts. This was precisely the attack made by Duquesne at Stromboli, and it there had precisely the consequences Clerk points out—confusion in the line, the van arriving first and getting the brunt of the fire of the defence, disabled ships in the van causing confusion in the rear, etc. Clerk further asserts, and he seems to be right, that as the action grew warm, the French, by running off to leeward, in their turn, led the English to repeat the same mode of attack; and so we find, at Stromboli, Ruyter giving ground in the same way, though his motive does not appear. Clerk also points out that a necessary corollary of the lee-gage, assumed for tactical reasons, is to aim at the assailant's spars, his motive power, so that his attack cannot be pushed farther than the defendant chooses. While therefore there cannot with certainty be attributed to Ruyter the deliberate choice of the lee-gage, for which there was as yet no precedent, it is evident that he reaped all its benefits, and that the character of the French officers of his day, inexperienced as seamen and of impetuous valor, offered just the conditions that gave most advantage to an inferior force standing on the defensive.

After the fight De Ruyter sailed to Palermo, one of his ships sinking on the way. Duquesne was joined outside Messina by the French division that had been lying there. The remaining incidents of the Sicilian war are unimportant to the general subject. On the 22nd of April, De Ruyter and Duquesne met again off Agosta. Duquesne had twenty-nine ships, the allied Spaniards and Dutch twenty-seven, of which ten were Spanish. Unfortunately the Spaniard commanded in chief, and took the centre of the line with the ships of his country, contrary to the advice of Ruyter, who, knowing how inefficient his allies were, wished to scatter them through the line and so support them better. Ruyter himself took the van, and the allies, having the wind, attacked; but the Spanish centre kept at long cannon range, leaving the brunt of the battle to fall on the Dutch van. The rear, following the commander-in-chief's motions, was

Left: *Abraham Duquesne was appointed Lieutenant General of the French fleet. Thought by many of his contemporaries to be the equal of Tourville, he was an energetic flag-officer who proved capable of taking advantage of De Ruyter's weakness in the war with Spain.*

also but slightly engaged. In this sorrowful yet still glorious fulfilment of hopeless duty, De Ruyter, who never before in his long career had been struck by an enemy's shot, received a mortal wound. He died a week later at Syracuse, and with him passed away the last hope of resistance on the sea. A month later the Spanish and Dutch fleets were attacked at anchor at Palermo, and many of them destroyed; while a division sent from Holland to reinforce the Mediterranean fleet was met by a French squadron in the Straits of Gibraltar and forced to take refuge in Cadiz.

The Sicilian enterprise continued to be only a diversion, and the slight importance attached to it shows clearly how entirely Louis XIV was bent on the continental war. As the years passed, the temper of the English people became more and more excited against France; the trade rivalries with Holland seemed to fall into the shade, and it became likely that England, which had entered the war as the ally of Louis, would, before it closed, take up arms against him. In addition to other causes of jealousy she saw the French navy increased to a number superior to her own. Charles for a while resisted the pressure of Parliament, but in January, 1678, a treaty of alliance, offensive and defensive, was made between the two sea countries; the king recalled the English troops which until now had been serving as part of the French army, and when Parliament opened again in February, asked for money to equip ninety ships and thirty thousand soldiers. Louis, who was expecting this result, at once ordered the evacuation of Sicily. He did not fear England by land, but on the sea he could not yet hold his own against the union of the two sea powers. At the same time he redoubled his attacks on the Spanish Netherlands.

The United Provinces were in truth the mainspring of the coalition. Though among the smallest in extent of the countries arrayed against Louis, they were strongest in the character and purpose of their ruler, the Prince of Orange, and in the wealth which, while supporting the armies of the confederates, also kept the poor and greedy German princes faithful to their alliance. Almost alone, by dint of mighty sea power, by commercial and maritime ability, they bore the burden of the war; and though they staggered and complained, they still bore it. Her commerce, preyed upon by French privateers, lost heavily; and there was added an immense indirect loss in the transfer of the carrying-trade between foreign countries, which had contributed to much to the prosperity of the Dutch.

The exhaustion of the United Provinces and the clamor of their merchants and peace party on the one hand, aided on the other by the sufferings of France, the embarrassment of her finances, and the threatened addition of England's navy to her already numerous enemies, inclined to peace the two principal parties to this long war. Difficulties were gradually smoothed away, and the Peace of Nijmegen between the United Provinces and France was signed August 11, 1678. The other powers shortly afterward acceded to it. The principal sufferer, as was natural, was the overgrown but feeble monarchy whose centre was Spain, which gave up to France Franche Comté and a number of fortified towns in the Spanish Netherlands, thus extending the boundaries of France to the east and northeast. Holland, for whose destruction Louis began the war, lost not a foot of ground in Europe; and beyond the seas only her colonies on the west coast of Africa and in Guyana. She owed her safety at first, and the final successful issue, to her sea power. That delivered her in the hour of extreme danger, and enabled her afterward to keep alive the general war. It may be said to have been one of the chief factors, and inferior to no other one singly, in determining the event of the great war which was formally closed at Nijmegen.

Above: *The funeral procession of De Ruyter at Syracuse.*

The effort none the less sapped her strength, and being followed by many years of similar strain broke her down. But what was the effect upon the vastly greater state, the extreme ambition of whose king was the principal cause of the exhausting wars of this time? Among the many activities which illustrated the brilliant opening of the reign of the then youthful king of France, none was so important, none so intelligently directed, as those of Colbert, who aimed first at restoring the finances from the confusion into which they had fallen, and then at establishing them upon a firm foundation of national wealth. For nearly twelve years all went well; the development of the greatness of France in all these directions went forward rapidly, if not in all with equal strides, and the king's revenues increased by bounds. Then came the hour in which he had to decide whether the exertions which his ambition naturally, perhaps properly, prompted should take the direction which, while imposing great efforts, did nothing to sustain but rather hindered the natural activities of his people, and broke down commerce by making control of the sea uncertain; or whether he should launch out in pursuits which, while involving expense, would keep peace on his borders, lead to the control of the sea, and by the impulse given to trade, and all upon which trade depends, would bring in money nearly if not quite equal to that which the State spent. This is not a fanciful picture; by his attitude toward Holland, and its consequences, Louis gave the first impulse to England upon the path which realized to her, within his own day, the results which Colbert and Leibnitz had hoped for France. Not all at once, but very rapidly, England pressed into the front place as a sea power; and however great her sufferings and the sufferings of individual Englishmen, it remained true of her that even in war her prosperity was great. Doubtless France could not forget her continental position, nor wholly keep free from continental wars; but it may be believed that if she had chosen the path of sea power, she might both have escaped many conflicts and borne those that were unavoidable with greater ease.

Below: *The ill-judged decision by the United Provinces to hire out their fleet to Spain for the defense of Sicily cost Holland dear. But in spite of losing her greatest admiral and much of her seaborne commerce, her sea power enabled her to defy the French attempt to destroy her. Eventually Louis XIV was forced to negotiate an unsatisfactory peace, whereas Holland lost only two small overseas colonies.*

Chapter 4

The Spanish Succession

VREEDE HANDEL
tusschen Engelandt en ons.

Above: *The accession of James II to the English throne triggered off more trouble for the continent of Europe. Not even his distinguished record as a fighting seaman, while still Duke of York, could save him from the consequences of his Catholic sympathies.*

The Peace of Nijmegen was followed by a period of ten years in which no extensive war broke out. They were, however, far from being years of political quiet. Louis XIV was as intent upon pushing on his frontiers to the eastward in peace as in war, and grasped in quick succession fragments of territory which had not been given him by the peace. The aggression most startling to Europe, and above all to the German Empire, was the seizure of the then imperial city of Strasburg on the 30th of September, 1681; and on the same day Casale, in Italy, was sold to him by the Duke of Mantua, showing that his ambitions were directed that way as well as to the north and east. Both of these were positions of great strategic importance, threatening, the one Germany, the other Italy, in case of war.

In the year that James II became king, 1685, a vast diplomatic combination against France began. July 9, 1686, there was signed at Augsburg a secret agreement between the emperor, the kings of Spain and Sweden, and a number of German princes. This compact took the name of the League of Augsburg, and from it the general war which followed two years later was called the War of the League of Augsburg.

The next year, 1687, the discontent of the English and the ambitions of the Prince of Orange, who hoped from his accession to the throne of England no ordinary personal aggrandizement, but the fulfilment of his strongest political wish and conviction, in curbing forever the power of Louis XIV, became more and more plain. But for his expedition into England, William needed ships, money, and men from the United Provinces; and they hung back, knowing that the result would be war with the French king, who proclaimed James his ally. Their action was at last decided by the course of Louis, who chose this moment to revoke concessions made at Nijmegen to Dutch trade. The serious injury thus done to Holland's material interests turned the wavering scale. This was in November, 1687. In the summer of the following year the birth of an heir to the English throne brought things to an issue. English loyalty might have put up with the reign of the father, now advanced in years, but could not endure the prospect of a continued Roman Catholic royalty.

Matters had at last reached the crisis to which they had been tending for years. Louis and William of Orange, longstanding enemies, and at the moment the two chief figures in European politics, alike from their own strong personalities and the cause which either represented, stood on the brink of great actions, whose effects were to be felt through many generations. Louis, holding all the power of France in his single grasp, facing eastward as before, saw the continent gathering against him; while on his flank was England heartily hostile, longing to enter on the strife against him, but as yet without a leader. If he attacked Holland by land, and sent his superior navy into the Channel, he might well keep William in his own country; the more so as the English navy, beloved and petted by the king, was likely to have more than the usual loyalty of seamen to their chief. Faithful to the bias of his life, perhaps unable to free himself from it, he turned toward the continent, and September 24, 1688, declared war against Germany and moved his armies toward the Rhine. William, overjoyed, saw removed the last obstacle to his ambition. He set sail from Holland on the 30th of October. The first start was foiled by a violent storm; but sailing again on the 10th of November, a fresh, fair breeze carried the ships through the Straits and the Channel, and William landed on the 15th at Torbay. Before the end of the year, James had fled from his kingdom. On the 21st of the following April, William and Mary were proclaimed sovereigns of Great Britain, and England and Holland were united for the war, which Louis had declared against the United Provinces as soon as he heard of William's invasion.

France thus entered the War of the League of Augsburg without a single ally. 'What her policy had most feared, what she had long averted, was come to pass. England and Holland were not only allied, but united under the same chief; and England entered the coalition with all the eagerness of passions long restrained by the Stuart policy.' As regards the sea war, the different battles have much less tactical value than those of De Ruyter. The chief points of strategic interest are the failure of

Louis, having a decided superiority at sea, properly to support James II in Ireland, which remained faithful to him, and the gradual disappearance from the ocean of the great French fleets, which Louis XIV could no longer maintain, owing to the expense of that continental policy which he had chosen for himself. A third point of rather minor interest is the peculiar character and large proportions taken on by the commerce-destroying and privateering warfare of the French, as their large fleets were disappearing. James, having fled from England in January, 1689, landed in Ireland in the following March, accompanied by French troops and a French squadron, and was enthusiastically welcomed everywhere but in the Protestant North. He made Dublin his capital, and remained in the country until July of the next year. During these fifteen months the

Above: *As Duke of York, James II had fought bravely against the Dutch and for a time commanded the loyalty of the Fleet. But his obstinacy led him to coerce his subjects on religious matters, and the desertion of the Fleet was a major factor in the Glorious Revolution of 1688. Without a loyal navy there was no way to prevent William of Orange from landing in England.*

French were much superior at sea; they landed troops in Ireland on more than one occasion; and the English, attempting to prevent this, were defeated in the naval battle of Bantry Bay. Although the French were superior to the united English and Dutch on the seas in 1689 and 1690; nevertheless, the English admiral Rooke was able, unmolested, to throw succors and troops into Londonderry, and afterward landed Marshal Schomberg, with a small army, near Carrickfergus. Rooke

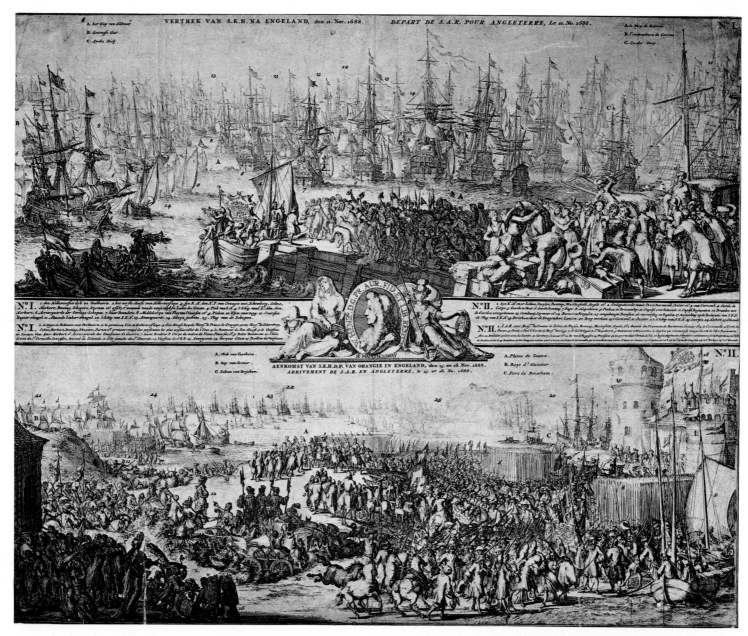

stopped intercourse between Ireland and Scotland, where were many Stuart partisans, and then with his small squadron passed along the east coast of Ireland, attempted to burn the shipping in Dublin harbor, failing only through lack of wind, and finally came off Cork, then occupied by James, took possession of an island in the harbor, and returned in safety to the Downs in October. There can be little doubt that an effective co-operation of the French fleet in the summer of 1689 would have broken down all opposition to James in Ireland, by isolating that country from England, with corresponding injury to William's power.

It is the nature of a merely military navy like that of France to be strongest at the beginning of hostilities; whereas that of the allied sea powers grew daily stronger, drawing upon the vast resources of their merchant shipping and their wealth. The disparity of force was still in favor of France in 1690, but it was not as great as the year before. The all-important question was where to direct it. There were two principal courses, involving two views of naval strategy. The one was to act against the allied fleet, whose defeat, if sufficiently severe, might involve the fall of William's throne in England; the other was to make the fleet subsidiary to the Irish campaign. The French king decided upon the former, which was undoubtedly the proper course; but there was no reason for neglecting, as he did, the important duty of cutting off the communications between the two islands. The English were gathering an army on their west coast,

Left: *The departure of William of Orange from the Netherlands (above) and his arrival in England (below). Although never loved, 'Dutch William' provided strong rule and crushed the Stuart supporters in Scotland and Ireland.*

Left below: *Although a confirmed landsman William of Orange knew how to make use of the Royal Navy. Command of the sea allowed him to cross to Ireland to defeat the Jacobites at the Battle of the Boyne, and thus secured his rear against attack.*

Below: *A somewhat exalted view of the Royal Navy escorting William of Orange across from Holland. Nevertheless the print pays due credit to the reason for William's bloodless accession, for without the connivance of the Navy it could not have taken place.*

and on the 21st of June, William embarked his forces at Chester on board two hundred and eighty-eight transports, escorted by only six men-of-war. On the 24th he landed in Carrickfergus. There is nothing more striking than the carelessness shown by both the contending parties, during the time that Ireland was in dispute, as to the communications of their opponents with the island; but this was especially strange in the French, as they had the larger forces, and must have received pretty accurate information of what was going on from disaffected persons in England.

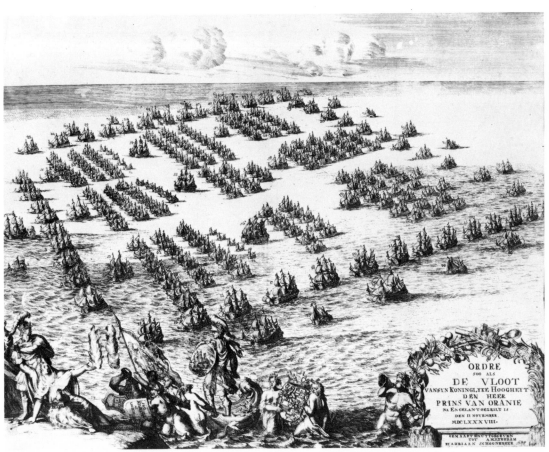

Above: *William's English wife, Queen Mary II, as seen by Kneller The device of joint rule was resorted to in order to preserve the Protestant Succession, but the Queen's inability to produce an heir led ultimately to the Hanoverian dynasty.*

Below: *The landing of William of Orange at Torbay in 1688.*

Tourville's fleet, complete in numbers, having seventy-eight ships, of which seventy were in the line-of-battle, with twenty-two fire-ships, got to sea June 22, the day after William embarked. On the 30th the French were off the Lizard, to the dismay of the English admiral, who was lying off the Isle of Wight in such an unprepared attitude that he had not even lookout ships to the westward. He got under way, standing offshore to the southeast, and was joined from time to time, during the next ten days, by other English and Dutch ships. The two fleets continued moving to the eastward, sighting each other from time to time.

The fight that followed on the 10th of July is known as the battle of Beachy Head. The ships engaged were, French seventy, English and Dutch according to their own account fifty-six, according to the French sixty. In the allied line of battle the Dutch were in the van; the English, commanded in person by Herbert, in the centre; and the rear was made up partly of English and partly of Dutch ships. The stages of the battle were as follows:

1 The allies, being to windward, bore down together in line abreast. As usual, this manoeuvre was ill performed, and as also generally happens, the van came under fire before the centre and rear, and bore the brunt of the injury.

2 Admiral Herbert, though commander-in-chief, failed to attack vigorously with the centre, keeping it at long range. The allied van and rear came to close action. Paul Hoste's account of this manoeuvre of the allies is that the admiral intended to fall mainly on the French rear. To that end he closed the centre to the rear and kept it to windward at long cannonshot (refused it), so as to prevent the French from tacking and doubling on the rear. If that were his purpose, his plan, though tolerably conceived in the main, was faulty in detail, for this

Right: *Contemporary diagram of the Battle of Beachy Head, fought on 30 June 1690 between Torrington and Tourville. The French lost a great opportunity to defeat the English and the Dutch, who did not concert their plans.*

Left: *The forces of William III landing at Carrickfergus on 24 June 1688. He was able to take his forces across the Irish Sea in 288 transports escorted by only half a dozen warships, in spite of Tourville's large fleet.*

A Prospect of the late Engagement at Sea between the English and the French Fleets on Monday the thirtieth of June 1690. the wind from NNE to the ENE with an exact List of ye English Dutch & French Ships Engraven by the Earle of Torringtons order & approbation

A List of the FRENCH Fleet										
	The Splendor	The Belliquer	The Henry	The Shining	The Proud	The George	The Flyer	The Vigilant	The Capable	The Positive
	The Conquerer	The Crown	The Serious	The Unstable	The Fierce	The Apollon	The S. Lewis	The Wife	The Tristy	The Passion
The Royal Sun	The Holy Ghost	Lionspride	The Harry born	The Grorme	The Marquee	The Dymond	The Prudent	The Hector	The L'Isle	The Count
The Royal Delphin	S. Philip	The Harry born	The Courtier	The Lovely	The Strong	The S. Michall	The Good	The Duke	The Neptune	The Light
The Great	The Thunder	The Splendor	The Bourbon	The Perfect	The Undertaker	The Faire hearted	The Moon	The Mulgrave	The Random	Lisbon
The Sovereign	The Haughty	The Brightest	The Eager	The Amiable	The Brave	The Precious	The Trident	The Indian	The Indian	The Pretty
	The Terrible	The Flower	The Firme	The Excellent	The Ambitious	The Aquillon	The Valiant	The Sea Horse	The Bizarre	The Patrice
	The Conquerer	The Pomp	The Toquer	The Prince	The Unparalell'd	The Fortune	The Bold	The Francis	The Solide	The Hardy

manoeuvre of the centre left a great gap between it and the van. He should rather have attacked, as Ruyter did at the Texel, as many of the rear ships as he thought he could deal with, and refused his van, assigning to it the part of checking the French van. The allied fleet was thus exposed to be doubled on at two points, both van and centre; and both points were attacked.

3 The commander of the French van, seeing the Dutch close to his line and more disabled than himself, pressed six of his leading ships ahead, where they went about, and so put the Dutch between two fires.

At the same time Tourville, finding himself without adversaries in the centre, having beaten off the leading division of the enemy's centre, pushed forward his own leading ships, which Herbert's dispositions had left without opponents; and these fresh ships strengthened the attack upon the Dutch in the van.

This brought about a *mêlée* at the head of the lines, in which the Dutch, being inferior, suffered heavily. Luckily for the allies the wind fell calm; and while Tourville himself and other French ships got out their boats to tow into action again, the allies were shrewd enough to drop anchor with all sail set, and before Tourville took in the situation the ebb-tide, setting southwest, had carried his fleet out of action. He finally anchored a league from his enemy.

At nine p.m., when the tide changed, the allies weighed and stood to the eastward. So badly had many of them been mauled, that, by English accounts, it was decided rather to destroy the disabled ships than to risk a general engagement to preserve them.

Tourville pursued; but instead of ordering a general chase, he kept the line-of-battle, reducing the speed of the fleet to that of the slower ships. The occasion was precisely one of those in which a *mêlée* is permissible, indeed, obligatory. The failure to order such general pursuit indicates the side on which Tourville's military character lacked completeness; and the failure showed itself, as is apt to be the case, at the supreme moment of his career. He never had such another opportunity as in this, the first great general action in which he commanded in chief, and which Hoste, who was on board the flag-ship, calls the most complete naval victory ever gained. It was so indeed at that time —the most complete, but not the most decisive, as it perhaps might have been.

Tourville's is the only great historical name among the seamen of this war, if we except the renowned privateersmen at whose head was Jean Bart. Tourville, who by this time had served afloat for nearly thirty years, was at once a seaman and a military man. He commanded in person all the largest fleets sent out during the earlier years of this war, and he brought to the command a scientific knowledge of tactics, based upon both theory and experience, joined to that practical acquaintance with the seaman's business which is necessary in order to apply tactical principles upon the ocean to the best advantage. But with all these high qualities he seems to have failed, where so many warriors fail, in the ability to assume a great responsibility. He was brave enough to do anything, but not strong enough to bear the heaviest burdens. Tourville was in fact the forerunner of the careful and skilful tacticians of the coming era, but with the savor still of the impetuous hard-fighting which characterized the sea commanders of the seventeenth century.

The day after the sea fight off Beachy Head, with its great but still partial results, the cause of James II was lost ashore in Ireland. James undertook to cover Dublin, taking up the line of the river Boyne, and there on the 11th of July the two armies met, with the result that James was wholly defeated. The result of the Irish campaign was to settle William safely on the English throne and establish the Anglo-Dutch alliance; and the union of the two sea peoples under one crown was the pledge, through their commercial and maritime ability, and the wealth they drew from the sea, of the successful prosecution of the war by their allies on the continent.

In 1692 there occurred the great disaster to the French fleet which is known as the battle of La Hougue. In itself, considered tactically, it possesses little importance, and the actual results have been much exaggerated; but popular report has made it one of the famous sea battles of the world, and therefore it cannot be wholly passed by.

Misled by reports from England, and still more by the representations of James, who fondly nursed his belief that the attachment of many English naval officers to his person was greater than their love of country or faithfulness to their trust, Louis XIV determined to attempt an invasion of the south coast of England, led by James in person. As a first step thereto, Tourville, at the head of between fifty and sixty ships-of-the-line, thirteen of which were to come from Toulon, was to engage the English fleet; from which so many desertions were expected as would, with the consequent demoralization, yield the French an easy and total victory. The first hitch was in the failure of the Toulon fleet, delayed by contrary winds, to join; and Tourville went to sea with only forty-four ships, but with a peremptory order from the king to fight when he fell in with the enemy, were they few or many, and come what might.

On the 29th of May, Tourville saw the allies to the northward and eastward; they numbered ninety-nine sail-of-the-line. The wind being southwest, he had the choice of engaging, but first summoned all the flag-officers on board his own ship, and put the question to them whether he ought to fight. They all said not, and he then handed them the order of the king. No one dared dispute that; though, had they known it, light vessels with contrary orders were even then searching for the fleet. The other officers then returned to their ships, and the whole fleet kept away together for the allies, who waited for them, on the starboard tack, heading south-southeast, the Dutch occupying the van, the English the centre and rear. When they were within easy range, the French hauled their wind on the same tack, keeping the weather-gage. Tourville, being so inferior in numbers, could not wholly avoid the enemy's line extending to the rear of his own, which was also necessarily weak from its extreme length; but he avoided Herbert's error at Beachy Head, keeping his van refused with long intervals between the ships, to check the enemy's van, and engaging closely with his centre and rear. It is not necessary to follow the phases of this unequal fight; the extraordinary result was that when the firing ceased at night, in consequence of a thick fog and calm, not a single French ship had struck her colors nor been sunk. No higher proof of military spirit and efficiency

Left: The Comte de Tourville, Vice-Admiral and Marshal of France. He brought a scientific approach to tactics, and was undoubtedly the finest French admiral bred in the age of sail.

Below: Obverse of the same medal, showing the Allied fleets put to flight by the sea god Neptune, upholding the dominion of the sea. It was to be a short-lived dominion.

Left below: Reverse of a medal commemorating the Battle of Bévéziers, showing the head of Louis XIV, Invictissimus Ludovicus Magnus.

could be given by any navy, and Tourville's seamanship and tactical ability contributed largely to the result, which it must also be confessed was not creditable to the allies.

Having amply vindicated the honor of his fleet, and shown the uselessness of further fighting, Tourville now thought of retreat, which was begun at midnight with a light northeast wind and continued all the next day. The allies pursued, the movements of the French being much embarrassed by the crippled condition of the flag-ship *Royal Sun*, the finest ship in the French navy, which the admiral could not make up his mind to destroy. The direction of the main retreat was toward the Channel Islands, thirty-five ships being with the admiral; of them twenty passed with the tidal current through the dangerous passage known as the Race of Alderney, between the island of that name and the mainland, and got safe to St Malo. Before the remaining fifteen could follow, the tide changed; and the anchors which had been dropped dragging, these ships were carried to the eastward and to leeward of the enemy. Three sought refuge in Cherbourg, which had then neither breakwater nor port, the remaining twelve at Cape La Hougue; and they were all burned either by their own crews or by the allies. The French thus lost fifteen of the finest ships in their navy, the least of which carried sixty guns; but this was little more than the loss of the allies at Beachy Head. La Hougue was also the last general action fought by the French fleet, which did rapidly dwindle away in the following years, so that this disaster seemed to be its death-blow. As a matter of fact, however,

Left: The stern of the Soleil Royal, 104 guns, Tourville's flag-ship at the Battle of Bévéziers (Beachy Head). This brand new 1st Rate, the pride of the French Navy, was badly mauled during the first part of the battle.

Tourville went to sea the next year with seventy ships, and the losses were at the time repaired. The decay of the French navy was not due to any one defeat, but to the exhaustion of France and the great cost of the continental war; and this war was mainly sustained by the two sea peoples whose union was secured by the success of William in the Irish campaign. Without asserting that the result would have been different had the naval operations of France been otherwise directed in 1690, it may safely be said that their misdirection was the immediate cause of things turning out as they did, and the first cause of the decay of the French navy.

The five remaining years of the War of the League of Augsburg, in which all Europe was in arms against France, are marked by no great sea battles, nor any single maritime event of the first importance. To appreciate the effect of the sea power of the allies, it is necessary to sum up and condense an account of the quiet, steady pressure which it brought to bear and maintained in all quarters against France.

The head of the opposition to Louis XIV was William III, and his tastes being military rather than naval combined with the direction of Louis' policy to make the action war continental rather than maritime; while the gradual withdrawal of the great French fleets, by leaving the allied navies without enemies on the sea, worked in the same way. Furthermore, the efficiency of the English navy, which was double in numbers that of the Dutch, was at this time at a low pitch; the demoralizing effects of the reign of Charles II could not be wholly overcome during the three years of his brother's rule.

After La Hougue, the direct military action of the allied navies was exerted in three principal ways, the first being in attacks upon the French ports, especially those in the Channel and near Brest. It may be said generally of all these enterprises

Above: *The Battle of La Hougue, more correctly known as Barfleur, more than wiped out the memory of Beachy Head. 17 May 1692 Russell met Tourville and drove his fleet into La Hougue, and then a daring boat attack two days later burnt a large part of the French Fleet. In all 15 sail of the line were destroyed, including the badly battered Soleil Royal, in addition to scores of lesser ships and transports.*

Right: *The French ships burning after Admiral Russell's pulling boats had followed them through the shoals of La Hougue. It is said that the exiled James II could not resist the temptation to say to his French hosts and backers, 'Who but brave English tars could do such a thing?'—in the circumstances a tactless observation typical of the Stuarts.*

against the French coast, in this and later wars, that they effected little, and even as a diversion did not weaken the French armies to any great extent.

In the second place, the allied navies were of great direct military value, though they fought no battles, when Louis XIV decided in 1694 to make his war against Spain offensive. Spain, though so weak in herself, was yet troublesome from her position in the rear of France; and Louis finally concluded to force her to peace by carrying the war into Catalonia, on the northeast coast. The movement of his armies was seconded by his fleet under Tourville; and the reduction of that difficult province went on rapidly until the approach of the allied navies

in largely superior force caused Tourville to retire to Toulon. This saved Barcelona; and from that time until the two sea nations had determined to make peace, they kept their fleets on the Spanish coast and arrested the French advance. When, in 1697, William had become disposed to peace and Spain refused it, Louis again invaded, the allied fleet did not appear, and Barcelona fell. At the same time a French naval expedition was successfully directed against Cartagena in South America, and under the two blows, both of which depended upon the control of the sea, Spain yielded.

The third military function of the allied navies was the protection of their sea commerce; and herein, if history may be trusted, they greatly failed. At no time has war against commerce been conducted on a larger scale and with greater results than during this period; and its operations were widest and most devastating at the very time that the great French fleets were disappearing, in the years immediately after La Hougue, apparently contradicting the assertion that such a warfare must be based on powerful fleets or neighboring seaports.

The decay of the French fleet was gradual, and the moral effect of its appearance in the Channel, its victory at Beachy Head, and gallant conduct at La Hougue remained for some time impressed on the minds of the allies. This impression caused their ships to be kept together in fleets, instead of scattering in pursuit of the enemy's cruisers, and so brought to the latter a support almost equal to an active warfare on the seas. Again, the efficiency of the English navy, as has been said, was low, and its administration perhaps worse; while treason in England gave the French the advantage of better information. It was immediately after La Hougue that the depredations of cruisers became most ruinous; and the reason was twofold: first, the allied fleet was kept together at Spithead for two months and more, gathering troops for a landing on the continent, thus leaving the cruisers unmolested; and in the second place, the French, not being able to send their fleet out again that summer,

Above: *Jean Bart rose from the humble rank of skipper of a Dunkerque coaster to chef d'escadre and was ennobled. Although he never commanded a major fleet he was an outstanding commander of light forces as well as a successful privateer.*

Above: *René Duguay-Trouin was the son of a family of Malouin merchant shippers who took to privateering with great dash. Only after a successful career of commerce-raiding was he given a royal commission as a naval officer.*

permitted the seamen to take service in private ships, thus largely increasing the numbers of the latter. The two causes working together gave an impunity and extension to commerce-destroying. As the pressure of the war became greater, and Louis continued to reduce the number of his ships in commission, another increase was given to the commerce-destroyers. 'The ships and officers of the royal navy were loaned, under certain conditions, to private firms, or to companies who wished to undertake privateering enterprises.' The commerce-destroying of this war was no mere business of single cruisers; squadrons of three or four up to half a dozen ships acted together under one man, and it is only just to say that under seamen like Jean Bart, Forbin, and Duguay-Trouin, they were even more ready to fight than to pillage. The largest of these private expeditions, and the only one that went far from the French shores, was directed in 1697 against Cartagena, on the Spanish Main. It numbered seven ships-of-the-line and six frigates, besides smaller vessels, and carried twenty-eight hundred troops. The chief object was to lay a contribution on the city of Cartagena; but its effect on the policy in Spain was marked, and led to peace. Although the allies continued to keep their large fleets together, still, as the war went on and efficiency of administration improved, commerce-destroying was brought within bounds.

Above: *The Battle of Barfleur eliminated the possibility of a French invasion of England and effectively ended any chance of a Stuart restoration. France was able to replace the lost ships but for the remaining five years of the war she turned to guerre de course rather than try another fleet engagement, and gradually lost the will to strive for true sea power.*

Above: *John Benbow won a royal commission from James II after gallantly defending his merchantman against an attack by pirates. He was Master of the Fleet at Beachy Head and Barfleur, and died of wounds in the West Indies in 1702, having been deserted by his captains during a battle. The French Admiral Du Casse wrote to express his disgust at their cowardice, and three were subsequently executed.*

At the same time, as an evidence of how much the unsupported cruisers suffered, even under these favorable conditions, it may be mentioned that the English report fifty-nine ships-of-war captured against eighteen admitted by the French during the war—a difference which a French naval historian attributes, with much probability, to the English failing to distinguish between ships-of-war properly so called, and those loaned to private firms. Captures of actual privateers do not appear in the list quoted from. The results of the war of 1689–1697 do not vitiate the general conclusion that 'a cruising, commerce-destroying warfare, to be destructive, must be seconded by a squadron warfare, and by divisions of ships-of-the-line; which,

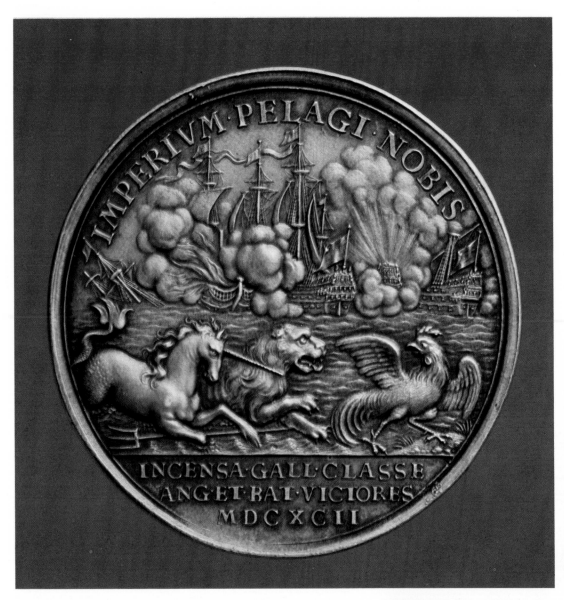

Left: *An English medal similar to the French one commemorating the Battle of Bévéziers on p113, but this time celebrating the victory at Barfleur. Note the similarity in style and the reference to Imperium Pelagi, dominion of the sea.*

Right below: *Shortly after Rooke began his abortive attack on Cadiz news was received of a fleet of Spanish galleons and their French escort, and he decided to attack immediately. The Spanish and French ships were trapped in harbor and totally destroyed.*

Below: *Admiral Sir George Rooke fought the Battle of Lagos Bay off the coast of Portugal in 1693, won a great victory at Vigo Bay in 1702 and topped an already distinguished career by capturing the Spanish fortress of Gibraltar in July 1704.*

forcing the enemy to unite his forces, permit the cruisers to make fortunate attempts upon his trade. Without such backing the result will be simply the capture of the cruisers.' Toward the end of this war the real tendency was becoming manifest, and was still more plainly seen in the next, when the French navy had sunk to a yet lower state of weakness.

Notwithstanding their losses, the sea nations made good their cause. The war, which began with the French taking the offensive, ended by reducing them everywhere to the defensive, and forced Louis to do violence at once to his strongest prejudices and his most reasonable political wishes, by recognizing as king of England him whom he looked upon as a usurper as well as his own inveterate enemy. On its surface, and taken as a whole, this war will appear almost wholly a land struggle, extending from the Spanish Netherlands down the line of the Rhine, to Savoy in Italy and Catalonia in Spain. Yet trade and shipping not only bore the burden of suffering, but in the main paid the armies that were fighting the French; and this turning of the stream of wealth from both sea nations into the coffers of their allies was perhaps determined, certainly hastened, by the misdirection of that naval supremacy with which France began the war. It was then possible, as it will usually be possible, for a really fine military navy of superior force to strike an overwhelming blow at a less ready rival; but the opportunity was allowed to slip, and the essentially stronger, better founded sea power of the allies had time to assert itself.

The peace signed at Ryswick in 1697 was most disadvantageous to France; she lost all that had been gained since the Peace

Above: *Sir George Rooke's flag-ship HMS* Royal Sovereign *returning from the attack on Cadiz in 1702, from a painting by Peter Monamy. This 100-gun 1st Rate was built at Woolwich in 1701 and then rebuilt at Chatham in 1728. She was finally broken up at Chatham in 1768. Already the rococo decoration of the seventeenth-century man-o'-war was giving way to a more austere form of gilding.*

Right: *The Battle of Malaga on 14 August 1704 was Rooke's last action but the gallant old Admiral's ships were short of ammunition after the capture of Gibraltar and in addition had very foul bottoms. After a fierce action lasting four hours the French extricated themselves and escaped, having missed yet another chance of scoring a victory and recapturing Gibraltar.*

of Nijmegen, nineteen years before, with the single important exception of Strasburg. To the two sea nations the terms of the treaty gave commercial benefits, which tended to the increase of their own sea power and to the consequent injury of that of France.

France had made a gigantic struggle; to stand alone as she did then, as as she has since done more than once, against all Europe is a great feat. Yet it may be said that as the United Provinces taught the lesson that a nation, however active and enterprising, cannot rest upon external resources alone, if intrinsically weak in numbers and territory, so France in its measure shows that a nation cannot subsist indefinitely off itself, however powerful in numbers and strong in internal resources, and the easiest way by which a nation can communicate with other peoples and renew its own strength is the sea.

During the last thirty years of the seventeenth century, amid all the strifes of arms and diplomacy, there had been clearly foreseen the coming of an event which would raise new and great

issues. This was the failure of the direct royal line in that branch of the House of Austria which was then on the Spanish throne; and the issues to be determined when the present king, infirm both in body and mind, should die, were whether the new monarch was to be taken from the House of Bourbon or from the Austrian family in Germany; and whether, in either event, the sovereign thus raised to the throne should succeed to the entire inheritance, the Empire of Spain, or some partition of that vast inheritance be made in the interests of the balance of European power. Before any arrangement was perfected, the actual king of Spain died, but before his death was induced by his ministers to sign a will, bequeathing all his States to the grandson of Louis XIV, then Duke of Anjou, known afterward as Philip V of Spain. By this step it was hoped to preserve the whole, by enlisting in its defence the nearest and one of the most powerful States in Europe—nearest, if are excepted the powers ruling the sea, which are always near any country whose ports are open to their ships.

Louis XIV accepted the bequest, and in so doing felt bound in honor to resist all attempts at partition. The union of the two kingdoms under one family promised important advantages to France, henceforth delivered from that old enemy in the rear, which had balked so many of her efforts to extend her frontiers eastward. The other countries at once realized the situation, and nothing could have saved war but some backward step on the part of the French king. Louis would not yield; on the contrary, he occupied, by connivance of the Spanish govenors, towns in the Netherlands which had been held by Dutch troops under treaties with Spain. Soon after, in February, 1701, the English Parliament met, and denounced any treaty which promised France the dominion of the Mediterranean. Holland began to arm, and the Emperor of Austria pushed his troops into northern Italy, where a campaign followed, greatly to the disadvantage of Louis.

In September of the same year, 1701, the two sea powers and the Emperor of Austria signed a secret treaty, which laid down

the chief lines of the coming war, with the exception of that waged in the Spanish peninsula itself. By it the allies undertook to conquer the Spanish Netherlands in order to place a barrier between France and the United Provinces; to conquer Milan as a security for the emperor's other provinces; and to conquer Naples and Sicily for the same security, and also for the security of the navigation and commerce of the subjects of his Britannic Majesty and of the United Provinces. The war begun, none of the allies could treat without the others, nor without having taken just measures—first, to prevent the kingdoms of France and Spain from ever being united under the same king; second, to prevent the French from ever making themselves masters of the Spanish Indies, or from sending ships thither to engage, directly or indirectly, in commerce; third, to secure to the subjects of his Britannic Majesty and of the United Provinces the commercial privileges which they enjoyed in all the Spanish States under the late king.

But though war was imminent, the countries about to engage hesitated. Holland would not move without England, and despite the strong feeling of the latter country against France, the manufacturers and merchants still remembered the terrible sufferings of the last war. Just then, as the scales were wavering, James II died. Louis, yielding to a sentiment of sympathy and urged by his nearest intimates, formally recognized the son of James as king of England; and the English people, enraged at what they looked on as a threat and an insult, threw aside all merely prudential considerations. The House of Lords declared that 'there could be no security till the usurper of the Spanish monarchy was brought to reason;' and the House of Commons voted fifty thousand soldiers and thirty-five thousand seamen, besides subsidies for German and Danish auxiliaries. William III died soon after, in March, 1702; but Queen Anne took up his policy, which had become that of the English and Dutch peoples.

France and Spain, whose cause was thenceforth known as that of the two crowns, went into the war without any ally save Bavaria. War was declared in May by Holland against the kings of France and Spain; by England against France and Spain, Anne refusing to recognize Philip V even in declaring war, because he had recognized James III as king of England; while the emperor was still more outspoken, declaring against the King of France and the Duke of Anjou. Thus began the great War of the Spanish Succession.

It is far from easy, in dealing with a war of such proportions, lasting for more than ten years, to disentangle from the general narrative that part which particularly touches our subject, without at the same time losing sight of the relation of the one part to the whole. It will conduce to clearness, however, to point out that the aim of William III was not to dispute the claim of Philip V to the throne—a matter of comparative indifference to the sea powers—but to seize, to the benefit of their commerce and colonial empire, such portions of the Spanish American possessions as he could, and at the same time to impose such conditions upon the new monarchy as would at least prevent any loss, to English and Dutch commerce, of the privileges they had had under the Austrian line. Such a policy would not direct the main effort of the sea nations upon the Spanish peninsula, but upon America; and the allied fleets might not have entered the Straits. Sicily and Naples were to go, not to England, but to Austria. Subsequent causes led to an entire change in this general plan. A new candidate, a son of the Emperor of Germany, was set up in 1703 by the coalition under the name of Carlos III, and the peninsula became the scene of a doubtful and bloody war, keeping the Anglo-Dutch fleets hovering round the coasts; with the result, as regards the sea powers, that nothing of deci-

sive importance was done in Spanish America, but that England issued from the strife with Gibraltar and Port Mahon in her hands, to be thenceforth a Mediterranean power.

When the war broke out, in pursuance of the original policy, Sir George Rooke, with a fleet of fifty ships-of-the-line and transports carrying fourteen thousand troops, was sent against Cadiz, which was the great European centre of the Spanish-American trade. Rooke's expedition against Cadiz failed, as it was nearly certain to do; for his instructions were so to act as to conciliate the Spanish people and discipline them to the Bourbon king. Such doubtful orders tied his hands; but after failing there, he learned that the galleons from the West Indies, loaded with silver and merchandise, had put into Vigo Bay under escort of French ships-of-war. He went there at once, and found the enemy in a harbor whose entrance was but three quarters of a mile wide, defended by fortifications and a heavy boom; but a passage was forced through the boom under a hot fire, the place seized, and all the shipping, with much of the specie, either taken or sunk. This affair, is known in history as that of the Vigo galleons.

The affair at Vigo had important political results, and helped to that change in the general plan of the sea powers which has been mentioned. The King of Portugal, moved by fear of the French, had acknowledged Philip V, but his heart was against him, for he dreaded French influence and power brought so near his little and isolated kingdom. The affair of Vigo, happening so near his own frontiers, impressed him with a sense of the power of the allied navies. The emperor transferred his claims to his second son, Charles; and the latter, after being proclaimed in Vienna and acknowledged by England and Holland, was taken by the allied fleets to Lisbon, where he landed in March, 1704. This necessitated the important change in the plans of the sea powers. Pledged to the support of Carlos, their fleets were thenceforth tied to the shores of the peninsula and the protection of commerce; while the war in the West Indies, becoming a side issue on a small scale, led to no results. From this time on, Portugal was the faithful ally of England. In and through all, Portugal, for a hundred years, had more to gain and more to fear from England than from any other power.

Great as were the effects of the maritime supremacy of the two sea powers upon the general result of the war, and especially upon that undisputed empire of the seas which England held for a century after, the contest is marked by no one naval action of military interest. This feature of the War of the Spanish Succession characterizes nearly the whole of the eighteenth century, with the exception of the American Revolutionary struggle. The noiseless, steady, exhausting pressure with which sea power acts, cutting off the resources of the enemy while maintaining its own, supporting war in scenes where it does not appear itself, or appears only in the background, and striking open blows at rare intervals, though lost to most, is emphasized to the careful reader by the events of this war and of the half-century that followed. The overwhelming sea power of England was the determining factor in European history during the period mentioned, maintaining war abroad while keeping its own people in prosperity at home, and building up the great empire which is now seen; but from its very greatness its action, by escaping opposition, escapes attention.

Immediately after landing Carlos III at Lisbon, Sir George Rooke sailed for Barcelona, which it was understood would be handed over when the fleets appeared; but the governor was faithful to his king and kept down the Austrian party. Rooke then sailed for Toulon, where a French fleet was at anchor. On his way he sighted another French fleet coming from Brest, which he chased but was unable to overtake; so that both the

Right: *A contemporary plan and illustration of the fortress of Gibraltar, captured by Sir George Rooke's Royal Marines in July 1704. The decision to attack was made on the spot by Rooke and Shovel, using the gunfire of 13 English and six Dutch ships to support the Marines' landing. Fortunately land troops were available to exploit the advantage gained, and before long the Spanish garrison capitulated. Since that day the Rock has remained in British hands, the key to the Western Mediterranean.*

Below: *Sir Cloudesley Shovel fought at Bantry Bay, Beachy Head, Gibraltar and Malaga and took Barcelona in 1705. On his return from an expedition to Toulon his flag-ship HMS Association ran aground in the Scilly Isles in 1707, and was drowned with his entire ship's company and those of three consorts. This disaster was recalled a few years back when divers recovered guns and other relics from the wreck.*

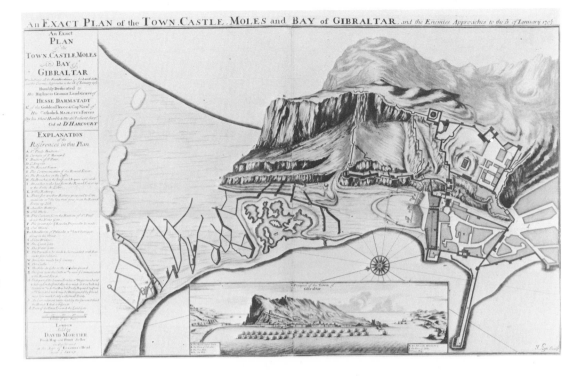

Right: *Toulon was the main French base in the Mediterranean. In 1707 it was attacked on land by the Duke of Savoy and from the sea by Sir Cloudesley Shovel. After a desperate defense, in which sailors helped to man the guns of the defenses and ships turned themselves into floating batteries, the Allies were forced to withdraw. But Toulon was put out of action for some time.*

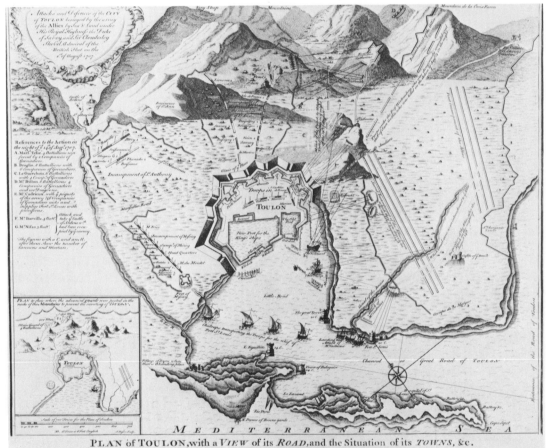

PLAN of TOULON, with a VIEW of its ROAD, and the Situation of its TOWNS, &c.

enemy's squadrons were united in the port. It is worth while to note here that the English navy did not as yet attempt to blockade the French ports in winter, as they did at a later date. At this period fleets, like armies, went into winter quarters. Another English admiral, Sir Cloudesley Shovel, had been sent in the spring to blockade Brest; but arriving too late, he found his bird flown, and at once kept on to the Mediterranean. Rooke and Shovel met off Lagos, and there held a council of war, in which the former, who was senior, declared that his instructions forbade his undertaking anything without the consent of the kings of Spain and Portugal. This was indeed tying the hands of the sea powers; but Rooke at last, chafing at the humiliating inac-

tion, and ashamed to go home without doing something, decided to attack Gibraltar for three reasons: because he heard it was insufficiently garrisoned, because it was of infinite importance as a port for the present war, and because its capture would reflect credit on the queen's arms. The place was attacked, bombarded, and then carried by an assault in boats. The English possession of Gibraltar dates from August 4, 1704, and the deed rightly keeps alive the name of Rooke, to whose judgment and fearlessness of responsibility England owes the key of the Mediterranean.

The following year, 1705, the allies moved against Philip V by two roads—from Lisbon upon Madrid, and by way of

Left: *The loss of HMS* Association *and her squadron on the rocks of the Scilly Isles on 22 October, 1707. Sir Cloudesley Shovel was returning to England from the Mediterranean, and was lost with all his men. In an age of crude navigation and even cruder provision of lights and buoys it is surprising that such disasters did not happen more often. In 1678 the French admiral D'Estrées ran a fleet of seven ships of the line aground in the West Indies.*

Below: *Both the Spanish and French navies attempted to starve Gibraltar into surrender, but the Royal Navy spared no effort to keep the garrison supplied with food and ammunition. This convoy arrived 28 May, 1708, lifting the blockade for good until the end of the war in 1713. With Minorca, Gibraltar enabled the Royal Navy to keep the Toulon Fleet under constant watch, guaranteeing control of the Western Mediterranean.*

Barcelona. The former attack, though based upon the sea, was mainly by land, and resultless; the Spanish people in that quarter showed unmistakably that they would not welcome the king set up by foreign powers. It was different in Catalonia. Barcelona surrendered on the 9th of October; all Catalonia welcomed Carlos, and the movement spread to Aragon and Valencia, the capital of the latter province declaring for Carlos.

The following year, 1706, the French took the offensive in Spain on the borders of Catalonia, while defending the passes of the mountains toward Portugal. In the absence of the allied fleet, and of the succors which it brought and maintained, the resistance was weak, and Barcelona was again besieged, this time by the French party supported by a French fleet of thirty sail-of-the-line and numerous transports with supplies from the neighboring port of Toulon. The siege, begun April 5, was going on hopefully; the Austrian claimant himself was within the walls, the prize of success; but on the 10th of May the allied fleet appeared, the French ships retired, and the siege was raised in disorder. The Portuguese and allied troops entered Madrid, June 26, 1706. The allied fleet, after the fall of Barcelona, seized Alicante and Cartagena.

In 1708 the allied fleets seized Sardinia, which from its fruitfulness and nearness to Barcelona became a rich storehouse to the Austrian claimant, so long as by the allied help he controlled the sea. The same year Minorca, with its valuable harbor, Port Mahon, was also taken, and from that time for fifty years remained in English hands. Blocking Cadiz and Cartagena by the possession of Gibraltar, and facing Toulon with Port Mahon, Great Britain was now as strongly based in the Mediterranean as either France or Spain; while, with Portugal as an ally, she controlled the two stations of Lisbon and Gibraltar, watching the trade routes both of the ocean and of the inland sea. By the end of 1708 the disasters of France by land and sea, the frightful sufferings of the kingdom, and the almost hopelessness of carrying on a strife which was destroying France, and easily borne by England, led Louis XIV to offer most humiliating concessions to obtain peace. The allies demanded the abandonment of the whole Spanish Empire without exception by the Duke of Anjou, refusing to call him king, and added thereto ruinous conditions for France herself. Louis would not yield these, and the war went on.

During the winter of 1709 and 1710 Louis withdrew all the French troops from Spain, thus abandoning the cause of his grandson. But when the cause of France was at the very lowest, and it seemed as though she might be driven to concessions which would reduce her to a second-class power, the existence of the coalition was threatened by the disgrace of Marlborough, who represented England in it. His loss of favor with the queen was followed by the accession to power of the party opposed to the war, or rather to its further continuance. This change took place in the summer of 1710, and the inclination toward peace was strengthened both by the favorable position in which England then stood for treating, and by the heavy burden she was bearing; which it became evident could bring in no further advantages commensurate to its weight. The weaker ally, Holland, had gradually ceased to contribute her stipulated share to the sea forces. Secret negotiations between England and France soon began, and received an additional impulse by the unexpected death of the Emperor of Germany, the brother of the Austrian claimant of the Spanish throne. There being no other male heir, Carlos became at once emperor of Austria, and was soon after elected emperor of Germany. England had no more wish to see two crowns on an Austrian head than on that of a Bourbon.

The demands made by England, as conditions of peace in 1711, showed her to have become a sea power in the purest sense of the word, not only in fact, but also in her own consciousness. She required that the same person should never be king both of France and Spain; that a barrier of fortified towns should be granted her allies, Holland and Germany, as a defensive line against France; that French conquests from her allies should be restored; and for herself she demanded the formal cession of Gibraltar and Port Mahon, whose strategic and maritime value has been pointed out, the destruction of the port of Dunkirk, the home nest of the privateers that preyed on English commerce, the cession of the French colonies of Newfoundland, Hudson's Bay, and Nova Scotia, the last of which she held at that time, and finally, treaties of commerce with France and Spain, and the concession of the monopoly of the slave trade with Spanish America, known as the Asiento, which Spain had given to France in 1701.

Negotiations continued, though hostilities did not cease; and in June, 1712, a four months' truce between Great Britain and France removed the English troops from the allied armies on the continent, their great leader Marlborough having been taken from their head the year before. The campaign of 1712 was favorable to France; but in almost any event the withdrawal

Above: *Duguay-Trouin's ship* le Français *capturing the British merchantman* Sans Pareil *in 1694, just one incident in a lifetime of daring attacks. Born in 1673, he went to sea at the age of 16 and died in 1736.*

Above: *On 10 October 1707 the corsair Forbin attacked an English troop convoy off the Lizard escorted by five ships of the line. After a stiff fight the 80-gun* Devonshire *blew up and the* Cumberland *struck her colors; the French took 60 ships out of a total of 80 in the convoy. Losses on this scale had a serious effect on the Allies' land campaign in Spain and contributed to the defeat of the Austrians at Almanza.*

of Great Britain made the end of the war a question of but a short time. April 11, 1713, an almost general peace, known as the Peace of Utrecht, one of the landmarks of history, was signed between France on the one hand, and England, Holland, Prussia, Portugal, and Savoy on the other. On the 7th of March, 1714, peace was signed between France and Austria.

The changes effected by this long war and sanctioned by the peace, neglecting details of lesser or passing importance, may be stated as follows: 1 The House of Bourbon was settled on the Spanish throne, and the Spanish empire retained its West Indian and American possessions. 2 The Spanish empire lost its possessions in the Netherlands, Gelderland going to the new kingdom of Prussia and Belgium to the emperor; the Spanish Netherlands thus became the Austrian Netherlands. 3 Spain lost also the principal islands of the Mediterranean; Sardinia being given to Austria, Minorca with its fine harbor to Great Britain, and Sicily to the Duke of Savoy. 4 Spain lost also her Italian possessions, Milan and Naples going to the emperor.

France, the backer of the successful claimant, came out of the strife worn out, and with considerable loss of territory. She had succeeded in placing a king of her own royal house on a neighboring throne, but her sea strength was exhausted, her population diminished, her financial condition ruined. The European territory surrendered was on her northern and eastern boundaries; and she abandoned the use of the port of Dunkirk, the centre of that privateering warfare so dreaded by English merchants. In America, the cession of Nova Scotia and Newfoundland was the first step toward that entire loss of Canada which befell half a century later; but for the present she retained Cape Breton Island, with its port Louisburg, the key to the Gulf and River St Lawrence.

The gains of England, by the treaty and the war, corresponded very nearly to the losses of France and Spain, and were all in the direction of extending and strengthening her sea power. Gibraltar and Port Mahon in the Mediterranean, and the colonies already mentioned in North America, afforded new bases to that power, extending and protecting her trade. Second only to the expansion of her own was the injury to the sea power of France and Holland, by the decay of their navies in consequence of the immense drain of the land warfare; further indications of that decay will be given later. It was the wisdom of England not to base her sea power solely on military positions nor even of fighting-ships, and the commercial advantages she had now gained by the war and the peace were very great. The grant of the slave trade with Spanish America, in itself lucrative, became yet more so as the basis for an immense smuggling intercourse with those countries, and the North American colonies ceded were valuable not merely nor chiefly as military stations, but commercially.

While England thus came out from the war in good running condition, and fairly placed in that position of maritime supremacy which she has so long maintained, her old rival in trade and fighting was left hopelessly behind. As the result of the war Holland obtained nothing at sea—no colony, no station. The gain which Holland made by land was that of military occupation only, of certain fortified places in the Austrian Netherlands, known to history as the 'barrier towns'; nothing was added by them to her revenue, population, or resources. Therefore, though the United Provinces attained the great object for which they began the war, and saved the Spanish Netherlands from the hands of France, the success was not worth the cost. Holland ceased to be numbered among the great powers of Europe, her navy was no longer a military factor in diplomacy, and her commerce also shared in the general decline of the State.

Such were the leading results of the War of the Spanish Succession, 'the vastest yet witnessed by Europe since the

Bottom: On 31 July 1718 Sir George Byng met a superior Spanish fleet South of Sicily, trying to recapture the island. In the battle which followed the Spanish lost seven ships captured or burned.

Below: In June 1711 Duguay-Trouin sailed from La Rochelle with 16 ships, bound for Rio de Janeiro. He captured the port in the teeth of heavy opposition, and withdrew on payment of a heavy ransom by the governor. This feat of privateering paid a 92 percent return to the expedition's backers.

Crusades.' It was a war whose chief military interest was on the land. Yet looking only, for the moment, to immediate and evident results, who reaped the benefit? Was it with those, who had waged war more and more exclusively by land, and set their eyes more and more on gains on the land, or was it not rather with England, who had indeed paid for that continental war and even backed it with her troops, but who meanwhile was building up her navy, strengthening, extending, and protecting her commerce, seizing maritime positions—in a word, founding and rearing her sea power upon the ruins of that of her rivals, friend and foe alike? By it she controlled the great commerce of the open sea with a military shipping that had no rival, and in the exhausted condition of the other nations could have none; and that shipping was now securely based on strong positions in all the disputed quarters of the world. The commerce which had sustained her in prosperity, and her allies in military efficiency, during the war, though checked and harassed by the

enemy's cruisers (to which she could pay only partial attention amid the many claims upon her), started with a bound into new life when the war was over.

The sea power of England therefore was not merely in the great navy, with which we too commonly and exclusively associate it; France had had such a navy in 1688, and it shrivelled away like a leaf in the fire. Neither was it in a prosperous commerce alone; a few years after the date at which we have arrived, the commerce of France took on fair proportions, but the first blast of war swept it off the seas as the navy of Cromwell had once swept that of Holland. It was in the union of the two, carefully fostered, that England made the gain of sea power over and beyond all other States; and this gain is distinctly associated with and dates from the War of the Spanish Succession. Before that war England was one of the sea powers; after it she was *the* sea power, without any second.

Is it meant, it may be asked, to attribute to sea power alone the greatness or wealth of any State? Certainly not. The due use and control of the sea is but one link in the chain of exchange by which wealth accumulates; but it is the central link, which lays under contribution other nations for the benefit of the one holding it, and which, history seems to assert, most surely of all gathers to itself riches. In England, this control and use of the sea seems to arise naturally, from the concurrence of many circumstances; the years immediately preceding the War of the Spanish Succession had, moreover, furthered the advance of her prosperity by a series of fiscal measures, which Macaulay speaks of as 'the deep and solid foundation on which was to rise the most gigantic fabric of commercial prosperity which the world had ever seen.' It may be questioned, however, whether the genius of the people, inclined to and developed by trade, did not make easier the taking of such measures; whether their adoption did not at least partially spring from, as well as add to, the sea power of the nation. However that may be, there is seen, on the opposite side of the Channel, a nation which started ahead of England in the race—a nation peculiarly well fitted, by situation and resources, for the control of the sea both by war and commerce. In 1672 France definitely chose expansion by land. At that time Colbert had administered her finances for twelve years, and from a state of terrible confusion had so restored them that the revenue of the King of France was more than double that of the King of England. Colbert's plans and hopes for France rested upon making her powerful on the sea.

The name of Duguay-Trouin can be mentioned, before finally leaving the War of the Spanish Succession, and his greatest privateering expedition, carried to a distance from home rarely reached by the seamen of his occupation, and which illustrates curiously the spirit of such enterprises in that day, and the shifts to which the French government was reduced. A small French squadron had attacked Rio de Janeiro in 1710, but being repulsed had lost some prisoners, who were said to have been put to death. Duguay-Trouin sought permission to avenge the insult to France. The king, consenting, advanced the ships and furnished the crews; and a regular contract was drawn up between the king on the one hand and the company employing Duguay-Trouin on the other, stipulating the expenses to be borne and supplies furnished on either hand; among which we find the odd, business-like provision that for every one of the troops embarked who shall die, be killed, or desert during the cruise, the company should pay a forfeit of thirty francs. Under provisions, enumerated in full in a long contract, Duguay-Trouin received a force of six ships-of-the-line, seven frigates, and over two thousand troops, with which he sailed to Rio de Janeiro in 1711; captured the place after a series of operations, and allowed it to be ransomed at the price of something under four hundred thousand dollars, probably nearly equal to a million in the present day, besides five hundred cases of sugar.

While the War of the Spanish Succession was engaging all western Europe, a strife which might have had a profound

Above: *This print shows Byng's fleet lying at Naples after the Battle of Cape Passaro in 1718.*

Many causes doubtless worked together to the disastrous result which marked the end of the reign of Louis XIV: constant wars, bad administration in the latter half of the period, extravagance throughout; but France was practically never invaded, the war was kept at or beyond her own frontiers with slight exceptions, her home industries could suffer little from direct hostilities. Why was France miserable and exhausted, while England was smiling and prosperous? The reason apparently was the difference in wealth and credit. France stood alone against many enemies; but those enemies were raised and kept moving by English subsidies.

influence upon its issue was going on in the east. Sweden and Russia were at war, the Hungarians had revolted against Austria, and Turkey was finally drawn in, though not till the end of the year 1710. Had Turkey helped the Hungarians, she would have made a powerful diversion, not for the first time in history, in favor of France. The English historian suggests that she was deterred by fear of the English fleet; at all events she did not move, and Hungary was reduced to obedience. The war between Sweden and Russia was to result in the preponderance of the latter upon the Baltic, the subsidence of Sweden, the old ally of France, into a second-rate State, and the entrance of Russia definitively into European politics. (Editor's note— *Following the deaths of Queen Anne in 1714 and Louis XIV in 1715, a period of instability followed in England and France. Spain's attempts to gain Sicily were decisively foiled by the English fleet off Cape Passaro in 1718. Mediterranean and Colonial rivalry continued, but European war was avoided until the 1730s.*)

Chapter 5

Anson and Hawke

We have now reached the opening of a series of great wars, destined to last with short intervals of peace for nearly half a century, and having, amid many misleading details, one broad characteristic distinguishing them from previous, and from many subsequent, wars. This strife embraced the four quarters of the world, and that not only as side issues here and there, the main struggle being in Europe; for the great questions to be determined by it, concerning the world's history, were the dominion of the sea and the control of distant countries, the possession of colonies, and, dependent upon these, the increase of wealth. The action of sea power is evident enough, the issue plainly indicated from the beginning; but for a long time there is no naval warfare of any consequence, because the truth is not recognized by the French government.

Such being the character of the coming wars, it is important to realize the relative positions of the three great powers in those quarters of the world, outside of Europe, where the strife was to engage.

In North America, England now held the thirteen colonies, control of the neighboring seas, or by such powerful diversion elsewhere as would relieve the pressure upon her.

Spain held Florida; under which name were embraced extensive regions beyond the peninsula, not accurately defined, and having little importance at any period of these long wars.

In the West Indies and South America, Spain held mainly what are still known as Spanish American countries, besides Cuba, Porto Rico, and part of Haiti; France had Guadeloupe, Martinique, and the western half of Haiti; England, Jamaica, Barbados, and some of the smaller islands. The smaller West India islands are singly too small to be strongly held except by a power controlling the sea. They had a twofold value in war: one as offering military positions for such a power; the other a commercial value, either as adding to one's own resources or diminishing those of the enemy. War directed against them may be considered as a war upon commerce, and the islands themselves as ships or convoys loaded with enemy's wealth. They will be found therefore changing hands like counters, and usually restored when peace comes; though the final result was to leave

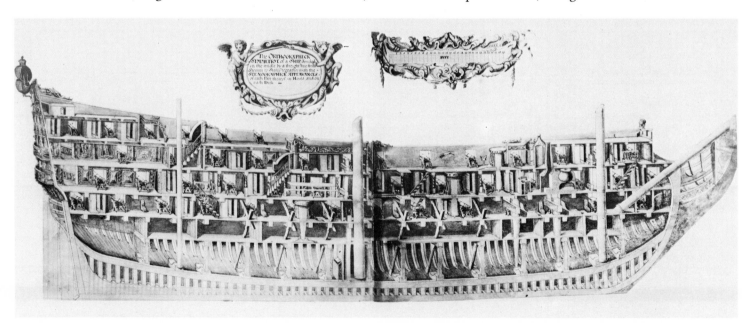

Above: *This 1680 engraving shows the longitudinal section of a 1st Rate three-decker ship-of-the-line. The science of naval architecture had advanced considerably by the end of the seventeenth century and ships were no longer designed by rule of thumb, although the availability of timbers of the correct shape determined the degree of latitude allowed to the shipwrights.*

the original United States, from Maine to Georgia.

France held Canada and Louisiana, a name much more extensive in its application then than now, and claimed the entire valley of the Ohio and Mississippi, by right of prior discovery, and as a necessary link between the St Lawrence and the Gulf of Mexico.

In 1750 the population of Canada was eighty thousand, that of the English colonies twelve hundred thousand. With such disparity of strength and resources, the only chance for Canada lay in the support of the sea power of France, either by direct

Right: *The Swedish naval architect Chapman (1721-1808) had a strong influence on eighteenth-century naval architecture. His composite drawing shows the details of hull and fittings of a French 40-gun frigate. Note the single gun deck which distinguished frigates from 5th Rates and upward, the round section of the hull and the large amount of space available for stores.*

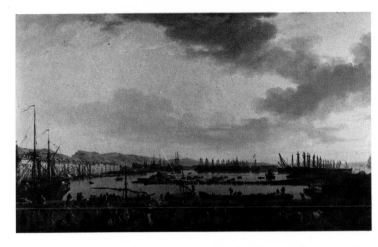

most of them in the hands of England. Nevertheless, the fact of each of the great powers having a share in this focus of commerce drew thither both large fleets and small squadrons, a tendency aided by the unfavorable seasons for military operations on the continent; and in the West Indies took place the greater number of the fleet-actions that illustrated this long series of wars.

In yet another remote region was the strife between England and France to be waged, and there, as in North America, finally decided by these wars. In India, the rival nations were represented by their East India companies, who directly administered both government and commerce. At this time the principal settlements of the English were—on the west coast, Bombay; on the east, Calcutta upon the Ganges, at some distance from the sea, and Madras; while a little south of Madras another town and station, known generally to the English as Fort St David, though sometimes called Cuddalore, had been established later.

France was established at Chandernagore, on the Ganges, above Calcutta; at Pondicherry, on the east coast, eighty miles

Above: Admiralty Board model of a 50-gun ship built to the 1733 Establishment. Although the identity is uncertain she is very like the Gloucester, *built at Sheerness in 1737.*

Above left: Vernet's view of the Arsenal at Toulon, painted in 1755. The French dockyards were much admired in England for their equipment and organization.

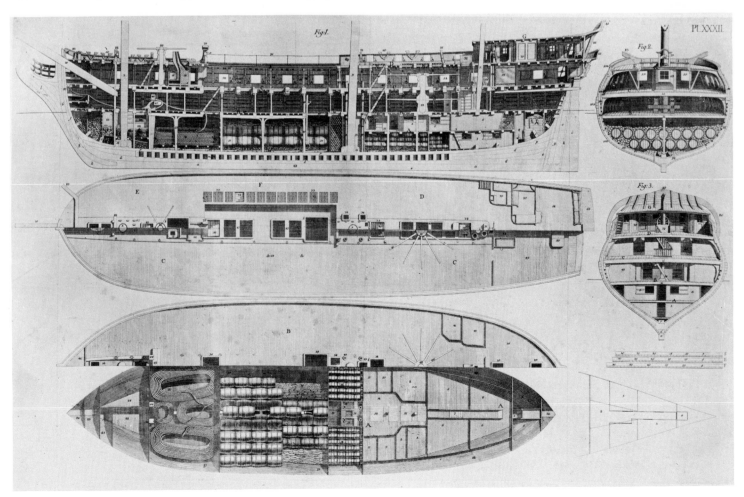

south of Madras; and on the west coast, far to the south of Bombay, she had a third station of inferior importance, called Mahé. The French, however, had a great advantage in the possession of the intermediate station already pointed out in the Indian Ocean, the neighboring islands of France and Bourbon. They were yet more fortunate in the personal character of the two men who were at this time at the head of their affairs in the Indian peninsula and the islands, Dupleix and La Bourdonnais—men to whom no rivals in ability or force of character had as yet appeared among the English Indian officials. Yet in these two men, whose cordial fellow-working might have ruined the English settlement in India, there appeared again that singular conflict of ideas, that hesitation between the land and the sea as the stay of power, a prophecy of which seems to be contained in the geographical position of France itself. The mind of Dupleix, though not inattentive to commercial interests, was fixed on building up a great empire in which France should rule over a multitude of vassal native princes. In the pursuit of this end he displayed great tact and untiring activity, perhaps also a somewhat soaring and fantastic imagination; but when he met La Bourdonnais, whose simpler and sounder views aimed at sea supremacy, at a dominion based upon free and certain communication with the home country instead of the shifting sands of Eastern intrigues and alliances, discord at once arose. It may be that with the weakness of Canada, compared to the English colonies, sea power could not there have changed the actual issue; but in the condition of the rival nations in India everything depended upon controlling the sea.

Such were the relative situations of the three countries in the principal foreign theatres of war. It is necessary to mention briefly the condition of the military navies, which were to have an importance as yet unrealized. Neither precise numbers nor an exact account of condition of the ships, can be given; but the relative efficiency can be fairly estimated. Campbell, the English contemporary naval historian, says that in 1727 the English navy had eighty four ships-of-the-line, from sixty guns up; forty 50-gun ships, and fifty-four frigates and smaller vessels. In 1734 this number had fallen to seventy ships-of-the-line and nineteen 50-gun ships. In 1744, after four years of war with Spain alone, the number was ninety ships-of-the-line and eighty-four frigates. The French navy at the same time he estimates at forty-five ships-of-the-line and sixty-seven frigates. In 1747, near the end of the first war, he says that the royal navy of Spain was reduced to twenty-two ships-of-the-line, that of France to thirty-one, while the English had risen to one hundred and twenty-six. This neglect of the French navy lasted more or less

throughout these wars, until 1760, when the sense of the nation was aroused to the importance of restoring it; too late, however, to prevent the most serious of the French losses. In England as well as in France discipline and administration had been sapped by the long peace; the inefficiency of the armaments sent out was notorious, and recalls the scandals that marked the outbreak of the Crimean War; while the very disappearance of the French ships led, by the necessity of replacing them, to putting afloat vessels superior singly, because more modern and scientific, to the older ships of the same class in England. It may be accepted as generally true that the French ships built between 1740 and 1800 were better designed and larger, class for class, than the English. The latter had the undoubted superiority both in the number and quality of the seamen and officers. Keeping some fleets always afloat, whether better or worse, the officers could not quite lose touch of their profession; whereas in France it is said that not one fifth of the officers were, in 1744, employed. This superiority was kept and increased by the practice, which

henceforth obtained, of blockading the French military ports with superior force; the enemy's squadrons when they put to sea found themselves at once at a disadvantage in point of practical skill. On the other hand, large as was the number of English seamen, the demands of commerce were so great that war found them scattered all over the world, and part of the fleet was always paralyzed for lack of crews. This constant employment assured good seamanship, but the absence of so many men had to be supplied by an indiscriminate press, which dragged in a class of miserable and sickly men, sadly diluting the quality of the whole. To realize the condition of ships' companies of that day, it will be necessary only to read the accounts of those sent to

Opposite: *A caricature of the press gang at work. At the outset of a war or an expedition, gangs of seamen under an officer toured the dockside inns and lodging houses to 'impress' trained seamen to make up numbers, for manpower was always in short supply.*

Right: *In 1740 Commodore Anson was sent in the 60-gun 4th Rate Centurion to attack Spanish possessions in the Pacific. He finished by circumnavigating the world, and captured a treasure galleon at Manila. Her cargo of bullion was sold for £400,000 at Canton.*

Left below: *Admiral Vernon achieved instant fame by his capture of Porto Bello in 1739 with only six ships, but he is better known today for his introduction of 'grog' or watered rum—from his grogram cloak he was known as 'Old Grog.'*

Anson starting for a cruise round the world, or to Hawke when fitting out for war service; the statements are now almost incredible, and the results most deplorable. It was not a question of sanitation only; the material sent was entirely unfit to meet the conditions of sea life under the most favorable circumstances. In both the French and English service a great deal of weeding among the officers was necessary.

War having been declared against Spain by England in October, 1739, the first attempts of the latter power were naturally directed against the Spanish-American colonies, the cause of the dispute, in which it was expected to find an easy and rich prey. The first expedition sailed under Admiral Vernon in November of the same year, and took Porto Bello by a sudden and audacious stroke, but found only the insignificant sum of ten thousand dollars in the port whence the galleons sailed. Returning to Jamaica, Vernon received large reinforcements of ships, and was joined by a land force of twelve thousand troops. With this increased force, attempts were made upon both Cartagena and Santiago de Cuba, in the years 1741 and 1742, but in both wretched failures resulted; the admiral and the general quarrelled, as was not uncommon in days when neither had an intelligent comprehension of the other's business.

Another expedition, justly celebrated for the endurance and perseverance shown by its leader, and famous both for the hardships borne and singular final success, was sent out in 1740 under Anson. Its mission was to pass round Cape Horn and attack the Spanish colonies on the west coast of South America. Passing the Cape at the worst season of the year, the ships met a series of tempests of the most violent kind; the squadron was scattered, never all to meet again, and Anson, after infinite peril, succeeded in rallying a part of it at Juan Fernandez. Two ships had put back to England, a third was lost to the southward of Chiloe. With the three left to him he cruised along the South American coast, taking some prizes and pillaging the town of Payta, intending to touch near Panama and join hands with Vernon for the capture of that place and the possession of the isthmus, if possible. Learning of the disaster at Cartagena, he then determined to cross the Pacific and waylay the two galleons that sailed yearly from Acapulco to Manila. In the passage across, one of the two ships now left to him was found in such bad condition that she had to be destroyed. With the other he succeeded in his last undertaking, capturing the great galleon with a million and a half dollars in specie. The expedition, from its many misfortunes, had no military result beyond the terror and consequent embarrassment caused to the Spanish settlements; but its very misfortunes, and the calm persistency which worked out a great success from them all, have given it a well-deserved renown.

Left: *Vernon's expedition to the West Indies in 1739 was to harry Spanish possessions, and so he attacked and captured the town of Porto Bello with the ships* Worcester, Hampton Court, Norwich, Princess Louisa, Burford *and* Strafford. *Promoted Vice-Admiral for this feat he failed in subsequent operations in the West Indies but was promoted Admiral in 1745. He was subsequently struck off the flag-list for publishing Admiralty letters, in the prevailing climate of political vindictiveness.*

Right: *The capture of the Spanish treasure ship* Nuestra Senora de Covadonga *by the* Centurion *in 1743. Anson's men, mostly Chelsea pensioners, suffered greatly throughout the voyage from the effects of scurvy and other diseases, but this did not prevent them from capturing the Spanish ship. The* Centurion *returning to England was nearly captured when she sailed through the French Fleet in the Channel.*

During the year 1740 happened two events which led to a general European war breaking in upon that in which Spain and England were already engaged. In May of that year Frederick the Great became king of Prussia, and in October the emperor Charles VI, formerly the Austrian claimant of the Spanish throne, died. He had no son, and left by will the sovereignty of his estates to his eldest daughter, the celebrated Maria Theresa, to secure whose succession the efforts of his diplomacy had been directed for many years. Meanwhile the failure of the Spanish-American expeditions and the severe losses of English commerce increased the general outcry against Walpole, who resigned early in 1742. England under the new

ministry became the open ally of Austria; and Parliament voted not only a subsidy to the empress-queen, but also a body of troops to be sent as auxiliaries to the Austrian Netherlands. At the same time Holland, under English influence, and bound like England by previous treaties to support the succession of Maria Theresa, also voted a subsidy. Here occurs again that curious view of international relations before mentioned. Both of these powers thus entered the war against France, but only as auxiliaries to the empress, not as principals; as nations, except the troops actually in the field, they were considered to be still at peace. In 1741, Spain, having now entered the continental war as an enemy of Austria, sent a body of fifteen thousand troops

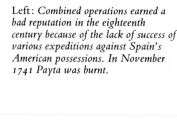

Left: *Combined operations earned a bad reputation in the eighteenth century because of the lack of success of various expeditions against Spain's American possessions. In November 1741 Payta was burnt.*

Right: *Frederick the Great of Prussia.*

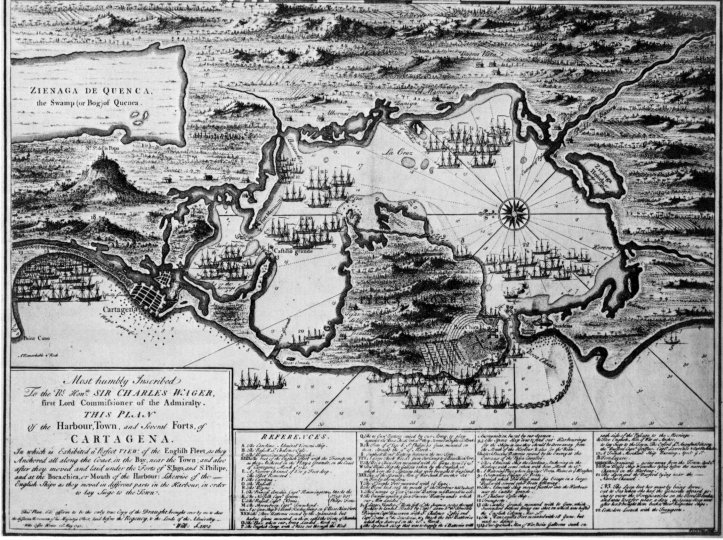

from Barcelona to attack the Austrian possessions in Italy. The English admiral Haddock, in the Mediterranean, sought and found the Spanish fleet; but with it was a division of twelve French sail-of-the-line, whose commander informed Haddock that he was engaged in the same expedition and had orders to fight, if the Spaniards, though formally at war with England, were attacked. As the allies were nearly double his force, the English admiral was obliged to go back to Port Mahon. He was soon after relieved; and the new admiral, Matthews, held at once the two positions of commander-in-chief in the Mediterranean and English minister at Turin, the capital of the King of Sardinia. In the course of the year 1742 an English captain in his fleet, chasing some Spanish galleys, drove them into the French port of St Tropez, and following them into the harbor burned them, in spite of the so-called neutrality of France. In the same year Matthews sent a division of ships under Commodore Martin to Naples, to compel the Bourbon king to withdraw his contingent of twenty thousand troops serving with the Spanish army in northern Italy against the Austrians. To the attempts to negotiate, Martin replied only by pulling out his watch and giving the government an hour to come to terms. There was nothing for it but submission; and the English fleet left the harbor after a stay of twenty-four hours, having relieved the empress of a dangerous enemy. Henceforward it was evident that the Spanish war in Italy could only be maintained by sending troops through France; England controlled the sea and the action of Naples. The moment was fast approaching when both France and England must quit the pretence of being only auxiliaries in the war.

In the latter part of 1743 the Infante Philip of Spain had sought to land on the coast of the Genoese Republic, which was unfriendly to the Austrians; but the attempt had been frustrated by the English fleet, and the Spanish ships forced to retreat into Toulon. They lay there for four months, unable to go out on account of the English superiority. In this dilemma the court of Spain applied to Louis XV and obtained an order for the French fleet, under the command of Admiral de Court, an old man of eighty years, a veteran of the days of Louis XIV, to escort the Spaniards either to the Gulf of Genoa or to their own ports, it does not clearly appear which. The French admiral was ordered not to fire unless he was attacked. In order to secure the

Above: *The action off Toulon in February 1744, following which Admirals Matthews and Lestock quarrelled over a failure to cooperate.*

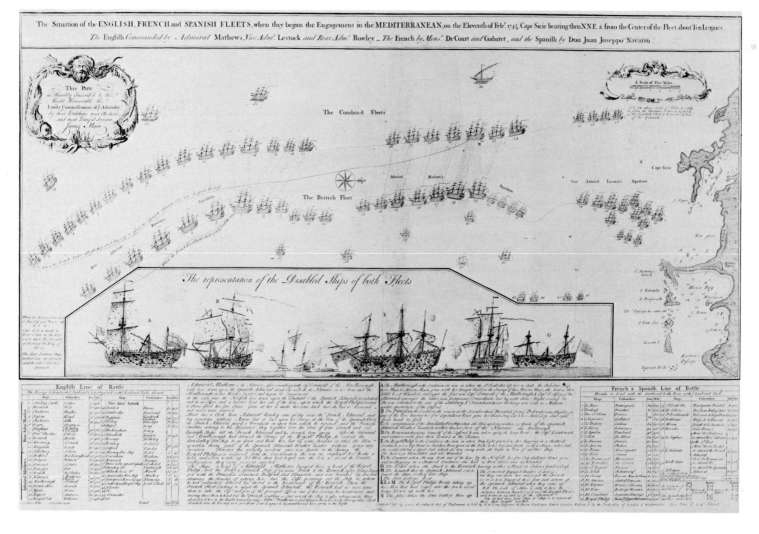

Left: *Contemporary plan of the attack on Cartagena in March 1741.*

Above: *Plan of the Toulon action. Admiral Matthews was cashiered for breaking the line of battle, setting the seal on sterile tactics for another 50 years.*

Left: *The Spanish ship* Nuestra Senora de los Remedios *driven ashore by English privateers near Beachy Head in February 1746.*

Right: *Edward Hawke was the only captain to emerge with credit from the Matthews-Lestock squabble, having taken the solitary prize of the action. Significantly he was later to be the first flag-officer to breach the Fighting Instructions.*

Below left: *The bombardment of Bastia in Corsica in 1745.*

best co-operation of the Spaniards, whose efficiency he probably distrusted, De Court proposed, as Ruyter had done in days long gone by, to scatter their ships among his own; but as the Spanish admiral, Navarro, refused, the line-of-battle was formed with nine French ships in the van, in the centre six French and three Spaniards, in the rear nine Spanish ships; in all, twenty-seven. In this order the combined fleets sailed from Toulon February 19, 1744. The English fleet, which had been cruising off Hyères in observation, chased, and on the 22nd its van and centre came up with the allies; but the rear division was then several miles to windward and astern, quite out of supporting distance. The wind was easterly, both fleets heading to the southward, and the English had the weather-gage. The numbers were nearly equal, the English having twenty-nine to the allied twenty-seven; but this advantage was reversed by the failure of the English rear to join. The course of the rear-admiral has been generally attributed to ill-will toward Matthews; for although he proved that in his separated position he made all sail to join, he did not attack later on when he could, on the plea that the signal for the line-of-battle was flying at the same time as the signal to engage; meaning that he could not leave the line to fight without disobeying the order to form line. Under the actual conditions Matthews, mortified and harassed by the inaction of his lieutenant, and fearing that the enemy would escape if he delayed longer, made the signal to engage when his own van was abreast the enemy's centre, and at once bore down himself out

of the line and attacked with his flag-ship of ninety guns the largest ship in the enemy's line, the 'Royal Philip,' of one hundred and ten guns, carrying the flag of the Spanish admiral. In doing this he was bravely supported by his next ahead and astern. The moment of attack seems to have been judiciously chosen; five Spanish ships had straggled far to the rear, leaving their admiral with the support only of his next ahead and astern, while three other Spaniards continued on with the French. The English van stood on, engaging the allied centre, while the allied van was without antagonists. Being thus disengaged, the latter was desirous of tacking to windward of the head of the English line, thus putting it between two fires, but was checked by the intelligent action of the three leading English captains, who, disregarding the signal to bear down, kept their commanding position and stopped the enemy's attempts to double. For this they were cashiered by the court-martial, but afterward restored. This circumspect but justifiable disregard of signals was imitated without any justification by all the English captains of the centre, save the admiral's seconds already mentioned, as well as by some of those in the van, who kept up a cannonade at long range while their commander-in-chief was closely and even furiously engaged. The one marked exception was Captain Hawke, afterward the distinguished admiral, who imitated the example of his chief, and after driving his first antagonist out of action, quitted his place in the van, brought to close quarters a fine Spanish ship that had kept at bay five other English ships, and took her—the only prize made that day. The commander of the English van, with his seconds, also behaved with spirit and came to close action. The general inefficiency and widespread misbehaviour of the English captains, after five years of declared war, will partly explain the failure of England to obtain from her undoubted naval superiority the results she might have expected in this war—the first act in a forty year's drama—and they give military officers a lesson on the necessity of having their minds prepared and stocked, by study of the conditions of war in their own day, if they would not be found unready and perhaps disgraced in the hour of battle. Attention may here fitly be drawn to the effect of a certain cordiality and good-will on the part of superiors toward their subordinates. It is not perhaps essential to military success, but it undoubtedly contributes to the other elements of that success a spirit, a breath of life, which makes possible what would otherwise be impossible.

Doubtless it is a natural gift. The highest example of it possibly ever known among seamen was Nelson. When he joined the fleet just before Trafalgar, the captains who gathered on board the flag-ship seemed to forget the rank of their admiral in their desire to testify their joy at meeting him. 'This Nelson,' wrote Captain Duff, who fell in the battle, 'is so lovable and excellent a man, so kindly a leader, that we all wish to exceed his desires and anticipate his orders.' He himself was conscious of this fascination and its value, when writing of the battle of the Nile to Lord Howe, he said, 'I had the happiness to command a band of brothers.'

The celebrity attained by Matthews's action off Toulon, certainly not due to the skill with which it was managed, nor to its results, sprang from the clamor at home, and chiefly from the number and findings of the courts-martial that followed. Both the admiral and his second, and also eleven captains out of the twenty-nine, had charges preferred against them. The admiral was cashiered because he had broken the line; that is, because his captains did not follow him when he left it to get at the enemy— a decision that smacks more of the Irish bull than of the Irish love of fighting. On the continent, the questions after 1745 reduced themselves to two—what part of the Austrian possessions should be given to Prussia, Spain, and Sardinia, and how peace was to be wrenched by France from England and Holland. Numerous places fell during the year of 1747, and the successes of the French inclined both Holland and England to come to terms. Negotiations went on during the winter; but in April, 1748, Saxe invested Maestricht. This forced a peace.

Meanwhile, though languishing, the sea war was not wholly uneventful. Two encounters between English and French squadrons happened during the year 1747, completing the destruction of the French fighting navy. In both cases the English were decidedly superior; and though there was given opportunity for some brilliant fighting by particular captains, and for the display of heroic endurance on the part of the French, greatly outnumbered but resisting to the last, only one tactical lesson is afforded. This lesson is, that when an enemy, either as

the result of battle or from original inequality, is greatly inferior in force, obliged to fly without standing on the order of his flying, the regard otherwise due to order must be in a measure at least dismissed, and a general chase ordered. The mistake of Tourville in this respect after Beachy Head has already been noted. In the first of the cases now under discussion, the English Admiral Anson had fourteen ships against eight French, weaker individually as well as in total number; in the second, Sir Edward Hawke had fourteen against nine, the latter being somewhat larger, ship for ship, than the English. In both cases the signal was made for a general chase, and the action which resulted was a *mêlée*. There was no opportunity for anything else; the one thing necessary was to overtake the running enemy, and that can only certainly be done by letting the fleetest or best situated ships get ahead, sure that the speed of the fastest pursuers is better than that of the slowest of the pursued, and that therefore either the latter must be abandoned or the whole force brought to bay. In the second case the French commander, Commodore l'Étenduère, did not have to be followed far. He had with him a convoy of two hundred and fifty merchant-ships; detaching one ship-of-the-line to continue the voyage with the convoy, he placed himself with the other eight between it and the enemy, awaiting the attack under his topsails. As the English came up

Top: *In May 1747 Admiral Anson met and defeated de la Jonquière off Finisterre, capturing six warships and nine transports.*

Left: *The 74-gun French man-o'-war* Terrible, *captured by Sir Edward Hawke off Finisterre in October 1747. The action was very similar to Anson's five months earlier, an attack on a big French convoy.*

Bottom: Robert Clive, who thwarted French ambitions to rule India and defeated Dupleix.

one after another they divided on either side of the French column, which was thus engaged on both sides. After an obstinate resistance, six of the French ships were taken, but the convoy was saved. The English had been so roughly handled that the two remaining French men-of-war got back safely to France. If, therefore, Sir Edward Hawke showed in his attack the judgment and dash which always distinguished that remarkable officer, it may be claimed for Commodore l'Étenduère that fortune, in assigning him the glorious disadvantage of numbers, gave him also the leading part in the drama, and that he filled it nobly. A French officer justly remarks that 'he defended his convoy as on shore a position is defended, when the aim is to save an army corps or to assure an evolution; he gave himself to be crushed. After an action that lasted from mid-day till eight p.m. the convoy was saved, thanks to the obstinacy of the defence; two hundred and fifty ships were saved to their owners by the devotion of L'Étenduère and of the captains under his orders. This devotion cannot be questioned, for eight ships had but few chances of surviving an action with fourteen; and not only did the commander of the eight accept an action which he might possibly have avoided, but he knew how to inspire his lieutenants with trust in him; for all supported the strife with honor, and yielded at last, showing the most indisputable proofs of their fine energetic defence. Four ships were entirely dismasted, two had only the foremast standing.' The whole affair, as conducted on both sides, affords an admirable study of how to follow up an advantage, original or acquired, and of the results that may be obtained by a gallant, even hopeless defence, for the furtherance of a particular object. It may be added that Hawke, disabled from further pursuit himself, sent a sloop of war express to the West Indies, with information of the approach of the convoy—a step which led to the capture of part of it, and gives a touch of completeness to the entire transaction, which cannot fail to be gratifying to a military student interested in seeing the actors in history fully alive to and discharging to the utmost their important tasks.

Before bringing to a close the story of this war and mentioning the peace settlement, an account must be given of the transactions in India, where France and England were then on equal terms. It has been said that affairs there were controlled by the East India companies of either nation; and that the French were represented in the peninsula by Dupleix, in the islands by La Bourdonnais. The latter was appointed to his post in 1735, and his untiring genius had been felt in all the details of administration, but especially in converting the Isle of France into a great naval station—a work which had to be built up from the foundations. In 1740, when war between France and England became probable, he obtained from the East India Company a squadron, though smaller than he asked, with which he proposed to ruin the English commerce and shipping; but when war actually began in 1744, he received orders not to attack the English, the

French company hoping that neutrality might exist between the companies in that distant region, though the nations were at war. The advantage won by the forethought of La Bourdonnais was thus lost; though first, and long alone, on the field, his hand was stayed. Meanwhile the English admiralty sent out a squadron and began to seize French ships between India and China; not till then did the company awake from its illusion. Having done this part of its work, the English squadron sailed to the coast of India, and in July, 1745, appeared off Pondicherry, the political capital of French India, prepared to sustain an attack which the governor of Madras was about to make by land. La Bourdonnais' time was now come.

Meanwhile, on the mainland of the Indian peninsula, Dupleix had been forming wide views and laying broad foundations for the establishment of French proponderance. He saw that through the progress and extension of the European races over the seas of the whole world the time had come when the Eastern peoples must be brought into ever-increasing contact with them; and he judged that India, so often conquered before, was now about to be conquered by Europeans. He meant that France should win the prize, and saw in England the only rival. His plan was to meddle in Indian politics: first, as head of a foreign and independent colony, which he already was; and

second, as a vassal of the Great Mogul, which he intended to become. To divide and conquer, to advance the French lines and influence by judicious alliances, to turn wavering scales by throwing in on one side or the other the weight of French courage and skill—such were his aims.

Let it be noted, however, that the kernel of the question now before Dupleix was not how to build up an empire out of the Indian provinces and races, but how to get rid of the English, and that finally. The wildest dreams of sovereignty he may have entertained could not have surpassed the actual performance of England a few years later. European qualities were bound to tell, if not offset by the opposition of other Europeans; and such opposition on the one side or the other depended upon the control of the sea. As everywhere and always, the action of sea power was here quiet and unperceived; but it will not be necessary to belittle in the least the qualities and career of Clive the English hero of this time and the founder of their empire, in order to prove the decisive influence which it exerted, despite the inefficiency of the English naval officers first engaged, and the lack of conclusive results in such naval battles as were fought.

The English, in 1745, made preparations to besiege Pondicherry, in which the royal navy was to support the land forces; but the effects of Dupleix's political schemes were at once seen. The Nabob of the Carnatic threatened to attack Madras, and the English desisted. The following year La Bourdonnais appeared on the scene, and an action took place between his squadron and that under Commodore Peyton; after which, although it had been a drawn fight, the English officer deserted the coast, taking refuge in Ceylon, and leaving the control at sea with the French.

During 1747 the disasters to the French navy in the Atlantic left the English undisturbed masters of the sea. In the following winter they sent to India the greatest European fleet yet seen in the East, with a large land force, the whole under the command of Admiral Boscawen, who bore a general's commission in addition to his naval rank. The fleet appeared off the Coromandel coast in August, 1748. Pondicherry was attacked by land and sea, but Dupleix made a successful resistance. The English fleet in its turn suffered from a hurricane, and the siege was raised in October. Shortly after came the news of the Peace of Aix-la-Chapelle, which ended the European war. Dupleix, with his home communications restored, could now resume his subtle and persevering efforts to secure a territorial base which should, as far as possible, shelter him from the chances of sea war. Pity that so much genius and patience should have been spent in an effort wholly vain; nothing could protect against that sea attack but a naval aid, which the home government could not give.

The Treaty of Aix-la-Chapelle, ending this general war, was signed April 30, 1748, by England, France, and Holland, and finally by all the powers in October of the same year. With the exception of certain portions shorn off the Austrian Empire—Silesia for Prussia, Parma for the Infante Philip of Spain, and some Italian territory to the east of Piedmont for the King of Sardinia—the general tenor of the terms was a return to the status before the war.

To conclude, France was forced to give up her conquests for want of a navy, and England saved her position by her sea power, though she had failed to use it to the best advantage.

Below: *The French fortress of Louisburg on Cape Breton Island defied capture in 1745 but in 1758 it fell, marking the beginning of the end of French rule in Canada.*

LES HÉROS DE LA PATRIE
Dupleix, conquérant des Indes

Right: *The Marquis Joseph François Dupleix, French governor-general of India, whose forces were finally defeated.*

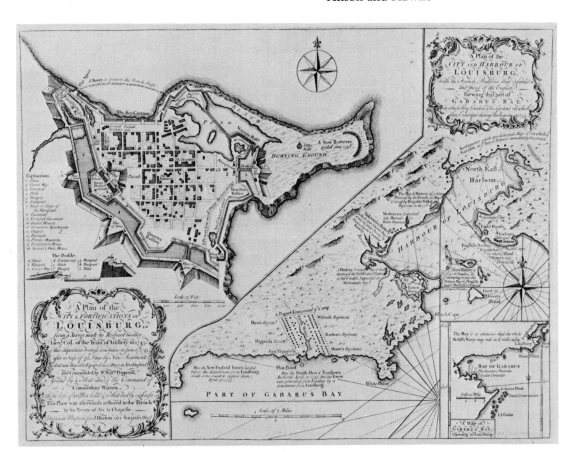

Left: *Plan of the fortress of Louisburg during the siege of 1745.*

Below: *Hogarth's depiction of Captain Lord Graham in his cabin, lying off Ostend in June 1745. He fought in the War of the Austrian Succession.*

Chapter 6

Quiberon Bay

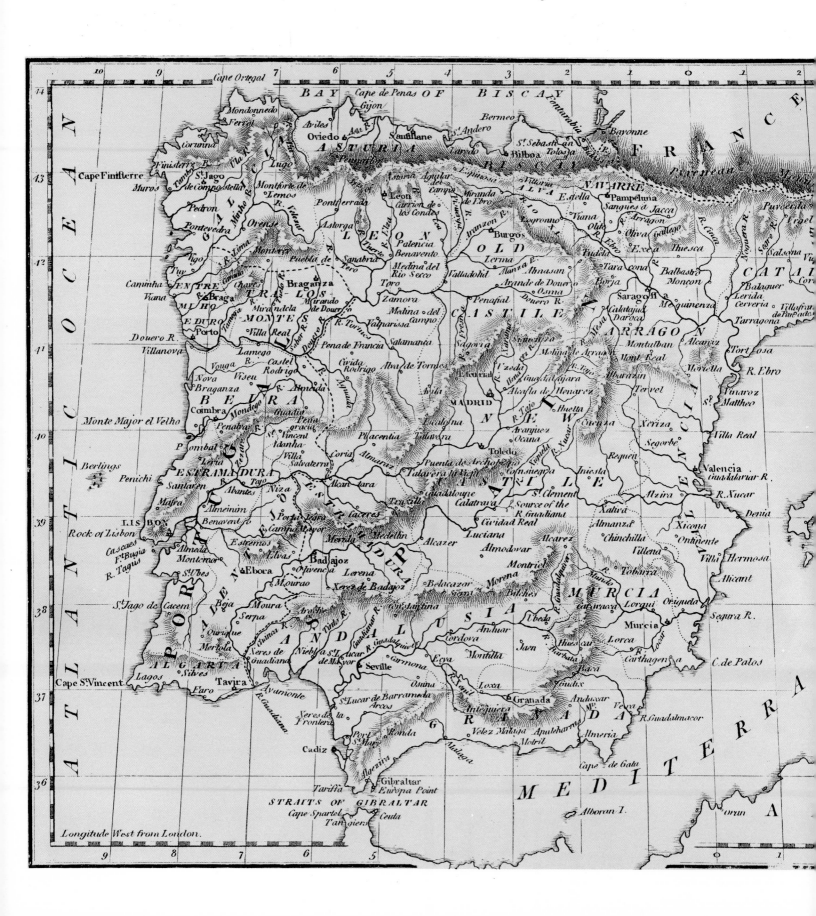

The urgency with which peace was desired by the principal parties to the War of the Austrian Succession may perhaps be inferred from the neglect to settle definitely and conclusively many of the questions outstanding between them, and notably the very disputes about which the war between England and Spain began. The right of uninterrupted navigation in West Indian seas, free from any search, was left undetermined, as were other kindred matters. The true character of the strife, shrouded for a moment by the continental war, was revealed by the so-called peace; though formally allayed, the contention continued in every part of the world. Before the end of 1755, three hundred trading vessels, valued at six million dollars, had been captured, and six thousand French seamen were imprisoned in England—enough to man nearly ten ships-of-the-line. All this was done while nominal peace still existed. War was not declared until six months later.

France seemed to submit, but she was biding her time, and preparing warily a severe stroke for which she had now ample provocation. Small squadrons, or detachments of ships, were sent to the West Indies and to Canada, while noisy preparations were made in the dock-yard of Brest, and troops assembled upon the shores of the Channel. England saw herself threatened with invasion—a menace to which her people have been peculiarly susceptible. The government of the day, weak at best,

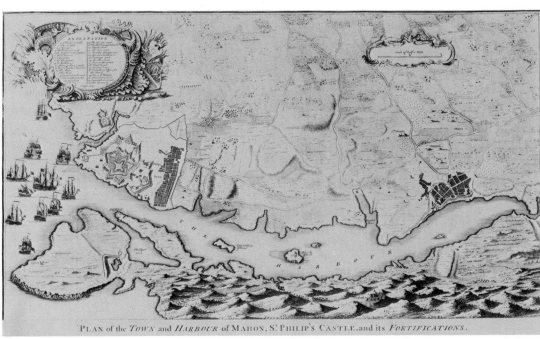

PLAN of the TOWN and HARBOUR of MAHON, St PHILIP'S CASTLE, and its FORTIFICATIONS.

Above: *Plan of Port Mahon, Minorca, a magnificent natural harbor with ample fresh water.*

was singularly unfit for waging war, and easily misled as to the real danger. Besides, England was embarrassed, as always at the beginning of a war, not only by the numerous points she had to protect in addition to her commerce, but also by the absence of a large number of her seamen in trading vessels all over the world. The Mediterranean was therefore neglected; and the French, while making loud demonstrations on the Channel, quietly equipped at Toulon twelve ships-of-the-line, which sailed on the 10th of April, 1756, under Admiral la Galissonière, convoying one hundred and fifty transports with fifteen thousand troops, commanded by the Duke of Richelieu. A week later the army was safely landed in Minorca, and Port Mahon invested, and the fleet established in blockade before the harbor.

Practically this was a complete surprise; for though the suspicions of the English government had been at last aroused, its action came too late. The garrison had not been reinforced, and numbered a scant three thousand men, from which thirty-five officers were absent on leave, among them the governor and the colonels of all the regiments. Admiral Byng sailed from Portsmouth with ten ships-of-the-line only three days before the French left Toulon. Six weeks later, when he reached the neighborhood of Port Mahon, his fleet had been increased to thirteen ships-of-the-line, and he had with him four thousand troops. It was already late; a practicable breach had been made in the fortress a week before. When the English fleet came in sight, la Galissonière stood out to meet it and bar the entrance to the harbor.

The battle that followed owes its historical celebrity wholly to the singular and tragic event which arose from it. Unlike

Left: *Spain and Portugal, showing Minorca (right), the key to the Central Mediterranean.*

Above: *Admiral the Hon John Byng was the son of Sir George Byng, victor of Cape Passaro and later Viscount Torrington. He had a distinguished career before he became a political scapegoat.*

Matthews' battle off Toulon, it does afford some tactical instruction, though mainly applicable to the obsolete conditions of warfare under sail; but it is especially linked to the earlier action through the effect produced upon the mind of the unfortunate Byng by the sentence of the court-martial upon Matthews. During the course of the engagement he repeatedly alluded to the censure upon the admiral for leaving the line, and seems to have accepted the judgment as justifying, if not determining, his own course. Briefly, it may be said that the two fleets, having sighted each other on the morning of the 20th of May, were found after a series of manoeuvres both on the port tack, with an easterly wind, heading southerly, the French to leeward, between the English and the harbor. Byng ran down in line ahead off the wind, the French remaining by it, so that when the former made the signal to engage, the fleets were not parallel, but formed an angle of from thirty to forty degrees. The attack which Byng by his own account meant to make, each ship against its opposite in the enemy's line, difficult to carry out under any circumstances, was here further impeded by the distance between the two rears being much greater than that between the vans; so that his whole line could not come into action at the same moment. When the signal was made, the van ships kept away in obedience to it, and ran down for the French so nearly head-on as to sacrifice their artillery fire in great measure; they received three raking broadsides, and were seriously dismantled aloft. The sixth English ship, counting from the van, had her foretopmast shot away, flew up into the wind, and came back, stopping and doubling up the rear of the

line. Then undoubtedly was the time for Byng, having committed himself to the fight, to have set the example and borne down, just as Farragut did at Mobile when his line was confused by the stopping of the next ahead: but according to the testimony of the flag-captain, Matthews' sentence deterred him.

The affair became entirely indecisive; the English van was separated from the rear and got the brunt of the fight. One French authority blames Galissonière for not tacking to windward of the enemy's van and crushing it. The true reason is probably that given and approved by one of the French authorities on naval warfare. Galissonière considered the support of the land attack on Mahon paramount to any destruction of the English fleet, if he thereby exposed his own. 'The French navy has always preferred the glory of assuring or preserving a conquest to that more brilliant perhaps, but actually less real, of taking some ships, and therein has approached more nearly the true end that has been proposed in war.' The justice of this conclusion depends upon the view that is taken of the true end of naval war. If it is merely to assure one or more positions ashore, the navy becomes simply a branch of the army for a particular occasion, and subordinates its action accordingly; but if the true end is to preponderate over the enemy's navy and so control the sea, then the enemy's ships and fleets are the true objects to be assailed on all occasions. A glimmer of this view seems to have been present to Morogues when he wrote that at sea there is no field of battle to be held, nor places to be won. If naval warfare is a war of posts, then the action of the fleets must be subordinate to the attack and defence of the posts; if its object is to break up the enemy's power on the sea, cutting off his communications with the rest of his possessions, drying up the sources of his wealth in his commerce, and making possible a closure of his ports, then the object of attack must be his organized military forces afloat; in short, his navy. During the remainder of this war the French fleets, except in the East Indies, appear only as the pursued in a general chase.

The action imposed upon the French fleets was, however, consistent with the general policy of the French government; and John Clerk was probably right in saying that there is apparent in this action off Minorca a tactic too well defined to be merely accidental—a tactic essentially defensive in its scope and aim. In assuming the lee-gage the French admiral not only covered Mahon, but took a good defensive position, imposing upon his enemy the necessity of attacking with all the consequent risks. Clerk seems to bring evidence enough to prove that the leading French ships did, after roughly handling their assailants, astutely withdraw thus forcing the latter to attack again with like results. The same policy was repeatedly followed during the American war twenty years later, and with pretty uniform success; so much so that, although formal avowal of the policy is wanting, it may be concluded that circumspection, economy, defensive war, remained the fixed purpose of the French authorities.

To return to Minorca; after the action of the 20th, Byng called a council of war, which decided that nothing more could be done, and that the English fleet should go to Gibraltar and cover that place from an attack. At Gibraltar, Byng was relieved by Hawke and sent home to be tried. The court-martial, while expressly clearing him of cowardice or disaffection, found him guilty of not doing his utmost either to defeat the French fleet or to relieve the garrison at Mahon; and, as the article of war prescribed death with no alternative punishment for this offence, it felt compelled to sentence him to death. The king refused to pardon, and Byng was accordingly shot.

The expedition against Minorca was begun while nominal peace still lasted. On the 17th of May, three days before Byng's

Above: *Sir Edward Hawke relieved Admiral Byng after his failure to relieve Minorca in 1756.*

battle, England declared war, and France replied on the 20th of June. On the 28th, Port Mahon surrendered, and Minorca passed into the hands of France.

The nature of the troubles between the two nations, and the scenes where they occurred, pointed out clearly enough the proper theatre of the strife, and we should by rights now be at the opening of a sea war, illustrated by great naval actions and attended with great modifications in the colonial and foreign possessions of the two powers. Of the two, England alone recognized the truth; France was again turned aside from the sea by causes which will shortly be given. Her fleets scarcely appeared; and losing the control of the sea, she surrendered one by one her colonies and all her hopes in India. Later in the struggle she drew in Spain as her ally, but it was only to involve that country in

Above: *The execution of Admiral Byng on the quarterdeck of HMS* Monarch *on 14 March 1757*, pour encourager les autres.

Below: *Byng's abortive attempt to relieve Minorca, 20 May 1756. He had consulted with his captains, who agreed that his squadron ought to withdraw to Gibraltar to refit and repair damage, but this did not help him to escape the firing squad.*

Left: *Major General James Wolfe, victor of Quebec. Although highly strung and volatile, his naval opposite number Admiral Saunders gave him steady support and sound advice.*

Right: *The attack on Quebec in September 1759 was a masterpiece of collaboration between the army and the navy, largely thanks to the patience of Saunders.*

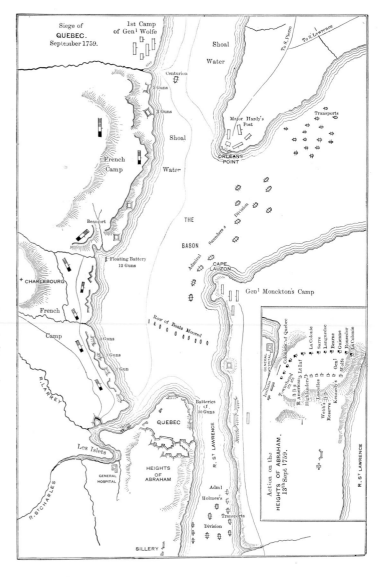

her own external ruin. England, on the other hand, defended and nourished by the sea, rode it everywhere in triumph. Secure and prosperous at home, she supported with her money the enemies of France. At the end of seven years the kingdom of Great Britain had become the British Empire.

It is far from certain that France could have successfully contended with England on the sea, without an ally. In 1756 the French navy had sixty-three ships-of-the-line, of which forty-five were in fair condition; but equipments and artillery were deficient. Spain had forty-six ships-of-the-line; but from the previous and subsequent performances of the Spanish navy, it may well be doubted if its worth were equal to its numbers. England at this time had one hundred and thirty ships-of-the-line; four years later she had one hundred and twenty actually in commission. Of course when a nation allows its inferiority, whether on land or sea, to become as great as that of France now was, it cannot hope for success.

Nevertheless, she obtained advantages at first. The conquest of Minorca was followed in November of the same year by the acquisition of Corsica. The republic of Genoa surrendered to France all the fortified harbors of the island. With Toulon, Corsica, and Port Mahon, she now had a strong grip on the Mediterranean. In Canada, the operations of 1756, under Montcalm, were successful despite the inferiority of numbers. At the same time an attack by a native prince in India took from the English Calcutta, and gave an opportunity to the French.

Instead of concentrating against England, France began another continental war, this time with a new and extraordinary alliance with Austria against Prussia. This alliance was further joined by Russia, Sweden, and Poland.

Frederick the Great, learning the combination against him, instead of waiting for it to develop, put his armies in motion and invaded Saxony, whose ruler was also King of Poland. This movement, in October, 1756, began the Seven Years' War; which, like the War of the Austrian Succession, but not to the same extent, drew some of the contestants off from the original cause of difference.

In the attack upon Canada there were two principal lines to be chosen—that by the way of Lake Champlain, and that by the way of the St Lawrence. The former was entirely inland, and as such does not concern our subject, beyond noting that not till after the fall of Quebec, in 1759, was it fairly opened to the English. In 1757 the attempt against Louisburg failed; the English admiral being unwilling to engage sixteen ships-of-the-line he found there, with the fifteen under his own command, which were also, he said, of inferior metal. Whether he was right in his decision or not, the indignation felt in England

clearly shows the difference of policy underlying the action of the French and English governments. The following year an admiral of a higher spirit, Boscawen, was sent out accompanied with twelve thousand troops, and, it must in fairness be said, found only five ships in the port. The troops were landed, while the fleet covered the siege from the only molestation it could fear, and cut off from the besieged the only line by which they could look for supplies. The island fell in 1758, opening the way by the St Lawrence to the heart of Canada, and giving the English a new base both for the fleet and army.

The next year the expedition under Wolfe was sent against Quebec. All his operations were based upon the fleet, which not only carried his army to the spot, but moved up and down the river as the various feints required. The landing which led to the decisive action was made directly from the ships. Montcalm, whose skill and determination had blocked the attacks by way of Lake Champlain the two previous years, had written urgently for reinforcements; but they were refused by the minister of war, who replied that in addition to other reasons it was too probable that the English would intercept them on the way, and that the more France sent, the more England would be moved to send. In a word, the possession of Canada depended upon sea power.

In 1760, the English, holding the course of the St Lawrence, with Louisburg at one end and Quebec at the other, seemed firmly seated. Nevertheless, the French governor, De Vaudreuil, still held out at Montreal, and the colonists still hoped for help from France. The English garrison at Quebec, though inferior in numbers to the forces of the Canadians, was imprudent

enough to leave the city and meet them in the open field. Defeated there, and pursued by the enemy, the latter nearly entered Quebec pell-mell with the English troops, and trenches were opened against the city. A few days later an English squadron came in sight, and the place was relieved. 'Thus,' says the old English chronicler of the navy, 'the enemy saw what it was to be inferior at sea; for, had a French squadron got the start of the English in sailing up the river, Quebec must have fallen.' Wholly cut off now, the little body of Frenchmen that remained in Montreal was surrounded by three English armies, which had come, one by way of Lake Champlain, the others from Oswego and from Quebec. The surrender of the city on the 8th of September, 1760, put an end forever to the French possession of Canada.

Stung by the constant lashing of the Power of the sea, France, despite the blindness and unwillingness of the rulers, was driven to undertake something against it. With a navy much inferior, unable to cope in all quarters of the world, it was rightly decided to concentrate upon one object; and the object chosen was Great Britain itself, whose shores were to be invaded. This decision, soon apprehended by the fears of the English nation, caused the great naval operations to centre for some years around the coast of France and in the Channel. Before describing

them, it will be well to sum up the general plan by which England was guided in the use of her overwhelming sea power.

Besides the operations on the North American continent already described, this plan was fourfold:

1 The French Atlantic ports were watched in force, especially Brest, so as to keep the great fleets or small squadrons from getting out without fighting.

2 Attacks were made upon the Atlantic and Channel coasts with flying squadrons, followed at times by the descent of small bodies of troops.

3 A fleet was kept in the Mediterranean and near Gibraltar to prevent the French Toulon fleet from getting round to the Atlantic. The action of the Mediterranean fleet, though an independent command, was subsidiary to that in the Atlantic.

4 Distant foreign expeditions were sent against the French colonies in the West India Islands and on the coast of Africa, and a squadron was maintained in the East Indies to secure the control of those seas, thereby supporting the English in the Peninsula, and cutting off the communications of the French. These operations in distant waters, never intermitted, assumed greater activity and larger proportions after the destruction of the French navy had relieved England from the fear of invasion, and when the ill-advised entrance of Spain into the war, in 1762, offered yet richer prizes to her enterprise.

The close blockade of the enemy's fleet in Brest, which was first systematically carried out during this war, may be considered rather a defensive than an offensive operation; for though the intention certainly was to fight if opportunity offered, the chief object was to neutralize an offensive weapon in the enemy's hands; the destruction of the weapon was secondary. The effect of the blockade in this and after wars was to keep the French in a state of constant inferiority in the practical handling of their ships, however fair-showing their outward appearance or equal their numerical force.

In the latter part of 1758, France, depressed by the sense of failure upon the continent, mortified and harassed by English descents upon her coasts, which had been particularly annoying that year, and seeing that it was not possible to carry on both the continental and sea wars with her money resources, determined to strike directly at England. Her commerce was annihilated while the enemy's throve. It was the boast of London merchants

Top: *A view of the taking of Quebec in 1759, by the English forces, showing the Heights of Abraham and the assault on the cliffs.*

Right: *The cutting out of the* Bienfaisant *and burning of the* Prudent *in the harbor of Louisburg on the night of 25–26 July 1758. The fortress capitulated next day.*

that under Pitt commerce was united with and made to flourish by war; and this thriving commerce was the soul also of the land struggle, by the money if lavished on the enemy of France.

At this time a new and active-minded minister, Choiseul, was called into power by Louis XV. From the beginning of 1759, preparations were made in the ocean and Channel ports. Flatboats to transport troops were built at Havre, Dunkirk, Brest, and Rochefort. It was intended to embark as many as fifty thousand men for the invasion of England, while twelve thousand were to be directed upon Scotland. Two squadrons were fitted out, each of respectable strength, one at Toulon, the other at Brest. The junction of these two squadrons at Brest was the first step in the great enterprise.

It was just here that it broke down, through the possession of Gibraltar by the English, and their naval superiority. It seems

Above: *In the Battle of Cape François in the West Indies in October 1757 three English 3rd Rates beat a force of seven French convoying a large fleet of merchantmen. Captain Forest commanded the* August *(60 guns) and Nelson's uncle, Maurice Suckling, commanded the* Dreadnought *(60 guns).*

Opposite: *Captain James Cook was much more than a competent navigator. His intellectual abilities made him a leading scientific figure and his achievements transformed the very nature of sea power. The improvements in navigation, astronomy and timekeeping in the second half of the eighteenth century made a vast expansion in overseas trade possible.*

Left: *The appointment of the Duc de Choiseul in 1761 to the post of Secretary of the Navy in addition to being Minister of War meant that for the first time the two services were under joint control. His drive and energy came too late to retrieve the disasters of the Seven Years' War but the results were seen in 1776.*

Below: *The great-grandson of the Sun King succeeded him in 1715 as the five-year old Louis XV. This meant a series of regencies during which great strides were made in regenerating French sea power. But the King when he assumed full power showed an unfortunate habit of conducting secret diplomacy without consulting his ministers.*

incredible that even the stern and confident William Pitt should, as late as 1757, have offered to surrender to Spain the watch-tower from which England overlooks the road between the Mediterranean and the Atlantic, as the price of her help to recover Minorca. Happily for England, Spain refused. In 1759, Admiral Boscawen commanded the English Mediterranean fleet. In making an attack upon French frigates in Toulon roads, some of his ships were so damaged that he sailed with his whole squadron to Gibraltar to refit; taking the precaution, however, to station lookout frigates at intervals, and to arrange signals by guns to notify him betimes of the enemy's approach. Taking advantage of his absence, and in obedience to orders, the French commodore, De la Clue, left Toulon with twelve ships-of-the-line on the 5th of August, and on the 17th found himself at the Straits of Gibraltar, with a brisk east wind carrying him out into the Atlantic. Everything seemed propitious, a thick haze and falling night concealing the French ships from the land, while not preventing their sight of each other, when an English frigate loomed up in the near distance. As soon as she saw the fleet, knowing they must be enemies, she hauled in for the land and began firing signal-guns. Pursuit was useless: flight alone remained. Hoping to elude the chase he knew must follow, the French commodore steered west-northwest for the open sea, putting out all lights; but either from carelessness or disaffection—for the latter is hinted by one French naval officer—five out of the twelve ships headed to the northward and put into Cadiz when on the following morning they could not see the commodore. The latter was dismayed when at daylight he saw his forces thus diminished. At eight o'clock some sails made their

appearance, and for a few minutes he hoped they were the missing ships. Instead of that, they were the lookouts of Boscawen's fleet, which numbering fourteen ships-of-the-line, was in full pursuit. The French formed their order on one of the close-hauled lines, and fled; but of course their fleet-speed was less than that of the fastest English ships. The general rule for all chases where the pursuer is decidedly superior, namely, that order must be observed only so far as to keep the leading ships within reasonable supporting distance of the slower ones, so that they may not be singly overpowered before the latter can come up, was by this time well understood in the English navy, and that is certainly the fitting time for a *mêlée*. Boscawen acted accordingly. The rear ship of the French, on the other hand, nobly emulated the example of L'Étenduère when he saved his convoy. Overtaken at two o'clock by the leading English ship, and soon after surrounded by four others, her captain made for five hours a desperate resistance, from which he could hope, not to save himself, but to delay the enemies long enough for the better sailers to escape. He so far succeeded that—thanks to the injury done by him and their better speed—they did that day escape action at close quarters, which could only have ended in their capture. When he hauled down his flag, his three topmasts were gone, the mizzen-mast fell immediately after, and the hull was so full of water that the ship was with difficulty kept afloat. M de Sabran—his name is worthy to be remembered—had received eleven wounds in this gallant resistance, by which he illustrated so signally the duty and service of a rearguard in retarding pursuit. That night two of the French ships hauled off to the westward, and so escaped. The other four continued their flight as before; but the next morning the commodore, despairing of escape, headed for the Portuguese coast, and ran them all ashore between Lagos and Cape St Vincent. The English admiral followed and attacked them, taking two and burning the others, without regard to the neutrality of Portugal.

The destruction or dispersal of the Toulon fleet stopped the invasion of England, though the five ships that got into Cadiz remained a matter of anxiety to Sir Edward Hawke, who cruised before Brest. Choiseul, balked of his main object, still clung to the invasion of Scotland. The French fleet at Brest, under Marshal de Conflans, a sea officer despite his title, numbered twenty sail-of-the-line, besides frigates. The troops to be embarked are variously stated at fifteen to twenty thousand. The original purpose was to escort the transports with only five ships-of-the-line, besides smaller vessels. Conflans insisted that the whole fleet ought to go. The minister of the navy thought that the admiral was not a sufficiently skilful tactician to be able to check the advance of an enemy, and so insure the safe arrival of the convoy at its destination near the Clyde without risking a decisive encounter. Believing therefore that there would be a general action, he considered that it would be better to fight it before the troops sailed; for if disastrous, the convoy would not be sacrificed, and if decisively victorious, the road would then be clear. The transports were assembled, not at Brest, but in the ports to the southward as far as the mouth of the Loire. The French fleet therefore put to sea with the expectation and purpose of fighting the enemy; but it is not easy to reconcile its subsequent course with that purpose, nor with the elaborate fighting instructions issued by the admiral before sailing.

About the 5th or 6th of November there came on a tremendous westerly gale. After buffeting it for three days, Hawke bore up and ran into Torbay, where he waited for the wind to shift, keeping his fleet in readiness to sail at once. The same, gale while keeping back the French already in Brest, gave the chance to a small squadron under M Bompart, which was expected from the West Indies, to slip in during Hawke's absence. Conflans made his preparations with activity, distributed Bompart's crews among his own ships, which were not very well manned, and got to sea with an easterly wind on the 14th. He stood at once to the southward, flattering himself that he had escaped Hawke. The latter, however, had sailed from Torbay on the 12th; and though again driven back, sailed a second time on the 14th, the same day that Conflans left Brest. He soon reached his station, learned that the enemy had been seen to the southward steering east, and easily concluding that they were bound to Quiberon Bay, shaped his own course for the same place under a press of sail. At eleven p.m. of the 19th the French admiral estimated his position to be seventy miles southwest by west from Belle Isle; (page 145) and the wind springing up fresh from the westward, he stood for it under short sail, the wind continuing to increase and hauling to west-northwest. At daybreak several ships were seen ahead, which proved to be the English squadron of Commodore Duff, blockading Quiberon. The signal was made to chase; and the English, taking flight, separated into two divisions—one going off before the wind, the other hauling up to the southward. The greater part of the French fleet continued its course after the former division, that is, toward the coast; but one ship hauled up for the second. Immediately after, the rear French ships made signal of sails to windward, which were also visible from aloft on board the flag-ship. It must have been about the same moment that the lookout frigate in advance of the English fleet informed her admiral of sails to leeward. Hawke's diligence had brought him up with Conflans, who, in his official reports, says he had considered it impossible that the enemy could have in that neighborhood forces superior or even equal to his own. Conflans now ordered his rear division to haul its wind in support of the ship chasing to the southward and eastward. In a few moments more it was discovered that the fleet to windward numbered twenty-three ships-of-the-line to the French twenty-one, and among them some three-deckers. Conflans then called in the chasing ships and got ready for action. It remained to settle his course under circumstances which he had not foreseen.

It was now blowing hard from the west-northwest, with every appearance of heavy weather, the fleet not far from a lee shore, with an enemy considerably superior in numbers; for besides Hawke's twenty-three of the line, Duff had four fifty-gun ships. Conflans therefore determined to run for it and lead his squadron into Quiberon Bay, trusting and believing that Hawke would not dare to follow, under the conditions of the weather, into a bay which French authorities describe as containing banks and shoals, and lined with reefs which the navigator rarely sees without fright and never passes without emotion. It was in the midst of these ghastly dangers that forty-four large ships were about to engage pell-mell; for the space was too contracted for fleet manoeuvres. Conflans flattered himself that he would get in first and be able to haul up close under the western shore of the bay, forcing the enemy, if he followed, to take position between him and the beach six miles to leeward. None of his expectations were fulfilled. In the retreat he took the head of his fleet; a step not unjustifiable, since only by leading in person could he have shown just what he wanted to do, but unfortunate for his reputation with the public, as it placed the admiral foremost in the flight. Hawke was not in the least, nor for one moment, deterred by the dangers before him, whose full extent he, as a skilful seaman, entirely realized; but his was a calm and steadfast as well as a gallant temper, that weighed risks justly, neither dissembling nor exaggerating. He has not left us his reasoning, but he doubtless felt that the French, leading, would serve partially as pilots, and must take the ground before him; he

believed the temper and experience of his officers, tried by the severe school of the blockade, to be superior to those of the French; and he knew that both the government and the country demanded that the enemy's fleet should not reach another friendly port in safety. On the very day that he was thus following the French, amid dangers and under conditions that have made this one of the most dramatic of sea fights, he was being burnt in effigy in England for allowing them to escape. As Conflans, leading his fleet, was rounding the Cardinals, as the southernmost rocks at the entrance of Quiberon Bay are called, the leading English ships brought the French rear to action. It was another case of a general chase ending in a *mêlée*, but under conditions of exceptional interest and grandeur from the surrounding circumstances of the gale of wind, the heavy sea, the lee shore, the headlong speed, shortened canvas, and the great number of ships engaged. One French seventy-four, closely pressed and out-numbered, ventured to open her lower-deck ports; the sea sweeping in carried her down with all on board but twenty men. Another was sunk by the fire of Hawke's

Above: *After Quiberon Bay Conflans admitted that he had never expected Hawke to follow him inshore. Hawke replied to his navigator, 'You have done your duty in pointing out the risk, now lay me alongside the French Admiral,' and even when the* Essex *and* Resolution *ran aground he pressed on to win the first truly decisive sea battle since the previous century.*

Above left: *On 20 November 1759 Sir Edward Hawke beat the Comte de Conflans at Quiberon Bay. By accepting the risk of going close inshore in a howling gale he was able to destroy the Brest fleet and remove all threat of invasion. More important, it marked the beginning of the end of subservience to the Fighting Instructions and the kindling of a new offensive spirit that reached its height at Trafalgar.*

Below: *The Battle of Quiberon Bay, 20 November 1759.*

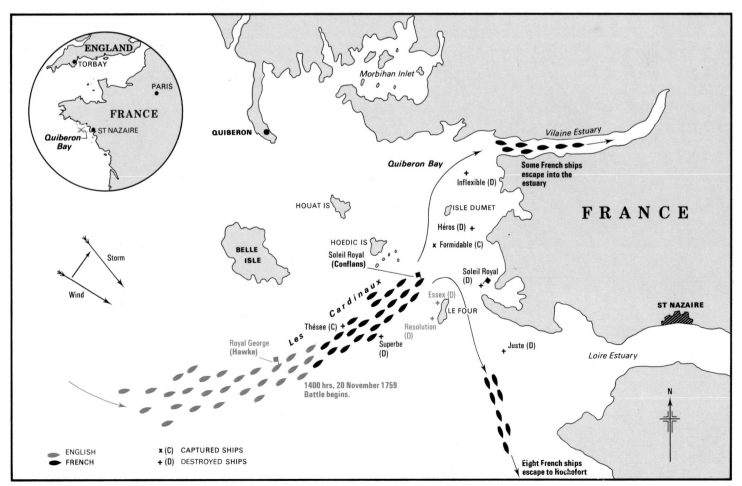

Above: *Vice-Admiral Sir George Pocock was Commander-in-Chief in the Indian Ocean in 1758-59. Although his three actions against D'Aché were indecisive his energetic collaboration with the land commanders helped to overthrow French rule in India.*

Above: *Robert Lord Clive, Baron of Plassey. His conquest of India was made easier by the constant bickering between the French Commodore D'Aché and his land Commander-in-Chief Comte Lally-Tollendal.*

flag-ship. Two others, one of which carried a commodore's pennant, struck their colors. The remainder were dispersed. Seven fled to the northward and eastward, and anchored off the mouth of the little river Vilaine, into which they succeeded in entering at the top of high water in two tides—a feat never before performed. Seven others took refuge to the southward and eastward in Rochefort. One, after being very badly injured, ran ashore and was lost near the mouth of the Loire. The flag-ship bearing the same name as that of Tourville burned at La Hougue, the *Royal Sun*, anchored at nightfall off Croisic, a little to the northward of the Loire, where she rode in safety during the night. The next morning the admiral found himself alone, and, somewhat precipitately it would seem, ran the ship ashore to keep her out of English hands. This step has been blamed by the French, but needlessly, as Hawke would never have let her get away. The great French fleet was annihilated; for the four-teen ships not taken or destroyed were divided into two parts, and those in the Vilaine only succeeded in escaping, two at a time, between fifteen months and two years later. The English lost two ships which ran upon a shoal, and were hopelessly wrecked; their losses in action were slight. At nightfall Hawke anchored his fleet and prizes in position to the southwest of Isle Dumet.

All possibility of an invasion of England passed away with the destruction of the Brest fleet. The battle of November 20,

Above: *The island of Dominica, attacked by Lord Rollo and Sir James Douglas in June 1760. It was retaken by the French during the American Revolutionary War.*

1759, was the Trafalgar of this war; and though a blockade was maintained over the fractions that were laid up in the Vilaine and at Rochefort, the English fleets were now free to act against the colonies of France, and later of Spain, on a grander scale than ever before. The same year that saw this great sea fight and the fall of Quebec witnessed also the capture of Guadeloupe in the West Indies, of Goree on the west coast of Africa, and the abandonment of the East Indian seas by the French flag after three indecisive actions between their commodore, D'Aché, and Admiral Pocock— an abandonment which necessarily led to the fall of the French power in India, never again to rise.

The conditions of India were such that a few Europeans, headed by men of nerve and shrewdness, dividing that they might conquer, and advancing their fortunes by judicious alliances, were able to hold their own, and more too, amidst overwhelming numerical odds; but it was necessary that they should not be opposed by men of their own kind, a few of whom could turn the wavering balance the other way. At the very time that Clive was acting in Bengal, Bussy invaded Orissa, seized the English factories, and made himself master of much of the coast regions between Madras and Calcutta; while a French squadron of nine ships, most of which, however, belonged to the East India Company and were not first-rate men-of-war, was on its way to Pondicherry with twelve hundred regular troops—an enormous European army for Indian operations of that day. The English naval force on the coast, though fewer in numbers, may be considered about equal to the approaching French squadron. It is scarcely too much to say that the future of India was still uncertain, and the first operations showed it.

The French division appeared off the Coromandel coast to the southward of Pondicherry on the 26th of April, 1758, and anchored on the 28th before the English station called Fort St David. Two ships kept on to Pondicherry, having on board the new governor, Comte de Lally, who wished to go at once to his seat of government. Meanwhile, the English admiral, Pocock,

The French effected upon the principal English ship a movement of concentration by defiling past her. The French now stood down to their two separated ships, while the English vessels that had been engaged were too much crippled to follow. This battle prevented the English fleet from relieving Fort St David, which surrendered on the 2nd of June.

After the fall of this place, the two opposing squadrons having refitted at their respective ports and resumed their station, a second action was fought in August, under nearly the same conditions and in much the same fashion. The French flag-ship met with a series of untoward accidents, which determined the commodore to withdraw from action; but the statement of his further reasons is most suggestive of the necessary final overthrow of the French cause. 'Prudence,' a writer of his own country says, 'commanded him not to prolong a contest from which his ships could not but come out with injuries very difficult to repair in a region where it was impossible to supply the almost entire lack of spare stores.' This was of so absolute a requisite for naval efficiency shows in a strong light the fatal tendency of that economy which always characterized French operations at sea, and was at once significant and ominous.

This was the end of the French power in India. The French fleet eventually abandoned the struggle; the English tenure there was never again shaken, even under the attacks of the skilful and bold Suffren, who twenty years later met difficulties as great

having news of the enemy's coming, and fearing specially for this post, was on his way to it, and appeared on the 29th of April, before the two ships with the governor were out of sight. The French at once got under way and stood out to sea on the starboard tack, heading to the northward and eastward, the wind being southeast, and signals were made to recall the ship and frigate escorting Lally; but they were disregarded by the latter's order, an act which must have increased, if it did not originate, the ill-will between him and Commodore d'Aché, through which the French campaign in India miscarried. The English, having formed to windward on the same tack as the French, made their attack in the then usual way, and with the usual results. The seven English ships were ordered to keep away together for the French eight, and the four leading ships, including the admiral's came into action handsomely; the last three, whether by their own fault or not, were late in doing so, but it will remembered that this was almost always the case in such attacks. The French commodore, seeing this interval between the van and the rear, formed the plan of separating them, and made signal to wear together, but in his impatience did not wait for an answer. Putting his own helm up, he wore round, and was followed in succession by the rear ships, while the van stood on.

as D'Aché's with a vigor and conduct which the latter at a more hopeful moment failed to show.

France having thus lost both Canada and India by the evident failure of her power to act at a distance by sea, it would seem scarcely possible that Spain, with her own weak navy and widely scattered possessions, would choose this moment for entering the war. Yet so it was. The maritime exhaustion of France was plain to all, and is abundantly testified to by her naval historians. 'The resources of France were exhausted,' says one, 'the year 1761 saw only a few single ships leave her ports, and all of them were captured. The alliance with Spain came too late. The

Above left: Admiral Keppel's attack on Belle Isle in April 1761. Although these raids were expensive and frequently unsuccessful they were undertaken partly to curb the nuisance of privateering and partly to tie down French forces.

Above: A feature of these raids was 'cutting-out,' or sending in boatloads of armed men to capture an enemy ship by surprise and sail it out to sea.

compact, into which the King of Naples was also to enter, guaranteed their mutual possessions by the whole power of both kingdoms. The grievances and claims of Spain were urged peremptorily, and the quarrel grew so fast that even the new English ministry, though ardently desiring peace, recalled their ambassador before the end of the year, and declared war on the 4th of January, 1762.

On the 5th of March, Pocock, who had returned from the East Indies, sailed from Portsmouth, convoying a fleet of transports to act against Havana; in the West Indies he was reinforced from the forces in that quarter, so that his command contained nineteen ships-of-the-line besides smaller vessels, and ten thousand soldiers.

In the previous January, the West India fleet, under the well-known Rodney, had acted with the land forces in the reduction of Martinique, the gem and tower of the French islands and the harbor of an extensive privateering system. It is said that fourteen hundred English merchantmen were taken during this war in the West Indian seas by cruisers whose principal port was Fort Royal in Martinique. With this necessary base fell also the privateering system resting upon it. Martinique was surrendered February 12, and the loss of this chief commercial and military centre was immediately followed by that of the smaller islands, Grenada, St Lucia, St Vincent. By these acquisitions the English colonies at Antigua, St Kitts, and Nevis, as well as the ships trading to those islands, were secured against the enemy, the commerce of England received large additions, and all the Lesser Antilles, or Windward Islands, became British possessions.

Admiral Pocock was joined off Cape St Nicholas by the West Indian reinforcement on the 27th of May, and as the season was so far advanced, he took his great fleet through the old Bahama channel instead of the usual route around the south side of Cuba. This was justly considered a great feat in those days of poor surveys, and was accomplished without an accident. Look-out and sounding vessels went first, frigates followed, and boats or sloops were anchored on shoals with carefully arranged signals for day or night. Having good weather, the fleet got through in a week and appeared before Havana. The operations will not be given in detail. After a forty days' siege the Moro Castle was taken on the 30th of July, and the city surrendered on the 10th of August. The Spaniards lost not only the city and port, but twelve ships-of-the-line, besides £3,000,000 in money and merchandise belonging to the Spanish king. The importance of Havana was not to be measured only by its own size, or its position as centre of a large and richly cultivated district; it was also the port commanding the only passage by which the treasure and other ships could sail from the Gulf of Mexico to Europe in those days. With Havana in an enemy's hands it would be necessary to assemble them at Cartagena and from there beat up against the trade-winds—an operation always difficult, and which would keep ships long in waters where they were exposed to capture by English cruisers. Not even an attack upon the isthmus would have been so serious a blow to Spain. This important result could only be achieved by a nation confident of controlling the communications by its sea power, to which the happy issue must wholly be ascribed, and which had another signal illustration in the timely conveying of four thousand American troops to reinforce the English ranks, terribly wasted by battle and fever.

While the long reach and vigor of England's sea power was thus felt in the West Indies, it was receiving further illustration in Portugal and in the far East. The allies declared war and invaded Portugal. They were for a time successful; but the 'tyrants of the seas' answered Portugal's call, sent a fleet and landed at Lisbon eight thousand soldiers, who drove the

occasional ships that went to sea in 1762 were taken, and the colonies still remaining to France could not be saved.' The destruction of French commerce, beginning by the capture of its merchant-ships, was consummated by the reduction of the colonies. It can hardly, therefore, be conceded that the Family Compact now made between the two courts, containing, as it did, not only an agreement to support each other in any future war, but also a secret clause binding Spain to declare war against England within a year, if peace were not made, 'was honorable to the wisdom of the two governments.' The possession of unlimited power, as the sea power of England then really was, is seldom accompanied by a profound respect for the rights of others. Without a rival upon the ocean, it suited England to maintain that enemy's property was liable to capture on board neutral ships, thus subjecting these nations not only to vexatious detentions, but to loss of valuable trade; just as it had suited her earlier in the war to establish a paper blockade of French ports. Neutrals of course chafed under these exactions; but the year 1761 was ill-chosen for an armed protest, and of all powers Spain risked most by a war. England had then one hundred and twenty ships-of-the-line in commission, besides those in reserve, manned by seventy thousand seamen trained and hardened by five years of constant warfare afloat, and flushed with victory. The navy of France, which numbered seventy-seven ships-of-the-line in 1758, lost as prizes to the English in 1759 twenty-seven, besides eight destroyed and many frigates lost; indeed, as has been seen, their own writers confess that the navy was ruined, root and branch. The Spanish navy contained about fifty ships; but the personnel, unless very different from the days before and after, must have been very inferior. Neutrality, too, though at times outraged, had been of great advantage to her, permitting her to restore her finances and trade and to re-establish her internal resources; but she needed a still longer period of it. Nevertheless, the king, influenced by family feeling and resentment against England, allowed himself to be drawn on by the astute Choiseul, and the Family Compact between the two crowns was signed on the 15th of August, 1761. This

Left: *Three ships of the line attacking Moro Castle during the siege of Havana. Ships bombarding forts were vulnerable to attack with red-hot shot, but a large ship's broadside could provide a greater concentration of fire. The hazards of working close inshore also made actions against forts unpopular.*

Below: *The reduction of the fortress of Havana was finally accomplished after a 40-day siege. This view of the landing of the troops was painted by Dominic Serres.*

Spaniards over the frontiers, and even carried the war into Spain itself.

Simultaneous with these significant events, Manila was attacked. With so much already on hand, it was found impossible to spare troops or ships from England. The successes in India and the absolute security of the establishments there, with the control of the sea, allowed the Indian officials themselves to undertake this colonial expedition. It sailed in August, 1762, and reaching Malacca on the 19th, was supplied at that neutral port with all that was needed for the siege about to be undertaken; the Dutch, though jealous of the English advance, not venturing to refuse their demands. The expedition, which depended entirely upon the fleet, resulted in the whole group of Philippine Islands surrendering in October and paying a ransom of four million dollars. At about the same time the fleet captured the Acapulco galleon having three million dollars on board, and an English squadron in the Atlantic took a treasure-ship from Lima with four million dollars in silver for the Spanish government.

The selection of the points of attack, due to the ministry of Pitt, was strategically good, cutting effectually the sinews of the enemy's strength; and if his plans had been fully carried out and Panama also seized, the success would have been yet more decisive. England had lost also the advantage of the surprise he would have effected by anticipating Spain's declaration of war; but her arms were triumphant during this short contest, through the rapidity with which her projects were carried into execution, due to the state of efficiency to which her naval forces and administration had been brought.

Before giving the terms of peace, it is necessary to trace in outline the effect of the war upon commerce, upon the foundations of sea power and national prosperity.

One prominent feature of this war may be more strongly impressed upon the mind by a startling, because paradoxical, statement that the prosperity of the English is shown by the magnitude of their losses.

'From 1756 to 1760,' states a French historian, 'French privateers captured from the English more than twenty-five hundred merchantmen. In 1761, though France had not, so to speak, a single ship-of-the-line at sea, and though the English had taken two hundred and forty of our privateers, their comrades still took eight hundred and twelve English vessels. The explanation of the number of these prizes lies in the prodigious growth of the English shipping. In 1760 it is claimed that the English had at sea eight thousand sail; of these the French captured nearly one tenth, despite escorts and cruisers. In the four years from 1756 to 1760 the French lost only nine hundred and fifty vessels.'

But this discrepancy is justly attributed by an English writer 'to the diminution of the French commerce and the dread of falling into the hands of the English, which kept many of their trading-vessels from going to sea;' and he goes on to point out that the capture of vessels was not the principal benefit resulting from the efficiency of England's fleets. The multiplication of French privateers was indeed a sad token to an instructed eye, showing behind them merchant shipping in enforced idleness, whose crews and whose owners were driven to speculative pillage in order to live. But while their commerce was nearly destroyed, and they had few merchant-ships at sea, the trading fleets of England covered the seas. Every year her commerce was increasing; the money which the war carried out was returned by the produce of her industry. Eight thousand vessels were employed by the traders of Great Britain.

No wonder, with such results to her commerce and such unvarying success attending her arms, and seeing the practical annihilation of the French navy, that the union of France and Spain, which was then lowering on her future and had once excited the fears of all Europe, was now beheld by Great Britain alone without the smallest fear of despondency. Spain was by her constitution and the distribution of her empire peculiarly open to the attack of a great sea people; and whatever the views of the government of the day, Pitt and the nation saw that the hour had come, which had been hoped for in vain in 1739,

The Taking of the Island of St Lucia by the Hon. Count Hervey (engraving)

because then years of peace and the obstinate bias of a great minister had relaxed the muscles of her fleet. Now she but reached forth her hand and seized what she wished; nor could there have been any limit to her prey, had not the ministry again been untrue to the interests of the country.

The preliminaries of peace were signed at Fontainebleau, November 3, 1762; the definitive treaty on the 10th of the following February, at Paris, whence the peace takes its name.

By its terms France renounced all claims to Canada, Nova Scotia, and all the islands of the St Lawrence; along with Canada she ceded the valley of the Ohio and all her territory on the east side of the Mississippi, except the city of New Orleans. At the same time Spain, as an equivalent for Havana, which England restored, yielded Florida, under which name were comprised all her continental possessions east of the Mississippi. Thus England obtained a colonial empire embracing Canada, from Hudson's Bay, and all of the present United States east of the Mississippi. The possibilities of this vast region were then only partially foreseen, and as yet there was no foreshadowing of the revolt of the thirteen colonies.

In the West Indies, England gave back to France the important islands of Guadeloupe and Martinique. The four so-called neutral islands of the Lesser Antilles were divided between the two powers; St Lucia going to France, St Vincent, Tobago, and Dominica to England, which also retained Grenada.

Minorca was given back to England; and as the restoration of the island to Spain had been one of the conditions of the alliance with the latter, France, unable to fulfil her stipulation, ceded to Spain Louisiana west of the Mississippi.

In India, France recovered the possessions she had held before Dupleix began his schemes of aggrandizement; but she gave up the right of erecting fortifications or keeping troops in Bengal, and so left the station at Chandernagore defenceless. In a word, France resumed her facilities for trading, but practically abandoned her pretentions to political influence. It was tacitly understood that the English company would keep all its

of the Seven Years' War, 'England had conquered France single-handed almost without allies, France having powerful auxiliaries. She had conquered solely by the superiority of her government.'

Yes! but by the superiority of her government using the tremendous weapon of her sea power. This made her rich, and in turn protected the trade by which she had her wealth. With her money she upheld her few auxiliaries, mainly Prussia and Hanover, in their desperate strife. Her power was everywhere that her ships could reach, and there was none to dispute the sea to her. Where she would she went, and with her went her guns and her troops. By this mobility her forces were multiplied, those of her enemies distracted. Ruler of the seas, she everywhere obstructed its highways.

The one nation that gained in this war was that which used the sea in peace to earn its wealth, and ruled it in war by the extent of its navy, by the number of its subjects who lived on the sea or by the sea, and by its numerous bases of operations scattered over the globe. Yet it must be observed that these bases themselves would have lost their value if their com-

Top: *The Royal Navy's capture of the French trading post of Chandernagore in India, 1757, during the Seven Years' War.*

Opposite: *The capture of St Lucia and Grenada in the West Indies in 1762 followed Rodney's capture of Martinique. The remaining French West Indian possessions were only saved because the Royal Navy turned its attentions to Spain's colonies.*

Left: *Although by no means well known today, the capture of Havana in 1762 was rightly seen as a bold and imaginative strategic stroke, and was commemorated by many artists.*

conquests.

The right of fishing upon the coasts of Newfoundland and in parts of the Gulf of St Lawrence, which France had previously enjoyed, was conceded to her by this treaty; but it was denied to Spain, who had claimed it for her fishermen. This concession was among those most attacked by the English opposition.

'For the first time since the Middle Ages,' says M Martin, speaking

munications remained obstructed. Therefore the French lost Louisburg, Martinique, Pondicherry; so England herself lost Minorca. The service between the bases and the mobile force between the ports and the fleets is mutual. In this respect the navy is essentially a light corps; it keeps open the communications between its own ports, it obstructs those of the enemy; but it sweeps the sea for the service of the land, it controls the desert that man may live and thrive on the habitable globe.

Chapter 7

From Ushant to Chesapeake Bay

If England had reason to complain that she had not reaped from the Treaty of Paris all the advantages that her military achievements and position entitled her to expect, France had every cause for discontent at the position in which the war left her. The gain of England was nearly measured by her losses; even the cession of Florida, made to the conqueror by Spain, had been bought by France at the price of Louisiana. Naturally the thoughts of her statesmen and of her people, as they bent under the present necessity to bear the burden of the vanquished, turned to the future with its possibilities of revenge and compensation. The Duc de Choiseul, able though imperious, remained for many years more at the head of affairs, and worked persistently to restore the power of France from the effects of the treaty.

He continued the restoration of the navy which was accompanied and furthered by a spirit of professional ambition and of desire to excel, among the officers of the navy, which has been before mentioned, and which, in the peculiar condition of the United States navy at the present day, may be commended as a model. The building of ships-of-war continued with great activity and on a large scale.

On the 10th of May, 1774, Louis XV died, at the time when the troubles in the North American colonies were fast coming to a head. Under his youthful successor, Louis XVI, the policy of peace on the continent, of friendly alliance with Spain, and of building up the navy in numbers and efficiency, was continued. This was the foreign policy of Choiseul, directed against the sea

Above: *Models such as this French 74* le Sceptre *were part of the design of eighteenth-century warships, enabling details to be discussed before the final plans were approved. Rigged models were more rare, and were often used for instruction of riggers.*

power of England as the chief enemy, and toward the sea power of France as the chief support, of the nation. The instructions which, according to a French naval author, the new king gave to his ministers show the spirit with which his reign up to the Revolution was inspired, whether or not they originated with the king himself:

'To watch all indications of approaching danger; to observe by cruisers the approaches to our islands and the entrance of the Gulf of Mexico; to keep track of what was passing on the banks of Newfoundland, and to follow the tendencies of English commerce; to observe in England the state of the troops and armaments, the public credit and the ministry; to meddle adroitly in the affairs of the British colonies; to give the insurgent colonists the means of obtaining supplies of war, while maintaining the strictest neutrality; to develop actively, but noiselessly, the navy; to repair our ships of war; to fill our storehouses and to keep on hand the means for rapidly equipping a fleet at Brest and at Toulon, while Spain should be fitting one at Ferrol; finally, at the first serious fear of rupture, to assemble numerous troops upon the shore of Brittany and Normandy, and get everything ready for an invasion of England, so as to force her to concentrate her forces, and thus restrict her means of resistance at the extremities of the empire.'

In the matter of developing the navy fifteen years of peace and steady work showed good results. When war openly broke out in 1778, France had eighty ships-of-the-line in good condition, and sixty-seven thousand seamen were borne on the rolls of the maritime conscription. Spain, when she entered the war in 1779 as the ally of France, had in her ports nearly sixty ships-of-the-line. To this combination England opposed a total number of two hundred and twenty-eight ships of all classes, of which about one hundred and fifty were of the line. The

Bottom: *A French 74-gun 3rd Rate. France took the lead in advancing the theoretical study of naval architecture in the early eighteenth century, and as a result French ships gained a reputation for being faster and handier. But these advantages were achieved at a cost of robust construction and ability to withstand weather damage. This suited the French strategic position, as they became more and more content to achieve 'sea denial,' but the British sought 'sea control' and so their ships needed weatherliness and heavier gunpowder.*

Below: *HMS* London, *a 90-gun 2nd Rate lying off Rame Head, near Plymouth, c 1781. She was launched at Chatham in 1766 and broken up in 1811. The system of Rates was adjusted as warships grew bigger during the eighteenth century but it remained broadly constant: 1st to 3rd Rates were fit to 'lie in the line' but 4th to 6th Rates (frigates), sloops and brigs were not. Elderly 1st Rates, for example, were often reduced to 2nd Rates by a slight reduction in armament, and on occasions two-deckers were 'razéed' by one deck, turning them into frigates.*

Left: *Louis XVI made an effort to remedy the indifference of Louis XV by appointing energetic officials to run the navy. During his reign the dire influence of the professional corps of administrators, la plume, was finally stamped out, but at the cost of putting the burden on the shoulders of sea officers.*

Below: The continent of North America in 1805. The War of 1812 did not disturb the boundaries between Canada and the United States settled at the end of the Revolutionary War.

NORTH AMERICA.

Right: The brig Lexington, one of the new ships acquired by the fledgling Continental Navy in 1776. Her first captain was Lieutenant John Paul Jones.

apparent equality in material which would result from these numbers was affected, to the disadvantage of England, by the superior size and artillery of the French and Spaniards; but on the other hand her strength was increased by the unity of aim imported by belonging to one nation. The allies were destined to feel the proverbial weakness of naval coalitions, as well as the degenerate administration of Spain, and the lack of habit—may it not even be said without injustice, of aptitude for the sea—of both nations. The naval policy with which Louis XVI began his reign was kept up to the end; in 1791, two years after the assembly of the States-General, the French navy numbered eighty-six ships-of-the-line, generally superior, both in dimen-

sions and model, to English ships of the same class.

We have come, therefore, to the beginning of a truly maritime war; which, as will be granted by those who have followed this narrative, had not been seen since the days of De Ruyter and Tourville. The magnificence of sea power and its value had perhaps been more clearly shown by the uncontrolled sway, and consequent exaltation, of one belligerent; but the lesson thus given, if more striking, is less vividly interesting than the spectacle of that sea power meeting a foe worthy of its steel, and excited to exertion by a strife which endangered, not only its most valuable colonies, but even its own shores. Waged, from the extended character of the British Empire, in all quarters of

Right: The fourth Earl of Sandwich, First Lord of the Admiralty before the Revolutionary War. Known to his opponents as 'Jemmy Twitcher,' his administration was harshly criticized but throughout the long and gruelling sea war of 1776–83 the Royal Dockyards proved faster and more proficient than the French at building and repairing warships. Even more important, they were able to introduce the radical improvement of coppering ships against shipworm, the Royal Navy's 'secret weapon' against the French. The painting is by Gainsborough.

the world at once, the attention of the student is called now to the East Indies and now to the West; now to the shores of the United States and thence to those of England; from New York and Chesapeake Bay to Gibraltar and Minorca, to the Cape Verde Islands, the Cape of Good Hope, and Ceylon. Fleets now meet fleets of equal size, and the general chase and the *mêlée*, which marked the actions of Hawke, Boscawen, and Anson, though they still occur at times, are for the most part succeeded by wary and complicated manoeuvres, too often barren of decisive results as naval battles, which are the prevailing characteristic of this coming war. The superior tactical science of the French succeeded in imparting to this conflict that peculiar feature of their naval policy, which subordinated the control of the sea by the destruction of the enemy's fleets, of his organized naval forces, to the success of particular operations, the retention of particular points, the carrying out of particular ulterior strategic ends. It is not necessary to endeavor to force upon others the conviction of the present writer that such a policy, however applicable as an exception, is faulty as a rule; but it is most desirable that all persons responsible for the conduct of naval affairs should recognize that the two lines of policy, in direct contradiction to each other, do exist. In the one there is a strict analogy to a war of posts; while in the other the objective is that force whose destruction leaves the posts unsupported and therefore sure to fall in due time. These opposing policies being recognized, consideration should also be had of the results of the two as exemplified in the history of England and France.

It was not, however, with such cautious views that the new king at first sought to impress his admirals. In the instructions addressed to the Count d'Orvilliers, commanding the first fleet sent out from Brest, the minister, speaking in the name of the king, says:

'Your duty now is to restore to the French flag the lustre with which it once shone; past misfortunes and faults must be buried out of sight; only by the most illustrious actions can the navy hope to succeed in doing this. His Majesty has the right to expect the greatest efforts from his officers. . . . Under whatever circumstances the king's fleet may be placed, his Majesty's orders, which he expressly charges me to impress upon you, as well as upon all officers in command, are that his ships attack with the greatest vigor, and defend themselves, on all occasions, to the last extremity.'

The brave words of Louis XVI were followed almost immediately by others, of different and qualifying tenor, to Admiral d'Orvilliers before he sailed. He was informed that the king, having learned the strength of the English fleet, relied upon his prudence as to the conduct to be followed at a moment when he had under his orders all the naval force of which France could dispose. As a matter of fact the two fleets were nearly equal; it would be impossible to decide which was the stronger, without detailed information as to the armament of every ship. D'Orvilliers found himself, as many a responsible man has before, with two sets of orders, on one or the other of which he was sure to be impaled, if unlucky; while the government, in the same event, was sure of a scape-goat.

It has been said before that, had the thirteen colonies been islands, the sea power of Great Britain would have so completely isolated them that their fall, one after the other, must have ensued. To this it may be added that the narrowness of the strip then occupied by civilized man, and the manner in which it was intersected by estuaries of the sea and navigable rivers, practically reduced to the condition of islands, so far as mutual support went, great sections of the insurgent country, which were not large enough to stand alone, yet too large for their fall not to have been a fatal blow to the common cause. The most familiar case is that of the line of the Hudson, where the Bay of New York was held from the first by the British, who also took the city in September, 1776, two months after the Declaration of Independence. The difficulties in the way of moving up and down such a stream were doubtless much greater to sailing vessels than they now are to steamers; yet it seems impossible to doubt that active and capable men wielding the great sea power of England could so have held that river and Lake Champlain with ships-of-war at intervals and accompanying galleys as to have supported a sufficient army moving between the head-waters of the Hudson and the lake, while themselves preventing any intercourse by water between New England and the States west of the river. This operation would have closely resembled that by which in the Civil War the United States fleets and armies gradually cut in twain the Southern Confederacy by mastering the course of the Mississippi, and the political results would have been even more important than the military; for at that early stage of the war the spirit of independence was far more general and bitter in the section that would have been cut off—in New England—than in New York and New Jersey, perhaps than anywhere except in South Carolina.

In 1777 the British attempted to accomplish this object by sending General Burgoyne from Canada to force his way by Lake Champlain to the Hudson. At the same time Sir Henry

Below: *George Washington, whose ragged army's survival ultimately depended on French sea power.*

Clinton moved north from New York with three thousand men, and reached West Point, whence he sent by shipping a part of his force up the river to within forty miles of Albany. While Burgoyne, with seven thousand regular troops, besides auxiliaries, was moving down to seize the head-waters of the river, fourteen thousand men were removed from its mouth to the Chesapeake. The eight thousand left in or near New York were consequently tied to the city by the presence of the American army in New Jersey. This disastrous step was taken in August; in October Burgoyne, isolated and hemmed in, surrendered. In the following May the English evacuated Philadelphia, and after a painful and perilous march through New Jersey, with Washington's army in close pursuit, regained New York.

This taking of the British fleet to the head of the Chesapeake, coupled with the ascent of the Potomac in 1814 by English sailing-frigates, shows another weak line in the chain of the American colonies; but it was not, like that of the Hudson and Champlain, a line both ends of which rested in the enemy's power—in Canada on the one hand, on the sea on the other.

As to the sea warfare in general, it is needless to enlarge upon the fact that the colonists could make no head against the fleets of Great Britain, and were consequently forced to abandon the sea to them, resorting only to a cruising warfare, mainly by privateers, for which their seamanship and enterprise well fitted them, and by which they did much injury to English commerce. By the end of 1778 the English naval historian estimates that American privateers had taken nearly a thousand merchant-ships, valued at nearly £2,000,000; he claims, however, that the losses of the Americans were heavier. They should have been; for the English cruisers were both better supported and individually more powerful, while the extension of American commerce had come to be the wonder of the statesmen of the mother-country. When the war broke out, it was as great as that of England herself at the beginning of the century.

An interesting indication of the number of the seafaring population of North America at that time is given by the statement in Parliament by the First Lord of the Admiralty, 'that the navy had lost eighteen thousand of the seamen employed in the last war by not having America,'—no inconsiderable loss to a sea power, particularly if carried over to the ranks of the enemy.

The course of warfare on the sea gave rise, as always, to grievances of neutrals against the English for the seizures of their ships in the American trade. Such provocation, however, was not necessary to excite the enmity and the hopes of France in the harassed state of the British government. The hour of reckoning, of vengeance, at which the policy of Choiseul had aimed, seemed now at hand. The question was early entertained at Paris what attitude should be assumed, what advantage drawn from the revolt of the colonies. It was decided that the latter should receive all possible support short of an actual break with England; and to this end a Frenchman named Beaumarchais was furnished with money to establish a business house which should supply the colonists with warlike stores. Beaumarchais' house was started in 1776; in December of that year Benjamin Franklin landed in France, and in May, 1777, Lafayette came to America. Meanwhile the preparations for war, especially for a sea war, were pushed on; the navy was steadily increased, and arrangements were made for threatening an invasion from the Channel, while the real scene of the war was to be in the colonies.

To this explosive condition of things the news of Burgoyne's surrender acted as a spark. The experience of former wars had taught France the worth of the Americans as enemies, and she was expecting to find in them valuable helpers in her schemes of revenge; now it seemed that even alone they might be able to take care of themselves, and reject any alliance. The tidings reached Europe on the 2nd of December, 1777; on the 16th the French foreign minister informed the commissioners of Congress that the king was ready to recognize the independence of the United States, and to make with them a commercial treaty and contingent defensive alliance. The speed with which the business was done shows that France had made up her mind; and the treaty, so momentous in its necessary consequences, was signed on the 6th of February, 1778.

It is not necessary to give the detailed terms of the treaty; but it is important to observe, first, that the express renunciation of Canada and Nova Scotia by France foreshadowed that political theory which is now known as the Monroe doctrine, the claims of which can scarcely be made good without an adequate sea-force; and next, that the alliance with France, and subsequently with Spain, brought to the Americans that which they above all needed—a sea power to counterbalance that of England. Will it be too much for American pride to admit that, had France refused to contest the control of the sea with England, the latter would have been able to reduce the Atlantic seaboard?

Before going on with the story of this maritime war, the military situation as it existed in the different parts of the world should be stated.

The three features which cause it to differ markedly from that at the opening of the Seven Years' War, in 1756, are— (1) the hostile relation of America to England; (2) the early appearance of Spain as the ally of France; and (3) the neutrality of the other continental States, which left France without preoccupation on the land side.

In Europe the most significant element to be noted is the state of preparedness of the French navy, and to some extent of the Spanish, as compared with previous wars. England stood wholly on the defensive, and without allies; while the Bourbon kings aimed at the conquest of Gibraltar and Port Mahon, and the invasion of England. The first two, however, were the dear objects of Spain, the last of France; and this divergence of aims was fatal to the success of this maritime coalition. In the introductory chapter allusion was made to the strategic question raised by these two policies.

In the West Indies the grip of the two combatants on the land was in fact about equal, though it should not have been so. Both France and England were strongly posted in the Windward Islands—the one at Martinique, the other at Barbadoes. It must be noted that the position of the latter, to windward of all others of the group, was a decided strategic advantage in the days of sail. As it happened, the fighting was pretty nearly confined to the neighborhood of the Lesser Antilles. Here, at the opening of the struggle, the English island of Dominica lay between the French Martinique and Guadeloupe; it was therefore coveted and seized. Next south of Martinique lay St Lucia, a French colony. Its strong harbor on the lee side, known as Gros Ilot Bay, was a capital place from which to watch the proceedings of the French navy in Fort Royal, Martinique. The English captured the island, and from that safe anchorage Rodney watched and pursued the French fleet before his famous action in 1782. The islands to the southward were of inferior military consequence. In the greater islands, Spain should have outweighed England, holding as she did Cuba, Porto Rico, and, with France, Haiti, as against Jamaica alone. Spain, however, counted here for nothing but a dead-weight; and England had elsewhere too much on her hands to attack her. The only point in America where the Spanish arms made themselves felt was in the great region east of the Mississippi, then known as Florida, which, though at that time an English possession, did not join the revolt of the colonies.

The very day the news of the outbreak of war reached Calcutta, July 7, 1778, Hastings sent orders to the governor of Madras to attack Pondicherry, and set the example by seizing Chandernagore. The naval force of each nation was insignificant; but the French commodore, after a brief action, forsook Pondicherry, which surrendered after a siege by land and sea of seventy days. The following March, 1779, Mahé, the last French settlement, fell, and the French flag again disappeared; while at the same time there arrived a strong English squadron of six ships-of-the-line under Admiral Hughes. The absence of any similar French force gave the entire control of the sea to the English until the arrival of Suffren, nearly three years later. In the mean while Holland had been drawn into the war, and her stations, Negapatam on the Coromandel coast, and the very important harbor of Trincomalee in Ceylon, were both captured, the latter in January, 1782, by the joint forces of the army and navy. The successful accomplishment of these two enterprises completed the military situation in Hindostan at the time when the arrival of Suffren, just one month later, turned the nominal war into a desperate and bloody contest. Suffren found himself with a decidedly stronger squadron, but without a port, either French or allied, on which to base his operations against the English.

Of these four chief theatres of the war, two, North America and the West Indies, as might be expected from their nearness, blend and directly affect each other. This is not so obviously the case with the struggles in Europe and India. The narrative therefore naturally falls into three principal divisions, which may to some extent be treated separately. After such separate consideration their mutual influence will be pointed out, together with any useful lessons to be gathered from the goodness or badness, the success or failure, of the grand combinations, and from the part played by sea power.

Above: John Paul Jones, the most dashing captain of the Continental Navy, whose exploits gave the Americans their first naval hero. However he finished his days in the service of foreign navies and died in Paris.

Above: *Commodore Esek Hopkins, Commander-in-Chief of the American Navy, in an engraving by J C Buttre.*

GREAT ENCOURAGEMENT FOR SEAMEN.

ALL GENTLEMEN SEAMEN and able-bodied LANDSMEN who have a Mind to diftinguifh themfelves in the GLORIOUS CAUSE of their Country, and make their Fortunes, an Opportunity now offers on board the Ship RANGER, of Twenty Guns, (for France) now laying in Portfmouth, in the State of New-Hampfhire, commanded by JOHN PAUL JONES Efq; let them repair to the Ship's Rendezvous in Portfmouth, or at the Sign of Commodore Manley, in Salem, where they will be kindly entertained, and receive the greateft Encouragement.—The Ship Ranger, in the Opinion of every Perfon who has feen her is looked upon to be one of the beft Cruizers in America.—She will be always able to Fight her Guns under a moft excellent Cover ; and no Veffel yet built was ever calculated for failing fafter, and making good Weather.

Any Gentlemen Volunteers who have a Mind to take an agreable Voyage in this pleafant Seafon of the Year, may, by entering on board the above Ship Ranger, meet with every Civility they can poffibly expect, and for a further Encouragement depend on the firft Opportunity being embraced to reward each one agreable to his Merit.

All reafonable Travelling Expences will be allowed, and the Advance-Money be paid on their Appearance on Board.

In CONGRESS, March 29, 1777.
Resolved,

THAT the Marine Committee be authorifed to advance to every able Seaman, that enters into the Continental Service, any Sum not exceeding FORTY DOLLARS, and to every ordinary Seaman or Landfman, any Sum not exceeding TWENTY DOLLARS, to be deducted from their future Prize-Money.

By Order of Congress,
JOHN-HANCOCK, President.

On the 13th of March, 1778, the French ambassador at London notified the English government that France had acknowledged the independence of the United States, and made with them a treaty of commerce and defensive alliance. England at once recalled her ambassador; but though war was imminent and England at disadvantage, the Spanish king offered mediation, and France wrongly delayed to strike. In June, Admiral Keppel sailed from Portsmouth, with twenty ships, on a cruise. Falling in with two French frigates, his guns, to bring them to, opened the war. Finding from their papers that thirty-two French ships lay in Brest, he at once returned for reinforcements. Sailing again with thirty ships, he fell in with the French fleet under D'Orvilliers to the westward of Ushant, and to windward, with a westerly wind. On the 27th of July was fought the first fleet action of the war, generally known as the battle of Ushant.

This battle, in which thirty ships-of-the-line fought on either side, was wholly indecisive in its results. No ship was taken or sunk; both fleets, after separating, returned to their respective ports. The action nevertheless obtained great celebrity in England from the public indignation at its lack of result, and from the storm of naval and political controversy which followed. The admiral and the officer third in command belonged to different political parties; they made charges, one against the other, and in the following courts-martial all England divided, chiefly on party lines. Public and naval sentiment generally favored the commander-in-chief, Keppel.

Above: *Lieutenant John Paul Jones hoists the Stars and Stripes aboard the* Lexington *for the first time 4 July 1776.*

Above: *The first salute to the Stars and Stripes by a foreign warship was given to the sloop* Ranger *by the French in Quiberon Bay.*

Top: *Broadsheets or recruiting posters were popular in the eighteenth century. This one recruited for John Paul Jones and the* Ranger.

Far left: *The Hon Augustus Keppel, whose action off Ushant in 1778 was marred by the public outcry against his second-in-command Palliser.*

Center left: *Rear Admiral Richard Kempenfeldt, who lost his life when his flag-ship HMS Royal George capsized in Spithead in 1782.*

Left: *The young Lord Howe, who became Commander-in-Chief during the Revolutionary War, painted by Gainsborough.*

Bottom: *The inconclusive fight off Ushant 27 July 1778, the first major battle of the Revolutionary War. Admiral d'Orvilliers failed to follow up an initial advantage and bad communications between Keppel and Palliser prevented a counterstroke.*

Tactically, the battle presents some interesting features, and involves one issue which is still living today. Keppel was to leeward and wished to force an action; in order to do this he signalled a general chase to windward, so that his fastest ships might overtake the slower ones of the enemy. Granting equal original fleet-speed, this was quite correct. D'Orvilliers, to windward, had no intention of fighting except on his own terms. As will generally be the case, the fleet acting on the offensive obtained its wish. At daybreak of the 27th both fleets were on the port tack, heading west-northwest, with a steady breeze at southwest. The English rear had fallen to leeward, and Keppel consequently made signal to six of its ships to chase to windward, so as to place them in a better position to support the main body if it could get into action. D'Orvilliers observed this movement, and construed it to show an intention to attack his rear with a superior force. The two fleets being then from six to eight miles apart, he wore his fleet in succession, by which he lost ground to leeward, but approached the enemy, and was able to see them better. At the completion of this evolution the wind hauled to the southward, favoring the English; so Keppel, instead of going about, stood on for half an hour more, and then tacked together in wake of the French. This confirmed D'Orvilliers' suspicions, and as the wind, which certainly favored the English that morning, now hauled back again to the westward, permitting them to lay up for the French rear, he wore his fleet together, thus bringing the rest to aid the rear, now

become the van, and preventing Keppel from concentrating on or penetrating it. The two fleets thus passed on opposite tacks, exchanging ineffective broadsides, the French running free to windward and having the power to attack, but not using it. D'Orvilliers then made the signal for his van, formerly the rear, to wear to leeward of the English rear, which was to leeward of its own main body, intending himself to remain to windward and so attack it on both sides; but the commander of that division, a prince of the blood royal, did not obey, and the possible advantage was lost. On the English side the same manoeuvre was attempted. The admiral of the van and some of his ships tacked, as soon as out of fire, and stood after the French rear; but for the most part the damage to rigging prevented tacking, and wearing was impossible on account of the ships coming up behind. The French now stood to leeward and formed line again, but the English were not in condition to attack. This was the end of the battle.

The failure of the Duc de Chartres, commanding the French van during the firing, to wear in obedience to orders, whether due to misunderstanding or misconduct, raises the question, which is still debated, as to the proper position for a naval commander-in-chief in action. Had D'Orvilliers been in the van, he could have insured the evolution he wished. From the centre the admiral has the extremities of his fleet equally visible, or invisible, as it may be. At the head he enforces his orders by his example. The French toward the end of this war solved the question by taking him out of the line altogether and putting him on board a frigate, for the avowed reasons that he could thus better see the movements of his fleet and of the enemy without being blinded by smoke or distracted by the occurrences on board his own ship, and that his signals could be better seen. This position, resembling somewhat that of a general on shore, being remote from personal risk, was also assumed by Lord Howe in 1778; but both that officer and the French abandoned the practice later. Nelson at Trafalgar, the end of his career, led his column; but it may be doubted whether he had any other motive than his ardor for battle. The two other great attacks in which he commanded in chief were directed against ships at anchor, and in neither did he take the head of the column; for the good reason that, his knowledge of the ground being imperfect, the leading ship was in most danger of grounding. The common practice in the days of broadside sailing-ships, except when a general chase was ordered, was for the admiral to be in the line, and in the centre of it. The departure from this custom on the part of both Nelson and Collingwood, each of whom led his own columns at Trafalgar, may have had some reason, and an ordinary man rather shrinks from criticising the action of officers of their eminence. The danger to which were exposed the two senior officers of the fleet, upon whom so much depended, is obvious; and had any serious injury befallen their persons, or the head of their columns, the lack of their influence would have been seriously felt. As it was, they were speedily obliterated, as admirals, in the smoke of the battle, leaving to those who came after them no guidance or control except the brilliancy of their courage and example. A French admiral has pointed out that the practical effect of the mode of attack at Trafalgar, two columns bearing down upon a line at right angles to them, was to sacrifice the head of the columns in making two breaches in the enemy's line. So far, very well; the sacrifice was well worth while; and into these breaches came up the rear ships of each column, nearly fresh, forming in fact a *reserve* which fell upon the shattered ships of the enemy on either side of the breaks. Now this idea of a reserve prompts a thought as to the commander-in-chief. The size of his ship was such as precluded its being out of the order; but would it not have been well had

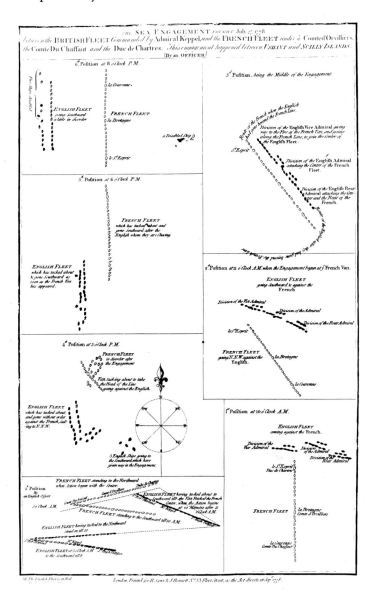

Above: Contemporary track chart of the Battle of Ushant. The differing political affiliations of Keppel and Palliser provided an excuse for a major political uproar and both officers were forced to resign. Sir Hugh Palliser was court-martialled for disobeying orders and even forced to vacate his seat in the House of Commons but Keppel was given the high office of First Lord of the Admiralty.

Below: The Battle of Negapatam, 6 July 1782, one of the series of five hard-fought actions between Hughes and Suffren in 1782–83, which are a byword for doggedness and equally matched skill.

the admiral of each column been with this reserve, keeping in his hands the power of directing it according to the chances of the action, making him a reality as well as a name for some time longer, and to a very useful purpose? The difficulty of arranging any system of signals or light despatch-boats which could take the place of the aids or messengers of a general, coupled with the fact that ships cannot stand still, as divisions of men do, waiting orders, but that they must have steerage-way, precludes the idea of putting an admiral of a fleet under way in a light vessel. By so doing he becomes simply a spectator; whereas by being in the most powerful ship of the fleet he retained the utmost weight possible after action is once engaged, and, if this ship be in the reserve, the admiral keeps to the latest possible moment the power of commander-in-chief in his own hands. 'Half a loaf is better than no bread'; if the admiral cannot, from the conditions of sea warfare, occupy the calmly watchful position of his brother on shore, let there be secured for him as much as may be.

On the 15th of April, 1778, Admiral Comte d'Estaing sailed from Toulon for the American continent, having under his command twelve ships-of-the-line and five frigates. With him went a passenger a minister accredited to Congress, who was instructed to decline all requests for subsidies, and to avoid explicit engagements relative to the conquest of Canada and other British possessions.

Above: *Charles Henri, Comte d'Estaing had been a dashing soldier before his appointment as* Chef d'Escadre *in 1760. His promotion to Vice-Admiral caused considerable jealousy among his fellow flag-officers, and this combined with his caution, caused many problems during the Revolutionary War. His orders to help the American colonists were vague, and although his forces outnumbered the British, Earl Howe was a more energetic and resolute commander.*

D'Estaing's progress was very slow. It is said that he wasted much time in drills, and even uselessly. However that may be, he did not reach his destination, the Capes of the Delaware, until the 8th of July—making a passage of twelve weeks, four of which were spent in reaching the Atlantic. The English government had news of his intended sailing; and in fact, as soon as they recalled their ambassador at Paris, orders were sent to America to evacuate Philadelphia, and concentrate upon New York. Fortunately for them, Lord Howe's movements were marked by a vigor and system other than D'Estaing's. First assembling his fleet and transports in Delaware Bay, and then hastening the embarkation of stores and supplies, he left Philadelphia as soon as the army had marched from there for New York. Ten days were taken up in reaching the mouth of the bay; but he sailed from it the 28th of June, ten days before D'Estaing arrived, though more than ten weeks after he had sailed. Once outside, a favoring wind took the whole fleet to Sandy Hook in two days. War is unforgiving; the prey that D'Estaing had missed by delays foiled him in his attempts upon both New York and Rhode Island.

On the 28th of July Howe was informed that the French fleet, which had disappeared to the southward, had been seen heading for Rhode Island. In four days his fleet was ready for sea, but owing to contrary winds did not reach Point Judith till the 9th of August. There he anchored, and learned that D'Estaing had run the batteries the day before and anchored between Gould and Canonicut Islands; the Seakonnet and Western passages had also been occupied by French ships, and the fleet was prepared to sustain the American army in an attack upon the British works.

The arrival of Howe, although his reinforcements did not raise the English fleet to over two thirds the strength of the French, upset D'Estaing's plans. With the prevailing summer southwest breezes blowing straight into the bay, he was exposed to any attempts his adversary might make. That same night the wind shifted unexpectedly to the northward, and D'Estaing at once got under way and stood out to sea. Howe, though surprised by this unlooked-for act—for he had not felt himself strong enough to attack—also made sail to keep the weather-gage. The next twenty-four hours passed in manoeuvring for the advantage; but on the night of the 11th of August a violent gale of wind dispersed the fleets. Great injury was done to the vessels of both, and among others the French flag-ship *Languedoc*, of ninety guns, lost all her masts and her rudder. Immediately after the gale two different English fifty-gun ships, in fighting order, fell in, the one with the *Languedoc*, the other with the *Tonnant*, of eighty guns, having only one mast standing. Under such conditions both English ships attacked; but night coming on, they ceased action, intending to begin again in the morning. When morning came, other French ships also came, and the opportunity was lost. It is suggestive to note that one of the captains was Hotham, who as admiral of the Mediterranean fleet, seventeen years later, so annoyed Nelson by his cool satisfaction in having taken only two ships: 'We must be contented; we have done very well.' This was the immediate occasion of Nelson's characteristic saying, 'Had we taken ten sail, and allowed the eleventh to escape, being able to get at her, I could never have called it well done.'

The English fell back on New York. The French rallied again off the entrance of Narragansett Bay; but D'Estaing decided that he could not remain on account of the damage to the squadron, and accordingly sailed for Boston on the 21st of August. Scarcely a shot had been exchanged between the two fleets, yet the weaker had thoroughly outgeneralled the stronger. With the exception of the manoeuvres for the weather-gage after D'Estaing left Newport, which have not been preserved, and of Howe's dispositions to receive the expected attack in New York Bay, the lessons are not tactical, but strategic, and of present application. Chief among them undoubtedly stands the value of celerity and watchfulness, combined with knowledge of one's profession. An English narrator in the fleet, speaking of the untiring labor between June 30, when the English army reached Navesink, and the arrival of the French fleet on the 11th of July, says: 'Lord Howe attended in person as usual, and by his presence animated the zeal and quickened the industry of officers and men.' In this quality he was a marked contrast to his amiable but indolent brother, General Howe.

The same industry and watchfulness marked his remaining operations. As soon as the French ships hauled off to the southward, lookout vessels followed them, and preparations continued (notably of fireships) for pursuit. The last ship that joined from England crossed the bar at New York on the 30th of July. On the 1st of August the fleet was ready for sea, with four fireships. The accident of the wind delayed his next movements; but, as has been seen, he came up only one day after the entrance of the enemy into Newport, which his inferior force could not have prevented. But the object of the enemy, which he could not oppose, was frustrated by his presence. D'Estaing was no sooner in Newport than he wished himself out. Howe's position

was strategically excellent. With his weatherly position in reference to the prevailing winds, the difficulty of beating a fleet out through the narrow entrance to the harbor would expose the French ships trying it to be attacked in detail; while if the wind unluckily came fair, the admiral relied upon his own skill to save his squadron.

D'Estaing, having repaired his ships, sailed with his whole force for Martinique on the 4th of November; on the same day Commodore Hotham left New York for Barbados, with five sixty-four and fifty-gun ships and a convoy of five thousand troops, destined for the conquest of St Lucia Island. On the way a heavy gale of wind injured the French fleet more than the English, the French flag-ship losing her main and mizzen topmasts. The loss of these spars, and the fact that twelve unencumbered ships-of-war reached Martinique only one day before the convoy of fifty-nine English transports reached Barbados, a hundred miles farther on, tells badly for the professional skill which then and now is a determining feature in naval war.

Admiral Barrington, commanding at Barbados, showed the same energy as Howe. The transports arrived on the 10th; the troops were kept on board; sailed on the morning of the 12th for St Lucia, and anchored there at three p.m. the 13th The same afternoon half the troops were landed, and the rest

Above: *The Bonhomme Richard was a converted French Indiaman armed with 42 guns, while the Serapis was a new 44-gun 5th Rate, a small two-decker. Apart from the difference in age the two ships were evenly matched, and the outcome of the fight on 23 September 1779 off Flamborough Head finally depended on the personal leadership of John Paul Jones.*

Left: *John Paul Jones hailing HMS Serapis during the fight, a latterday reconstruction of Jones' reply to a call to surrender, 'I have not yet begun to fight.' Lithograph from a painting by Paul Moran.*

the next morning. They seized at once a better port, to which the admiral was about to move the transports when the appearance of D'Estaing prevented him. All that night the transports were being warped inside the ships-of-war, and the latter anchored across the entrance to the bay, especial care being taken to strengthen the two extremities of the line, and to prevent the enemy from passing inside the weather end, as the English ships in after years did at the battle of the Nile. The French was much more than double the English fleet; and if the latter were destroyed, the transports and troops would be trapped.

D'Estaing stood down along the English order twice from north to south, cannonading at long range, but did not anchor. Abandoning then his intentions against the fleet, he moved to another bay, landed some French soldiers, and assaulted the position of the English troops. Failing here also, he retired to Martinique; and the French garrison, which had been driven into the interior of the island, surrendered.

It seems scarcely necessary to point out the admirable diligence of Admiral Barrington, to which and to the skill of his dispositions he owed this valuable strategic success; for such it was. St Lucia was the island next south of Martinique, and the harbor of Gros Ilot at its northern end was especially adapted to the work of watching the French depot at Fort Royal, their principal station in the West Indies. Thence Rodney pursued them before his great action in 1782.

The English had thus retrieved the capture of Dominica, which had been taken on the 8th of September by the French governor of the West India Islands. There being no English squadron there, no difficulty had been met. The value of Dominica to the French has been pointed out; and it is necessary

men surrendered the island. Meanwhile Byron, hearing of the loss of St Vincent and probable attack on Grenada, sailed with a large convoy of vessels carrying troops, and with twenty-one ships-of-the-line, to regain the one and relieve the other. Receiving on the way definite information that the French were before Grenada, he kept on for it, rounding the northwest point of the island at daybreak of July 6. His approach had been reported the day before to D'Estaing, who remained at anchor,

here to use the example of both Dominica and St Lucia to enforce what has before been said, that the possession of these smaller islands depended solely upon the naval preponderance. Upon the grasp of this principle held by any one will depend his criticism upon the next action of D'Estaing, to be immediately related.

Six months of almost entire quiet followed the affair of St Lucia. The English were reinforced by the fleet of Byron, who took chief command; but the French, being joined by ten more ships-of-the-line, remained superior in numbers. About the middle of June, Byron sailed with his fleet to protect a large convoy of merchant-ships, bound for England, till they were clear of the islands. D'Estaing then sent a very small expedition which seized St Vincent, June 16, 1779, without difficulty; and on the 30th of June he sailed with his whole fleet to attack Grenada. Anchoring off Georgetown on the 2nd of July, he landed his soldiers, and on the 4th the garrison of seven hundred

Above: *The Spanish* Santo Domingo *blowing up during the Moonlight Battle of St Vincent. Only four ships-of-the-line escaped, out of the eleven under Don Juan de Langara's command at the outset of the battle.*

Above left: *Known as the 'Moonlight Battle' to distinguish it from the later Battle of Cape St Vincent, Rodney's action of 16 January 1780 relieved the hard-pressed garrison of Gibraltar. The British met 11 ships-of-the-line and two frigates under Don Juan de Langara off Cape St Vincent. The Spanish lost their flag-ship and six others, of which two were driven ashore and a third blew up.*

Right: *Rodney's action off Cape St Vincent was fought with 18 sail of the line, the escort for a large convoy carrying reinforcements and supplies for Gibraltar and Minorca.*

Left: *In the Battle of Grenada on 6 July 1779 Vice-Admiral Byron was caught in a trap by D'Estaing, with a single squadron facing the whole French Fleet. His ships were badly mauled and the 3rd Rate Lion was nearly sunk. But the French obsession with the 'mission' dictated that D'Estaing should break off action just when he had Byron at his mercy. The British sustained a severe tactical defeat for they failed to recapture Grenada but avoided a strategic defeat.*

fearing lest with the currents and light winds he might drop too far to leeward if he let go the bottom. When the English came in sight, the French got under way; but the confused massing of their ships prevented Byron from recognizing at once the disparity of numbers, they having twenty-five ships-of-the-line. He made signal for a general chase, and as the disorder of the French fleet forced it to form on the leewardmost ships, the English easily retained the advantage of the wind with which they approached. As the action began, therefore, the French were to the westward with a partly formed line, on the starboard tack, heading north, the rear in disorder, and to windward of the van and centre. The English stood down with a fair wind, steering south by west on the port tack, between the island and the enemy, their leading ships approaching at a slight angle, but heading more directly for his yet unformed rear; while the English convoy was between its own fleet and the island, under

GEORGE·III

Above: *King George III of England.*

Below: *Plan of the Siege of Yorktown.*

special charge of three ships, which were now called in. As the signal so far commanded a general chase, the three fastest of the English, among which was the flag of the second in command, Admiral Barrington, came under fire of the French centre and rear, apparently unsupported, and suffered much from the consequent concentration of fire upon them. When they reached the sternmost ships they wore upon the same tack with them and stood north, after and to windward of them; and at about the same time Byron, who had not before known of the surrender, saw the French flag flying over the forts. Signals followed to wear in succession, and for the advanced ships to form line for mutual support, ceasing the general chase under which the engagement had hitherto been fought. While the main body was still standing south on the port tack, three ships— *Cornwall*, *Grafton*, and *Lion*—obeying literally the signal for close action, had passed much to leeward of the others, drawing upon themselves most of the fire of the enemy's line. They thus suffered very severely in men and spars; and though finally relieved by the advanced ships, as these approached from the southward on the opposite tack, they were unable, after wearing to keep up with the fleet, and so dropped astern and toward the French. The bulk of the injury sustained by the English fell upon these three, upon the three advanced ships under Barrington, and upon two others in the rear, which, seeing the van so heavily engaged, did not follow the successive movement, but bore down straight out of the order, and took their places at the head of the column—an act strongly resembling that which won Nelson such high renown at Cape St Vincent, but involving less responsibility.

So far Byron had conducted his attack, using the initiative permitted him by the advantage of the wind and the disorder of the French rear. It will be observed that, though it was desirable to lose no time in assailing the latter while in confusion, it is questionable whether Barrington's three ships should have been allowed to separate as far as they seem to have done from the rest of the fleet. A general chase is permissible and proper when, from superiority of numbers, original or acquired, or from the general situation, the ships first in action will not be greatly outnumbered, or subjected to overpowering concentration before support comes up, or when there is probability that the enemy may escape unless promptly struck. This was not so here. Nor should the *Cornwall*, *Grafton*, and *Lion* have been permitted to take a course which allowed, almost compelled, the enemy to concentrate rather than diffuse his fire.

The French had up to this time remained strictly on the defensive, in accordance with their usual policy. There was now offered an opportunity for offensive action which tested D'Estaing's professional qualities, and to appreciate which the situation at the moment must be understood. Both fleets were by this on the starboard tack, heading north, the French to leeward. The latter had received little injury in their motive power, though their line was not in perfect order; but the English, owing to the faulty attack, had seven ships seriously crippled, four of which—the *Monmouth*, *Grafton*, *Cornwall*, and *Lion*—were disabled. The last three, by three p.m., were a league astern and much to leeward of their line, being in fact nearer the French than the English; while the speed of the English fleet was necessarily reduced to that of the crippled ships remaining in line. These conditions bring out strongly the embarrassments of a fleet whose injuries are concentrated upon a few ships, instead of being distributed among all; the ten or twelve which were practically untouched had to conform to the capabilities of the others. D'Estaing, with twenty-five ships, now had Byron to windward of him with seventeen or eighteen capable of holding together, but slower and less handy than their enemies, and saw him tactically embarrassed by the care of a convoy to windward and three disabled ships to leeward. Under these circumstances three courses were open to the French admiral: (1) He might stretch ahead, and, tacking in succession, place himself between Byron and the convoy, throwing his frigates among the latter; (2) He might tack his fleet together and stand up to the English line to bring on a general action; or (3) he could after going about, cut off the three disabled ships, which might bring on a general action with less exposure.

None of these did he do. As regards the first, he, knowing the criticisms of the fleet, wrote home that his line was too much disordered to allow it. Whatever the technical irregularity, it is difficult to believe that, with the relative power of motion in the two fleets, the attempt was hopeless. The third alternative probably presented the greatest advantage, for it insured the separation between the enemy's main body and the crippled ships, and might very probably exasperate the British admiral into an attack under most hazardous conditions. It is stated by English authorities that Byron said he would have borne down again, had any attack been made on them. At three p.m. D'Estaing tacked all together, forming line on the lee ship, and stood to the southward again. The English imitated this movement, except the van ship *Monmouth*, which being too badly hurt to manoeuvre kept on to the northward, and the three separated ships. Two of these kept on north and passed once more under the French broadsides; but the *Lion*, unable to keep the wind, kept broad off before it across the bows of the enemy, for Jamaica, a thousand miles away. She was not pursued; a single transport was the sole maritime trophy of the French. 'Had the admiral's seamanship equalled his courage,' wrote the celebrated Suffren, who commanded the French van ship, 'we would not have suffered four dismasted vessels to escape.' 'D'Estaing, at the age of thirty, had been transferred from the army to the navy with the premature rank of rear-admiral.

The navy did not credit him with nautical ability when the war broke out, and it is safe to say that its opinion was justified by his conduct during it.' 'Brave as his sword, D'Estaing was always the idol of the soldier, the idol of the seaman; but moral authority over his officers failed him on several occasions, notwithstanding the marked protection extended to him by the king.'

Another cause than incapacity as a seaman has usually been assigned by French historians for the impotent action of D'Estaing on this occasion. He looked upon Grenada, they say, as the real objective of his efforts, and considered the English fleet a very secondary concern. Ramatuelle, a naval tactician who served actively in this war and wrote under the Empire, cites this case, which he couples with that of Yorktown and others, as exemplifying the true policy of naval war. His words, which probably reflect the current opinion of his service in that day, as they certainly do the policy of French governments, call for more than passing mention, as they involve principles worthy of most serious discussion:

'The French navy has always preferred the glory of assuring or preserving a conquest to that, more brilliant perhaps, but actually less real, of taking a few ships; and in that it has approached more nearly the true end to be proposed in war. What in fact would the loss of a few ships matter to the English? The essential point is to attack them in their possessions, the immediate source of their commercial wealth and of their maritime power. The war of 1778 furnishes examples which prove the devotion of the French admirals to the true interests of the country. The preservation of the island of Grenada, the reduction of Yorktown where the English army surrendered, the conquest of the island of St Christopher, were the result of great battles in which the enemy was allowed to retreat undisturbed, rather than risk giving him a chance to succor the points attacked.'

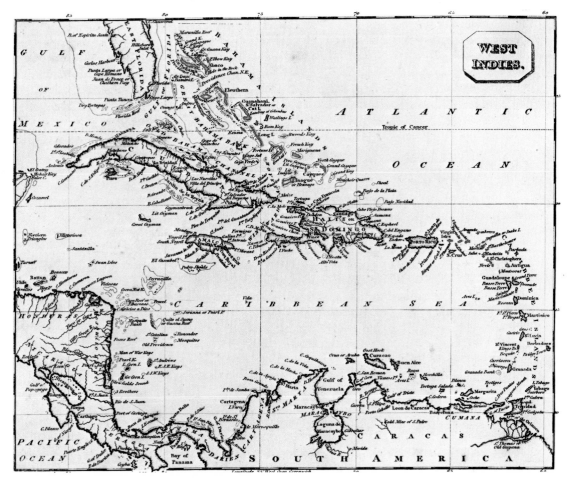

Above: *It was said of Comte d'Estaing after the Battle of Grenada by Suffren, 'If only Monsieur d'Estaing were as able as a naval officer as he is brave as a man.' During the Revolutionary War his moments of strength were punctuated by long intervals of indecision.*

Left: *The West Indies at the end of the great struggle for naval supremacy. Only Guadeloupe and Martinique remained in French hands, but thanks to Napoleon's ill-advised invasions of Spain and the Netherlands the two countries became allies of Britain and retained their possessions after 1815.*

Grenada was no doubt very dear in the eyes of D'Estaing, because it was his only success. After making the failures at the Delaware, at New York, and at Rhode Island, with the mortifying affair at St Lucia, it is difficult to understand the confidence in him expressed by some French writers. Gifted with a brilliant and contagious personal daring, he distinguished himself most highly, when an admiral, by leading in person assaults upon intrenchments at St Lucia and Grenada, and a few months later in the unsuccessful attack upon Savannah.

During the absence of the French navy in the winter of 1778–79, the English, controlling now the sea with a few of their ships that had not gone to the West Indies, determined to shift the scene of the continental war to the Southern States, where there was believed to be a large number of loyalists. The expedition was directed upon Georgia, and was so far successful that Savannah fell into their hands in the last days of 1778. The whole State speedily submitted. Operations were thence extended into South Carolina, but failed to bring about the capture of Charleston.

Arriving off the coast of Georgia on the 1st of September, D'Estaing took the English wholly at unawares; but the fatal lack of promptness, which had previously marked the command of this very daring man, again betrayed his good fortune. Dallying at first before Savannah, the fleeting of precious days again brought on a change of conditions, and the approach of the bad-weather season impelled him, too slow at first, into a premature assault. In it he displayed his accustomed gallantry, fighting at the head of his column, as did the American general; but the result was a bloody repulse. The siege was raised, and D'Estaing sailed at once for France, not only giving up his project upon New York, but abandoning the Southern States to the enemy. The value of this help from the great sea power of France, thus cruelly dangled before the eyes of the Americans only to be withdrawn, was shown by the action of the English, who abandoned Newport in the utmost haste when they learned the presence of the French fleet. Withdrawal had been before decided upon, but D'Estaing's coming converted it into flight.

The fragments of D'Estaing's late fleet were joined by a reinforcement from France under the Comte de Guichen, who assumed chief command in the West Indian seas March 22, 1780. The next day he sailed for St Lucia, which he hoped to find unprepared; but a crusty, hard-fighting old admiral of the traditional English type, Sir Hyde Parker, had so settled himself at the anchorage, with sixteen ships, that Guichen with his twenty-two would not attack. The opportunity, if it were one, did not recur. De Guichen, returning to Martinique, anchored there on the 27th; and the same day Parker at St Lucia was joined by the new English commander-in-chief, Rodney.

This since celebrated, but then only distinguished, admiral was sixty-two years old at the time of assuming a command where he was to win an undying fame. Of distinguished courage and professional skill, but with extravagant if not irregular habits, money embarrassments had detained him in exile in France at the time the war began. Despite his brilliant personal courage and professional skill, which in the matter of tactics was far in advance of his contemporaries in England, Rodney, as a commander-in-chief, belongs rather to the wary, cautious school of the French tacticians than to the impetuous, unbounded eagerness of Nelson. As in Tourville we have seen the desperate fighting of the seventeenth century, unwilling to leave its enemy, merging into the formal, artificial—we may almost say trifling—parade tactics of the eighteenth, so in Rodney we shall see the transition from those ceremonious duels to an action which, while skilful in conception, aimed at serious results. For it would be unjust to Rodney to press the comparison to the

French admirals of his day. With a skill that De Guichen recognized as soon as they crossed swords, Rodney meant mischief, not idle flourishes. Whatever incidental favors fortune might bestow by the way, the objective from which his eye never wandered was the French fleet—the organized military force of the enemy on the sea. And on the day when Fortune forsook the opponent who had neglected her offers, when the conqueror of Cornwallis failed to strike while he had Rodney at a disadvantage, the latter won a victory which redeemed England from the depths of anxiety, and restored to her by one blow all those islands which the cautious tactics of the allies had for a moment gained, save only Tobago.

De Guichen and Rodney met for the first time on the 17th of April, 1780, three weeks after the arrival of the latter. The French fleet was beating to windward in the Channel between Martinique and Dominica, when the enemy was made in the southeast. A day was spent in manoeuvring for the weather-gage, which Rodney got. The two fleets being now well to leeward of the islands, both on the starboard tack heading to the northward and the French on the lee bow of the English, Rodney, who was carrying a press of sail, signalled to his fleet that he meant to attack the enemy's rear and centre with his whole force; and when he had reached the position he thought suitable, ordered them to keep away eight points (90°) together. De Guichen, seeing the danger of the rear, wore his fleet all together and stood down to succor it. Rodney, finding himself foiled, hauled up again on the same tack as the enemy, both fleets now heading to the southward and eastward. Later, he again made signal for battle, followed an hour after, just at noon, by the order (quoting his own despatch), 'for every ship to bear down and steer for her opposite in the enemy's line.' This, which sounds like the old story of ship to ship, Rodney explains to have meant her opposite at the moment, not her opposite in numerical order. His own words are: 'In a slanting position, that my leading ships might attack the van ships of the enemy's centre division, and the whole British fleet be opposed to only two thirds of the enemy.' The difficulty and misunderstanding which followed seem to have sprung mainly from the defective character of the signal book. Instead of doing as the admiral wished, the leading ships carried sail so as to reach their supposed station abreast their numerical opposite in the order. Rodney stated afterward that when he bore down the second time, the French fleet was in a very extended line of battle; and that, had his orders been obeyed, the centre and rear must have been disabled before the van could have joined.

There seems every reason to believe that Rodney's intentions throughout were to double on the French, as asserted. The failure sprang from the signal-book and tactical inefficiency of the fleet; for which he, having lately joined, was not answerable. But the ugliness of his fence was so apparent to De Guichen, that he exclaimed, when the English fleet kept away the first time, that six or seven of his ships were gone; and sent word to Rodney that if his signals had been obeyed he would have had him for his prisoner. A more convincing proof that he recognized the dangerousness of his enemy is to be found in the fact that he took care not to have the lee-gage in their subsequent encounters. Rodney's careful plans being upset, he showed that with them he carried all the stubborn courage of the most downright fighter; taking his own ship close to the enemy and ceasing only when the latter hauled off, her foremast and mainyard gone, and her hull so damaged that she could hardly be kept afloat.

An incident of this battle mentioned by French writers and by Botta, who probably drew upon French authorities, but not found in the English accounts, shows the critical nature of the attack in the apprehension of the French. According to them,

Rodney, marking a gap in their order due to a ship in rear of the French admiral being out of station, tried to break through; but the captain of the *Destin*, seventy-four, pressed up under more sail and threw himself across the path of the English ninety-gun ship.

'The action of the *Destin* was justly praised,' says Lapeyrouse-Bonfils. 'The fleet ran the danger of almost certain defeat, but for the bravery of M de Goimpy. Such, after the affair, was the opinion of the whole French squadron. Yet, admitting that our line was broken, what disasters then would necessarily threaten the fleet? Would it not always have been easy for our rear to remedy the accident by promptly standing on to fill the place of the vessels cut off? That movement would necessarily have brought about a *mêlée*, which would have turned to the advantage of the fleet having the bravest and most devoted captains. But then, as under the empire, it was an acknowledged principle that ships cut off were ships taken, and the belief wrought its own fulfilment.'

The effect of breaking an enemy's line, or order-of-battle, depends upon several conditions. The essential idea is to divide the opposing force by penetrating through an interval found, or made, in it, and then to concentrate upon that one of the fractions which can be least easily helped by the other. In a column of ships this will usually be the rear. The compactness of the order attacked, the number of the ships cut off, the length of time during which they can be isolated and outnumbered, will all affect the results. A very great factor in the issue will be the moral effect, the confusion introduced into a line thus broken. Ships coming up toward the break are stopped, the rear doubles up, while the ships ahead continue their course. Such a moment is critical, and calls for instant action; but the men are

rare who in an unforeseen emergency can see, and at once take the right course, especially if, being subordinates, they incur responsibility. In such a scene of confusion the English, without presumption, hoped to profit by their better seamanship; for it is not only 'courage and devotion,' but skill, which then tells. All these effects of 'breaking the line' received illustration in Rodney's great battle in 1782.

De Guichen and Rodney met twice again in the following month, but on neither occasion did the French admiral take the favorite lee-gage of his nation. Meanwhile a Spanish fleet of twelve ships-of-the-line was on its way to join the French. Rodney cruised to windward of Martinique to intercept them; but the Spanish admiral kept a northerly course, sighted Guadeloupe, and thence sent a despatch to De Guichen, who joined his allies and escorted them into port. The great preponderance of the coalition, in numbers, raised the fears of the English islands; but lack of harmony led to delays and hesitations, a terrible epidemic raged in the Spanish squadron, and the intended operations came to nothing. In August De Guichen sailed for France with fifteen ships. Rodney, ignorant of his destination, and anxious about both North America and Jamaica, divided his fleet, leaving one half in the islands, and with the remainder sailing for New York, where he arrived on the 12th of September. The risk thus run was very great, and scarcely justifiable; but no ill effect followed the dispersal of forces. Had De Guichen intended to turn upon Jamaica, or, as was expected by Washington, upon New York, neither part of Rodney's fleet could well have withstood him. Two chances of disaster, instead of one, were run, by being in small force on two fields instead of in full force on one.

Rodney's anxiety about North America was well grounded. On the 12th of July of this year the long expected French succor arrived—five thousand French troops under Rochambeau and seven ships-of-the-line under De Ternay. Hence the English, though still superior at sea, felt forced to concentrate at New York, and were unable to strengthen their operations in Carolina. The difficulty and distance of movements by land gave such an advantage to sea power that Lafayette urged the French government further to increase the fleet; but it was still naturally and properly attentive to its own immediate interests in the Antilles. It was not yet time to deliver America.

Rodney, having escaped the great hurricane of October, 1780, by his absence, returned to the West Indies later in the year, and soon after heard of the war between England and Holland; which, proceeding from causes which will be mentioned later, was declared December 20, 1780. The admiral at once seized the Dutch islands of St Eustatius and St Martin, besides numerous merchant-ships, with property amounting

Above: *The surrender of Cornwallis at Yorktown in October 1781, the last
straw for the British Government in its long struggle to subdue the American
rebel colonists. This major disaster was brought about because of Admiral Graves'
defeat in Chesapeake Bay the month before. In tactical terms the sea battle was a
minor affair, almost a draw, but it prevented the vital relief getting through to
Yorktown, and it is the classic example of a relatively minor sea battle influencing
major events on land.*

in all to fifteen million dollars. These islands, while still neutral,
had played a rôle similar to that of Nasau during the American
Civil War, and had become a great depot of contraband goods,
immense quantities of which now fell into the English hands.

The year 1780 had been gloomy for the cause of the United
States. The battle of Camden had seemed to settle the English
yoke on South Carolina, and the enemy formed high hopes of
controlling both North Carolina and Virginia. The treason of
Arnold following had increased the depression, which was
but partially relieved by the victory at King's Mountain. The
substantial aid of French troops was the most cheerful spot in the
situation. Yet even that had a checkered light, the second division
of the intended help being blocked in Brest by the English fleet;
while the final failure of De Guichen to appear, and Rodney
coming in his stead, made the hopes of the campaign fruitless.

A period of vehement and decisive action was, however, at
hand. At the end of March, 1781, the Comte de Grasse sailed
from Brest with twenty-six ships-of-the-line and a large convoy.
When off the Azores, five ships parted company for the East
Indies, under Suffren, of whom more will be heard later on. De
Grasse came in sight of Martinique on the 28th of April.
Admiral Hood (Rodney having remained behind at St Eustatius)
was blockading before Fort Royal, the French port and arsenal
on the lee side of the island, in which were four ships-of-the-
line, when his lookouts reported the enemy's fleet. Hood had
two objects before him—one to prevent the junction of the four
blockaded ships with the approaching fleet, the other to keep the
latter from getting between him and Gros Ilot Bay in St Lucia.
Instead of effecting this in the next twenty-four hours, by beating
to windward of the Diamond Rock, his fleet got so far to leeward that De Grasse, passing through the channel on the 29th,
headed up for Fort Royal, keeping his convoy between the fleet
and the island. For this false position Hood was severely blamed

by Rodney, but it may have been due to light winds and the lee
current. However that be, the four ships in Fort Royal got
under way and joined the main body. The English had now
only eighteen ships to the French twenty-four, and the latter
were to windward; but though thus in the proportion of four
to three, and having the power to attack, De Grasse would not
do it. The fear of exposing his convoy prevented him from
running the chance of a serious engagement. Great must have
been his distrust of his forces, one would say. When is a navy to
fight, if this was not a time? He carried on a distant cannonade,
with results so far against the English as to make his backward-
ness yet more extraordinary. Can a policy or a tradition which
justifies such a line of conduct be good?

The invasion of the Southern States by the English, beginning
in Georgia and followed by the taking of Charleston and the
military control of the two extreme States, had been pressed on
to the northward by way of Camden into North Carolina. On
the 16th of August, 1780, General Gates was totally defeated at
Camden; and during the following nine months the English
under Cornwallis persisted in their attempts to overrun North
Carolina. Cornwallis, too weak to dream of controlling, or even
penetrating, into the interior of an unfriendly country, had
now to choose between returning to Charleston, to assure there
and in South Carolina the shaken British power, and moving
northward again to Virginia, there to join hands with a small
expeditionary force operating on the James River under
Generals Phillips and Arnold. Cornwallis, taking the matter into
his own hands, marched from Wilmington on the 25th of
April, 1781, joining the British already at Petersburg on the 20th
of May. The forces thus united numbered seven thousand men.
Driven back from the open country of South Carolina into
Charleston, there now remained two centres of British power—
at New York and in the Chesapeake. With New Jersey and

Pennsylvania in the hands of the Americans, communication between the two depended wholly upon the sea.

Despite his unfavorable criticism of Cornwallis's action, Clinton had himself already risked a large detachment in the Chesapeake. A body of sixteen hundred men under Benedict Arnold had ravaged the country of the James and burned Richmond in January of this same year. In the hopes of capturing Arnold, Lafayette had been sent to Virginia with a nucleus of twelve hundred troops, and on the evening of the 8th of March the French squadron at Newport sailed, in concerted movement, to control the waters of the bay. Admiral Arbuthnot, commanding the English fleet lying in Gardiner's Bay, at the eastern end of Long Island learned the departure by his lookouts, and started in pursuit on the morning of the 10th, thirty-six hours later. Favored either by diligence or luck, he made such good time that when the two fleets came in sight of each other, a little outside of the capes of the Chesapeake, the English were leading. They at once went about in order to meet their enemy, who on his part, formed a line-of-battle. The wind at this time was west, so that neither could head directly into the bay.

The two fleets were nearly equal in strength, there being eight ships on each side; but the English had one ninety-gun ship, while of the French one was only a heavy frigate, which

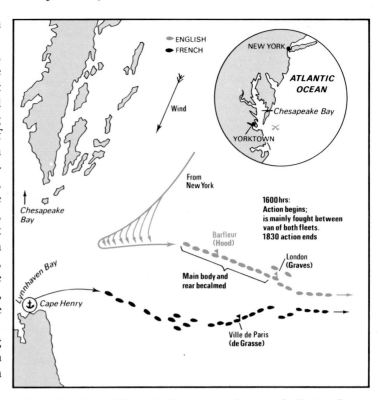

Below: A French engraving commemorating George Washington's crowning victory at Yorktown. France had got her revenge for the humiliations of the Seven Years' War, but it was to be a hollow victory for her. The financial strains set up by the war were already attacking the very fabric of France, leading ultimately to the Revolution. Furthermore her navy, built up for this purpose by Choiseul, never again reached the peak that it attained in 1781.

Above: The Battle of Chesapeake Bay, otherwise known as the Virginia Capes, 5 September 1781, in which Admiral de Grasse prevented a British squadron under Vice-Admiral Thomas Graves from entering Chesapeake Bay, intent on landing reinforcements for Yorktown. With 19 ships of the line to the 24 French, Graves delayed until he had formed a line of battle, as laid down in the Fighting Instructions, giving the enemy time to out maneuver him. Thereupon he retired to New York to repair damage to rigging.

Iournée mémorable du 19 Octobre 1781 à York en Virginie

Gravé d'après le Tableau de N:Piehle peint d'après nature à Philadelphie en 1783

was put into the line. Nevertheless, the case was eminently one for the general French policy to have determined the action of a vigorous chief, and the failure to see the matter through must fall upon the good-will of Commodore Destouches, or upon some other cause than that preference for the ulterior objects of the operations, of which the reader of French naval history hears so much. The weather was boisterous and threatening, and the wind, after hauling once or twice, settled down to northeast, with a big sea, but was then fair for entering the bay. The two fleets were by this time both on the port tack standing out to sea, the French leading, and about a point on the weather

bow of the English. From this position they wore in succession ahead of the latter, taking the lee-gage, and thus gaining the use of their lower batteries, which the heavy sea forbade to the weather-gage. The English stood on till abreast the enemy's line, when they wore together, and soon after attacked in the usual manner, and with the usual results. The three van ships were very badly injured aloft, but in their turn, throwing their force mainly on the two leaders of the enemy, crippled them seriously in hulls and rigging. The French van then kept away, and Arbuthnot, in perplexity, ordered his van to haul the wind again. M Destouches now executed a very neat movement by defiling. Signalling his van to haul up on the other tack, he led the rest of his squadron by the disabled English ships, and after giving them the successive broadsides of his comparatively fresh ships, wore, and out to sea. This was the end of the battle, in which the English certainly got the worst; but with their usual tenacity of purpose, being unable to pursue their enemy afloat, they steered for the bay, made the junction with Arnold, and thus broke up the plans of the French and Americans, from which so much had been hoped by Washington. There can be no doubt, after careful reading of the accounts, that after the fighting the French were in better force than the English, and they in fact claimed the victory; yet the ulterior objects of the expedition did not tempt them again to try the issue with a fleet of about their own size.

The way of the sea being thus open and held in force, two thousand more English troops sailing from New York reached Virginia on the 26th of March, and the subsequent arrival of Cornwallis in May raised the number to seven thousand. The operations of the contending forces during the spring and summer months, in which Lafayette commanded the Americans, do not concern our subject. Early in August, Cornwallis, acting under orders from Clinton, withdrew his troops into the peninsula between the York and James rivers, and occupied Yorktown.

Washington and Rochambeau had met on the 21st of May, and decided that the situation demanded that the effort of the French West Indian fleet, when it came, should be directed against either New York of the Chesapeake. This was the tenor of the despatch found by De Grasse at Cap Français, and meantime the allied generals drew their troops toward New York, where they would be on hand for the furtherance of one object, and nearer the second if they had to make for it.

In either case the result, in the opinion of Washington and of the French government, depended upon superior sea power; but Rochambeau had privately notified the admiral that his own preference was for the Chesapeake as the scene of the intended operations, and moreover the French government had declined to furnish the means for a formal siege of New York. The enterprise therefore assumed the form of an extensive military combination, dependent upon ease and rapidity of movement, and upon blinding the eyes of the enemy to the real objective—purposes to which the peculiar qualities of a navy admirably lent themselves. The shorter distance to be traversed, the greater depth of water and easier pilotage of the Chesapeake, were further reasons which would commend the scheme to the judgment of a seaman; and De Grasse readily accepted it, without making difficulties or demanding modifications which would have involved discussion and delay.

Having made his decision, the French admiral acted with great good judgment, promptitude, and vigor. The same frigate that brought despatches from Washington was sent back, so that by August 15th the allied generals knew of the intended coming of the fleet. Thirty-five hundred soldiers were spared by the governor of Cap Français, upon the condition of a Spanish squadron anchoring at the place, which De Grasse procured. He also raised from the governor of Havana the money urgently needed by the Americans; and finally, instead of weakening his force by sending convoys to France, as the court had wished, he took every available ship to the Chesapeake. To conceal his coming as long as possible, he passed through the Bahama Channel, as a less frequented route, and on the 30th of August anchored in Lynnhaven Bay, just within the capes of the Chesapeake, with twenty-eight ships-of-the-line. Three days before, August 27, the French squadron at Newport, eight ships-of-the-line with four frigates and eighteen transports under M de Barras, sailed for the rendezvous; making, however, a wide

circuit out to sea to avoid the English. This course was the more necessary as the French siege-artillery was with it. The troops under Washington and Rochambeau had crossed the Hudson on the 24th of August, moving toward the head of Chesapeake Bay. Thus the different armed forces, both land and sea, were converging toward their objective, Cornwallis.

Admiral Graves was painfully surprised, on making the Chesapeake, to find anchored there a fleet which from its numbers could only be an enemy's. Nevertheless, he stood in to meet it, and as De Grasse got under way, allowing his ships to be counted, the sense of numerical inferiority—nineteen to twenty-four—did not deter the English admiral from attacking. The clumsiness of his method, however, betrayed his gallantry; many of his ships were roughly handled, without any advantage being gained. De Grasse, expecting De Barras, remained outside five days, keeping the English fleet in play without coming to action; then returning to port he found De Barras safely at anchor. Graves went back to New York, and with him disappeared the last hope of succor that was to gladden Cornwallis's eyes. The siege was steadily endured, but the control of the sea made only one issue possible, and the English forces were surrendered October 19, 1781. With this disaster the hope of subduing the colonies died in England. The conflict flickered through a year longer, but no serious operations were undertaken. (See Map page 171.)

Before quitting that struggle for independence, it must again be affirmed that its successful ending, at least at so early a date, was due to the control of the sea—to sea power in the hands of the French, and its improper distribution by the English authorities. This assertion may be safely rested on the authority of the one man who, above all others, thoroughly knew the resources of the country, the temper of the people, the difficulties of the struggle, and whose name is still the highest warrant for sound, quiet, unfluttered goodsense and patriotism.

The keynote to all Washington's utterances is set in the 'Memorandum for concerting a plan of operations with the French army,' dated July 15, 1780, and sent by the hands of Lafayette:

'The Marquis de Lafayette will be pleased to communicate the following general ideas to Count de Rochambeau and the Chevalier de Ternay, as the sentiments of the underwritten:

In any operation, and under all circumstances, a decisive naval superiority is to be considered as a fundamental principle, and the basis upon which every hope of success must ultimately depend.'

This, however, though the most formal and decisive expression of Washington's views, is but one among many others equally distinct. Ships and money are the burden of his cry. May 23, 1781, he writes to the Chevalier de la Luzerne: 'I do not see how it is possible to give effectual support to the Southern States, and avert the evils which threaten, while we are inferior in naval force in these seas.'

Such, in the opinion of the revered commander-in-chief of the American armies, was the influence of sea power upon the contest which he directed with so much skill and such infinite patience, and which, amidst countless trials and discouragements, he brought to a glorious close.

It will be observed that the American cause was reduced to these straits, notwithstanding the great and admitted losses of British commerce by the cruisers of the allies and by American privateers. This fact, and the small results from the general war, dominated as it was by the idea of commerce-destroying, show strongly the secondary and indecisive effect of such a policy upon the great issues of war.

Chapter 8

Europe and the Indies

The last chapter closed with the opinions of Washington, as to the effect of sea power upon the struggle for American independence. In Europe the results turned yet more entirely upon the same factor. There the allies had three several objectives, at each of which England stood strictly upon the defensive. The first of these was England herself, involving, as a preliminary to an invasion, the destruction of the Channel fleet—a project which, if seriously entertained, can scarcely be said to have been seriously attempted; the second was the reduction of Gibraltar; the third, the capture of Minorca. The last alone met with success. Thrice was England threatened by a largely superior fleet, thrice the threat fell harmless. Thrice was Gibraltar reduced to straits; thrice was it relieved by the address and fortune of English seamen, despite overpowering odds.

After Keppel's action off Ushant, no general encounter took place between fleets in European seas during the year 1778 and the first half of 1779. Meantime Spain was drawing toward a rupture with England and an active alliance with France. War was declared by her on the 16th of June, 1779; but as early as April 12, a treaty between the two Bourbon kingdoms, involving active war upon England, had been signed. By its terms the invasion of Great Britain or Ireland was to be undertaken, every effort made to recover for Spain, Minorca, Pensacola, and Mobile, and the two courts bound themselves to grant neither peace, nor truce, nor suspension of hostilities, until Gibraltar should be restored.

The declaration of war was withheld until ready to strike; but the English government, doubtless, should have been upon its guard in the strained relations of the two countries, and prepared to prevent a junction of the two fleets. As it was, no efficient blockade of Brest was established, and twenty-eight French sail-of-the-line went out unopposed June 3, 1779, under D'Orvilliers, Keppel's opponent of the year before. The fleet steered for the coasts of Spain, where it was to find the Spanish ships; but it was not till the 22nd of July that the full contingent

175

Opposite top left: *A French squadron c 1779.*

Opposite top right: *The Battle of the Dogger Bank in 1781. As the tide of war went against the British in North America her old antagonists the Dutch threw in their lot with France and Spain. As always, both sides dispensed with elegant maneuvers and simply closed for a bloody yardarm-to-yardarm fight. After a few hours both sides were too battered to continue and the Dutch broke off the engagement.*

Opposite below: *General Sir George Elliot, created Baron Heathfield for his defense of Gibraltar. Between 1779 and 1782 the Rock was constantly under siege, and although its defense was a heavy drain on the Royal Navy's resources the siege tied down French and Spanish ships during the last gruelling period of the war. The siege also set the seal on the reputation of the Royal Marines, who formed the main part of the garrison.*

Below: *A Dutch print of the Dogger Bank battle. The Dutch were commanded by Admiral Zoutman and the English by Sir Hyde Parker.*

joined. Seven precious summer weeks thus slipped by unimproved, but that was not all the loss; the French had been provisioned for only thirteen weeks, and this truly great armada of sixty-six ships-of-the-line and fourteen frigates had not more than forty working-days before it. Sickness, moreover, ravaged the fleet; and although it was fortunate enough to enter the Channel while the English were at sea, the latter, numbering little more than half their enemies, succeeded in passing within them. The flabbiness of coalitions increased the weakness due to inefficient preparation; a great and not unnatural panic on the English Channel coast, and the capture of one ship-of-the-line, were the sole results of a cruise extending, for the French, over fifteen weeks.

The year 1781, decisive of the question of the independence of the United States, was marked in the European seas by imposing movements of great fleets followed by puny results. At the end of March De Grasse sailed from Brest with twenty-six ships-of-the-line. On the 29th he detached five under Suffren to the East Indies, and himself continued on to meet success at

Yorktown and disaster in the West Indies. On the 23rd of June De Guichen sailed from Brest with eighteen ships-of-the-line for Cadiz, where he joined thirty Spanish ships. This immense armament sailed on the 22nd of July for the Mediterranean, landed fourteen thousand troops at Minorca, and then moved upon the English Channel.

The English had this year first to provide against the danger to Gibraltar. Amid the horrors and uproar of one of the longest and most exciting sieges of history, the sufferings of the combatants were intensified by the presence of many peaceful inhabitants, including the wives and families of soldiers as well as of officers. A great fleet of twenty-eight ships-of-the-line sailed from Portsmouth on the 13th of March, convoying three hundred merchant-ships for the East and West Indies, besides ninety-seven transports and supply-ships for the Rock. A delay on the Irish coast prevented its falling in with De Grasse, who had sailed nine days after it. Arriving off Cape St Vincent, it met no enemy, and looking into Cadiz saw the great Spanish fleet at anchor. The latter made no move, and the English admiral,

Above: *View from Gibraltar of the Spanish batteries erected during the siege of September 1782, still known as La Lineas or The Lines.*

Algeciras, on the opposite side of the bay from Gibraltar, to support a grand combined attack by land and sea, which, it was hoped, would reduce to submission the key to the Mediterranean. With the ships already there, the total rose to nearly fifty ships-of-the-line. The details of the mighty onslaught scarcely belong to our subject, yet cannot be wholly passed by, without at least such mention as may recognize and draw attention to their interest.

The three years' siege which was now drawing to its end had been productive of many brilliant feats of arms, as well as of less striking but more trying proofs of steadfast endurance, on the

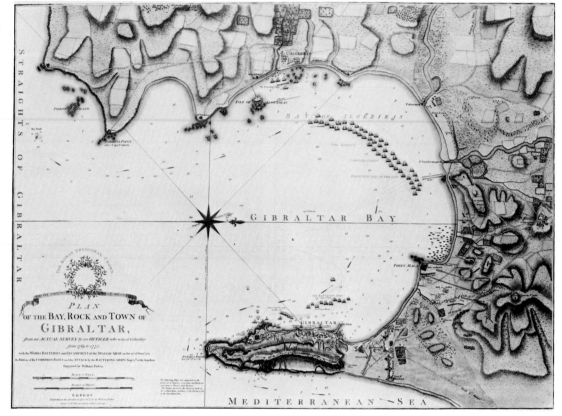

Right: *Plan of the Bay of Gibraltar showing the great attack by the Combined Fleet and the Spanish floating batteries in September 1782.*

Derby, threw his supplies into Gibraltar on the 12th of April, undisturbed. At the same time he, like De Grasse, detached to the East Indies a small squadron, which was destined before long to fall in with Suffren.

Gibraltar relieved, England untouched, were the results of these gigantic gatherings; they can scarcely be called efforts. A mortifying disaster closed the year for the allies. De Guichen sailed from Brest with seventeen sail, protecting a large convoy of merchantmen and ships with military supplies. The fleet was pursued by twelve English ships under Admiral Kempenfeldt, an officer whose high professional abilities have not earned the immortality with which poetry has graced his tragical death. Falling in with the French one hundred and fifty miles west of Ushant, he cut off a part of the convoy, despite his inferior numbers. A few days later a tempest dispersed the French fleet. Only two ships-of-the-line and five merchantmen out of one hundred and fifty reached the West Indies.

The year 1782 opened with the loss of the English of Port Mahon, which surrendered on the 5th of February, after a siege of six months—a surrender induced by the ravages of scurvy, consequent upon the lack of vegetables and confinement in the foul air of bombproofs and casemates, under the heavy fire of an enemy. On the last night of the defence the call for necessary guards was four hundred and fifteen, while only six hundred and sixty men were fit for duty, thus leaving no reliefs.

On the 10th of September the allied fleets sailed thence for

part of the garrison. How long the latter might have held out cannot be said, seeing the success with which the English sea power defied the efforts of the allies to cut off the communications of the fortress; but it was seemingly certain that the place must be subdued by main force or not at all, while the growing exhaustion of the belligerents foretold the near end of the war. Accordingly Spain multiplied her efforts of preparation and military ingenuity; while the report of them and of the approaching decisive contest drew to the scene volunteers and men of eminence from other countries of Europe. Two French Bourbon princes added, by their coming, to the theatrical interest with which the approaching drama was invested. The presence of royalty was needed adequately to grace the sublime catastrophe; for the sanguine confidence of the besiegers had determined a satisfactory *dénouement* with all the security of a playwright.

Besides the works on the isthmus which joins the Rock to the mainland, where three hundred pieces of artillery were now mounted, the chief reliance of the assailants was upon ten floating batteries elaborately contrived to be shot and fire proof, and carrying one hundred and fifty-four heavy guns. These were to anchor in a close north-and-south line along the west face of the works, at about nine hundred yards distance. They were to be supported by forty gunboats and as many bomb vessels, besides the efforts of the ships-of-the-line to cover the attack and distract the garrison. Twelve thousand French troops were brought to reinforce the Spaniards in the grand assault, which was to be made when the bombardment had sufficiently injured and demoralized the defenders. At this time the latter numbered seven thousand, their land opponents thirty-three thousand men.

The final act was opened by the English. At seven o'clock on the morning of September 8, 1782, the commanding general, Elliott, began a severe and most injurious fire upon the works on the isthmus. Having effected his purpose, he stopped; but the enemy took up the glove the next morning, and for four days successively poured in a fire from the isthmus alone of six thousand five hundred cannon-balls and one thousand one

hundred bombs every twenty-four hours. So approached the great closing scene of September 13. At seven a.m. of that day the ten battering-ships unmoored from the head of the bay and stood down to their station. Between nine and ten they anchored, and the general fire at once began. The besieged replied with equal fury. The battering-ships seem in the main, and for some hours, to have justified the hopes formed of them; cold shot glanced or failed to get through their sides, while the self-acting apparatus for extinguishing fires balked the hot shot.

About two o'clock, however, smoke was seen to issue from the ship of the commander-in-chief, and though controlled for

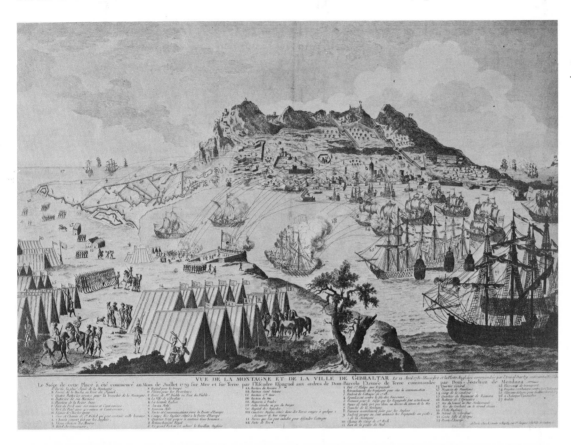

Left: A French view of the Siege of Gibraltar, with the tents of the investing army in the foreground and ships and bomb vessels bombarding the fortress.

VUE DE LA MONTAGNE ET DE LA VILLE DE GIBRALTAR

Left: Ten floating batteries were specially built for the big attack on Gibraltar. With three-foot thick sides packed with wet sand and cork and mounting 36-pounder guns, they were towed into action by ships' boats. Despite the elaborate precautions against fire the garrison's red-hot shot finally set them on fire one by one. The French designer, D'Arçon, claimed that they had been rushed into service without adequate trials and that they had not been supported by other ships. What is more likely is that the sheer volume of hits wore down their system of protection.

Above: *Table Bay at the Cape of Good Hope, by W Hodges. This strategic foothold on the route to India was taken over by the British after the Netherlands fell under French control, but was not handed back in 1815.*

Below right: *When dawn came on 14 September 1782 the great attack on Gibraltar by the Combined Fleet had failed. It was the last major assault as Lord Howe fought a big convoy through to bring supplies to the garrison a month later.*

Below: *D'Arcon's floating batteries burning to the waterline after being pounded for hours by the British artillery.*

some time, the fire continued to gain. The same misfortune befell others; by evening, the fire of the besieged gained a marked superiority, and by one o'clock in the morning the greater part of the battering-ships were in flames. Their distress was increased by the action of the naval officer commanding the English gunboats, who now took post upon the flank of the line and raked it effectually—a service which the Spanish gunboats should have prevented. In the end, nine of the ten blew up at their anchors, with a loss estimated at fifteen hundred men, four hundred being saved from the midst of the fire by the English seamen. The tenth ship was boarded and burned by the English boats. The hopes of the assailants perished with the failure of the battering-ships.

There remained only the hope of starving out the garrison. To this end the allied fleets now gave themselves. It was known that Lord Howe was on his way out with a great fleet, numbering

thirty-four ships-of-the-line, besides supply vessels. On the 10th of October a violent westerly gale injured the combined ships, driving one ashore under the batteries of Gibraltar, where she was surrendered. The next day Howe's force came in sight, and the transports had a fine chance to make the anchorage, which, through carelessness, was missed by all but four. The rest, with the men-of-war, drove eastward into the Mediterranean. The allies followed on the 13th; but though thus placed between the port and the relieving force, and not encumbered, like the latter, with supply-ships, they yet contrived to let the transports, with scarcely an exception, slip in and anchor safely. Not only provisions and ammunition, but also bodies of troops carried by the ships-of-war, were landed without molestation. On the 19th the English fleet repassed the straits with an easterly wind, having within a week's time fulfilled its mission, and made Gibraltar safe for another year.

The conclusion continually recurs. Whatever may be the determining factors in strifes between neighbouring continental States, when a question arises of control over distant regions, politically weak—whether they be crumbling empires, anarchical republics, colonies, isolated military posts, or islands below a certain size—it must ultimately be decided by naval power, by the organized military force afloat, which represents the communications that form so prominent a feature in all strategy. The magnificent defence of Gibraltar hinged upon this; upon this depended the military results of the war in America; upon this the final fate of the West India Islands; upon this certainly the possession of India. Upon this will depend the control of the Central American Isthmus, if that question take a military coloring; and though modified by the continental position and surroundings of Turkey, the same sea power must be a weighty factor in shaping the outcome of the Eastern Question in Europe.

The very interesting and instructive campaign of Suffren in the East Indies, although in itself by far the most noteworthy and meritorious naval performance of the war of 1778, failed, through no fault of his, to affect the general issue. It was not till 1781 that the French Court felt able to direct upon the East naval forces adequate to the importance of the issue. Yet the conditions of the peninsula at that time were such as to give an unusual opportunity for shaking the English power. Hyder Ali, the most skilful and daring of all the enemies against whom the English had yet fought in India, was then ruling over the kingdom of Mysore, which, from its position in the southern part of the peninsula, threatened both the Carnatic and the Malabar coast. In the summer of 1780 swarms of his horsemen descended without warning from the hills, and appeared near the gates of Madras. In September one body of English troops, three thousand strong, was cut to pieces, and another of five thousand was only saved by a rapid retreat upon Madras, losing its artillery and trains. Unable to attack Madras, Hyder turned upon the scattered posts separated from each other and the capital by the open country, which was now wholly in his control.

Such was the state of affairs when, in January, 1781, a French squadron of six ships-of-the-line and three frigates appeared on the coast. The English fleet under Sir Edward Hughes had gone to Bombay. To the French commodore, Count d'Orves, Hyder appealed for aid in an attack upon Cuddalore. Deprived of support by sea, and surrounded by the myriads of natives, the place must have fallen. D'Orves, however, refused, and returned to the Isle of France. At the same time one of the most skilful of the English Indian soldiers, Sir Eyre Coote, took the field against Hyder. The latter at once raised the siege of the beleaguered posts, and after a series of operations extending through the spring months, was brought to battle on the 1st of

Above: *Sir Edward Hughes as a captain. The artist, Madame Cerroit painted him holding a letter inscribed 'Captain Hughes on the* Somerset *at Quebec,' because in 1761 the* Somerset *was at Leghorn. In 1759 Hughes was commanding the* Lowestoft *at Quebec.*

Below: *An 18-gun ordnance storeship with a cargo of fresh fruit for the Gibraltar garrison fighting her way between a Spanish 36-gun frigate, a xebec of 18 guns and four oared gunboats. These gunboats were particularly dangerous to sailing warships when they lay becalmed.*

July, 1781. His total defeat restored to the English the open country, saved the Carnatic, and put an end to the hopes of the partisans of the French in their late possession of Pondicherry. A great opportunity had been lost.

Meanwhile a French officer of very different temper from his predecessors was on his way to the East Indies. It will be remembered that when De Grasse sailed from Brest, March 22, 1781, for the West Indies, there went with his fleet a division of five ships-of-the-line under Suffren. The latter separated from the main body on the 29th of the month, taking with him a few transports destined for the Cape of Good Hope, then a Dutch colony. The French government had learned that an expedition from England was destined to seize this important halting-place on the road to India, and Suffren's first mission was to secure it. In fact, the squadron under Commodore Johnston had got away first, and had anchored at Porto Praya, in the Cape Verde Islands, a Portuguese colony, on the 11th of April. It numbered two ships-of-the-line, and three of fifty guns, with frigates and smaller vessels, besides thirty-five transports, mostly armed. Without apprehension of attack, not because he trusted to the neutrality of the port but because he thought his destination secret, the English commodore had not anchored with a view to battle.

It so happened that at the moment of sailing from Brest one of the ships intended for the West Indies was transferred to Suffren's squadron. She consequently had not water enough for the longer voyage, and this with other reasons determined Suffren also to anchor at Porto Praya. On the 16th of April, five days after Johnstone, he made the island early in the morning and stood for the anchorage, sending a coppered ship ahead to reconnoitre. Approaching from the eastward, the land for some time hid the English squadron; but at quarter before nine the advance ship, the *Artésien*, signalled that enemy's ships were anchored in the bay. The latter is open to the southward, and extends from east to west about a mile and a half; the conditions are such that ships usually lie in the northeast part, near the shore. The English were there, stretching irregularly

in a west-northwest line. Both Suffren and Johnstone were surprised, but the latter more so; and the initiative remained with the French officer. Few men were fitter, by natural temper and the teaching of experience, for the prompt decision required. Of ardent disposition and inborn military genius, Suffren had learned, in the conduct of Boscawen toward the squadron of De la Clue, in which he had served, not to lay weight upon the power of Portugal to enforce respect for her neutrality. He knew that this must be the squadron meant for the Cape of Good Hope. The only question for him was whether to press on to the Cape with the chance of getting there first, or to attack the English at their anchors, in the hope of so crippling them as to prevent their further progress. He decided for the latter; and although the ships of his squadron, not sailing equally well, were scattered, he also determined to stand in at once, rather than lose the advantage of a surprise. Making signal to prepare for action at anchor, he took the lead in his flag-ship, the *Héros*, of seventy-four guns, hauled close round the southeast point of the bay, and stood for the English flag-ship. He was closely followed by the *Hannibal*, seventy-four; the advance ship *Artésien*, a sixty-four, also stood on with him; but the two rear ships were still far astern.

The English commodore got ready for battle as soon as he made out the enemy, but had no time to rectify his order. Suffren anchored five hundred feet from the flag-ship's starboard beam (by a singular coincidence the English flag-ship was also called *Hero*), thus having enemy's ships on both sides, and opened fire. The *Hannibal* anchored ahead of her commodore, and so close that the latter had to veer cable and drop astern; but her captain, ignorant of Suffren's intention to disregard the neutrality of the port, had not obeyed the order to clear for action, and was wholly unprepared—his decks lumbered with water-casks which had been got up to expedite watering, and the guns not cast loose. He did not add to this fault by any hesitation, but followed the flag-ship boldly, receiving passively the fire, to which for a time he was unable to reply. Luffing to the wind, he passed to windward of his chief, chose his position with skill, and atoned by his death for his first fault. These two ships were so placed as to use both broadsides. The *Artésien*, in the smoke, mistook an East India ship for a man-of-war. Running alongside, her captain was struck dead at the moment he was about to anchor, and the critical moment being lost by the absence of a head, the ship drifted out of close action, carrying the East-Indiaman along with her. The remaining two vessels, coming up late, failed to keep close enough to the wind, and they too were thrown out of action. Then Suffren, finding himself with only two ships to bear the brunt of the fight, cut his cable and made sail. The *Hannibal* followed his movement; but so much injured was she that her fore and main masts went over the side—fortunately not till she was pointed out from the bay, which she left shorn to a hulk.

Putting entirely aside questions of international law, the wisdom and conduct of Suffren's attack, from the military point of view, invite attention. To judge them properly, we must consider what was the object of the mission with which he was charged, and what were the chief factors in thwarting or forwarding it. His first object was to protect the Cape of Good Hope against an English expedition; the chief reliance for effecting his purpose was to get there first; the obstacle to his success was the English fleet. To anticipate the arrival of the latter, two courses were open to him—to run for it in the hope of winning the race, or to beat the enemy and so put him out of the running altogether. So long as his whereabouts was unknown, a search, unless with very probable information, would

be a waste of time; but when fortune had thrown his enemy across his path, the genius of Suffren at once jumped to the conclusion that the control of the sea in southern waters would determine the question, and should be settled at once. To use his own strong expression, 'The destruction of the English squadron would *cut off the root* of all the plans and projects of that expedition, gain us for a long time the superiority in India, a superiority whence might result a glorious peace, and hinder the English from reaching the Cape before me—an object which has been fulfilled and was the principal aim of my mission.'

Owing to a combination of misfortunes, the attack at Porto Praya had not the decisive result it deserved. Commodore Johnstone got under way and followed Suffren; but he thought his force was not adequate to attack in face of the resolute bearing of the French, and feared the loss of time consequent upon chasing to leeward of his port. He succeeded, however, in retaking the East India ship which the *Artésien* had carried out. Suffren continued his course and anchored at the Cape, in Simon's Bay, on the 21st of June. Johnstone followed him a fortnight later; but learning by an advance ship that the French troops had been landed, he gave up the enterprise against the colony, made a successful commerce-destroying attack upon five Dutch India ships in Saldanha Bay, which poorly repaid the failure of the military undertaking, and then went back himself to England, after sending the ships-of-the-line on to join Sir Edward Hughes in the East Indies.

Having seen the Cape secured, Suffren sailed for the Isle of

Opposite left: Suffren was an exception to the general run of French admirals in disdaining the Fighting Instructions, preferring to bring his enemy to action whenever he could.

Opposite right: Sir Edward Hughes was overshadowed by the galaxy of brilliant admirals who came after him, but his feat in holding Suffren to five drawn battles makes him an outstanding fighter.

Above: An East Indiaman wearing by bringing the wind around her stern, in a large convoy. Painted c 1789 by Pocock.

France, arriving there on the 25th of October, 1781. Count d'Orves, being senior, took command of the united squadron. The necessary repairs were made, and the fleet sailed for India, December 17. On the 22nd of January, 1782, an English fifty-gun ship, the *Hannibal*, was taken. On the 9th of February Count d'Orves died, and Suffren became commander-in-chief, with the rank of commodore. A few days later the land was seen to the northward of Madras; but owing to head-winds the city was not sighted until February 15. Nine large ships-of-war were found anchored in order under the guns of the forts. They were the fleet of Sir Edward Hughes, not in confusion like that of Johnstone.

Here, at the meeting point between these two redoubtable champions, each curiously representative of the characteristics of his own race—the one of the stubborn tenacity and seamanship of the English, the other of the ardor and tactical science of the French, too long checked and betrayed by a false system—is the place to give an accurate statement of the material forces. The French fleet had three seventy-fours, seven sixty-fours, and two fifty-gun ships, one of which was the lately captured English *Hannibal*. To these Sir Edward Hughes opposed two seventy-fours, one seventy, one sixty-eight, four sixty-fours, and one fifty-gun ship. The odds, therefore, twelve to nine, were decidedly against the English; and it is likely that the advantage in single-ship power, class for class, was also against them.

It must be recalled that at the time of his arrival Suffren found no friendly port or roadstead, no base of supplies or repair. The French posts had all fallen by 1779; and his rapid movement, which saved the Cape, did not bring him up in time to prevent the capture of the Dutch Indian possessions.

Suffren having sighted Hughes's fleet at Madras, February 15, anchored his own four miles to the northward. Considering the enemy's line, supported by the batteries, to be too strong for attack, he again got under way at four p.m., and stood south. Hughes also weighed, standing to the southward all that night under easy sail, and at daylight found that the enemy's squadron had separated from the convoy, the ships of war being about twelve miles east, while the transports were nine miles southwest, from him. This dispersal is said to have been due to the carelessness of the French frigates, which did not keep touch of the English. Hughes at once profited by it, chasing the convoy, knowing that the line-of-battle ships must follow. His copper-bottomed ships came up with and captured six of the enemy, five of which were English prizes. The sixth carried three hundred troops with military stores. Hughes had scored a point.

Suffren of course followed in a general chase, and by three p.m. four of his best sailers were two or three miles from the sternmost English ships. Hughes's ships were now much scattered, but not injudiciously so, for they joined by signal at seven p.m. Both squadrons stood to the southeast during the night, under easy sail.

At daylight of the 17th—the date of the first of four actions fought between these two chiefs within seven months—the fleets were six or eight miles apart, the French bearing north-northeast from the English. The latter formed line-ahead on the

Below: *Shipping lying off Bombay, as seen c 1740 by Lambert and Scott.*

port tack, with difficulty, owing to the light winds and frequent calms. Admiral Hughes explains that he hoped to weather the enemy by this course so as to engage closely, counting probably on finding himself to windward when the sea-breeze made. The wind continuing light, but with frequent squalls, from north-northeast, the French, running before it, kept the puffs longer and neared the English rapidly, Suffren's intention to attack the rear being aided by Hughes's course. The latter finding his rear straggling, bore up to line abreast, retreating to gain time for the ships to close on the centre. These movements in line abreast continued till twenty minutes before four p.m., when, finding he could not escape attack on the enemy's terms, Hughes hauled his wind on the port tack and awaited it. Whether by his own fault or not, he was now in the worst possible position, waiting for an attack by a superior force at its pleasure. The rear ship of his line, the *Exeter*, was not closed up; and there appears no reason why she should not have been made the van, by forming on the starboard tack, and thus bringing the other ships to her.

The method of Suffren's attack is differently stated by him and by Hughes, but the difference is in detail only; the main facts are certain. Hughes says the enemy 'steered down on the rear of our line in an irregular double line-abreast,' in which formation they continued till the moment of collision, when 'three of the enemy's ships in the first line bore right down upon the *Exeter*, while four more of their second line, headed by the *Héros*, in which M de Suffren had his flag, hauled *along the outside of the first line* toward our centre. At five minutes past four the enemy's three ships began their fire upon the *Exeter*, which was returned by her and her second ahead; the action became general from our rear to our centre, the commanding ship of the enemy, with three others of their second line, leading down on our centre, yet never advancing farther than opposite to the *Superbe*, our centre ship, with little or no wind and some heavy rain during the engagement. Under these circumstances, the enemy brought eight of their best ships to the attack of five of ours, as the van of our line, consisting of the *Monmouth*, *Eagle*, *Burford*, and *Worcester*, could not be brought into action without tacking on the enemy,' for which there was not enough wind.

Here we will leave them, and give Suffren's account of how he took up his position. In his report to the Minister of Marine he says:

'I should have destroyed the English squadron, less by superior numbers than by the advantageous disposition in which I attacked it. I attacked the rear ship and stood along the English line as far as the sixth. I thus made three of them useless, so that we were twelve against six. I began the fight at half-past three in the afternoon, taking the lead and making signal to form line as best could be done; without that I would not have engaged. At four I made signal to three ships to double on the enemy's rear, and to the squadron to approach within pistol-shot. This signal, though repeated, was not executed. I did not *myself* give the example, in order that I might hold in check the three van ships, which by tacking would have doubled on me. However, except the *Brilliant*, which doubled on the rear, no ship was as close as mine, nor received as many shots.'

The principal point of difference in the two accounts is, that Suffren asserts that his flag-ship passed along the whole English line, from the rear to the sixth ship; while Hughes says the French divided into two lines, which, upon coming near, steered, one on the rear, the other on the centre, of his squadron.

The inefficiency which showed itself on the field of battle disappeared in the general conduct of the campaign where the qualities of the chief alone told. The battle of February 17th ended with a shift of wind to the southeast at six p.m., after two hours action. The English were thus brought to windward, and their van ships enabled to share in the fight. Night falling, Suffren, at half-past six, hauled his squadron by the wind on the starboard tack, heading northeast) while Hughes steered south under easy sail. It is said by Captain Chevalier, of the French navy, that Suffren intended to renew the fight next day. In that case he should have taken measures to keep within reach. It was too plainly Hughes's policy not to fight without some advantage—to allow the supposition that with one ship, the *Exeter*, lost to him through the concentration of so many enemies upon her, he would quietly await an attack. This is so plain as to make it probable that Suffren saw sufficient reason, in the results to his fleet and the misconduct of his officers, not to wish to renew action at once. The next morning the two fleets were out of sight of each other. The continuance of the north wind, and the crippled state of two of his ships, forced Hughes to go to Trincomalee, where the sheltered harbor allowed them to repair.

Meanwhile Suffren, anxious to act against his principal objective, had sailed again on the 23rd of March. It was his hope to cut off two ships-of-the-line which were expected from England. For this he was too late; the two seventy-fours joined the main body at Madras, March 30th. Hughes had refitted at Trincomalee in a fortnight, and reached Madras again on the 12th of March. Soon after the reinforcement had joined him, he sailed again for Trincomalee with troops and military stores for the garrison. On the 8th of April Suffren's squadron was seen to the northeast, also standing to the southward. Hughes kept on, through that and the two following days, with light northerly winds. On the 11th he made the coast of Ceylon, fifty miles north of Trincomalee, and bore away for the port. On the morning of the 12th the French squadron in the northeast was seen crowding sail in pursuit. It was the day on which Rodney and De Grasse met in the West Indies, but the parts were reversed; here the French, not the English, sought action.

The speed of the ships in both squadrons was very unequal; each had some coppered ships and some not coppered. Hughes found that his slow sailers could not escape the fastest of his enemy—a condition which will always compel a retreating force to hazard an action, unless it can resolve to give up the rear ships, and which makes it imperative for the safety, as well as the efficiency, of a squadron that vessels of the same class should all have a certain minimum speed. The same cause—the danger of a separated ship—led the unwilling De Grasse, the same day, in another scene, to a risky manoeuvre and a great mishap. Hughes, with better reason, resolved to fight; and at nine a.m. formed his line on the starboard tack, standing in-shore, the squadron in good order, with intervals of two cables between the ships. His account, which again varies from that of Suffren, giving a radically different idea of the tactics used by the French commodore, and more to the credit of the latter's skill, will be followed. He says:

'The enemy, bearing north by east, distant six miles, with wind at north by east, continued manoeuvring their ships and changing their positions in line, till fifteen minutes past noon, when they bore away to engage us, five sail of their van stretching along to engage the ships of our van, and the other seven sail steering directly on our three centre ships, the *Superbe*, the *Monmouth*, her second ahead, and the *Monarca*, her second astern. At half-past one the engagement began in the van of both squadrons; three minutes after, I made the signal for battle. The French admiral in the *Héros* and his second astern in *L'Orient* (both seventy-fours) bore down on the *Superbe* within pistol-shot. The *Héros* continued in her position, giving and receiving a severe fire for nine minutes, and then stood on, greatly damaged, to

'attack the *Monmouth*, at that time engaged with another of the enemy's ships, making room for the ships in his rear to come up to the attack of our centre, where the engagement was hottest. At three the *Monmouth* had her mizzen-mast shot away, and in a few minutes her mainmast, and bore out of the line to leeward; and at forty minutes past three the wind unexpectedly continuing far northerly without any sea-breeze, and being careful not to entangle our ships with the land, I made signal to wear and haul by the wind in a line-of-battle on the larboard tack, still engaging the enemy.'

Now here, practically, was concentration with a vengeance. In this, the hardest fight between these two hard fighters, the English loss was 137 killed and 430 wounded in eleven ships. Of this total, the two centre ships, the flag-ship and her next ahead, lost 104 killed and 198 wounded—fifty-three per cent of the entire loss of the squadron, of which they formed eighteen per cent. The casualties were very much heavier, in proportion to the size of the ships, than those of the leaders of the two columns at Trafalgar. The material injury to hulls, spars, etc., was yet more serious. The English squadron, by this concentration of the enemy upon a small fraction of it, was entirely crippled. Inferior when the action began, its inferiority was yet more decisive by the subtraction of two ships, and Suffren's freedom to move was increased.

It is evident that the French chief intended an attack elementary in conception and difficult of execution. To keep a fleet on a line of bearing, sailing free, requires much drill, especially when the ships have different rates of speed, as had Suffren's. The extreme injury suffered by the *Superbe* and *Monmouth*, undeniably due to a concentration, cannot be attributed to Suffren's dispositions. 'The injuries which the *Heros* received at the beginning of the action did not allow her to remain by the *Superbe*. Not being able to back her topsails in time, the braces having been cut, she passed ahead, and was only stopped on the beam of the *Monmouth*.' This accounts for the suffering of the latter ship, already injured, and now contending with a much larger opponent. The *Superbe* was freed from Suffrens only to be engaged by the next Frenchman, an equally heavy ship; and when the *Monmouth* drifted or bore up, to leeward, the French flag-ship also drifted so that for a few moments she fired her stern guns into the *Superbe's* bow. The latter at the same time was engaged on the beam and quarter by two French ships, who, either with or without signal, came up to shield their commodore.

It is not likely that Suffren erred on the side of excessive caution. On the contrary, his most marked defect as a commander-in-chief was an ardor which, when in sight of the enemy, became impatience, and carried him at times into action hastily and in disorder. But if, in the details and execution of his battles, in his tactical combinations, Suffren was at times foiled by his own impetuosity and the short-comings of most of his captains, in the general conduct of the campaign, in strategy, where the personal qualities of the commander-in-chief mainly told, his superiority was manifest, and achieved brilliant success. Then ardor showed itself in energy, untiring and infectious. The eagerness of his hot Provençal blood overrode difficulty, created resources out of destitution, and made itself felt through every vessel under his orders. No military lesson is more instructive nor of more enduring value than the rapidity and ingenuity with which he, without a port or supplies, continually refitted his fleet and took the field, while his slower enemy was dawdling over his repairs.

The battle forced the English to remain inactive for six weeks, till the *Monmouth* was repaired. Unfortunately, Suffren's situation did not allow him to assume the offensive at once. He was short of men, provisions, and especially of spare spars and rigging. In an official letter after the action he wrote: 'I have no spare stores to repair rigging; the squadron lacks at least twelve spare topmasts.'

Hughes meantime, having rigged jury-masts to the *Monmouth*, had gone to Trincomalee, where his squadron refitted and the sick were landed for treatment; but it is evident, as has before been mentioned, that the English had not held the port long enough to make an arsenal or supply port, for he says, "I will be able to remast the *Monmouth* from the spare stores on board the several ships.' His resources were nevertheless superior to those of his adversary. During the time that Suffren was at Tranquebar, worrying the English communications between Madras and Trincomalee, Hughes still stayed quietly in the latter port, sailing for Negapatam on the 23rd of June, the day after Suffren reached Cuddalore. The two squadrons had thus again approached each other, and Suffren hastened his preparations for attack as soon as he heard that his enemy was where he could get at him. Hughes awaited his movement.

Before sailing, however, Suffren took occasion to say in writing home: 'Since my arrival in Ceylon, partly by the help of the Dutch, partly through the prizes we have taken, the squadron has been equipped for six months' service, and I have rations of wheat and rice assured for more than a year.' This achievement was indeed a just source of pride and self-congratulation. Without a port, and destitute of resources, the French commodore had lived off the enemy; the store ships and commerce of the latter had supplied his wants. To his fertility of resource and the activity of his cruisers, inspired by himself, this result was due. Yet he had but two frigates, the class of vessel upon which an admiral must mainly depend for this predatory warfare. On the 23rd of March, both provisions and stores had been nearly exhausted. Six thousand dollars in money, and the provisions in the convoy, were then his sole resources. Since then he had fought a severe action, most expensive in rigging and men, as well as in ammunition. After that fight of April 12 he had left only powder and shot enough for one other battle of equal severity. Three months later he was able to report as above, that he could keep the sea on his station for six months without further supplies. This result was due wholly to himself —to his self-reliance, and what may without exaggeration be called his greatness of soul. It was not expected at Paris; on the contrary, it was expected there that the squadron would return to the Isle of France to refit. It was not thought possible that it could remain on a hostile coast, so far from its nearest base, and be kept in efficient condition. Suffren thought otherwise; he considered, with true military insight and a proper sense of the value of his own profession, that the success of the operations in India depended upon the control of the sea, and therefore upon the uninterrupted presence of his squadron. He did not shrink from attempting that which had always been thought impossible. This firmness of spirit, bearing the stamp of genius, must, to be justly appreciated, be considered with reference to the circumstances of his own time, and of the preceding generations in which he grew up.

Suffren was born July 17, 1729, and served during the wars of 1739 and 1756. He was first under fire at Matthews's action off Toulon, February 22, 1744. He was the contemporary of D'Estaing, De Guichen, and De Grasse, before the days of the French Revolution, when the uprising of a people had taught men how often impossibilities are not impossible; before Napoleon and Nelson had made a mock of the word. His attitude and action had therefore at the time the additional merit of originality, but his lofty temper was capable of yet higher proof. Convinced of the necessity of keeping the squadron on its station, he ventured to disregard not only the murmurs of his officers but the express orders of the Court. When he reached Batacalo, he found despatches directing him to return to the Isle of France. Instead of taking them as a release from the great burden of responsibility, he disobeyed, giving his reasons, and asserting that he on the spot could judge better than a minister in Europe what the circumstances demanded. Such a leader deserved better subordinates, and a better colleague than he had in the commander of the forces on shore. Whether or no the conditions of the general maritime struggle would have permitted the overthrow of the English East Indian power may be doubtful; but it is certain that among all the admirals of the three nations there was none so fitted to accomplish that result as Suffren. We shall find him enduring severer tests, and always equal to them.

In the afternoon of the 5th of July Suffren's squadron came in sight of the English, anchored off Cuddalore. An hour later, a sudden squall carried away the main and mizzen topmasts of one of the French ships. Admiral Hughes got under way, and the two fleets manoeuvred during the night. The following day the wind favored the English, and the opponents found themselves in line of battle on the starboard tack, heading south-southeast, with the wind at southwest. The disabled French ship having by unpardonable inactivity failed to repair her injuries, the numbers about to engage were equal—eleven on each side. At eleven a.m. the English bore down together and engaged ship against ship; but as was usual under those conditions, the rear ships did not come to as close action as those ahead of them. Captain Chevalier carefully points out that their failure was a fair offset to the failure of the French rear on the 12th of April, but fails to note in this connection that the French van, both on that occasion and again on the 3rd of September, bungled as well as the rear. There can remain little doubt, in the mind of the careful reader, that most of the French captains were inferior, as seamen, to their opponents. During this part of the engagement the fourth ship in the French order, the *Brilliant*, lost her mainmast, bore up out of the line, and dropped gradually astern and to leeward.

At one p.m., when the action was hottest, the wind suddenly shifted to south-southeast, taking the ships on the port bow.

Below: *The fourth action between Hughes and Suffren, when the French admiral made a surprise attack on Trincomalee. Suffren had numerical superiority but his impetuosity and the poor discipline of his captains made it impossible to bring more than 40 percent of his strength into action.*

Four English ships, the *Burford, Sultan, Worcester,* and *Eagle,* seeing the breeze coming, kept off to port, toward the French line; the others were taken aback and paid off to starboard. The French ships, on the other hand, with two exceptions, the *Brilliant* and *Sévère,* paid off from the English. The effect of the change of wind was therefore to separate the main parts of the two squadrons, but to bring together between the lines four English and two French ships. Technical order was destroyed. The *Brilliant,* having dropped far astern of her position, came under the fire of two of the English rear, the *Worcester* and the *Eagle,* who had kept off in time and so neared the French. Suffren in person came to her assistance and drove off the English, who were also threatened by the approach of two other French ships that had worn to the westward in obedience to signal. While this partial action was taking place, the other endangered French ship, the *Sévère,* was engaged by the English *Sultan,* and, if the French captain M de Cillart can be believed, by two other English ships. It is probable, from her place in the line, that the *Burford* also assailed her. However this may be, the *Sévère* hauled down her flag; but while the *Sultan* was wearing away from her, she resumed her fire, raking the English ship. The order to surrender, given by the French captain and carried into execution by the formal well-established token of submission, was disregarded by his subordinates, who fired upon their enemy while the flag was down. In effect, the action of the French ship amounted to using an infamous *ruse de guerre*; but it would be unjust to say that this was intended. The positions of the different vessels were such that the *Sultan* could not have secured her prize; other French ships were approaching and must have retaken it. The indignation of the French juniors at the weakness of their captain was therefore justified; their refusal to be bound by it may be excused to men face to face with an unexpected question of propriety, in the heat of battle and under the sting of shame. Nevertheless, scrupulous good faith would seem to demand that their deliverance should be awaited from other hands, not bound by the action of their commander; or at least that the forbearing assailant should not have suffered from them. The captain, suspended and sent home by Suffren, and cashiered by the king, utterly condemned himself by his attempted defence: 'When Captain de Cillart saw the French squadron drawing off—for all the ships except the *Brilliant* had fallen off on the other tack—he thought it useless to prolong his defence, and had the flag hauled down. *The ships engaged with him immediately ceased their fire,* and the one on the starboard side moved away. At this moment the *Sévère* fell off to starboard and her sails filled; Captain de Cillart then ordered the fire to be resumed by his lower-deck guns, the only ones still manned, and he rejoined his squadron.'

It is immediately after the action of the 6th of July that Suffren's superior energy and military capacity begin markedly to influence the issue between himself and Hughes. The tussle had been severe; but military qualities began to tell, as they surely must. The losses of the two squadrons in men, in the last action, had been as one to three in favor of the English; on the other hand, the latter had apparently suffered more in sails and spars—in motive power. Both fleets anchored in the evening, the English off Negapatam, the French to leeward, off Cuddalore. On the 18th of July Suffren was again ready for sea; whereas on the same day Hughes had but just decided to go to Madras to finish his repairs. Suffren was further delayed by the political necessity of an official visit to Hyder Ali, after which he sailed to Batacalo, arriving there on the 9th of August, to await reinforcements and supplies from France. On the 21st, these joined him; and two days later he sailed, now with fourteen ships-of-the-line, for Trincomalee, anchoring off the town on

the 25th. The following night the troops were landed, batteries thrown up, and the attack pressed with vigor. On the 30th and 31st the two forts which made the defensive strength of the place surrendered, and this all-important port passed into the hands of the French. Convinced that Hughes would soon appear, Suffren granted readily all the honors of war demanded by the governor of the place, contenting himself with the substantial gain. Two days later, on the evening of September 2nd, the English fleet was sighted by the French lookout frigates.

The action of September 3, like that of July 6, was brought to a close by a shift of wind to the southeast. When it came, the English line wore, and formed again on the other tack. The French also wore; and their van ships, being now to windward, stood down between their crippled ships and the enemy's line. Toward sundown Hughes hauled off to the northward, abandoning the hope of regaining Trincomalee, but with the satisfaction of having inflicted this severe retaliation upon his successful opponent.

At this season the monsoon wind, which has come for four or five months from southwest, changes to northeast, blowing upon the east coast of the peninsula, where are no good harbors. The consequent swell made the shore often unapproachable, and so forbade support from fleet to army. The change of the monsoon is also frequently marked by violent hurricanes. The two commanders, therefore, had to quit a region where their stay might be dangerous as well as useless. Had Trincomalee not been lost, Hughes, in the condition of his squadron, might have awaited there the reinforcements and supplies expected soon from England; for although the port is not healthy, it is secure and well situated. Bickerton had already reached Bombay, and was on his way now to Madras with five ships-of-the-line. As things were, Hughes thought necessary to go to Bombay for the season, sailing or rather being driven to sea by a hurricane, on the 17th of October. Four days later Bickerton reached Madras, not having fallen in with the admiral. With an activity which characterized him he sailed at once, and was again in Bombay on the 28th of November. Hughes's ships, scattered and crippled by tempest, dropped in one by one, a few days later.

It is not necessary to follow the trivial operations of the next few months. Tippoo being engaged on the other side of the peninsula and General de Bussy displaying little vigor, while Hughes was in superior force off the coast, the affairs of the French on shore went from bad to worse, unaided by inadequate support from the home government. Suffren, having but fifteen ships to eighteen English, was unwilling to go to leeward of Trincomalee, lest it should fall before he could return to it. Under these conditions the English troops advanced from Madras, passing near but around Cuddalore, and encamped to the southward of it, by the sea. The supply-ships and light cruisers were stationed off the shore near the army; while Admiral Hughes, with the heavy ships, anchored some twenty miles south, where, being to windward, he covered the others.

In order to assure to Suffren the full credit of his subsequent course, it is necessary to emphasize the fact that Bussy, though commander-in-chief both by land and sea, did not venture to order him to leave Trincomalee and come to his support. Allowing him to feel the extremity of the danger, he told him not to leave port unless he heard that the army was shut up in Cuddalore, and blockaded by the English squadron. This letter was received on the 10th of June. Suffren waited for no more. The next day he sailed, and forty-eight hours later his frigates saw the English fleet. The same day, the 13th, after a sharp action, the French army was shut up in the town, behind very weak walls. Everything now depended on the action of the fleets.

Upon Suffren's appearance, Hughes moved away and anchored four or five miles from the town. Baffling winds prevailed for three days; but the monsoon resuming on the 16th, Suffren approached. The English admiral not liking to accept action at anchor, and to leeward, in which he was right, got under way; but attaching more importance to the weather-gage than to preventing a junction between the enemy's land and sea forces, he stood out into the offing with a southerly, or south-southeast wind, notwithstanding his superior numbers. Suffren formed on the same tack, and some manoeuvring ensued during that night and the next day. At eight p.m. of the 17th the French squadron, which had refused to be drawn to sea, anchored off Cuddalore and communicated with the commander-in-chief. Twelve hundred of the garrison were hastily embarked to fill the numerous vacancies at the guns of the fleet.

Until the 20th the wind, holding unexpectedly at west, denied Hughes the advantage which he sought; and finally on that day he decided to accept action and await the attack. It was made by Suffren with fifteen ships to eighteen, the fire opening at quarter-past four p.m. and lasting until half-past six. The loss on both sides was nearly equal; but the English ships, abandoning both the field of battle and their army, returned to Madras. Suffren anchored before Cuddalore.

The embarrassment of the British army was now very great. The supply-ships on which it had depended fled before the action of the 20th, and the result of course made it impossible for them to return. The sultan's light cavalry harassed their communications by land. On the 25th, the general commanding wrote that his 'mind was on the rack without a moment's rest since the departure of the fleet, considering the character of M de Suffren, and the infinite superiority on the part of the French now that we are left to ourselves.' From this anxiety he was relieved by the news of the conclusion of peace, which reached Cuddalore on the 29th by flag-of-truce from Madras.

On the 6th of October, 1783, Suffren finally sailed from Trincomalee for France, stopping at the Isle of France and the Cape of Good Hope. The homeward voyage was a continued and spontaneous ovation.

Alike in the general conduct of his operations and on the battlefield under the fire of the enemy, lofty resolve was the distinguishing merit of Suffren; and when there is coupled with it the clear and absolute conviction which he held of the necessity to seek and crush the enemy's fleet, we have probably the leading traits of his military character. The latter was the light that led him, the former the spirit that sustained him. As a tactician, in the sense of a driller of ships, imparting to them uniformity of action and manoeuvring, he seems to have been deficient, and would probably himself have admitted, with some contempt, the justice of the criticism made upon him in these respects. Whether or no he ever actually characterized tactics—meaning thereby elementary or evolutionary tactics—as the veil of timidity, there was that in his actions which makes the *mot* probable.

Still, he was a very great man. When every deduction has been made, there must still remain his heroic constancy, his fearlessness of responsibility as of danger, the rapidity of his action, and the genius whose unerring intuition led him to break through the traditions of his service and assert for the navy that principal part which befits it, that offensive action which secures the control of the sea by the destruction of the enemy's fleet.

Below: *Lord Howe's relief of Gibraltar 11 October 1782. Even though the Franco-Spanish Fleet was in Algeciras Bay it made virtually no attempt to prevent his storeships running into the harbor. On the way back the escorting fleet fought a running battle off Cape Spartel, but it was too late.*

Chapter 9

The Battle of the Saints

The surrender of Cornwallis marked the end of the active war upon the American continent. The issue of the struggle was indeed assured upon the day when France devoted her sea power to the support of the colonists; but, as not uncommonly happens, the determining characteristics of a period were summed up in one striking event. From the beginning, the military question, owing to the physical characteristics of the country, a long seaboard with estuaries penetrating deep into the interior, and the consequent greater ease of movement by water than by land, had hinged upon the control of the sea and the use made of that control. Its misdirection by Sir William Howe in 1777, when he moved his army to the Chesapeake instead of supporting Burgoyne's advance, opened the way to the startling success at Saratoga, when amazed Europe saw six thousand regular troops surrendering to a body of provincials. During the four years that followed, until the surrender of Yorktown, the scales rose and fell according as the one navy or the other appeared on the scene, or as English commanders kept touch with the sea or pushed their operations far from its support. Finally, at the great crisis, all is found depending upon the question whether the French or the English fleet should first appear, and upon their relative force.

The maritime struggle was at once transferred to the West Indies. The events which followed there were antecedent in time both to Suffren's battles and to the final relief of Gibraltar; but they stand so much by themselves as to call for separate treatment, and have such close relation to the conclusion of the war and the conditions of peace, as to form the dramatic finale of the one and the stepping-stone of transition to the other. It is fitting indeed that a brilliant though indecisive naval victory should close the story of an essentially naval war.

The capitulation of Yorktown was completed on the 19th of October, 1781, and on the 5th of November, De Grasse, resisting the suggestions of Lafayette and Washington that the fleet should aid in carrying the war farther south, sailed from the Chesapeake. He reached Martinique on the 26th, the day after the Marquis de Bouillé, commanding the French troops in the West Indies, had regained by a bold surprise the Dutch island of St Eustatius. The two commanders now concerted a joint expedition against Barbados, which was frustrated by the violence of the trade winds.

Foiled here, the French proceeded against the island of St Christopher, or St Kitt's. On the 11th of January, 1782, the fleet, carrying six thousand troops, anchored on the west coast off Basse Terre, the chief town. No opposition was met, the small garrison of six hundred men retiring to a fortified post ten miles to the northwest, on Brimstone Hill, a solitary precipitous height overlooking the lee shore of the island. The French

Above: *Sir William Sidney Smith, brilliant but erratic flag-officer, victor of Acre.*

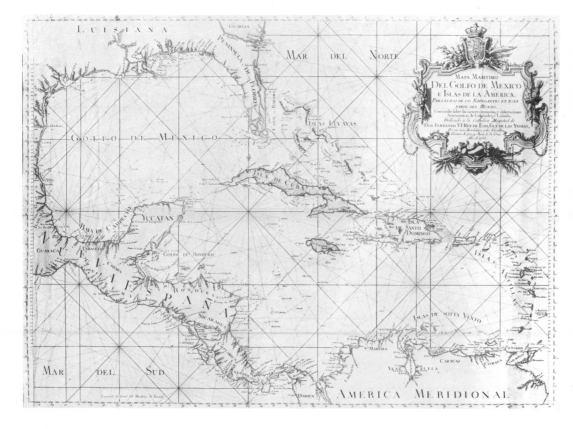

Left: *A chart of the West Indies and Gulf of Mexico c 1755.*

troops landed and pursued, but the position being found too strong for assault, siege operations were begun.

The French fleet remained at anchor in Basse Terre road. Meanwhile, news of the attack was carried to Sir Samuel Hood, who had followed De Grasse from the continent, and, in the continued absence of Rodney, was naval commander-in-chief on the station. He sailed from Barbados on the 14th, anchored at Antigua on the 21st, and there embarked all the troops that could be spared—about seven hundred men. On the afternoon of the 23rd the fleet started for St Kitt's, carrying such sail as would bring it within striking distance of the enemy at daylight next morning.

The English having but twenty-two ships to the French twenty-nine, and the latter being generally superior in force, class for class, it is necessary to mark closely the lay of the land in order to understand Hood's original plans and their subsequent modifications; for, resultless at his attempt proved, his conduct during the next three weeks forms the most brilliant military effort of the whole war. The islands of St Kitt's and Nevis being separated only by a narrow channel, impracticable for ships-of-the-line, are in effect one, and their common axis lying northwest and southeast, it is necessary for sailing ships, with the trade wind, to round the southern extremity of Nevis, from which position the wind is fair to reach all anchorages on the lee side of the islands. Basse Terre is about twelve miles distant from the western point of Nevis (Fort Charles), and its roadstead lies east and west. The French fleet were anchored there in disorder, three or four deep, not expecting attack, and the ships at the west end of the road could not reach those at the east without beating to windward—a tedious, and under fire a perilous process. A further most important point to note is that all the eastern ships were so placed that vessels approaching from the southward could reach them with the usual wind.

Hood, therefore, we are told, intended to appear at early daylight, in order of and ready for battle, and fall upon the eastern ships, filing by them with his whole fleet, thus concentrating the fire of all upon a few of the enemy; then turning away, so as to escape the guns of the others, he proposed, first wearing and then tacking, to keep his fleet circling in long procession past that part of the enemy's ships chosen for attack. The plan was audacious, but undeniably sound in principle; some good could hardly fail to follow, and unless De Grasse showed more readiness than he had hitherto done, even decisive results might be hoped for.

The best-laid plans, however, may fail, and Hood's was balked by the awkwardness of a lieutenant of the watch, who hove-to (stopped) a frigate at night ahead of the fleet, and was consequently run down by a ship-of-the-line. The latter also received such injury as delayed the movement, several hours being lost in repairing damages. The French were thus warned of the enemy's approach, and although not suspecting his intention to attack, De Grasse feared that Hood would pass down to leeward of him and disturb the siege of Brimstone Hill, an undertaking so rash for an inferior force that it is as difficult to conceive how he could have supposed it, as to account for his overlooking the weakness of his own position at anchor.

At one p.m. of the 24th the English fleet was seen rounding the south end of Nevis; at three De Grasse got under way and stood to the southward. Toward sundown Hood also went about and stood south, as though retreating; but he was well to windward of his opponent, and maintained this advantage through the night. At daybreak both fleets were to leeward of Nevis—the English near the island, the French about nine miles distant. Some time was spent in manoeuvring, with the object on Hood's part of getting the French admiral yet more to leeward; for,

having failed in his first attempt, he had formed the yet bolder intention of seizing the anchorage his unskilful opponent had left, and establishing himself there in an impregnable manner. In this he succeeded, as will be shown; but to understand the justification for a movement confessedly hazardous, it must be pointed out that he thus would place himself between the besiegers of Brimstone Hill and their fleet; or, if the latter anchored near the hill, the English fleet would be between it and its base in Martinique, ready to intercept supplies or detachments approaching from the southward. In short, the position in which Hood hoped to establish himself was on the flank of the enemy's communications, a position the more advantageous because the island alone could not long support the large body of troops so suddenly thrown upon it. Moreover, both fleets were expecting reinforcements; Rodney was on his way and might arrive first, which he did, and in time to save St Kitt's, which he did not. It was also but four months since Yorktown; the affairs of England were going badly; something must be done, something left to chance, and Hood knew himself and his officers. It may be added that he knew his opponent.

Below: *An engraving of a portrait of Lord Rodney, from the painting by Reynolds.*

Above: *Admiral Comte Louis de Bougainville was a great explorer in the South Pacific. As a result of the acrimony after France's humiliating defeat at the Saints in 1782 he and Coriolis d'Espinouse were publicly admonished for failing to set a proper example as Chefs d'Escadre after the line was broken. He was fortunate to escape the Reign of Terror and was loaded with honors by Napoleon.*

At noon, when the hillsides of Nevis were covered with expectant and interested sightseers, the English fleet rapidly formed its line on the starboard tack and headed north for Basse Terre. The French, at the moment, were in column steering south, but went about at once and stood for the enemy in a bow-and-quarter line. (When a fleet is in line ahead, close to the wind, on one tack, and the ships go about together, they will, on the other tack, be on the same line, but not one ahead of the other. This formation was called bow-and-quarter line.) At two the British had got far enough for Hood to make signal to anchor. At twenty minutes past two the van of the French came within gunshot of the English centre, and shortly afterward the firing began, the assailants very properly directing their main effort upon the English rear ships, which, as happens with most long columns, had opened, out, a tendency increased in this case by the slowness of the fourth ship from the rear, the *Prudent*. The French flag-ship, *Ville de Paris*, of one hundred and twenty guns, bearing De Grasse's flag, pushed for the gap thus made, but was foiled by the *Canada*, seventy-four, whose captain, Cornwallis, the brother of Lord Cornwallis, threw all his sails aback, and dropped down in front of the huge enemy to the support of the rear—an example nobly followed by the *Resolution* and the *Bedford* immediately ahead of him. The scene was now varied and animated in the extreme. The English van, which had escaped attack, was rapidly anchoring in its appointed position. The commander-in-chief in the centre, proudly reliant upon the skill and conduct of his captains, made signal for

the ships ahead to carry a press of sail, and gain their positions regardless of the danger to the threatened rear. The latter, closely pressed and outnumbered, stood on unswervingly, shortened sail, and came to anchor, one by one, in a line ahead, under the roar of the guns of their baffled enemies. The latter filed by, delivered their fire, and bore off again to the southward, leaving their former berths to their weaker but clever antagonists.

The anchorage thus brilliantly taken by Hood was not exactly the same as that held by De Grasse the day before; but as it covered and controlled it, his claim that he took up the place the other had left is substantially correct. The following night and morning were spent in changing and strengthening the order, which was finally established as follows. The van ship was anchored about four miles southeast from Basse Terre, so close to the shore that a ship could not pass inside her, nor, with the prevailing wind, even reach her, because of a point and shoal just outside, covering her position. From this point the line extended in a west-northwest direction to the twelfth or thirteenth ship (from a mile and a quarter to a mile and a half), where it turned gradually but rapidly to north, the last six ships being on a north and south line. Hood's flag-ship, the *Barfleur*, of ninety guns, was at the apex of the salient angle thus formed.

It would not have been impossible for the French fleet to take the anchorage they formerly held; but it and all others to leeward were forbidden by the considerations already stated, so long as Hood remained where he was. It became necessary therefore to dislodge him, but this was rendered exceedingly difficult by the careful tactical dispositions that have been described. His left flank was covered by the shore. Any attempt to enfilade his front by passing along the other flank was met by the broadsides of the six or eight ships drawn up *en potence* to the rear. The front commanded the approaches to Basse Terre. To attack him in the rear, from the northwest, was forbidden by the trade-wind. To these difficulties was to be added that the attack must be made under sail against ships at anchor, to whom loss of spars would be of no immediate concern; and which, having springs out (a spring is a rope taken from the stern or quarter of a ship at anchor, to an anchor properly placed, by which means the ship can be turned in a desired direction), could train their broadsides over a large area with great ease.

Nevertheless, both sound policy and mortification impelled De Grasse to fight, which he did the next day, January 26. The method of attack, in single column of twenty-nine ships against a line so carefully arranged, was faulty in the extreme; but it may be doubted whether any commander of that day would have broken through the traditional fighting order. Hood had intended the same, but he hoped a surprise on an ill-ordered enemy, and at the original French anchorage it was possible to reach their eastern ships, with but slight exposure to concentrated

fire. Not so now. The French formed to the southward and steered for the eastern flank of Hood's line. As their van ship drew up with the point already mentioned, the wind headed her, so that she could only reach the third in the English order, the first four ships of which, using their springs, concentrated their guns upon her. This vessel was supposed by the English to be the *Pluton*, and if so, her captain was D'Albert de Rions, in Suffren's opinion the foremost officer of the French navy. 'The crash occasioned by their destructive broadsides,' wrote an English officer who was present, 'was so tremendous that whole pieces of plank were seen flying from her off side ere she could escape the cool, concentrated fire of her determined adversaries. As she proceeded along the British line, she received the first fire of every ship in passing. She was indeed in so shattered a state as to be compelled to bear away for St Eustatius.' And so ship after ship passed by, running the length of the line, distributing their successive fires in gallant but dreary, ineffectual monotony over the whole extent. A second time that day De Grasse attacked in the same order, but neglecting the English van, directed his effort upon the rear and centre. This was equally fruitless, and seems to have been done with little spirit.

From that time until the 14th of February, Hood maintained his position in sight of the French fleet, which remained cruising in the offing and to the southward. On the 1st a despatch vessel arrived from Kempenfeldt, informing him of the dispersal of the French reinforcements for the West Indies, which must have renewed his hopes that his bold attempt would be successful through Rodney's arrival. It was not, however, to be so. Brimstone Hill surrendered on the 12th, after a creditable defence. On the 13th De Grasse took his fleet, now amounting to thirty-three ships-of-the-line, to Nevis, and anchored there. On the night of the 14th Hood summoned all his captains on board, had them set their watches by his, and at eleven p.m., one after another, without noise or signal, cut their cables and made sail to the northward, passing round that end of the island unnoticed, or at least unmolested, by the French.

Both strategically and tactically Hood's conceptions and dispositions were excellent, and their execution was most honorable to the skill and steadiness of himself and his captains. Regarded as a single military operation, this was brilliant throughout; but when considered with reference to the general situation of England at the time, a much higher estimate must

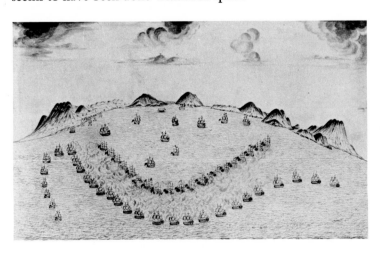

Top: *Contemporary painting of the Saints by Captain William Elliot, exhibited at the Royal Academy in 1787.*

Opposite: *The aftermath of the Battle of the Saints in France was almost as grisly as the battle itself. Not only were Bougainville and D'Espinouse publicly reprimanded; the captains of the* Neptune *and* Jason *were admonished, those of the* Zélé *and* Ardent *were dismissed their ships and the captain of the* Caton *was sentenced to life imprisonment.*

Left: *Diagram of Commodore Samuel Hood's action, 26 January 1782, against De Grasse at St Kitts (known to the French as St Christopher). Afterward the French tried to prevent the English from leaving the anchorage but by fixing false riding lights on buoys they were able to cut their cables and slip away.*

be formed of the admiral's qualities. St Kitt's in itself might not be worth a great risk; but it was of the first importance that energy and audacity should be carried into the conduct of England's naval war, that some great success should light upon her flag. Material success was not obtained. The chances, though fair enough, turned against Hood; but every man in that fleet must have felt the glow of daring achievement, the assured confidence which follows a great deed nobly done. Had this man been in chief command when greater issues were at stake, had he been first instead of second at the Chesapeake, Cornwallis might have been saved. The operation—seizing an anchorage left by the enemy—would have been nearly the same; and both situations may be instructively compared with Suffren's relief of Cuddalore.

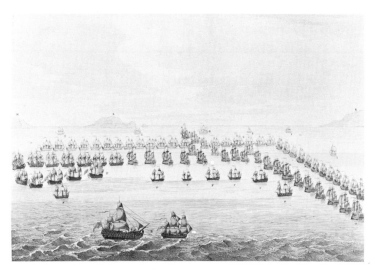

Above: *A very stylized view of the Saints, an engraving based on a painting by Walker, published in 1786.*

The hour was now close at hand when the French admiral should feel, even if he did not admit, the consequences of this mistake, by which he had won a paltry island and lost an English fleet. Rodney had sailed from Europe on the 15th of January, with twelve ships-of-the-line. On the 19th of February he anchored at Barbados, and the same day Hood reached Antigua from St Kitt's. On the 25th the squadrons of Rodney and Hood met to windward of Antigua, forming a united fleet of thirty-four ships-of-the-line. The next day De Grasse anchored in Fort Royal, thus escaping the pursuit which Rodney at once began. The English admiral then returned to St Lucia, where he was joined by three more ships-of-the-line from England, raising his force to thirty-seven. Knowing that a large convoy was expected from France, before the arrival of which nothing could be attempted, Rodney sent a part of his fleet to cruise to windward and as far north as Guadeloupe; but the officer in charge of the French convoy, suspecting this action, kept well north of that island, and reached Fort Royal, Martinique, on the 20th of March. The ships-of-war with him raised De Grasse's fleet to thirty-three effective sail-of-the-line and two fifty-gun ships.

The object of the united efforts of France and Spain this year was the conquest of Jamaica. It was expected to unite at Cap Français (now Cap Haïtien), in Haiti, fifty ships-of-the-line and twenty thousand troops. Part of the latter were already at the rendezvous; and De Grasse, appointed to command the combined fleets, was to collect in Martinique all the available troops and supplies in the French islands, and convoy them to the rendezvous. It was this junction that Rodney was charged to prevent.

The region within which occurred the important operations of the next few days covers a distance of one hundred and fifty miles, from south to north, including the islands of St Lucia, Martinique, Dominica, and Guadeloupe, in the order named. At this time the first was in English, the others in French, hands. The final, and for the moment decisive, encounter took place between, and a little to westward of, Dominica and Guadeloupe.

These are twenty-three miles apart; but the channel is narrowed to thirteen by three islets called the Saints, lying ten miles south of Guadeloupe. It is said to have been De Grasse's intention, that instead of sailing direct for Cap Français he in fact intended to take a circuitous course near the islands, which, being friendly or neutral, would give refuge to the convoy if pressed. The close pursuit of the English, who came up with him off Dominica, led him to forsake this plan, sending the convoy into Basse Terre at the south end of Guadeloupe, while with the fleet he tried to beat through the channel and pass east of the island, thus drawing the English away from the transports and ridding himself of the tactical embarrassment due to the latter's presence. Accidents to various ships thwarted this attempt, and brought about a battle disastrous to him and fatal to the joint

Above: The Ville de Paris *finally strikes her colors to the* Formidable *after a terrible battering. Painting by T Whitcombe.*

Opposite top: Rodney's flag-ship the 90-gun 2nd Rate Formidable *engaging the French flag-ship, the 104-gun 1st Rate* Ville de Paris *at the Saints (center). The Frenchman's resistance cost her more casualties than Rodney's entire fleet, and toward the end of the day her gun crews were reduced to scooping gunpowder out of kegs in the hold as all cartridges had been expended. She was repaired as HMS* Ville de Paris *but foundered in a gale off Newfoundland five months later.*

Below: The Battle of the Saints, 12 April 1782.

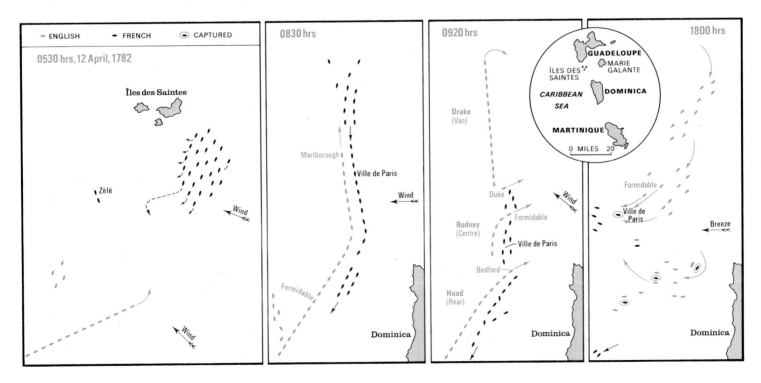

Left: *The Prince George, a 90-gun 2nd Rate in tow of the 28-gun frigate* Triton *after the Battle of the Saints. She lost her foremast and suffered other damage but was soon repaired, and served for another half a century. Holes in a wooden hull were relatively easy to repair with wooden plugs.*

Opposite: *Sir Samuel Hood receiving the sword of Comte de Grasse on the deck of the* Ville de Paris—*a tranquil view of what by most accounts must have been a bloody tangle of dead and dying. Indeed, after the battle the French reported on the British 'secret weapon'—the carronade. A short-barrelled large-caliber gun, known as the 'smasher,' it had a considerable impact used in close-range action.*

enterprise.

The anchorages of the two fleets, in Martinique and St Lucia, were thirty miles apart. The prevailing east wind is generally fair to pass from one to the other; but a strong westerly current, and the frequency of calms and light airs, tend to throw to leeward sailing-ships leaving St Lucia for the northern island. A chain of frigates connected the English lookout ships off Martinique, by signal, with Rodney's flag-ship in Gros Ilot Bay. Everything was astir at the two stations, the French busy with the multitudinous arrangements necessitated by a great military undertaking, the English with less to do, yet maintaining themselves in a state of expectancy and preparation for instant action, that entails constant alertness and mental activity.

On the 5th of April Rodney was informed that the soldiers were being embarked, and on the 8th, soon after daylight, the lookout frigates were seen making signal that the enemy was leaving port. The English fleet at once began to get under way, and by noon was clear of the harbor to the number of thirty-six of the line. At half-past two p.m. the advanced frigates were in sight of the French fleet, which was seen from the mastheads of the main body just before sundown. The English stood to the northward all night, and at daybreak of the 9th were abreast Dominica, but for the most part becalmed. In-shore of them, to the northward and eastward, were seen the French fleet and convoy: the men-of-war numbering thirty-three of the line, besides smaller vessels; the convoy a hundred and fifty sail, under special charge of the two fifty-gun ships. The irregular and uncertain winds, common to the night and early hours of the day near the land, had scattered these unwieldy numbers. Fifteen sail-of-the-line were in the channel between Dominica and the Saints, with a fresh trade-wind, apparently beating to windward; the remainder of the ships-of-war and most of the convoy were still becalmed close under Dominica.

Gradually, however, and one by one, the French ships were catching light airs off the land; and by favor of these, which did not reach so far as the English in the offing, drew out from the island and entered the more steady breeze of the channel, reinforcing the group which was thus possessed of that prime element of naval power, mobility. At the same time light airs

from the southeast crept out to the English van under Hood, fanning it gently north from the main body of the fleet toward two isolated French ships, which, having fallen to leeward during the night, had shared the calms that left the English motionless, with their heads all round the compass. They had come nearly within gunshot, when a light puff from the northwest enabled the Frenchmen to draw away and approach their own ships in the channel.

The farther the English van advanced, the fresher grew their wind, until they fairly opened the channel of the Saints and felt the trade-wind. De Grasse signalled to the convoy to put into Guadeloupe, which order was so well carried out that they were all out of sight to the northward by two in the afternoon, and will appear no more in the sequel. The two French ships, already spoken of as fallen to leeward, not being yet out of danger from the English van, which had now a commanding breeze, and the latter being much separated from their rear and centre, De Grasse ordered his van to bear down and engage. This was obeyed by the ships signalled and by three others, in all by fourteen or fifteen, the action beginning at half-past nine a.m., and lasting with intermissions until quarter-past one p.m. Hood was soon forced to heave-to, in order not to increase too much his separation from the main fleet; the French kept under way, approaching from the rear and passing in succession at half cannon-shot to windward.

As each ship drew ahead, she tacked, standing back to the southward until in position to resume her place in the order of attack, thus describing a continuous irregular curve of elliptical form, to windward of their opponents. The brunt of the attack fell upon eight or nine of the English, this number being successively increased as one ship after another, as the baffling airs served, drew out from the calm space under Dominica; but the French received similar accessions. While this engagement was going on, part of the English centre, eight ships with Rodney's own flag-ship among them, by carefully watching the puffs and cat's-paws, had worked in with the land and caught the sea breeze, which was felt there sooner than in the offing. As soon as they had it, about eleven a.m., they stood to the north, being now on the weather quarter (weather quarter is behind, but on the windward side) both of the English van and also of its assailants. The latter, on seeing this, tacked, and abandoning the contest for the moment, steered south to join their centre, lest Rodney's eight ships should get between them. At half-past eleven the French again formed line on the starboard tack, most of their ships being now clear of the land, while the English rear was still becalmed. The greater numbers of the French enabled them to extend from north to south along the length of the English line, whereas the latter was still broken by a great gap between the van and centre.

The attack upon Hood was therefore hotly renewed; but the French centre and rear, having the wind, kept their distance, and held Rodney's division at long range. At quarter-past one the French, finding that the whole British line was coming up with the wind, ceased firing, and at two Rodney hauled down the signal for battle, the enemy having withdrawn. However, the action of the 9th of April amounted actually to no more than an artillery duel.

By daylight, April 12, (about half-past five) the English fleet, which had gone about at two a.m., was standing on the starboard tack, with the wind at southeast, an unusual amount of southing for that hour (Map, page 193). It was about fifteen miles from the Saints, which bore north-northeast, and ten from the French fleet, which bore northeast. The latter, owing to the events of the night, was greatly scattered, as much as eight or ten miles separating the weather, or easternmost, ships from the lee, the flag-ship *Ville de Paris* being among the latter. Anxiety for

the *Zélé* kept the French admiral, with the ships in his company, under short canvas, standing to the southward on the port tack.

The English on the starboard tack, with the wind as they had it, headed east-northeast, and thus, as soon as there was light to see, found the French 'broad on the lee bow, and one of M de Grasse's ships (the *Zélé*) towed by a frigate, square under our lee with his bowsprit and foremast prostrate across his fore-castle.' To draw the French farther to leeward, Rodney detached four ships to chase the *Zélé*. As soon as De Grasse saw this he signalled his fleet to keep away, as Rodney wished, and at the same time to form the line-of-battle, thus calling down to him the ships to windward. The English line was also formed rapidly, and the chasing ships recalled at seven a.m. De Grasse, seeing that if he stood on he would lose the weather-gage altogether, hauled up again on the port tack; and the breeze changing to east-southeast and east in his favor and knocking the English off, the race of the two fleets on opposite tacks, for the advantage of the wind, became nearly equal. The French, however, won, thanks to a superiority in sailing which had enabled them to draw so far to windward of the English on the previous days, and, but for the awkwardness of the *Zélé*, might have cleared them altogether (0830 hours). Their leading ships first reached and passed the point where the rapidly converging tracks intersected, while the English leader, the *Marlborough*, struck the French line between the sixth and tenth ships (variously stated). The battle, of course, had by this time begun, the ninth ship in the French line, the *Brave*, opening fire at twenty

minutes before eight a.m. upon the *Marlborough*. As there was no previous intention of breaking the line, the English leader kept away, in obedience to a signal from Rodney, and ran close along under the enemy's lee, followed in succession by all the ships as they reached her wake. The battle thus assumed the common and indecisive phase of two fleets passing on opposite tacks, the wind very light, however, and so allowing a more heavy engagement than common under these circumstances, the ships 'sliding by' at the rate of three to four knots. Since the hostile lines diverged again south of their point of meeting, De Grasse made signal to keep away four points to south-southwest, thus bringing his van into action with the English rear, and not permitting the latter to reach his rear unscathed. There were, however, two dangers threatening the French if they continued their course. Its direction, south or south-southwest, carried them into the calms that hung round the north end of Dominica; and the uncertainty of the wind made it possible that by its hauling to the southward the enemy could pass through their line and gain the wind, and with it the possibility of forcing the decisive battle which the French policy had shunned; and this was in fact what happened. De Grasse therefore made signal at half-past eight to wear *together* and take the same tack as the English. This, however, was impossible; the two fleets were too close together to admit the evolution. He then signalled to haul close to the wind and wear *in succession*, which also failed to be done, and at five minutes past nine the dreaded contingency arose; the wind hauled to the southward, knocking off all the French ships that had not yet kept away; that is, all who had English ships close under their lee (0920 hours). Rodney, in the *Formidable*, was at this time just drawing up with the fourth ship astern of De Grasse's flag. Luffing to the new

wind, he passed through the French line, followed by the five ships next astern of him, while nearly at the same moment, and from the same causes, his six astern led through the interval abreast him, followed by the whole English rear. The French line-of-battle was thus broken in two places by columns of enemies' ships in such close order as to force its vessels aside, even if the wind had not conspired to embarrass their action. Every principle upon which a line-of-battle was constituted, for mutual support and for the clear field of fire of each ship, was thus overthrown for the French, and preserved for the English divisions which filed through; and the French were forced off to leeward by the interposition of the enemy's columns, besides being broken up. Compelled thus to forsake the line upon which they had been ranged, it was necessary to re-form upon another, and unite the three groups into which they were divided—a difficult piece of tactics under any circumstances, but doubly so under the moral impression of disaster, and in presence of a superior enemy, who, though himself disordered, was in better shape, and already felt the glow of victory.

It does not appear that any substantial attempt to re-form was made by the French. To reunite, yes; but only as a flying, disordered mass. The various shifts of wind and movements of the divisions left their fleet, by noontime that day, with the centre two miles northwest of and to leeward of the van, the rear yet farther from the centre and to leeward of it. Calms and short puffs of wind prevailed now through both fleets. At half-past one p.m. a light breeze from the east sprang up, and De Grasse made signal to form the line again on the port tack; between three and four, not having succeeded in this, he made signal to form on the starboard tack. The two signals and the general tenor of the accounts show that at no time were the

French re-formed after their line was broken; and all the manoeuvres tended toward, even if they did not necessitate, taking the whole fleet as far down as the most leewardly of its parts. In such a movement, it followed of course that the most crippled ships were left behind, and these were picked up, one by one, by the English, who pursued without any regular order, for which there was no need, as mutual support was assured without it. Shortly after six p.m. De Grasse's flag-ship, the *Ville de Paris*, struck her colors to the *Barfleur*, carrying the flag of Sir Samuel Hood. The French accounts state that nine of the enemy's ships then surrounded her, and there is no doubt that she had been fought to the bitter end. Her name, commemorating the great city whose gift she had been to the king, her unusual size, and the fact that no French naval commander-in-chief had before taken prisoner in battle, conspired to bestow a peculiar brilliancy upon Rodney's victory. Four other ships-of-the-line were taken and, singularly enough, upon these particular ships was found the whole train of artillery intended for the reduction of Jamaica. Such were the leading features of the Battle of the Saints, or, as it is sometimes styled, of the 12th of April, known to the French as the Battle of Dominica.

Independently of the tactical handling of the two fleets, there were certain differences of equipment which conferred tactical advantage, and are therefore worth noting. The French appear to have had finer ships, and, class for class, heavier armaments. Sir Charles Douglas, an eminent officer of active and ingenious turn of mind, who paid particular attention to gunnery details, estimated that in weight of battery the thirty-three French were superior to the thirty six English by the force of four 84-gun ships; and that after the loss of the *Zélé*, *Jason*, and *Caton* there still remained an advantage equal to two seventy-fours.

The French admiral La Gravière admits the generally heavier calibre of French cannon at this era. The better construction of the French ships and their greater draught caused them to sail and beat better, and accounts in part of for the success of De Grasse in gaining to windward.

There were gunnery innovations, in some at least of the English ships, which by increasing the accuracy, the rapidity, and the field of fire, greatly augmented the power of their batteries. These were the introduction of locks, by which the man who aimed also fired; and the fitting to the gun-carriages of breast-pieces and sweeps, so that the guns could be pointed farther ahead or astern—that is, over a larger field than had been usual. In fights between single ships, not controlled in their movements by their relations to a fleet, this improvement would at times allow the possessor to take a position whence he could train upon his enemy without the latter being able to reply.

These matters of antiquated and now obsolete detail carry with them lessons that are never obsolete; they differ in no respect from the more modern experiences with the needle-gun and the torpedo. This whole action of April 12, 1782, is fraught with sound military teaching. Perseverance in pursuit, gaining advantage of position, concentration of one's own effort, dispersal of the enemy's force, the efficient tactical bearing of small but important improvements in the material of war are all indicated. To insist further upon the necessity of not letting slip a chance to beat the enemy in detail, would be thrown away on any one not fully convinced by the bearing of April 9 on April 12. The abandonment of the attack upon Jamaica, after the defeat of the French fleet, shows conclusively that the true way to secure ulterior objects is to defeat the force which threatens them.

Above: *Death of Lord Manners at the Battle of the Saints. Death came from enemy shot, but also from splinters of timber, falling rigging and the personal weapons of boarding parties.*

Opposite left: *Sir George Rodney, raised to the peerage after his much needed victory at the Saints. He was criticized by his subordinates for not pursuing the French after the battle but posterity recognizes the magnitude of his victory.*

Left: *Dodd's painting of the Battle of the Saints, 'Lord Rodney's Victory over the French off Dominica 1782.'*

Chapter 10

A discussion of the War of 1778

The war of 1778, between Great Britain and the House of Bourbon, which is so inextricably associated with the American Revolution, stands by itself in one respect. It was purely a maritime war. Not only did the allied kingdoms carefully refrain from continental entanglements, which England in accordance with her former policy strove to excite, but there was between the two contestants an approach to equality on the sea which had not been realized since the days of Tourville. The points in dispute, the objects for which the war was undertaken or at which it aimed, were for the most part remote from Europe; and none of them was on the continent with the single exception of Gibraltar, the strife over which, being at the extreme point of a rugged and difficult salient, and separated from neutral nations by the whole of France and Spain, never threatened to drag in other parties than those immediately interested.

No such conditions existed in any war between the accession of Louis XIV and the downfall of Napoleon. There was a period during the reign of the former in which the French navy was superior in number and equipment to the English and Dutch; but the policy and ambition of the sovereign was always directed to continental extension, and his naval power, resting on inadequate foundations, was ephemeral. During the first three-quarters of the eighteenth century there was practically no check to the sea power of England; great as were its effects upon the issues of the day, the absence of a capable rival made its operations barren of military lessons. In the later wars of the French Republic and Empire, the apparent equality in numbers of ships and weight of batteries was illusive, owing to the demoralization of the French officers and seamen by causes upon which it is not necessary here to enlarge. After some years of courageous but impotent effort, the tremendous disaster of Trafalgar proclaimed to the world the professional inefficiency of the French and Spanish navies.

The student of naval war will therefore expect to find a particular interest in the plans and methods of the parties to this great contest, and especially where they concern the general conduct of the whole war, or of certain large and clearly defined portions of it. The principal parties of the War of 1778 were, on the one hand, Great Britain; on the other, the House of Bourbon, controlling the two great kingdoms of France and Spain. The American colonies, being already engaged in an unequal struggle with the mother-country, gladly welcomed an event so important to them; while in 1780 Holland was deliberately forced by England into a war from which she had nothing to gain and all to lose.

With Great Britain also the object of the war was very simple. Having been led into a lamentable altercation with her most promising colonies, the quarrel had gone on step by step till she was threatened with their loss. To maintain forcible control when willing adhesion had departed, she had taken up arms against them, and her object in so doing was to prevent a break in those foreign possessions with which, in the eyes of that generation, her greatness was indissolubly connected.

The views and objects of France and Spain were more complex. The moral incentives of hereditary enmity and desire of revenge for the recent past doubtless weighed strongly, as in France did also the sympathy of the *salons* and philosophers with the colonists' struggle for freedom. The principal objects at which France aimed were the English West Indies and that control of India which had passed into English hands, and also to secure in due time the independence of the United States, after they had wrought a sufficient diversion in her favor. With the policy of exclusive trade which characterized that generation, the loss of these important possessions was expected to lessen that commercial greatness upon which the prosperity of England depended—to weaken her and to strengthen France. In fact, the strife which should be greater may be said to have been the animating motive of France; all objects were summed up in the one supreme end to which they contributed—maritime and political superiority over England.

Preponderance over England, in combination with France, was also the aim of the equally humbled but less vigorous kingdom of Spain; but there was a definiteness in the injuries suffered and the objects specially sought by her which is less easily found in the broader views of her ally. Although no Spaniard then living could remember the Spanish flag flying over Minorca, Gibraltar, or Jamaica, the lapse of time had not reconciled the proud and tenacious nation to their loss; nor was there on the part of the Americans the same traditional objection to the renewal of Spanish sovereignty over the two Floridas that was felt with reference to Canada.

In short, as regards the *objects* of the war the allies were on the offensive, as England was thrown upon the defensive. The tyrannical empire which England was thus accused, and not unjustly, of exercising over the seas, rested upon her great sea power, actual or latent; upon her commerce and armed shipping, her commercial establishments, colonies, and naval stations in all parts of the world. Up to this time her scattered colonies had been bound to her by ties of affectionate sentiment, and by the still stronger motive of self-interest through the close commercial connection with the mother-country and the protection afforded by the constant presence of her superior navy. Now a break was made in the girdle of strong ports upon which her naval power was based, by the revolt of the continental colonies; while the numerous trade interests between them and the West Indies, which were injured by the consequent hostilities, tended to divide the sympathies of the islands also. The struggle was not only for political possessions and commercial use. It involved a military question of the first importance—whether a chain of

Above: *The East River shore in 1750.*

Opposite: *New York in 1746 showing the Ferry House on the East River.*

naval stations covering one of the shores of the Atlantic, linking Canada and Halifax with the West Indies, and backed by a thriving seafaring population, should remain in the hands of a nation which had so far used its unprecedented sea power with consistent, resolute aggressiveness, and with almost unbroken success.

In a sea war, as in all others, two things are from the first essential—a suitable base upon the frontier, in this case the seaboard, from which the operations start, and an organized military force, in this case a fleet, of size and quality adequate to the proposed operations. If the war, as in the present instance, extends to distant parts of the globe, there will be needed in each of those distant regions secure ports for the shipping, to serve as secondary, or contingent, bases of the local war. Between these secondary and the principal, or home, bases there must be reasonably secure communication, which will depend upon military control of the intervening sea. This control must be exercised by the navy, which will enforce it either by clearing the sea in all directions of hostile cruisers, thus allowing the ships of its own nation to pass with reasonable security, or by accompanying in force (convoying) each train of supply-ships necessary for the support of the distant operations. The former method aims at a widely diffused effort of the national power, the other at a concentration of it upon that part of the sea where the convoy is at a given moment. Whichever be adopted, the communications will doubtless be strengthened by the military holding of good harbors, properly spaced yet not too numerous, along the routes, as, for instance, the Cape of Good Hope and the Mauritius. Stations of this kind have always been necessary, but are doubly so now, as fuel needs renewing more frequently than did the provisions and supplies in former days. These combinations of strong points at home and abroad, and the condition of the communications between them, may be called the strategic features of the general military situation, by which, and by the relative strength of the opposing fleets, the nature of the operations must be determined. In each of the three divisions of the field, Europe, America, and India, under which for sake of clearness the narrative has been given, the control of the sea has been insisted upon as the determining factor, and the hostile fleet therefore indicated as the true objective. Let the foregoing considerations now be applied to the whole field of war, and see how far the same conclusion holds good of it, and if so, what should have been the nature of the operations on either side.

In Europe the home base of Great Britain was on the English Channel, with the two principal arsenals of Plymouth and Portsmouth. The base of the allied powers was on the Atlantic, the principal military ports being Brest, Ferrol, and Cadiz. Behind these, within the Mediterranean, were the dock-yards of Toulon and Cartagena, over against which stood the English

station Port Mahon, in Minorca. The latter, however, may be left wholly out of account, being confined to a defensive part during the war, as the British fleet was not able to spare any squadron to the Mediterranean. There was a difference in the parts played by Port Mahon and Gibraltar. The former, being at the time wholly unimportant, received no attention from the allies until late in the war, when it fell after a six months' siege; whereas the latter, being considered of the first importance, absorbed from the beginning a very large part of the allied attack, and so made a valuable diversion in favor of Great Britain.

In North America the local bases of the war at its outbreak were New York, Narragansett Bay, and Boston. The two former were then held by the English, and were the most important stations on the continent, from their position, susceptibility of defence, and resources. Boston had passed into the hands of the Americans, and was therefore at the service of the allies.

The principal local bases of the war in the West Indies are already known through the previous narrative. They were for the English, Barbados, St Lucia, and to a less degree Antigua. A thousand miles to leeward was the large island of Jamaica, with a dock-yard of great natural capabilities at Kingston. The allies held, in the first order of importance, Fort Royal in Martinique, and Havana; in the second order, Guadeloupe and Cap Français. A controlling feature of the strategic situation in that day, and one which will not be wholly without weight in our own, was the trade-wind, with its accompanying current. A passage to windward against these obstacles was a long and serious undertaking even for single ships, much more for larger bodies. It followed that fleets would go to the western islands only reluctantly, or when assured that the enemy had taken the same direction, as Rodney went to Jamaica after the Battle of the Saints, knowing the French fleet to have gone to Cap Français. This condition of the wind made the windward, or eastern, islands points on the natural lines of communication between Europe and America, as well as local bases of the naval war, and tied the fleets to them. Hence also it followed that between the two scenes of operations, between the continent and the Lesser Antilles, was interposed a wide central region into which the larger operations of war could not safely be carried except by a belligerent possessed of great naval superiority, or unless a decisive advantage had been gained upon one flank.

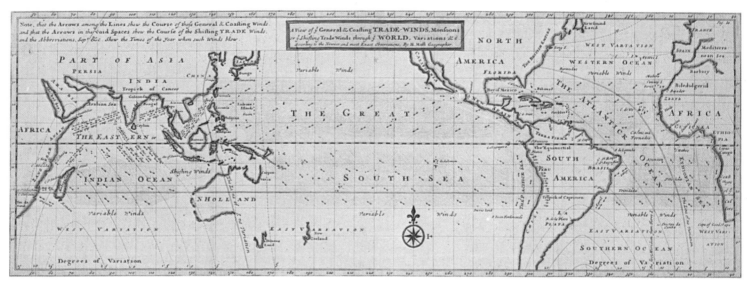

In India the political conditions of the peninsula necessarily indicated the eastern, or Coromandel, coast as the scene of operations. Trincomalee, in the adjacent island of Ceylon, though unhealthy, offered an excellent and defensible harbor, and thus acquired first-rate strategic importance, all the other anchorages on the coast being mere open roadsteads. From this circumstance the trade-winds, or monsoons, in this region also had strategic bearing. The 'change of the monsoon,' in September and October, is often marked by violent hurricanes. Active operations, or even remaining on the coast, were therefore unadvisable from this time until the close of the northeast monsoon. The question of a port to which to retire during this season was pressing. Trincomalee was the only one, and its unique strategic value was heightened by being to windward, during the fine season, of the principal scene of war. The English harbor of Bombay on the west coast was too distant to be considered a local base, and rather falls, like the French islands Mauritius and Bourbon, under the head of stations on the line of communications with the mother-country.

Such were the principal points of support, or bases, of the belligerent nations, at home and abroad. Of those abroad it must be said, speaking generally, that they were deficient in resources—an important element of strategic value. Naval and military stores and equipments, and to a great extent provisions for sea use, had to be sent them from the mother-countries. Hence the strategic question of communications assumed additional importance. To intercept a large convoy of supply-ships was an operation only secondary to the destruction of a body of ships-of-war; while to protect such by main strength,

or by evading the enemy's search, taxed the skill of the governments and naval commanders in distributing the ships-of-war and squadrons at their disposal, among the many objects which demanded attention.

Thus the navies, by which alone these vital streams could be secured or endangered, bore the same relation to the maintenance of the general war that has already been observed of the separate parts. They were the links that bound the whole together, and were therefore indicated as the proper objective of both belligerents.

The distance from Europe to America was not such as to make intermediate ports of supply absolutely necessary; while if difficulty did arise from an unforeseen cause, it was always possible, barring meeting an enemy, either to return to Europe or to make a friendly port in the West Indies. The case was different with the long voyage to India by the Cape of Good Hope. A voyage of such duration could rarely be made without a stop for water, for fresh provisions, often for such refitting as called for the quiet of a harbor, even when the stores on board furnished the necessary material. A perfect line of communications required, as has been said, several such harbors, properly spaced, adequately defended, and with abundant supplies, such as England in the present day holds on some of her main commercial routes, acquisitions of her past wars. In the war of 1778 none of the belligerents had such ports on this route, until, by by the accession of Holland, the Cape of Good Hope was put at the disposal of the French and suitably strengthend by Suffren. With this and the Mauritius on the way, and Trincomalee at the far end of the road, the communications of the allies with France

Left: *Fitting out a French privateer. The size of ship and quality of her armament depended on the purse of her owners, but the lucrative profits from privateering always attracted 'risk capital,' especially for a well known captain.*

Left: *Chart of world trade showing the direction of prevailing winds. Ultimately sea power was about shipborne trade, for navies only exist to ensure safe passage from one land mass to another.*

Right: *John Harrison's chronometer, one of the most important aids to navigation, which opened the distant oceans to trade after the middle of the eighteenth century. Accurate timekeeping enabled longitude to be calculated, and this combined with advances in astronomy made it possible for ships' navigators to proceed by 'dead reckoning.'*

Above: *The back of the Harrison chronometer (front—see left), his fourth c 1759, in a series made between 1735 and 1760. With a diameter of only 5.2 inches it was hardly bigger than a pocket watch, and it won the £20,000 prize offered by the Board of Longitude.*

Above: *The top plate of Larcum Kendall's timekeeper, a copy of Harrison's chronometer used by Captain Cook on his second Pacific voyage and gave an error of less than eight miles in longitude over the whole circumference of the world.*

were reasonably guarded. England, though then holding St Helena, depended, for the refreshment and refitting of her India-bound squadrons and convoys in the Atlantic, upon the benevolent neutrality of Portugal, extended in the islands of Madeira and Cape Verde and in the Brazilian ports.

This combination of useful harbors and the conditions of the communications between them constitute, as has been said, the main strategic outlines of the situation. The navy, as the organized force linking the whole together, has been indicated as the principal objective of military effort.

A condition peculiar to the sea, and affecting the following discussion, must be briefly mentioned; that is the difficulty of obtaining information. Armies pass through countries more or less inhabited by a stationary population, and they leave behind them traces of their march. Fleets move through a desert over which wanders flit, but where they do not remain; and as the waters close behind them, an occasional waif from the decks may indicate their passage, but tells nothing of their course. The sail spoken by the pursuer may know nothing of the pursued, which yet passed the point of parley but a few days or hours before. Of late, careful study of the winds and currents of the ocean has laid down certain advantageous routes, which will be habitually followed by a careful seaman, and afford some presumption as to his movements; but in 1778 the data for such precision were not collected, and even had they been, the quickest route must often have been abandoned for one of the many possible ones, in order to elude pursuit or lying-in-wait. In such a game of hide-and-seek the advantage is with the sought, and the great importance of watching the outlets of

an enemy's country, of stopping the chase before it has got away into the silent desert, is at once evident.

The defensive was necessarily accepted by England in 1778, and the fact remains that, notwithstanding the notorious probability of France and Spain joining in the war, the English navy was inferior in number to that of the allies. In what have been called the strategic features of the situation, the home bases, and the secondary bases abroad, the advantage upon the whole lay with her. Her positions, if not stronger in themselves, were at least better situated, geographically, for strategic effect; but in the second essential for war, the organized military force, or fleet, adequate to offensive operations, she had been allowed to become inferior. It only remained, therefore, to use this inferior force with such science and vigor as would frustrate the designs of the enemy, by getting first to sea, taking positions skilfully, anticipating their combinations by greater quickness of movement, harassing their communications with their objectives, and meeting the principal divisions of the enemy with superior forces.

It is sufficiently clear that the maintenance of this war, everywhere except on the American continent, depended upon the mother-countries in Europe and upon open communication with them. The key of the situation was in Europe, and in Europe in the hostile dock-yards. If England were unable, as she proved to be, to raise up a continental war against France, then her one hope was to find and strike down the enemy's navy. Nowhere was it so certainly to be found as in its home ports; nowhere so easily met as immediately after leaving them. This dictated her policy in the Napoleonic wars, when the moral

Left: *Louis XVI discussing with La Pérouse his voyage of exploration. He left France in 1785 and was last heard of at Botany Bay three years later, but then disappeared. Only 40 years later was it confirmed that his frigate had been wrecked on the uncharted Santa Cruz Islands East of New Guinea, and all the survivors had been massacred.*

Left: *Rowlandson's view of Portsmouth conveys the sense of bustle of England's premier naval dockyard at the turn of the century. It remains the most important naval yard to this day, and is the home of Nelson's flag-ship HMS Victory.*

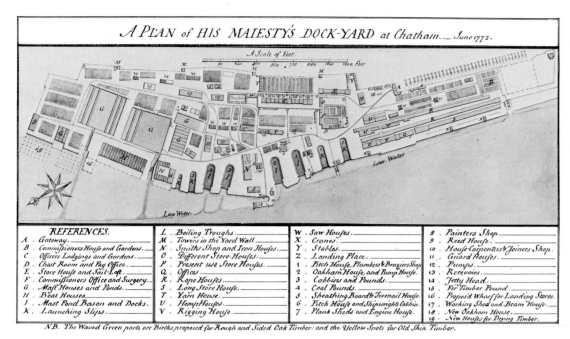

A PLAN of HIS MAIESTY'S DOCK-YARD at Chatham.— June 1772.

A Scale of Feet.

Left: Chatham Dockyard was well placed to control the southern half of the North Sea, and had been vital in the long wars against the Dutch in the seventeenth century. A hundred years later it blocked French access to Northern Europe, and with Plymouth and Portsmouth its slipways, docks and myriad facilities were a most important factor in the Royal Navy's final triumph over adversity.

REFERENCES.

A . Gateway.	L . Boiling Troughs.	W . Saw Houses.
B . Commissioners House and Gardens.	M . Towers in the Yard Wall.	X . Cranes.
C . Officers Lodgings and Gardens.	N . Smiths Shop and Iron Houses.	Y . Stables.
D . Chest Room and Pay Office.	O . Different Store-Houses.	Z . Landing Place.
E . Store House and Sail-Loft.	P . Present use Store Houses.	1 . Pitch House, Plumbers & Braziers Shop.
F . Commissioners Office and Surgery.	Q . Offices.	2 . Oakham House, and Pump House.
G . Mast Houses and Ponds.	R . Rope Houses.	3 . Cabbins and Pounds.
H . Boat Houses.	S . Long Store House.	4 . Coal Pounds.
I . Mast Pond Bason and Docks.	T . Yarn House.	5 . Sheathing Board & Treenail House.
K . Launching Slips.	U . Hemp Houses.	6 . Pitch House and Shipwrights Cabbin.
	V . Rigging House.	7 . Plank Sheds and Engine House.

8 . Painters Shop.	
9 . Reed House.	
10 . House-Carpenters & Joiners Shop.	
11 . Guard Houses.	
12 . Pumps.	
13 . Receivoirs.	
14 . Jetty Head.	
15 . Fir Timber Pound.	
16 . Propos'd Wharf for Landing Stores.	
17 . Working Shed and Beam House.	
18 . New Oakham House.	
19 . New Houses for Drying Timber.	

N.B. The Waved Green parts are Births proposed for Rough and Sided Oak Timber: and the Yellow Spots for Old Ship Timber.

superiority of her navy was so established that she dared to oppose inferior forces to the combined dangers of the sea and of the more numerous and well-equipped ships lying quietly at anchor inside.

The ships of 1805 were essentially the same as those of 1780. There had doubtless been progress and improvement; but the changes were in degree, not in kind. Not only so, but the fleets of twenty years earlier, under Hawke and his fellows, had dared the winters of the Bay of Biscay. If it be urged that the condition of the French navy was better, the character and training of its officers higher, than in the days of Hawke and Nelson, the fact must be admitted; nevertheless, the admiralty could not long have been ignorant that the number of such officers was still so deficient as seriously to affect the quality of the deck service, and the lack of seamen so great as to necessitate filling up the complements with soldiers. As for the *personnel* of the Spanish navy, there is no reason to believe it better than fifteen years later, when Nelson, speaking of Spain giving certain ships to France, said, 'I take it for granted not manned [by Spaniards], as that would be the readiest way to lose them again.'

In the use of the ships at its disposal, taking the war of 1778 as a whole, the English ministry kept their foreign detachments in America, and in the West and East Indies, equal to those of the enemy. At particular times, indeed, this was not so; but speaking generally of the assignment of ships, the statement is correct. In Europe, on the contrary the British fleet was habitually much inferior to that in the French and Spanish ports. It therefore could be used offensively only by great care, and through good fortune in meeting the enemy in detail; and even so an expensive victory, unless very decisive, entailed considerable risk from the consequent temporary disability of the ships engaged. It followed that the English home (or Channel) fleet upon which depended also the communications with Gibraltar and the Mediterranean, was used very economically both as to battle and weather, and was confined to the defence of the home coast, or to operations against the enemy's communications.

India was so far distant that no exception can be taken to the policy there. Ships sent there went to stay, and could be neither reinforced nor recalled with a view to sudden emergencies. The field stood by itself. But Europe, North America, and the West Indies should have been looked upon as one large theatre of war, throughout which events were mutually dependent, and whose different parts stood in close relations of greater or less importance, to which due attention should have been paid.

As regards the strategic question, it may be said pithily that the phrase 'ulterior objects' embodies the cardinal fault of the allies' naval policy. Ulterior objects brought to nought the hopes of the allies, because, by fastening their eyes upon them, they thoughtlessly passed the road which led to them. Desire eagerly directed upon the ends in view—or rather upon the partial, though great, advantages which they constituted their ends—blinded them to the means by which alone they could be surely attained; hence, as the result of the war, everywhere failure to attain them. Their object was 'to avenge their respective injuries, and to put an end to that tyrannical empire which England claims to maintain upon the ocean.' The revenge they had obtained was barren of benefit to themselves. They had, so that generation thought, injured England by liberating America; but they had not righted their wrongs in Gibraltar and Jamaica, the English fleet had not received any such treatment as would lessen its haughty self-reliance, the armed neutrality of the northern powers had been allowed to pass fruitlessly away, and the English empire over the seas soon became as tyrannical and more absolute than before.

Barring questions of preparation and administration, of the fighting quality of the allied fleets as compared with the English, and looking only to the indisputable fact of largely superior numbers, it must be noted as the supreme factor in the military conduct of the war, that, while the allied powers were on the offensive and England on the defensive, the attitude of the allied fleets in presence of the English navy was habitually defensive. Neither in the greater strategic combinations, nor upon the battlefield, does there appear any serious purpose of using superior numbers to crush fractions of the enemy's fleet, to make the disparity of numbers yet greater, to put an end to the empire of the seas by the destruction of the organized force which sustained it. With the single brilliant exception of Suffren, the allied navies avoided or accepted action; they never imposed it. Yet so long as the English navy was permitted thus with impunity to range the seas, not only was there no security that it would not frustrate the ulterior objects of the campaign, as it did again and again, but there was always the possibility that by some happy chance it would, by winning an important victory, restore the balance of strength. That it did not do so is to be imputed as a fault to the English ministry; but if England was wrong in permitting her European fleet to fall so far below that of the allies, the latter were yet more to blame for their failure to profit by the mistake. The stronger party, assuming the

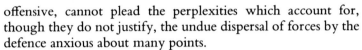

offensive, cannot plead the perplexities which account for, though they do not justify, the undue dispersal of forces by the defence anxious about many points.

The national bias of the French, which found expression in the line of action here again and for the last time criticised, appears to have been shared by both the government and the naval officers of the day. It is the key to the course of the French navy, and, in the opinion of the author, to its failure to achieve more substantial results to France from this war. It is instructive, as showing how strong a hold tradition has over the minds of men, that a body of highly accomplished and gallant seamen should have accepted, apparently without a murmur, so inferior a rôle for their noble profession. It carries also a warning, if these criticisms are correct, that current opinions and plausible impressions should always be thoroughly tested; for if erroneous they work sure failure, and perhaps disaster.

There was such an impression largely held by French officers of that day, and yet more widely spread in the United States now, of the efficacy of commerce-destroying as a main reliance in war, especially when directed against a commercial country like Great Britain. 'The surest means in my opinion,' wrote a distinguished officer, Lamotte-Picquet, 'to conquer the English is to attack them in their commerce.' The harassment and distress caused to a country by serious interference with its commerce will be conceded by all. It is doubtless a most important secondary operation of naval war, and is not likely to be abandoned till war itself shall cease; but regarded as a primary and fundamental measure, sufficient in itself to crush an enemy, it is probably a delusion, and a most dangerous delusion, when presented in the fascinating garb of cheapness to the representatives of a people. Especially is it misleading when the nation against whom it is to be directed possesses, as Great Britain did and does, the two requisites of a strong sea power—a widespread healthy commerce and a powerful navy. Where the revenues and industries of a country can be concentrated into a few treasure-ships, like the flota of Spanish galleons, the sinew of war may perhaps be cut by a stroke; but when its wealth is scattered in thousands of going and coming ships, when the roots of the system spread wide and far, and strike deep, it can stand many a cruel shock and lose many a goodly bough without the life being touched. Only by military command of the sea by prolonged control of the strategic centres of commerce, can such an attack be fatal; and such control can be wrung from a powerful navy only by fighting and overcoming it. For two

hundred years England has been the great commercial nation of the world. More than any other her wealth has been intrusted to the sea in war as in peace; yet of all nations she has ever been most reluctant to concede the immunities of commerce and the rights of neutrals. Regarded not as a matter of right, but of policy, history has justified the refusal; and if she maintain her navy in full strength, the future will doubtless repeat the lesson of the past.

The preliminaries of the peace between Great Britain and the allied courts, which brought to an end this great war, were signed at Versailles, January 20, 1783, an arrangement having been concluded between Great Britain and the American Commissioners two months before, by which the independence of the United States was conceded. This was the great outcome of the war. As between the European belligerents, Great Britain received back from France all the West India Islands she had lost, except Tobago, and gave up St Lucia. The French stations in India were restored; and Trincomalee being in the possession of the enemy, England could not dispute its return to Holland, but she refused to cede Negapatam. To Spain, England surrendered the two Floridas and Minorca, the latter a serious loss had the naval power of Spain been sufficient to maintain possession of it; as it was, it again fell into the hands of Great Britain in the next war. Some unimportant redistribution of trading-posts on the west coast of Africa was also made.

Trivial in themselves, there is but one comment that need be made upon these arrangements. In any coming war their permanency would depend wholly upon the balance of sea power, upon that empire of the seas concerning which nothing conclusive had been established by the war.

The definitive treaties of peace were signed at Versailles, September 3, 1783.

(Editor's note— *The social and political developments in Europe during the decade following the Treaty of Versailles greatly influenced the later decade of war. The stirring events of the French Revolution, leading to the execution of Louis XVI on 21 January 1793, made war between Revolutionary France and the established powers of Europe virtually inevitable. On 1 February the French Republic declared war against Great Britain and Holland. It was already at war with Austria, Prussia and Sardinia. The virtual isolation of France was completed by the declaration against Spain on the 7th of March, and the later involvement of Russia.*

The relative strength of the navies involved in these wars was quite unevenly distributed. In Spain, for example, though it boasted a large

Above: *Rowlandson's caricatures of four naval types. First, the sailor, the good-natured Jack Tar of popular fiction.*

Above: *Second, the carpenter, responsible for woodwork aboard ship, and his adze and calipers.*

Above: *Third, the cook, one-legged because traditionally the job was given to maimed seamen as a form of pension.*

Above: *Fourth, the purser, traditionally a rascal who swindled the illiterate seaman of his pay and victuals.*

Right: *Rowlandson's view of naval justice. Although the penalty for mutiny was death the Admiralty dealt fairly mildly with the Spithead mutineers in 1797, recognizing that their grievances were over bad pay. However when the Nore mutineers blockaded London they lost public sympathy by their arrogance and republican pronouncements. The ringleaders were hanged at the yard-arm of HMS* Sandwich *after the rest of the Nore Fleet deserted the cause. In fact all the grievances which caused the mutiny had been dealt with by Lord Howe after Spithead.*

number of ships-of-the-line, the navy was but a relic of the glorious and distant past. The British navy, on the other hand, though suffering from the usual problems resulting from prolonged inaction was basically sound. It had a large body of extremely capable officers and seamen, with reasonably strict discipline, reinforced by a tradition of naval excellence. The French navy had sunk into such a state of feeble disrepair (characterized by mutiny, unskilled officers and insufficient supplies), that on 27 August 1793 the vital Mediterranean port of Toulon was simply handed over to the British and Spanish by royalists in the city. Although the subsequent siege was successful the French lost as a result of this action about one sixth of their ships-of-the-line.

British objectives in the West Indies at the start of the war were to protect this important source as well as market of British trade, and to deprive the French of every possible friendly anchorage. The British did maintain superiority in the region, but at great cost to themselves.

Here follow the abridged extracts from Mahan's The Influence of Sea Power upon the French Revolution 1793-1812. *This work was published in 1892, two years after* The Influence of Sea Power upon History 1660-1783. *Mahan went on to write other naval histories, including a biography of Nelson, but these major studies of sea power were to establish his international reputation.)*

Right: *A French sailor late in the eighteenth century, with a 'tarpaulin' hat on his head and cutlass belt slung over his shoulder. Sailors had no official uniform until the nineteenth century and made most of their clothes rather than buy officially issued clothing from the 'slop chest.' Half a day each week was set aside for repairing or making clothes, and a rest period is still known as a 'make and mend.'*

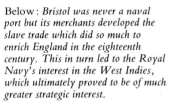

THE MERRY SHIPS CREW, or *Nautical Philosophers.*

Below: *Bristol was never a naval port but its merchants developed the slave trade which did so much to enrich England in the eighteenth century. This in turn led to the Royal Navy's interest in the West Indies, which ultimately proved to be of much greater strategic interest.*

Above: *A satirical cartoon on the rough justice of naval discipline: 'The happy ship's crew or the nautical philosophers.'*

Chapter 11

The Glorious First of June

The pressure of the allied armies upon all her frontiers, combined with the British mastery of the sea, had thrown France largely upon her own resources during the year 1793; while the distracted condition of the country and a bad harvest had united to cause a scarcity of bread-stuffs, which threatened a famine, with all its consequences of sufferings to the army and the people, and inevitable increase of disturbance and sedition.

The eyes of the government had therefore turned beyond the sea to the United States, and its representatives there had been directed to accumulate a quantity of provisions to be shipped to France. It was intended to despatch these in a great convoy, to be protected on the voyage by a force of ships-of-war; while its approach to the shores of Europe would be covered by a sortie of the great fleet from Brest and Rochefort, to occupy the attention of, and, if necessary, forcibly to contest the control of the sea with, the British navy.

The convoying squadron of two ships-of-the-line and three smaller vessels sailed from Brest for the United States in December, 1793, under the command of Rear-Admiral Van Stabel, an active and judicious officer. On the 12th of February it anchored in Chesapeake Bay, and sailed again for France on the 11th of April. The merchant ships under its charge numbered one hundred and thirty, among them being many laden with produce from the French West India islands, which, not venturing to make the passage home direct and unattended, for fear of British cruisers, had collected at Hampton Roads to await the time of sailing.

On the 16th of May the great fleet, comprising twenty-five ships-of-the-line, one of which carried one hundred and twenty guns and three others one hundred and ten, sailed under the command of Rear-Admiral Villaret Joyeuse. The admiral's orders were to cruise in the same station that had already been assigned to Nielly, with whom he was expected to form a junction, and to protect the approach of the convoy at all hazards, but not to fight unless essential to secure that end, to which all other objects were subordinated. The time of waiting was to be utilized for fleet manoeuvres, in which the representative and admiral had too much reason to fear that the captains were unskilled.

On the 2nd of May the Channel fleet, numbering thirty-four ships-of-the-line and attended by fifteen frigates and smaller ships-of-war, sailed from Spithead. It had under its charge one hundred and forty-eight sail of merchantmen, bound to Newfoundland and to the East and West Indies. Upon arriving two days later off the Lizard, a promontory near the southwest extremity of England and a hundred miles due north of the Island of Ushant, Howe detached eight ships-of-the-line to accompany the convoy to the latitude of Cape Finisterre, on the northwest coast of Spain. After performing this service, six, under Admiral Montagu, were to cruise between Cape Ortegal and the latitude of Belle-Isle, to intercept the convoy from America. The width, over two hundred miles, of the belt of ocean to be covered by these six ships with their accompanying frigates, taken in connection with the chances which night and fog might give the French convoy for passing unobserved, illustrates the comparative disadvantages of lying in wait at the supposed point of arrival, instead of at the known port of departure, for a body of vessels whose precise destination is in doubt.

On the morning of May 28, the French numbered twenty-six ships-of-the-line and were, when they first formed line, from ten to twelve miles to windward of the British, also numbering twenty-six. On the evening of May 29, in consequence of Howe's various movements and the course to which Villaret was by them constrained—for he acted purely on the defensive and had to conform to the initiative of the enemy—the French fleet was to leeward of the British. As Howe had succeeded within so short a time in forcing action from to leeward, there was every reason to apprehend that from the windward position —decidedly the more favorable upon the whole, though not without its drawbacks—he would be able to compel a decisive battle, which the French naval policy proscribed generally, and in the present case particularly. Besides this adverse change in circumstance, the balance of loss was still more against the French. On the first day the *Révolutionnaire* on one side and the *Audacious* on the other had been compelled to quit their fleets; but the force of the latter was not over two thirds that of the former. By the action of the 29th the *Indomptable*, of eighty guns, was driven from the French fleet, and the admiral thought necessary to send with her a seventy-four and a frigate. The *Tyrannicide*, seventy-four, had lost all her upper masts; she had consequently to be towed by one of her consorts through the next two days and in the battle of the First of June. If Villaret had had any expectation of escaping Howe's pursuit, the presence of this disabled ship would have destroyed it, unless he was willing to abandon her. Besides the mishaps already stated, the leading ship, *Montagnard*, had been so much injured in the early part of the engagement that she could not go about. Continuing to stand west, while the body of the fleet was running east to the aid of the *Indomptable* and *Tyrannicide*, this ship separated from her consorts and was not able to regain them. To this loss of four ships actually gone, and one per-

manently crippled, may be added that of the *Audacieux*, one of Nielly's squadron, which joined on the morning of the 29th, but was immediately detached to seek and protect the *Révolutionnaire*. On the other hand, the British had by no means escaped unscathed; but on the morning of the 30th, in reply to an interrogatory signal from the admiral, they all reported readiness to renew the action, except one, the *Caesar*, which was not among the most injured. This ship, however, did not leave the fleet, and was in her station in the battle of the First.

Towards the close of the day the weather grew thick, and so continued, with short intervals of clearing, for the next thirty-six hours. At half-past seven the body of the French bore from the British flag-ship northwest, distant nine or ten miles; both fleets standing very slowly to the westward and a little northerly,

Opposite: A French 74-gun ship modelled in bone by prisoners-of-war. What was originally a hobby among the thousands of French prisoners during the Napoleonic Wars became a well organized industry, for their captors were willing to buy the models or barter them for such luxuries as tobacco. However, to please the buyer, ships with distinctive French characteristics were often given an English name, and they are generally not as accurate as Navy Board models.

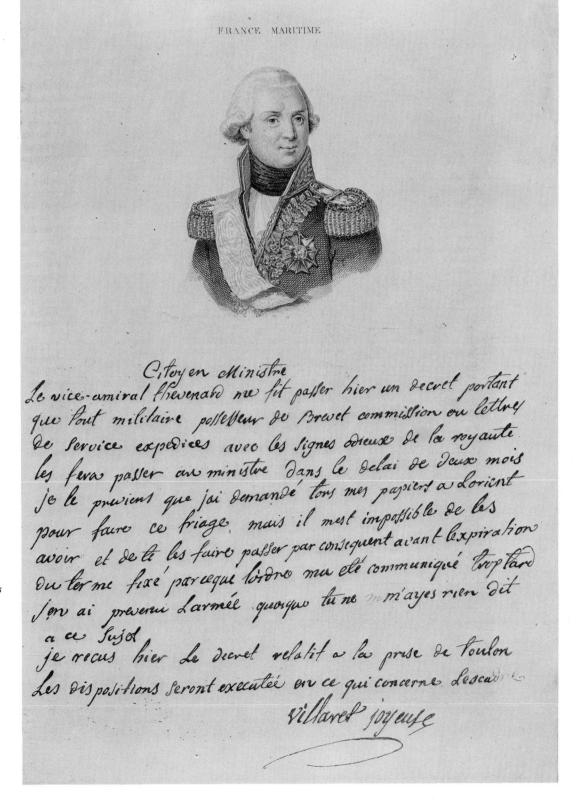

FRANCE MARITIME

Right: Vice-Admiral Villaret-Joyeuse had been a junior officer in the old French Navy but after the Revolution he was reinstated by the Directory and given flag rank. He was a brave fighter who never lacked the courage to tell his political masters what they were doing wrong. Considering the poor material he was given he did well to achieve what he did, and he ranks as the best of the French senior officers who served between 1793 and 1814. The letter refers to the new orders to relinquish the old commissions of office with the 'odious royal stamp' for the new commissions of the Revolutionary navy. He ends saying that he has received the orders to take Toulon and that they will be carried out accordingly.

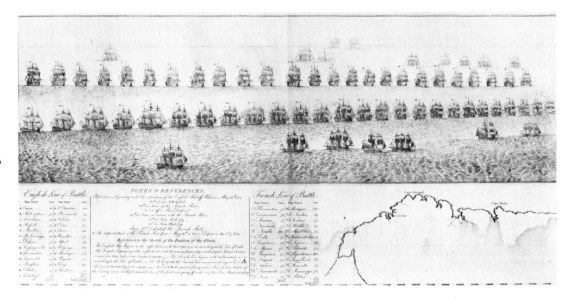

with wind from the southward and westward. During most of
the 30th, none of the British fleet could be seen from the flag-
ship, but they all, as well as the French, kept together. On that
day also, by a piece of great good fortune considering the state
of the weather, Admiral Nielly joined Villaret with the three
ships still under his command, as did also another seventy-four
belonging to the Cancale squadron. These four fresh ships
exactly replaced the four disabled ones that had parted company,
and again made the French twenty-six to Howe's twenty-five.

About ten o'clock in the morning of May 31st, the fog lifted
for a moment, allowing Howe to count twenty-seven sail of his
ships and frigates; and, after again shutting down for a couple of
hours, it finally dispersed shortly after noon. The French were
then seen bearing from west to northwest. The British made
sail in chase and by six p.m. had approached to within about
three miles. They were not, however, able to reach the position
Howe wished—abreast the enemy—early enough to permit the
intended general engagement, unless by a night action; which
for more than one reason the admiral was not willing to undertake. He therefore hauled again to the wind, heading to the
westward in order of battle. The French had formed on a
parallel line and were running in the same direction. During the

night both fleets carried all the sail their masts would stand. In
the morning the French, thanks to the better sailing of their
vessels, were found to have gained somewhat on their enemies,
but not sufficiently to avoid or postpone the battle, which they
had been directed if possible to shun. Villaret therefore formed
his fleet in close order, and stood on slowly under short canvas,
which at once allowed irregularities in the order to be more
easily corrected and also left the crews free to devote themselves
exclusively to fighting the ships. Howe, by carrying sail, was
thus able to choose his position prior to bearing down. Having
reached it and formed his line, the French being now hove-to to
await the attack, the British fleet was also hove-to, and the
crews went to breakfast. At twelve minutes past eight it again
filled-away by signal, and stood slowly down for the enemy
(see Map page 210). The intention being to attack along the
whole line, ship to ship, advantage was taken of this measured
approach to change the place of the three-decked ships in the
order, so that they should oppose the heaviest of the French.

Howe's plan, as communicated to the fleet by signal, was not
merely to attack on the side from which he approached, but to
pass through the intervals between the enemy's ships, and to
engage them on the further, or lee side. This method conferred

Left: *The sinking of the 74-gun* Vengeur du Peuple *during the Glorious First of June battle, with English boats rescuing survivors. She had been pounded by the two-decker* Brunswick *and discipline was such that her captain and crew deserted their wounded and jumped overboard. The ship sank before the boats could get closer.*

the advantage of a raking fire while passing through the line, and cut off the retreat of disabled enemies; for a crippled ship could only retire to leeward. To carry out the design, however, required not only that the enemy should leave wide enough intervals, but also that the assailants should be able to see where the intervals were.

The British ships were steering each for its opposite in the enemy's order, heading about northwest; so that, as the French line was east and west, the approach was not perpendicular but in a slanting direction. At twenty minutes before nine, the formation was so accurate that Lord Howe shut the signal book with an air of satisfaction, as though his work as admiral was done and all that remained was to show the gallant bearing and example which had ever been associated with his name. The gesture was, however, premature, and eccentricities of conduct on the part of some captains compelled him again to open the book and order them into their stations. Shortly after nine o'clock the French van began firing. The British ship *Caesar*, on the left flank of her line, and therefore corresponding to the leader of the French, instead of pressing on to her station for battle, hauled to the wind and began firing while still five hundred yards distant—a position inconsistent with decisive

results under the gunnery conditions of that day.

The rest of the fleet stood on. The *Queen Charlotte*, in order to reach her position, had to steer somewhat more to the westward. Either the French line had drawn a little ahead, or some other incident had thrown this ship astern of her intended point of arrival. Her course, therefore, becoming more nearly parallel to the enemy's, she passed within range of the third vessel behind Villaret's flag-ship, the *Montagne*, her destined opponent. This ship, the *Vengeur*, opened fire upon her at half-past nine. The *Queen Charlotte*, not to be crippled before reaching her place, made more sail and passed on. The next ahead of the *Vengeur*, the *Achille*, also engaged her, and to this the *Charlotte* replied at eight minutes before ten. The assailant suffered severely, and her attention was quickly engrossed by the *Brunswick*, the supporter of Howe's flag-ship on her starboard side, which tried to break through the line ahead of the *Achille*.

The *Queen Charlotte* (June 1, the battle) continued on for the *Montagne*. Seeing her evident purpose to pass under the stern, the captain of this ship threw his sails aback, so as to fall to the rear and close the interval. At the same moment the French ship next astern, the *Jacobin*, increased her sail, most properly, for the same object. The two thus moving towards each other, a

Right: *The Glorious First of June showed that despite the neglect and parsimony which had reigned in peacetime the Royal Navy had little difficulty in returning to the form which it had known under Rodney in 1782. Although not a decisive victory such as Nelson was to make standard, it showed that revolutionary fervour was no substitute for training and discipline.*

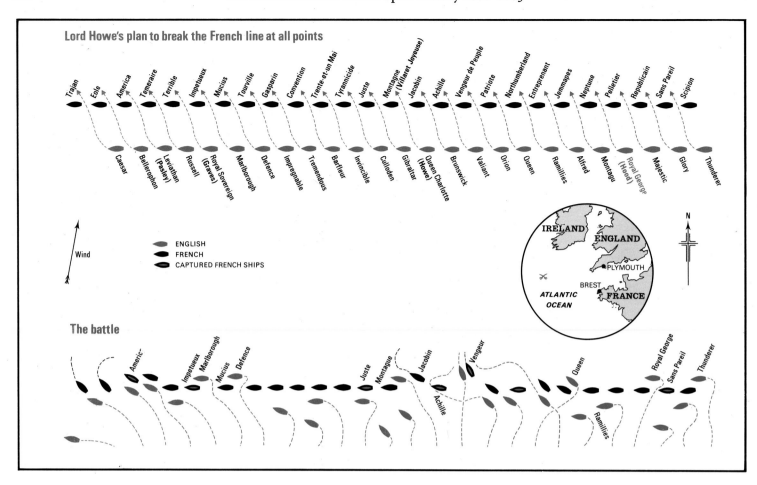

Lord Howe's plan to break the French line at all points

Trajan, Eole, America, Temeraire, Terrible, Impetueux, Mucius, Tourville, Gasparin, Convention, Trente-et-un Mai, Tyrannicide, Juste, Montagne (Villaret Joyeuse), Jacobin, Achille, Vengeur de Peuple, Patriote, Northumberland, Entreprenant, Jemmapes, Neptune, Pelletier, Republicain, Sans Pareil, Scipion

Caesar, Bellerophon, Leviathan (Pasley), Russell, Royal Sovereign (Graves), Marlborough, Defence, Impregnable, Tremendous, Barfleur, Invincible, Culloden, Gibraltar, Queen Charlotte (Howe), Brunswick, Valiant, Orion, Queen, Ramilies, Alfred, Montagu, Royal George (Hood), Majestic, Glory, Thunderer

Wind

🔘 ENGLISH
⬛ FRENCH
◼ CAPTURED FRENCH SHIPS

IRELAND   ENGLAND   PLYMOUTH   BREST   FRANCE   ATLANTIC OCEAN   N

The battle

Americ, Impetueux, Marlborough, Mucius, Defence, Juste, Montagne, Jacobin, Achille, Vengeur, Queen, Ramilies, Royal George, Sans Pareil, Thunderer

collision was threatened. As the only alternative, the *Jacobin* put her helm up and steered for the starboard, or lee, side of the *Montagne*. At this moment the *Queen Charlotte* drew up. Putting her helm hard over, she kept away perpendicularly to the *Montagne*, and passed under her stern, so close that the French flag brushed the side of the British ship. One after another the fifty guns of the latter's broadside swept from stern to stem of the enemy—three hundred of her crew falling at once, her captain among the number. The *Jacobin* having moved to the starboard side of the *Montagne*, in the place the *Queen Charlotte* had intended to take, it was thought that the latter would have to go to leeward of both; but, amid all the confusion of the scene, the quick eye of the gallant man who was directing her movements caught a glimpse of the *Jacobin's* rudder and saw it moving to change the ship's direction to leeward. Quickly seizing his opportunity, the helm of the British flag-ship was again shifted, and she came slowly and heavily to the wind in her appointed place, her jib-boom in the movement just clearing the *Jacobin*, as her side a few minutes before had grazed the flag of the *Montagne*. The latter, it is said, made no reply to this deadly assault. The *Jacobin* fired a few shots, one of which cut away the foretopmast of the *Queen Charlotte*; and then, instead of imitating the latter's movement and coming to the wind again, by which the British ship would have been placed between his

Top: *The Battle of the First of June 1794.*

Left: *The Glorious First of June was unusual by eighteenth century standards in being fought 400 miles out in the Atlantic. The huge grain convoy of 117 ships was under the command of Contre-Amiral Vanstabel, sailing from American ports bound for Brest. With a famine threatening it was essential to get the convoy through, and Villaret-Joyeuse had orders to this effect.*

fire and that of the *Montagne*, the captain weakly kept off and ran to leeward out of action.

By this time the engagement was general all along the line. Smoke, excitement and the difficulties of the situation broke somewhat the simultaneousness of the shock of the British assault; but, with some exceptions, their fire from van to rear opened at nearly the same time. Six ships only passed at once through the enemy's line, but very many of the others brought their opponents to close action to windward.

There was one episode of so singular, so deadly, and yet so dramatic an interest, occurring in the midst of this extensive *mêlée*, that it cannot be passed by. As long as naval history shall be written, it must commemorate the strife between the French ship *Vengeur de Peuple* and the British ship *Brunswick*. The latter went into action on the right hand of the *Queen Charlotte*; its duty therefore was to pierce the French line astern of the *Jacobin*. This was favored by the movement of the latter to support the *Montagne*; but, as the *Brunswick* pressed for the widened gap, the *Achille* made sail ahead and threw herself in the way. Foiled here, the *Brunswick* again tried to traverse the line astern of the *Achille*, but the *Vengeur* now came up, and, as the *Brunswick* persisted, the two collided and swung side to side, the anchors of the British ship hooking in the rigging and channels of the French. Thus fastened in deadly embrace, they fell off before the wind and went away together to leeward (see Map).

As the contact of the two ships prevented opening the lower ports as usual, the British crew blew off the lids. The *Vengeur* having already been firing from the side engaged, hers were probably open; but, owing to the hulls touching, it was not possible to use the ordinary sponges and rammers, with rigid wooden staves, and the French had no others. The British, however, were specially provided for such a case with sponges and rammers having flexible rope handles, and with these they were able to carry on the action. In this way the contest continued much to the advantage of the British on the lower decks, where the French, for the reason given, could use only a few of the forward and after guns, the form of a ship at the extremities causing the distance there between the combatants to be greater. But while such an inequality existed below, above the balance was reversed; the heavy carronades of the *Vengeur*, loaded with langrage, and the superiority of her musketry—re-enforced very probably by the men from the useless cannon below—beating

down the resistance of the British crew on the upper deck and nearly silencing their guns. The captain of the *Brunswick* received three wounds, from one of which he afterwards died; and a number of others, both officers and men, were killed and wounded. This circumstance encouraged the *Vengeur's* commander to try to carry his opponent by boarding; but, when about to execute the attempt, the approach of two other British ships necessitated calling off the men, to serve the guns on the hitherto disengaged side.

Meanwhile the *Brunswick's* crew maintained an unremitting fire, giving to their guns alternately extreme elevation and depression, so that at one discharge the shot went up through the

Top right: *The 1st Rate* Queen Charlotte *at a review in Spithead in 1790. She had been launched at Chatham in April that year, and was blown up by an accidental explosion ten years later off Leghorn.*

Center right: *The triumphant 3rd Rate* Brunswick, *minus her mizzenmast but with the* Vengeur du Peuple *sinking (left) and the* Achille *having struck her colors (right).*

Right: *The two captured 74s* le Juste *and* l'Amérique *on their arrival in Portsmouth after the Glorious First of June. Having been dismasted they are under 'jury rig.' The former was recommissioned under the same name but the latter was renamed* Impétueux *as the name* America *was already in use. Both ships remained in service until 1811–13.*

Vengeur's decks, ripping them open, while at the other they tended to injure the bottom. The fight had thus continued for an hour when the *Achille*, with only her foremast standing, was seen approaching the *Brunswick* on her port, or disengaged, side. The threatened danger was promptly met and successfully averted. Before the new enemy could take a suitable position, half-a-dozen guns' crews on each of the lower decks shifted to the side on which she was, and in a few moments their fire brought down her only remaining and already damaged mast. The *Achille* had no farther part in the battle and was taken possession of by the British a few hours later.

At quarter before one the uneasy motions of the two ships wrenched the anchors one after another from the *Brunswick's* side, and after a grapple of three hours they separated. The character of the contest, as described, had caused the injury to fall mainly upon the hulls and crews, while the spars and rigging, contrary to the usual result in so fierce an action, had largely escaped. As they were parting, the *Brunswick* poured a few final shots into the *Vengeur's* stern, injuring the rudder, and increasing the leaks from which the doomed ship was already suffering. Immediately afterwards the mizzen-mast of the British vessel went overboard; and, being already well to leeward of her own fleet and threatened by the approach of the French admiral, she stood to the northward under such sail as her spars would bear, intending to make a home port, if possible. In this long and desperate conflict, besides the injuries to be expected to hull and spars, the *Brunswick* had twenty-three of her seventy-four guns dismounted, and had lost forty-four killed and one hundred and fourteen wounded out of a crew of six hundred men.

Soon after the dismasting of the *Achille*, the British ship *Ramillies*, commanded by the brother of the *Brunswick's* captain, had been seen coming slowly down toward the two combatants. She arrived but a few moments before their separation, and, when they were far enough apart for her fire not to endanger the *Brunswick*, she also attacked the *Vengeur*, but not longer after left again in order to secure the *Achille*. This fresh onslaught, however, brought down all the *Vengeur's* masts except the mizzen, which stood for half an hour longer. The French ship was helpless. With numerous shot-holes at or near the water line, with many of her port lids gone, she was rolling heavily in the waves, unsteadied by masts, and taking in water on all sides. Guns were thrown overboard, pumps worked and assisted by bailing, but all in vain—the *Vengeur* was slowly but surely sinking. At half-past one the danger was so evident that signals of distress were made; but among the disabled or pre-occupied combatants they for a long time received no attention. About six p.m., fortunately, two British ships and a cutter drew near, and upon learning the state of the case sent all their boats that remained unhurt. It was too late to save every survivor of this gallant fight, but nearly four hundred were taken off; the remainder, among whom were most of the badly wounded, went down with their ship before the British boats had regained their own. 'Scarcely had the boats pulled clear of the sides, when the most frightful spectacle was offered to our gaze. Those of our comrades who remained on board the *Vengeur du Peuple*, with hands raised to Heaven, implored with lamentable cries the help for which they could no longer hope. Soon disappeared the ship and the unhappy victims which it contained. In the midst of the horror with which this scene inspired us all, we could not avoid a feeling of admiration mingled with our grief. As we drew away, we heard some of our comrades still making prayers for the welfare of their country; the last cries of these unfortunates were: "Vive la République!" They died uttering them.'

Left: The text of Nelson's inspiring message at Trafalgar, but actually a commemorative plaque for the Glorious First of June, with the Royal Arms and portraits of Howe, his second-in-command Hood and two of the junior admirals.

Below: HMS Queen Charlotte *leading the prizes into Spithead 19 June 1794. Howe and his men received a rapturous welcome for their victory showed that the Royal Navy was more than equal to the French.*

Long before the *Vengeur* and the *Brunswick* separated, the fate of the battle had been decided, and the final action of the two commanders-in-chief taken. It was just ten o'clock when the British flag-ship passed under the stern of the *Montagne*. At ten minutes past ten the latter, whose extensive injuries were mainly to the hull, made sail in advance—a movement which the *Queen Charlotte*, having lost both fore and main topmasts, was unable to follow. Many of the French ships ahead of the *Montagne* had already given ground and left their posts; others both before and behind her had been dismasted. Between half past ten and eleven the smoke cleared sufficiently for Villaret to see the situation on the field of battle.

Opposite: The fight between the Vengeur du Peuple (left) *and* Achille (right) *against the* Brunswick (center). *Once rigging started to fall on the upper deck the task of gun crews became almost impossible, and fallen masts were if possible cut loose.*

Right: Carnage on the deck of the flag-ship Queen Charlotte. *Howe (left) with his First Captain Sir Roger Curtis, observes as Captain Henry Neville of the Queen's Regiment, mortally wounded, is carried below. The painting is by Mather Brown.*

Above: *The laurels of victory for Howe and his captains. Ironically Howe was notorious for his difficulty in communicating his meaning to his subordinates despite having introduced an improved method of signalling in 1782.*

Below: *The scene of devastation on the evening of the Glorious First of June.*

Ships dismasted not only lose their power of motion, but also do not drift to leeward as rapidly as those whose spars are up, but which are moving very slowly. In consequence, the lines having some movement ahead, the dismasted ships of both parties had tended astern and to windward of the battle. There they lay, British and French, pell-mell together. Of the twelve ahead of the French admiral when the battle began, seven had soon run out of action to leeward. Two of these, having hauled to the wind on the other tack, were now found to be astern and to windward of both fleets; to windward even of the dismasted ships. Of the rest of the twelve, one, having lost main and mizzen masts, was unavoidably carried to leeward, and the remaining four were totally dismasted. Of these four, three finally fell into the hands of the British. Of the thirteen ships astern of the *Montagne*, six had lost all their masts, and one had only the foremast standing; the remaining six had their spars left in fairly serviceable condition, and had, some sooner and some later, retreated to leeward. Four of the dismasted ships in the rear, including among them the *Vengeur*, were captured by the British.

When Admiral Villaret Joyeuse had recognized the situation, as thus briefly described, he directed the *Montagne* also to be headed to leeward, and made signals to gather the serviceable ships round the commander-in-chief. A column of twelve was thus formed (June 1, the battle) on the starboard tack, standing, that is, to the eastward again—the *Montagne* leading and the rear being brought up by the *Terrible*, the flag-ship of the second in command, which had only her foremast left and was therefore taken in tow by an uninjured seventy-four. Villaret considered it imprudent, if not impossible, to get far enough to windward to interpose in favor of the dismasted vessels. He determined, therefore, to place himself to leeward of them, in such position as to receive and cover those that could run down to him, or which his frigates could reach and tow away. In this manner the *Scipion*, the *Jemappes*, and the *Mucius*, totally disabled, were restored to the French fleet between two and four o'clock. The last named had actually struck to a British ship, but had not been taken into possession. Villaret remained for some time, hove-to in this position, until satisfied that no more of the separated vessels could join him, and then made sail in a northwesterly direction.

Lord Howe was unable to follow with his own ship the comparatively rapid movements of the French commander-in-chief. At eleven o'clock, however, a signal was made for those that could to close around the admiral, and the *Queen Charlotte* was with difficulty put on the other tack. Howe then led the column which thus formed to the eastward, a step that was necessary not only in order to cover dismantled British ships and secure the prizes, but also to relieve the *Queen*, which was threatened by Villaret and in a critical situation. This ship, which had behaved with so much forwardness and gallantry in the British van on the 29th of May, had on the First of June been stationed in the rear. The antagonist which she attacked went away rapidly to leeward; and the *Queen*, following with unrelenting ardor, found herself at the end of the engagement again between the lines, with a dismantled enemy, indeed, near by, but with her own mainmast gone and other spars tottering. Eight of Villaret's column cannonaded her as they passed, but without doing much harm, and Howe's approach extricated her.

Some attention is now due to the naval strategy, to the general conduct and results of this short maritime campaign, which covered only four weeks. The object of the French was to insure the arrival of the convoy from America. For this purpose they had at sea, at the first, two detachments—one of five ships-of-the-line under Nielly, the other of twenty-five under Villaret.

The rendezvous for the two was the same, and the important point where their intended junction should take place was known to their admirals and unknown to the British. It may be again said that the instructions of the French government to its officers compelled the latter to avoid, if possible, any decisive engagement.

The object of the British was twofold: to intercept the expected convoy, and to bring the French fleet to battle. The two might, and did, interfere with each other—might, by divergence of interest, prompt a separation of the force. Of the two, fighting the French fleet was indisputably the more important, and was doubtless so considered by Howe, in accordance with the usual British naval policy, which aimed at the destruction of the enemy's organized force afloat. The ships at his disposal, including Montagu's squadron, amounted to thirty-two of the line. He was ignorant of the rendezvous of the French fleets and of the exact course that would be followed by the convoy; but of both he could form approximate estimates.

The strategic aim of the French admiral, after he had been so unfortunate as to be found by the British fleet, was to draw it away from the rendezvous appointed for the convoy. Both his orders and the tactical condition of his fleet forbade the attempt to secure this by bringing the enemy to battle. When first met, the French were to windward, south of the British. If they had been north, with the same advantage of the wind, the situation would have been most satisfactory to them; for the convoy was approaching from the west-southwest, and by retreating to the northward and westward Villaret would have led the enemy directly from the position endangering it. As things were, it was impossible to steer to the northward without bringing on the battle he had to avoid; and if defeated where he then was, the victorious fleet would be left too near the convoy. Villaret, therefore, kept the advantage of the wind and steered a west course, which diverged slowly from the convoy's path, and, if long enough continued, would allow it to pass out of sight. The slowness of this divergence, however, doubtless contributed to reconcile him to the loss of the weather gage on the 29th, and immediately upon finding himself north of the enemy he went to the northward and westward during the two following days. The result was eminently successful. It is stated by the latest French authorities that on the 30th the convoy passed over the ground where the partial engagement of the 29th was fought. If so, it must have been under cover of the dense fog which then prevailed, as the fleets had not moved very far.

After the two fleets separated, each made the best of its way to a home port. Lord Howe waited until the morning of the 3rd, securing and refitting his prizes and disabled ships, and reached Portsmouth on the 13th of June. Villaret Joyeuse went to Brest. On the morning of the 9th he fell in with Montagu's squadron, a little south of Ushant. The condition of the French encumbered with injured ships, would have afforded an opportunity to a quick-moving fleet; but two of the British were excessively slow and the admiral did not dare approach a much superior force. Villaret pursued for a short distance, but, fearing to be drawn to leeward of his port in his crippled state, he soon gave over the chase. On the 11th of June, all his fleet anchored in Bertheaume roads, outside of Brest. Montague, on the 10th, departed for England, a movement which finally closed the campaign on the part of the British. On the night of the 12th the French crews saw a number of lights in the Raz de Sein, the southern passage by which Brest is approached. They were those of the long-expected convoy. Admiral Van Stabel, fearing to find a hostile fleet before the usual and safer entrance, had steered for the Penmarcks, a rocky promontory thirty miles south of the port, and thence for the Raz de Sein. On the same day that Van Stabel made the land Montagu anchored in Plymouth. Two days later, June 14, the convoy and the remnant of Villaret's squadron entered Brest together. Thus ended the cruise, which was marked, indeed, by a great naval disaster, but had insured the principal object for which it was undertaken.

(Editor's note—During the winter of 1794 the British fleet was largely inactive, staying in the channel ports. The French fleet at Brest took advantage of the slackening of the blockade, slipping out on 24 December 1794. Inexperience, lack of supplies and damaged ships hindered the operations which was brought to a disastrous end by the harsh weather. Both sides committed tremendous tactical errors. 1794 also saw the rise of Robespierre and the Reign of Terror. He was finally consumed by the passion he had called forth; he was himself executed 28 July 1794.

Meanwhile, the French armies were triumphant on the Continent. They pushed into Prussia, Spain, and Holland, forcing them in 1795 to sign treaties ceding territory and rights to France. Holland reversed its allegiance, serving as an important naval center on the British flank. In 1795 France, after a twelve-month of victory, came near losing all her conquests. Threatened with dangerous internal reaction, she succeeded only with great difficulty in freeing herself from embarrassments and modifying the defects of her institutions. The leadership of France shifted to the Executive Directory.

In 1796 the British fleet had been three years in the Mediterranean, and since the acquisition of Corsica had effected little. During this time Napoleon was enjoying tremendous success in Italy. The Spanish allied themselves with the French, bringing a large fleet to the Mediterranean. Fear of the overwhelming numbers of the combined fleets drove the British to evacuate Corsica and leave the sea to their enemies. England desperately needed a victory, to regain control over the seas and boost morale.)

Above: *Lord Keith's attack on the Cape of Good Hope on 7 August 1796. His forces seized the important pass of Muigzenburg near Cape Town after defeating a Dutch squadron in Saldanha Bay.*

Chapter 12

Cape St Vincent

The meeting which took place between the Spanish and British fleets was the result of the following movements. Towards the end of 1796 the Directory, encouraged by Bonaparte's successes and by the Spanish alliance, and allured by the promises of disaffected Irish, determined on an expedition to Ireland. As the first passage of the troops and their subsequent communications would depend upon naval superiority, five ships-of-the-line were ordered from Toulon to Brest. This force, under Admiral Villeneuve, sailed on the 1st of December, accompanied by the Spanish fleet of twenty-six ships, which, since October, had remained in Toulon. On the 6th Langara went into Cartagena, leaving Villeneuve to himself, and on the 10th the French passed Gibraltar in full sight of the British fleet, driving before the easterly gale, which then did so much harm to Jervis's squadron and prevented pursuit. They did not, however, reach Brest soon enough for the expedition. The Spaniards remained in Cartagena nearly two months, during which time Admiral Cordova took command; but under urgent pressure from the Directory they finally sailed for Cadiz on the 1st of February, passing the Straits on the 5th with heavy

easterly weather, which drove them far to the westward. They numbered now twenty-seven ships-of-the-line.

Sir John Jervis, after leaving Lisbon on January 18, 1797, had convoyed to the westward some Portuguese merchant ships bound to Brazil, and then beaten back towards his station off Cape St Vincent. On the 6th of February he was joined by a re-enforcement of five ships, which were sent from England as soon as the scare about Ireland had passed. With these fifteen he cruised off the Cape, knowing that he there must meet any squadron, from either the Mediterranean or the Atlantic, bound to Cadiz. At five a.m. of February 14, the frigate *Niger*, which had kept sight of the Spanish fleet for some days, joined the admiral, and informed him that it was probably not more than ten or twelve miles distant, to the southward and westward. The wind, which had been strong southeasterly for several days, had changed during the night to west by south, enabling the Spaniards to head for Cadiz, after the weary battling of the past week; but this otherwise fortunate circumstance became a very dangerous incident to a large, ill-officered, and ill-commanded body of ships, about to meet an enemy so skilful, so alert, and so

Above: *It is difficult not to sympathize with the Comte de Villeneuve. His political master wanted spectacular results from him but lacked the most elementary understanding of the sea. Under strong pressure from Napoleon he put to sea from Ferrol only to find himself trapped in Cadiz. When he emerged it was to meet Nelson and the British Fleet.*

Right: *On 14 February 1797 Sir John Jervis met the Spanish Fleet off Cape St Vincent and inflicted a severe defeat. It was distinguished by the conduct of Commodore Horatio Nelson, who showed great initiative in leaving the line to cut off the Spanish weather division. He boarded the 80-gun San Nicolas and then captured the 112-gun San Josef alongside her.*

thoroughly drilled as Jervis's comparatively small and manageable force. At day break, about 6.30, the Spaniards were seen, stretching on the horizon from southwest to south in an ill-defined body, across the path of the advancing British. Their distance, though not stated, was probably not less than fifteen to twenty miles. The British fleet being close hauled on the starboard tack, heading from south to south by west, while the Spaniards, bound for Cadiz, were steering east-southeast, the two courses crossed nearly at right angles. At this moment there was a great contrast between the arrays presented by the approaching combatants. The British, formed during the night in two columns of eight and seven ships respectively, elicited the commendation of their exacting chief 'for their admirable close order.' The Spaniards, on the contrary, eager to get to port, and

in confusion through the night shift of wind and their own loose habits of sailing, were broken into two bodies. Of these the leading one, as all were sailing nearly before the wind, was most to leeward. It was composed of six ships, the interval between which and the other twenty-one was probably not less than eight miles. Even after the British fleet was seen, no attempt was for some time made to remedy this fatal separation; a neglect due partly to professional nonchalance and inefficiency, and partly misinformation concerning the enemy's force, which they had heard through a neutral was only nine ships-of-the-line.

The weather being hazy and occasionally foggy, some time passed before the gradually approaching enemies could clearly see each other. At nine a.m. the number and rates of the Spaniards could be made out from the masthead of the British flag-

Left: *Nelson, now Sir Horatio, attempted to cut out a Spanish treasure ship at Tenerife in the Canary Islands, but lost his right arm during the unsuccessful attack.*

Right: *Vice-Admiral Cuthbert Collingwood was a great personal friend of Nelson and his second-in-command at Trafalgar. His most endearing attribute was planting acorns on his estate in Northumberland to ensure that the Royal Navy's supply of oak never failed.*

Far right: *Sir George Cockburn, who under the patronage of Admiral Lord Hood, gained rapid promotion in the Royal Navy. By 1793, a year after being appointed Lieutenant, he was already a post-captain. He served with Nelson in actions off the coast of Italy in 1796.*

ship, so that they were then probably distant from twelve to fifteen miles. At half-past nine Jervis sent three ships ahead to chase, and a few minutes later supported them with three others. This advanced duty enabled these six to take the lead in the attack. About ten the fog lifted and disclosed the relative situations. The British, still in two columns, were heading fair for the gap in the Spanish order. The six lee ships of the latter had realized their false position, and were now close to the wind on the port tack, heading about north-northwest, in hopes that they could rejoin the main body to windward, which still continued its course for Cadiz. Jervis then made signal to form a single column, the fighting order of battle, and pass through the enemy's line. It soon became evident that the lee Spanish ships could not cross the bows of the British. For a moment they wavered and bore up to southeast; but soon after five of them resumed their northwest course, with the apparent purpose of breaking through the hostile line whose advance they had not been able to anticipate. The sixth continued to the southeast and disappeared.

The weather division of the Spaniards now also saw that it was not possible for all its members to effect a junction with the separated ships. Three stood on, and crossed the bows of the advancing enemy; the remainder hauled up in increasing disorder to the northward, steering a course nearly parallel, but directly opposite, to the British, and passing their van at long cannon shot. At half-past eleven the *Culloden*, Captain Troubridge, heading Jervis's column, came abreast the leading ships of this body, and opened fire. Sir John Jervis now saw secured to him the great desire of commanders-in-chief. His own force, in

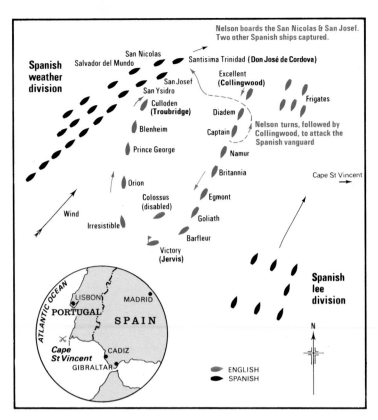

Above: *The Battle of Cape St Vincent, 14 February 1797.*

Above: *When Nelson captured the two-decker* San Nicolas *he led his boarding parties across her decks to capture the three-decker* San Josef, *which was hopelessly entangled alongside. This was termed 'Nelson's patent boarding bridge.'*

Center: *Jervis' Inshore Squadron blockading the Spanish in Cadiz, July 1797, where the survivors of the February battle had taken refuge.*

compact fighting order, was interposed between the fractions of the enemy, able to deal for a measurable time with either, undisturbed by the other. Should he attack the eighteen weather, or the eight lee ships, with his own fifteen? With accurate professional judgment he promptly decided to assail the larger body; because the smaller, having to beat to windward, would be kept out of action longer than he could hope if he chose the other alternative. The decision was in principle identical with that which determined Nelson's tactics at the Nile. The signal was therefore made to tack in succession, in pursuit of the weather ships. Troubridge, anticipating the order, had already hoisted at the masthead his answering flag of recognition, rolled up after the manner of the sea, needing but a turn of the wrist to unloose it. Quick as the admiral's signal flew the reply fluttered out, and the *Culloden's* sails were already shaking as she luffed up into the wind. 'Look at Troubridge,' shouted Jervis, in exultation: 'he handles his ship as if the eyes of all England were upon him! and would to God they were!' The rear of the Spaniards was just passing the *Culloden* as she thus went round. Ship after ship of the British line tacked in her wake and stood on in pursuit; while those still on the first course, south by west, interposed between the two Spanish divisions. Of these the lee, led by a hundred-gun ship under a vice-admiral's flag, headed towards Jervis's flag-ship, the *Victory*, the seventh in the British order, as though to go through the line ahead of her. The *Victory* was too prompt; and the Spaniards, to avoid collision, went about close under the British broadsides. In doing this he was exposed to and received a raking fire, which drove him out of action, accompanied by his consorts. The *Victory*, which had backed a topsail a moment to aim more accurately, then stood on and tacked in the wake of the *Culloden*, followed by the rest of the British column.

It was now nearly one o'clock. The action so far had consisted, first, in piercing the enemy's line, cutting off the van and greater part of the centre from the rear; and, second, in a cannonade between two columns passing on opposite parallel courses—the Spanish main division running free, the British close to the wind. Naval history abounds in instances of these brushes, and pronounces them commonly indecisive. Jervis, who had been such, meant decisive action when he ordered the *Culloden* to tack and follow the enemy. But a stern chase is a long chase, and the Spanish ships were fast sailers. Some time must pass before Troubridge and his companions could overtake them; and, as each succeeding vessel of the British line had to reach the common point of tacking, from which the Spaniards were steadily receding, the rear of Jervis's fleet must be long in coming up.

Thus, one by one, the British ships were changing their course from south by west to north-northeast in pursuit of the Spanish main division, and the latter was gradually passing to the rear of their enemy's original order. When they saw the sea clear to the southeast, about one o'clock, they bore up, altering their course to east-southeast, hoping to pass behind the British and so join the lee division. Fortunately for Jervis, Nelson was in the third ship from the rear. Having fully divined his chief's purpose, he saw it on the point of defeat, and, without waiting for orders, wore at once out of the line, and threw the *Captain*, alone, in front of the enemy's leading ships. In this well-timed but most daring move, which illustrates to the highest degree the immense difference between a desperate and a reckless action, Nelson passed to the head of the British column, crossing the bows of five large Spanish vessels, and then with his seventy-four engaged the *Santisima Trinidad*, of one hundred and thirty guns, the biggest ship at that time afloat. The enemy, apparently dashed by this act of extraordinary temerity, and as little under control as a flock of frightened sheep, hauled up in a body again to north-northeast, resuming what can only be described as their flight.

Their momentary change of course had, however, caused a delay which enabled the British leaders to come up. Troubridge in the *Culloden* was soon right behind Nelson, to whom he was dear beyond all British officers, and three other ships followed in as close array as was consistent with the free use of their guns. The Spaniards, never in good order, lay before them in confusion, two or three deep, hindering one another's fire, and presenting a target that could not easily be missed. This closing scene of the battle raged round the rear ships of the Spanish main body, and necessarily became a *mêlée*, each British captain acting according to his own judgment and the condition of his ship. A very distinguished part fell to Collingwood, likewise a close associate of Nelson's, whose ship, the *Excellent*, had brought up the rear of the order. Having, probably from this circumstance, escaped serious injury to her spars, she was fully under her captain's control, and enabled him to display the courage and skill for which he was so eminently distinguished. Passing along the enemy's rear, he had compelled one seventy-four to strike, when his eye caught sight of Nelson's ship lying disabled on the starboard side, and within pistol shot, of the *San Nicolas*, a Spanish eighty; 'her foretopmast and wheel shot away, not a sail, shroud, or rope left,' and being fired upon by five hostile ships. With every sail set he pressed ahead, passing between the *Captain* and her nearest enemy, brushing the latter at a distance of ten feet, and pouring in one of those broadsides of which he used to assure his practised crew that, if they could fire three in five minutes, no vessel could resist them. The *San Nicolas*, either intentionally or from the helmsman being killed, luffed and fell on board the *San Josef*, a ship of one hundred and twelve guns, while the *Excellent*, continuing her course, left the ground again clear for Nelson. The latter, seeing the *Captain* powerless for continued manoeuvre, put the helm to starboard; the British ship came up to the wind, fetched over to the *San Nicolas*, and grappled her. Nelson, having his men ready on deck, rushed at their head on board the Spaniard, drove her crew below, and captured her. The *San Josef*, which was fast to the *San Nicolas* on the other side, now opened a fire of musketry; but the commodore, first stationing sentinels to prevent the *San Nicolas's* men regaining their deck, called upon his own ship for a re-enforcement, with which he boarded the three-decker and carried her also. On her quarter-deck, surrounded by his followers still hot from the fight, he received the swords of the Spanish officers.

This dramatic ending to the distinguished part played by him, and the promptitude of his previous action, by which, while assuming a great responsibility, he saved the success of the day, have made Nelson the most striking figure in the battle of Cape St Vincent; or, as it is sometimes called, of St Valentine's Day. This splendid movement of his genius in no way detracts from the credit due to the commander-in-chief; as it was no lessening of Nelson's own fame that the leader of the van at the Nile conceived on the moment the happy thought of passing inside the French line. To Jervis alone belongs the honor of attacking such heavy odds, as well as of the correct and sufficient combination by which he hoped to snatch victory from superior numbers. He was happy, indeed, in having such a lieutenant, so right a man in so right a place, and at so critical a moment; but the whole responsibility and the whole original plan was his, and no man can take it from him. To him, too, was primarily due the admirable efficiency of his fleet, which removed from his enterprise the reproach of rashness to bestow upon it the praise of daring. A yet higher meed of glory is due to this bold admiral. As the dull morning light showed him the two fleets,

he was heard to say, 'A victory is very essential to England at this moment.' Honor to the chief who can rise above his own anxieties and his local responsibilities to think of the needs of his country, and who is willing to risk his own reputation to support her credit.

Among the numerous rewards bestowed for this action, the admiral was advanced to the peerage as Earl St Vincent, while upon Nelson was bestowed the then distinguished honor of Knight of the Bath. On the 20th of February he was made a rear-admiral. The captains of the fleet received medals, and the senior lieutenant of each ship was promoted.

(Editor's note—*17 October 1797 Napoleon Bonaparte as the sole representative of France, signed the treaty of Campo Formio—dividing the territory of Venice, giving the city itself to Austria, ceding the Netherlands to France and providing for the pacification and re-arrangement of the German Empire. In November 1799 Napoleon, leaving his army in Egypt, lead a coup d'état, so seizing control of France. Thus his military achievements on the Continent were consolidated by diplomatic victories. Yet, his fortunes in Egypt and Syria, by late 1799, had been mixed.*)

Below: *Another commemorative plaque, this time to Jervis and his captains after Cape St Vincent.*

Chapter 13

The Nile and the East

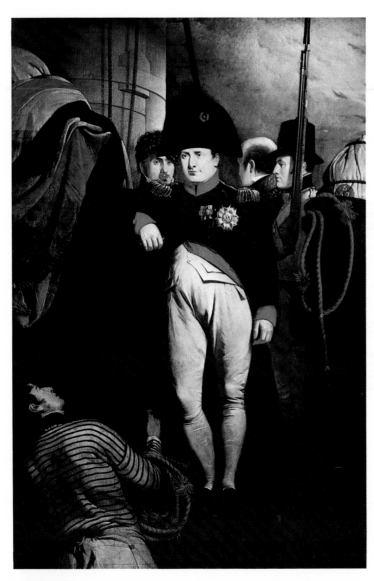

'When the Cisalpine has the best military frontier in Europe, when France gains Mayence and the Rhine, when she has in the Levant Corfu, extremely well fortified, and the islands, what more would you wish? To scatter our force, in order that England may continue to take from us, from Spain, from Holland, our colonies, and postpone yet further the restoration of our trade and our navy? . . . Either our government must destroy the English monarchy, or must expect itself to be destroyed by the corruption and intrigue of those active islanders. The present moment offers us a fine game. Let us concentrate all our activity upon the navy, and destroy England. That done, Europe is at our feet.' Thus did Bonaparte demonstrate that, after Campo Formio, the scene of strife was to be transferred to the sea.

During the year 1797 no British fleet, and, with the rare exception of one or two scattered cruisers, no British ship-of-war, had entered the Mediterranean. The gathering of the Spanish navy at Cadiz, and of the greater part of the French in Brest, with the apparent design to invade Ireland or England, had dictated the concentration of the British navy before those two ports; either immediately, as St Vincent at Cadiz, or by the dispositions—less fitted to compass their purpose—of the Channel fleet, by which bodies of ships were gathered at points other than Brest, with the hope of combining them against any sortie from that port. Great Britain, during the time following St Vincent's retreat from the Mediterranean, was in the position of a nation struggling for existence—for so she felt it—which had been compelled to contract her lines through loss of force, due to the gradual submission of her allies to her enemies. To this had further conduced the threatening attitude of the Dutch navy in the Texel, requiring a strong North Sea fleet. Toward the end of 1797 several circumstances occurred to relieve the pressure. In October Admiral Duncan inflicted upon the Dutch fleet, off the Texel, a defeat so decisive and complete as to throw it out of the contest for a long time. Of fifteen ships opposed to him, nine were taken. The condition of the French fleet in Brest, if not accurately known to be as bad as Bonaparte represented it, was still sufficiently understood. When the opening spring of 1798 permitted the Channel fleet in a body to keep the sea, the ministry felt it safe to detach a force to the Mediterranean.

Sir Horatio Nelson sailed from England on the 10th of April, and joined the fleet off Cadiz on the 30th. Lord St Vincent

detachments from Genoa, Corsica, and Civita Vecchia—the total number of troops amounting to between thirty and thirty-five thousand.

On the same day that Nelson parted from St Vincent, May 2, the admiralty wrote to the latter that it was essential to send twelve ships-of-the-line into the Mediterranean to counteract the French armament; and that to replace them eight ships had been ordered from England. The junction of the latter with the main fleet was made May 24, out of sight of the port; and during the night Captain Troubridge sailed with the inshore ships, their places being taken by vessels similarly painted, so that no suspicion of the transaction might arise in Cadiz. On the 7th of June Troubridge joined Nelson, having picked up two more ships by the way; so that the British were now thirteen seventy-

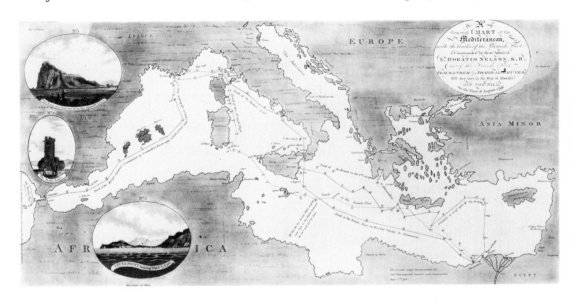

welcomed him gladly, and at once sent him with three ships-of-the-line to the Mediterranean, to watch the impending armament, and, if possible, learn its destination. Nelson left the fleet on the 2nd of May, the day before Bonaparte quitted Paris. On the night of the 20th, in a violent gale of wind, his ship was dismasted and with difficulty saved from going ashore. On the 19th Bonaparte had sailed with the Marseille and Toulon divisions of the expedition. He was to be joined on the way by the

Above: *A contemporary map of the Mediterranean illustrating the fleet movements which led up to the Battle of the Nile in 1798.*

Above: *Sir Thomas Troubridge, of whom the usually imperturbable Jervis said, 'Look at Troubridge, he handles his ship as if the eyes of all England were upon him!' when he took the* Culloden *into action at Cape St Vincent. Sadly he was drowned in 1804 when the* Blenheim *capsized in a storm.*

Opposite left: *Napoleon's tireless energy and military mind could not cope with the vagaries of wind and tide. Repeatedly his grand designs against England were frustrated until they were finally smashed at Trafalgar.*

Opposite right: *The young Nelson.*

Right: *A track chart of the Battle of the Nile (Aboukir) drawn in Nelson's own hand. After Tenerife he taught himself to write with his left hand.*

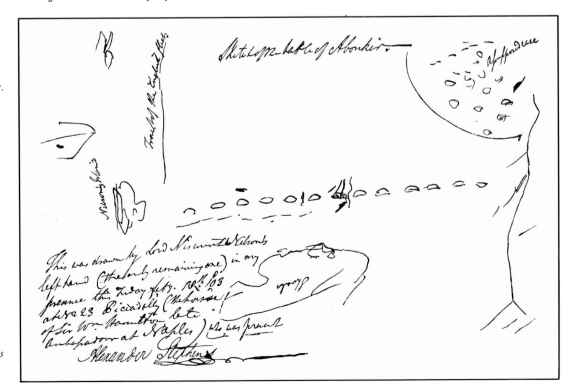

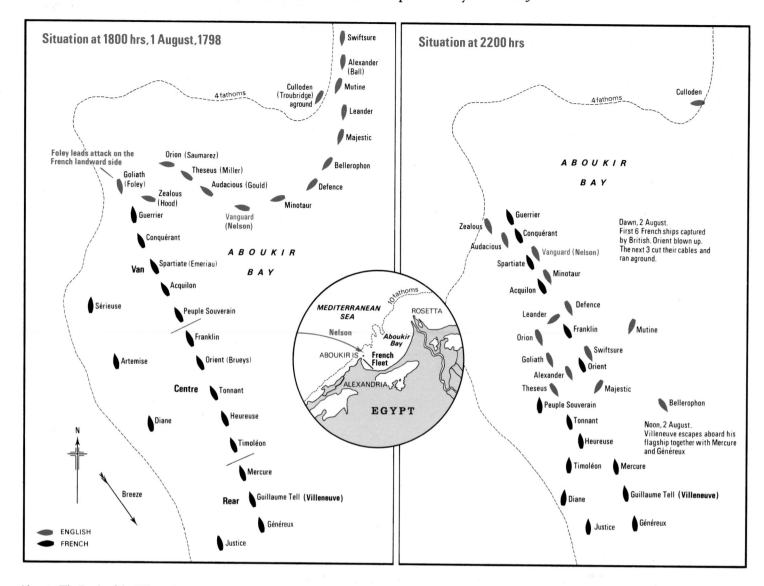

Situation at 1800 hrs, 1 August, 1798

Swiftsure
Alexander (Ball)
Mutine
Culloden (Troubridge) aground
Leander
Majestic
Foley leads attack on the French landward side
Orion (Saumarez)
Theseus (Miller)
Bellerophon
Goliath (Foley)
Audacious (Gould)
Defence
Zealous (Hood)
Minotaur
Guerrier
Vanguard (Nelson)
Conquérant
ABOUKIR BAY
Van
Spartiate (Emeriau)
Acquilon
Sérieuse
Peuple Souverain
Franklin
Artemise
Orient (Brueys)
Centre
Tonnant
Diane
Heureuse
Timoléon
N
Mercure
Rear
Guillaume Tell (Villeneuve)
Breeze
Généreux
Justice
ENGLISH
FRENCH

Situation at 2200 hrs

Culloden
4 fathoms
ABOUKIR BAY
Zealous
Guerrier
Audacious
Conquérant
Vanguard (Nelson)
Spartiate
Minotaur
Acquilon
Defence
Leander
Franklin
Mutine
Orion
Goliath
Swiftsure
Alexander
Orient
Theseus
Majestic
Peuple Souverain
Bellerophon
Tonnant
Heureuse
Timoléon
Mercure
Diane
Guillaume Tell (Villeneuve)
Justice
Généreux

Dawn, 2 August. First 6 French ships captured by British. Orient blown up. The next 3 cut their cables and ran aground.

Noon, 2 August. Villeneuve escapes aboard his flagship together with Mercure and Généreux.

MEDITERRANEAN SEA
Nelson
ROSETTA
Aboukir Bay
ABOUKIR IS
French Fleet
ALEXANDRIA
EGYPT
10 fathoms

Above: *The Battle of the Nile, 1 August 1798.*

Right: *The Battle of the Nile, fought in Aboukir Bay near Alexandria on 1 August 1798 was the first of Nelson's annihilating victories. He destroyed the fleet supporting Napoleon's invasion of Egypt.*

fours and one of fifty guns. By a very strange fatality, however, the frigates at first with Nelson had parted company the night his ship was dismasted, and had never rejoined. Troubridge brought only one little brig; and, as it was inadmissible to scatter the ships-of-the-line, the want of lookout vessels seriously affected all Nelson's movements in the long and harassing pursuit, covering nearly eight weeks, that lay ahead.

The British fleet, after its junction, was becalmed for several days. It then made the best of its way round the north end of Corsica, and thence south between Italy and the islands. Not till June 14, off Civita Vecchia, was probable information received that the French had been seen ten days before off the southwest point of Sicily, steering to the eastward. As yet there was no certainty as to their destination, and Nelson had no light vessels for scouts. St Vincent in his instructions had said, reflecting the ideas of the government, that the enemy's 'object appears to be either an attack upon Naples or Sicily, the conveyance of an army to some part of Spain to invade Portugal, or to pass through the Straits with the view of proceeding to Ireland.' The whole situation vividly illustrates the difficulty of pursuit by sea, and the necessity of stationing and keeping the detaining force near the point of the enemy's departure before he can get away. By whatsoever fault, certainly not that of Nelson or St Vincent, the British fleet was a fortnight too late in entering the Mediterranean.

An easterly course, however, with a fresh northwest wind,

Right: Plan of the Battle of the Nile showing the double envelopment of Brueys' fleet. In the center is the huge 120-gun flag-ship l'Orient blowing up and at bottom right is Troubridge's Culloden hard aground on a shoal.

Below right: The scene the next morning. Three of the nine prizes taken had to be burned as they were too damaged to be worth sailing back home, and only two of the French ships of-the-line escaped.

Below: The carnage at the Nile was all the more lurid because the action took place at night. Just before midnight Brueys' flag-ship l'Orient blew up in a colossal explosion (right) killing most of her crew.

indicated that neither Spain nor the Atlantic was the destination of the French armament; and Nelson at once decided it must be Malta, to be used as a base of operations against Sicily. '*Malta is in the direct road to Sicily*,' said he. Pausing a moment to communicate with Naples, he there heard, on the 17th of June, that the French had landed at Malta; and pushing on, received off Messina the news of its surrender. This was on the 20th, the day after Bonaparte sailed from the island for Egypt. On the 22nd, off Cape Passaro, the southeast extremity of Sicily, a vessel was spoken, from which Nelson gained the information of Bona-

numerous a body of vessels, would not have served him, had the British admiral had those active purveyors of information, those eyes of the fleet, which are so essential to naval as to land warfare. On leaving Malta, Bonaparte directed the expedition to steer first for Candia. After a week's quiet navigation he was off the side of the island, and on the 27th of June was joined by a frigate from Naples, to tell him of Nelson, with fourteen sail, being off that port ten days before. At this moment the British admiral had already outstripped his chase. When Bonaparte knew that his enemy was somewhere near upon his heels, he again changed

parte's departure, supposed to be for Sicily; but he had meantime learned from Naples that the French had no intention of molesting any part of that kingdom. Utterly in the dark, and without frigates, he concluded, after weighing all the chances, that Egypt was the enemy's destination, and with a fair wind and a press of sail shaped his course for Alexandria. On the 28th the fleet came off the port, and sent a boat ashore. No French vessels had been seen on the coast.

This remarkable miscarriage, happening to a man of so much energy and intuition, was due primarily to his want of small lookout ships; and secondly, to Bonaparte's using the simple, yet at sea sufficient, ruse of taking an indirect instead of a direct course to his object. This, however, in a narrow sea, with so

the course, ordering the fleet to make the land seventy miles west of Alexandria, and sending a frigate direct to the port to reconnoitre. On the 29th of June, the day Nelson sailed away from Alexandria, the light squadron signalled the coast, along which the fleet sailed till July 1st, when it anchored off the city. Determined to run no chance of an enemy's frustrating his objects, the commander-in-chief landed his army the same evening.

If, in this celebrated chase, Nelson made a serious mistake, it was upon his arrival at Alexandria. Knowing the time when the French left Malta, as he did, and that they were accompanied by so great a train of transports, it seems a fair criticism that he should have trusted his judgment a little further, and waited off the suspected port of destination to see whether so cumbrous a body had not been outsailed by his compact homogeneous force. 'His active and anxious mind,' wrote Sir Edward Berry, who, as captain of the flagship, was witness of his daily feelings, 'would not permit him to rest a moment in the same place; he therefore shaped his course to the northward for the coast of Caramania.' His one thought now was to get back to the westward, taking a more northerly course on the return, so as to increase the chance of information. The fleet accordingly stretched to the northward until the coast of Asia Minor was made, and then beat back along the south shore of Candia, not seeing a single vessel until it had passed that island. The squadron now filled with water, which was running short, and on the 24th again sailed for Alexandria; the admiral having satisfied himself that the French were at least neither in Corfu nor to the westward. On the 1st of August the minarets of the city were seen, and soon after the port full of shipping, with the French flag upon the walls, but, to Nelson's bitter disappointment, no large ships of war. At one in the afternoon, however, one of his fleet made signal that a number of ships-of-the-line were at anchor in Aboukir Bay, twelve or fifteen miles east of Alexandria; and Nelson, prompt to attack as Bonaparte had been to disembark, gave slippery fortune, so long unkind, no chance again to balk him, but with a brisk breeze flew at once upon the foe.

The Bay of Aboukir, in the western portion of which the French fleet was anchored, and where was fought the celebrated Battle of the Nile, is an open roadstead, extending from the promontory of Aboukir, fifteen miles east of Alexandria, to the Rosetta mouth of the Nile. The distance between the two ex-

treme points is about eighteen miles. In the western part, where the French were lying, the shore-line, after receding some distance from Aboukir Point, turns to the southeast and continues in that direction in a long narrow tongue of sand, behind which lies the shallow Lake Madieh. Northeast from the point is a line of shoals and rocks, rising at two and a half miles' distance into a small island, then bearing the same name, Aboukir, but since known as Nelson's Island; beyond which the same stretch of foul ground continues for another mile and a quarter. Behind this four-mile barrier there is found fair shelter from the prevailing northwest summer wind; but as, for three miles from the beach, there were only four fathoms of water, the order of battle had to be established somewhat beyond that distance. The northwestern ship, which with the prevailing wind would be to windward and in the van, was moored a mile and a half southeast from Aboukir Island, in five fathoms of water. The few guns established by Brueys on Aboukir island were so light as to be entirely ineffective, in range and weight, at the distance between them and the flank they pretended to strengthen. They were a mere toy defence, as futile as the other general dispositions taken.

Below: *The blowing up of l'Orient inspired the poem 'Casabianca' written by Mrs Hemans in 1829, for Brueys' flag-captain, the Comte de Casa Bianca who had his ten-year old son on board. It was this child who 'stood on the burning deck,' too frightened to leave his dead father.*

The evening before the eventful first of August, as the British fleet expected to make Alexandria the next day, the *Alexander* and *Swiftsure* were sent ahead to reconnoitre. In consequence of this dispatchment, made necessary by the want of frigates, these ships, when the main body at one p.m. sighted the French fleet, were considerably to leeward, and did not get into action until two hours after their consorts. As soon as the enemy were seen, the British fleet hauled sharp up on the wind, heading about northeast, to weather Aboukir Island and shoal; the admiral at the same time making signal to prepare for action, anchoring by the stern. As they drew by the shoal, being in eleven fathoms, Nelson hailed Captain Hood, of the *Zealous*, and asked if he thought they were far enough to the eastward to clear it; for the only chart in the fleet was a rough sketch taken from the captured merchant vessel, and no British officer knew the ground. Hood replied that he would bear up, sounding as he went, so that the other ships keeping outside of him would be safe. Thus the fleet was piloted into action; one ship, the *Goliath*, being ahead of the *Zealous*, but on her outer bow, and the admiral very properly allowing others to pass him, until he was sixth in the order, so as to be reasonably certain the flag-ship would not touch the bottom. Captain Foley of the *Goliath*, still keeping the lead, crossed ahead of the French column, over the ground left open by Brueys's oversight, intending to attack the van ship, the *Guerrier*; but the anchor hung for a moment, so that he brought up on the inner quarter of the second, the *Conquérant*, while Hood, following close after, anchored on the bow of the *Guerrier*. These two British ships thus came into action shortly before sundown, the French having opened fire ten minutes before. Five minutes later, just as the sun was sinking below the horizon, the foremast of the *Guerrier* went overboard. 'So auspicious a commencement of the attack was greeted with three cheers by the whole British fleet.' The *Orion* followed with a much wider sweep, passing round her two leaders, between them and the shore, and anchored on the inner side of the fifth French ship; while the *Theseus*, which came next, brought up abreast the third, having gone between the *Goliath* and *Zealous* and their antagonists. The *Audacious*, the fifth of the British to come up, chose a new course. Steering between the *Guerrier* and the *Conquérant*, she took her place on the bow of the latter, already engaged on the quarter by the *Goliath*. These five all anchored on the inner (port) side of the French. Nelson's ship, the *Vanguard*, coming next, anchored outside the third of the enemy's vessels, the *Spartiate*, thus placed between her and the *Theseus*. The *Minotaur*, five minutes later, took the outer side of the fourth, heretofore without an opponent; and the *Defence* attacked, also on the outer side, the fifth ship, already engaged on her inner side by the *Orion*. Five French seventy-fours were thus in hot action with eight British of the same size, half an hour after the first British gun was fired, and only five hours from the time Brueys first knew that the enemy were near.

This most gallant, but most unfortunate, man had passed suddenly from a condition of indolent security face to face with an appalling emergency. When Nelson's fleet was first reported, numbers of men were ashore, three miles or more away, getting water for the ships. They were recalled, but most of them did not return. Brueys still cherished the belief, with which indeed he could not have parted without despair, that the enemy would not brave the unknown perils of the ground with night falling; nor could he tell their purpose until they had passed Aboukir Island and opened the bay. A hurried council of senior officers renewed the decision previously reached, to fight, if fight they must, at anchor; but Brueys betrayed the vacillations of an unsteady purpose by crossing the light yards, a step which could have no other significance than that of getting under way. Still,

Below: *The brand new 3rd Rate* Hércule *was intercepted by HMS* Mars *off the Bec du Raz on 21 April 1798 and captured before completing her maiden voyage from Lorient to Brest.*

Above: *Nelson coming on deck at the Nile, having had a slight wound in the temple bandaged.*

he hoped for the respite of a night to make the preparations so long neglected. Little did he know the man whom England herself still hardly knew. Without a moment's pause, without a tremor of uncertainty, yet with all the precautions of a seaman, Nelson came straight onward, facing with a mind long prepared for the difficulties of navigation, the doubts and obscurity of a night action. Hurriedly the French prepare for battle; and, secure that the enemy will not dare go within the line, the batteries on that side are choked with the numerous encumbrances of ship economy, the proper disposal of which is termed 'clearing for action.'

Left: *Nelson having his head wound dressed in the cockpit of HMS Vanguard during the Battle of the Nile. All but the most seriously wounded preferred to leave the ghastly sights and sounds in the cockpit and return to their post of action. Nelson also knew that his reappearance on deck would hearten his men.*

Below: *Nelson as the destroyer of revolutionary crocodiles or 'The British hero cleansing ye mouth of ye Nile'—James Gillray's sardonic view of the victory of the Nile, published in 1798.*

For half an hour Brueys was a helpless and hopeless, though undaunted, spectator of an overwhelming attack, which he had never expected at all, delivered in a manner he had deemed impossible upon the part of his order he thought most secure. Soon he was freed from the agony of mere passive waiting by the opportunity to act. The *Bellerophon* and *Majestic*, both seventy-fours, anchored outside and abreast, respectively, of the flag-ship *Orient*, of one hundred and twenty guns, and of the *Tonnant*, eighty, next astern. Darkness had just settled down upon the water as the arrival of these two ships completed the first scene of the tragedy; and the British vessels, which were fighting under their white ensign as more easily seen at night, now hoisted also four lanterns, horizontally arranged, whereby to recognize each other.

Meanwhile a woful mishap had befallen Nelson's chosen brother-in-arms, Troubridge. His ship, the *Culloden*, had been some distance from the main body of the fleet when the latter rounded the shoal, and, doing her own piloting, ran upon its outer extremity at a quarter before seven. There she stuck, despite all the efforts of her most able commander, until two o'clock the next morning, when the battle was over. There also, however, she served as a beacon to the two remaining ships, *Alexander* and *Swiftsure*, who had to make the perilous passage in the dark. These vessels, with the *Leander*, fifty, arriving after eight o'clock, at a critical moment of the battle, played the part of a reserve in a quarter where the British were meeting with disaster.

Neither the *Bellerophon* nor the *Majestic* was equally matched with the French ship opposed to it; but the *Bellerophon* especially, having to do with a vessel double her own force and having brought up fairly abreast, where she got her full fire, was soon nearly a wreck. In three quarters of an hour her main and mizzen masts were shot away, and in thirty minutes more, unable longer to endure her punishment, the cable was cut and she wore out of action. As she did so, the foremost also fell, and, with forty-nine killed and one hundred and forty-eight wounded, out of a ship's company of six hundred and fifty men, the *Bellerophon* drifted down the line, receiving the successive broadsides of the French rear. As she thus passed, without flag or light, the *Swiftsure* came up. Withholding his fire, Captain Hallowell

hailed, and finding her to be a British ship, let go at once his anchor, bringing up on the starboard bow of the *Orient*. Immediately afterwards the *Alexander* arrived and anchored on the port quarter of the three-decker, while the *Leander*, with the discretion becoming her size, placed herself on the port bow of the *Franklin*, the next ahead of the *Orient*, in a position of comparative impunity, and thus raked both the French ships. The French centre was thus in its turn the victim of a concentration, similar to that with which the action began in the van, and destined to result in a frightful catastrophe.

At about nine in the evening the French flag-ship was observed to be on fire, from what cause has never been certainly known. The British guns, trained on the part in flames, helped to paralyze all efforts to extinguish them, and they gained rapidly. The brave and unfortunate Brueys was spared the sight of this last calamity. Already twice wounded, at half-past eight a cannon-ball carried away his left leg at the thigh. He refused to be taken below, and passed away calmly and nobly a few moments before the fire broke out. At ten the *Orient* blew up. Five ships ahead of her had already surrendered, and the eighty-gun ship *Franklin* also hauled down her flag before midnight.

Six of the French still had their colors flying; but either from their cables being cut by shot, or from the necessity of slipping to avoid the explosion of the *Orient*, they had drifted far astern.

Above: *François Brueys d'Aiguilliers was discharged in 1793 for royalist sympathies but was reinstated by the Directory in 1795 and promoted to Rear-Admiral.*

Right: *The opening phase of the engagement at the Nile, as Nelson's 74s approached the line of anchored French ships.*

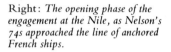

Above: *It was typical of Nelson's magnanimity toward his 'band of brothers' that he recommended Troubridge for the Nile medal even though the* Culloden *had been aground throughout the action.*

Above: *Fearful bloodshed aboard the* Tonnant *at the Nile, as Captain Dupetit-Thouars with both legs shot off above the knees, orders his men to place him upright in a barrel. From here he encouraged his men for a few more minutes, but to no avail. Next morning the dismasted hulk was forced to strike her colors.*

The three in the extreme rear had been but slightly engaged; of the others, the *Tonnant* was totally dismasted, while the *Heureux* and *Mercure* had received considerable injury. The following morning these vessels were attacked by some of the least injured of the British, with the result that the *Tonnant*, *Mercure*, *Heureux* and *Timoléon*, the last of which had been the extreme rear, or flank, ship of the original order, ran ashore. There the three first named afterwards hauled down their flags, and the fourth was burned by her officers. The two other French ships, *Guillaume Tell* and *Généreux*, escaped. The former bore the flag of Rear-Admiral Villeneuve, who had commanded the rear in this battle, and was hereafter to be commander-in-chief of the allied fleet at the memorable disaster of Trafalgar.

Such was, in its main outlines, the celebrated Battle of the Nile, the most complete of naval victories, and among the most decisive, at least of the immediate course of events. In it the French lost eleven out of thirteen ships-of-the-line and thirty-five hundred men, killed, wounded, or drowned; among them being the commander-in-chief and three captains killed, a rear-admiral and six captains wounded. The British loss was two hundred and eighteen killed—of which one captain—and six hundred and seventy-eight wounded, among whom was the admiral himself, struck in the head by a heavy splinter. The hurt, which he at first thought fatal, disabled him for the moment and seriously affected his efficiency for some days. 'I think,' wrote he, four weeks later, 'that if it had pleased God I had not been wounded, not a boat would have escaped.'

The particular circumstances under which the British attack was undertaken, the admirable skill as well as conduct shown by all the captains, and the thoroughly scientific character of the tactical combination adopted, as seen in its execution, unite with the decisiveness of the issue to cast a peculiar lustre upon this victory of Nelson's. Lord Howe, inferior to none as a judge of merit, said to Captain Berry that the Battle of the Nile 'stood unparalleled and singular in this instance, that every captain distinguished himself.'

'The consequences of this battle,' sums up a brilliant French naval writer, 'were incalculable. Our navy never recovered from this terrible blow to its consideration and its power. This was the combat which for two years delivered the Mediterranean to the English, and called thither the squadrons of Russia; which shut up our army in the midst of a rebellious population, and decided the Porte to declare against us; which put India out of the reach of our enterprise, and brought France within a hair's-breadth of her ruin; for it rekindled the scarcely extinct war with Austria, and brought Suwarrow and the Austro-Russians to our very frontiers.'

While Bonaparte's Oriental castles were thus crumbling, through the destruction in Aboukir Bay of the foundation upon which they rested—while Ionia was falling, Malta starving, and Egypt isolated, through the loss of the sea—the Franco-Spanish allies were deprived of another important foothold for maritime power. On the 15th of November Minorca with its valuable harbor, Port Mahon, was surrendered to a combined British

military and naval expedition, quietly fitted out by St Vincent from Gibraltar.

The year 1798 in the Mediterranean closed with these operations in progress. At its beginning France was in entire control of the land-locked sea, and scarcely a sail hostile to her, except furtive privateers, traversed its surface. When it closed, only two French ships-of-the-line fit for battle remained upon the waters, which swarmed with enemy's squadrons. Of these two, refugees from the fatal bay of Aboukir, one was securely locked in Malta, whence she never escaped; the other made its way to Toulon, and met its doom in a vain effort to carry relief to the beleaguered island.

After the destruction of his fleet, Bonaparte resumed the task of subduing and organizing Egypt, which had by that misfortune become more than ever essential to his projects. In the original conception of his eastern adventure the valley of the Nile had borne a twofold part. It was, in the first place, to become a permanent acquisition of France, the greatest of her colonies—great not only by its own natural resources, susceptible as was believed of immense development, but also by its singular position, which, to a power controlling the Mediterranean waters, gave the military and commercial link between the eastern and western worlds. To France, bereft of the East and the West Indies, childless now of her richest colonies, Egypt was to be the great and more than equal compensation. But this first object obtained, though in itself a justification, was but the necessary step to the more dazzling, if not more useful, achievement of the destruction of the British power in India, and the creation there of an empire tributary to France.

The singular position of isolation in which the French in Egypt were placed, by the loss of the control of the sea, must be realized, in order to understand the difficulties under which Bonaparte labored in shaping his course of action, from time to time, with reference to the general current of events. Separated from Palestine by two hundred miles of desert, and by a yet wider stretch of barren sand from any habitable land to the west, Egypt is aptly described by Napoleon himself as a great oasis, surrounded on all sides by the desert and the sea.

Bonaparte had hoped to cajole the Porte into an attitude of neutrality, upon the plea that his quarrel was solely with the Mamelukes on account of injury done by them to French

Opposite: Sir William Sidney Smith had a flair for independent operations but was temperamentally unsuited to cooperate with senior officers.

Left: Napoleon's repulse by Sir William Sidney Smith in St Jean d'Acre early in 1799 put an end to his plans to attack Turkey, making him 'miss his destiny' as he put it.

1799. The Turks were by him routed and driven from the oasis, and the fort besieged. Bonaparte himself arrived on the 15th, and on the 20th the garrison capitulated. The corps destined for the expedition, numbering in all thirteen thousand men, having now assembled, the advance from El Arish began on the 22nd. On the 25th Gaza was taken. On the 3rd of March the army encamped before Jaffa, and on the 7th the place was carried by storm. A port, though a very poor one, was thus secured. The next day there entered, from Acre, a convoy of Turkish coasters laden with provisions and ammunition, which fell a welcome prize to the French, and was sent back to Haifa, a small port seven miles south of Acre, for the use of the troops upon arrival. On the 12th of March the army resumed its march upon Acre, distant about sixty miles. On the 17th, at five in the afternoon, a detachment entered and held Haifa, to provide a place of safety for the flotilla, which, coasting the beach, slowly followed the advance of the troops. From Haifa Bonaparte could see the roadstead of Acre, and lying there two British ships-of-the-line, the *Tigre* and the *Theseus*, both under the command of Sir Sidney Smith, the captain of the former; who, as ranking officer on the spot, represented the naval power of Great Britain, about to foil the plans of the great French leader.

It was on the morning of the 18th they were seen approaching Acre, under convoy of a small corvette. The *Tigre* at once gave chase, and captured all but the corvette and two of the coasters. The cannon that should have been turned against the walls were landed and served to defend them; while the prizes, receiving British crews, thenceforth harassed the siege works, flanking the two walls against which the attacks were addressed, and enfilading the trenches. The French, having by this mishap lost all their siege guns proper, had to depend upon field-pieces to breach the walls until the 25th of April, when half a dozen heavy cannon were received from Jaffa.

On the 4th of May, when the besieged and besiegers had been mining, countermining, and daily fighting, for over six weeks—separated by but a stone's throw one from the other—a breach thought practicable by the French general was made, the mine for blowing in the counterscarp was finished, and a general assault was ordered for the 5th; but the engineers of the besieged countermined so industriously that by daybreak they had ruined the mine before being discovered. This caused the assault to be postponed to the 9th. On the 7th, towards evening, some thirty or forty sail were seen on the western horizon. They bore the long expected Turkish succors from Rhodes; whose commander even now had only been induced to approach by a peremptory exercise of Sir Sidney Smith's powers as British minister. Bonaparte saw that no more time could be lost, and ordered the assault at once; the weather being calm, twenty-four hours might still elapse before the re-enforcements could enter the place. Under a heavy fire from one side and the other, the attack was made; and in the morning the British seamen saw the French flag flying on the outer angle of one of the towers. It marked the high water of Bonaparte's Syrian expedition.

On the 8th the assault was renewed. As the French columns advanced, the Turkish ships were still detained in the offing by calms, and the soldiers were being brought ashore in boats, but still far from the landing. Then it was that Sir Sidney Smith, seeing that a few critical moments might determine the success or failure of his weary struggle, manned the boats of his ships, and pulling rapidly ashore led the British seamen, armed with pikes, to help hold the breach till the troops could arrive. The French carried the first line, the old fortifications of the town; but that done, they found themselves confronted with a second, which Phélippeaux, now dead, had formed by connecting together the houses and garden walls of the seraglio within. The

commerce. On the 11th of December he had sent to Constantinople a M Beauchamp, recently consul at Muscat, with instructions how to act in the twofold contingency of war having been declared or not. At that time he expected that Talleyrand would be found in Constantinople as Ambassador of France. The news by the Ragusan enlightened him as to the actual relations with Turkey; but the disquieting rumors before received, coinciding with his ultimate purpose to advance upon India through Syria, had already determined him to act as the military situation demanded. He had learned that troops were assembling in Syria and in the island of Rhodes, and divined that he was threatened with a double invasion—by the desert of Suez and by the Mediterranean Sea. True to his sound and invariable policy, he determined to use his central position to strike first one and then the other, and not passively to wait on the defensive until a simultaneous attack might compel him to divide his force. During the violent winter weather, which would last yet for six weeks or two months, landing on the Egyptian coast was thought impracticable. For that period, probably for longer, he could count upon security on the side of the sea. He would improve the interval by invading Syria, driving back the enemy there, breaking up his army, and seizing his ports. Thus he would both shut the coast to the British cruisers off Alexandria, which drew supplies from thence, and make impossible any future invasion from the side of the desert.

The first essential point in the campaign was to possess El Arish, just occupied by the troops of Djezzar. General Reynier advanced against it with his division on the 5th of February,

strife raged throughout the day, with varied success in different quarters; but at nightfall, after a struggle of twenty-four hours, the assailants withdrew and Acre was saved. On the 20th the siege was raised, the French retreating during the night. Upon the 25th they reached Jaffa, and on the 29th Gaza. Both places were evacuated; and the army, resuming its march, next day entered the desert. On the 2nd of June it encamped in the oasis of El Arish. The garrison of the fort there was re-enforced, the works strengthened with more artillery, and the place provisioned for six months. It was the one substantial result of the Syrian expedition, an outpost which, like Acre, an invader must subdue before advancing. On the 7th, after nine days' march through the desert under the scorching heat of the June sun, the army re-entered Egypt. It had lost since its departure fifteen hundred killed or dead of disease, and more than two thousand wounded.

(Editor's note— *The operations in the Atlantic during this period were, with few exceptions, reduced to the destruction of commerce, the harassment of the enemy's communications on the sea and, on the part of the British, a more or less vigilant observation of the proceedings in the enemy's naval ports, of which Brest was the most important. The strategy of the blockade of Brest rested on the fact that the French fleet could not sail in such westerly weather as forced the British to take refuge in port, and upon the expectation that the latter, by diligence, could regain their station with the first of the east wind in time to prevent the enemy's escape.*

On 15 December 1796 a large French fleet slipped out of Brest undetected by the few British look-outs, destined for Ireland. Extremely harsh weather and incompetent seamanship marred the expedition from the outset, though the French achieved the Irish coast without once encountering enemy ships. Once there however, lack of experience,

poor planning and rough seas prevented them from landing troops. On retreating to Brest they again avoided detection and returned ingloriously with five ships-of-the-line lost to the sea. The expedition was marked by serious tactical blunders on both sides.

In August 1797 Earl St Vincent succeeded Bridport and took control of the blockade of Brest. His untiring vigilance and efficiency are a model of military excellence. The rules he laid down—centering the fleet closer to Brest, tightening the discipline of the blockades—and maintaining a large body of ships at sea at all times—prevented the French from again quitting Brest.

In October, 16 small Dutch ships-of-the-line put to sea by themselves, and on the 11th met the fleet of Admiral Duncan, of equal numbers but distinctly superior in broadside force. The British, having the wind, bore down and attacked—passing when possible through the enemy's line so as to cut off his retreat to the Dutch coast, less than ten miles distant. This battle, known by the name of Camperdown from a village on the adjoining shore, was fought with all the desperation that in every age has marked the meetings of the British and the Dutch. It closed with the defeat of the latter, which put an end to the Texel expedition.

In 1798 France was in a position of extreme weakness internally and externally. Under Napoleon's leadership in the land campaigns she rebounded. By 1801 France had destroyed Austrian power, reconquered Italy, and formed a Second Coalition against Great Britain in an effort to smash her sea power. British blockade policy involved the search of neutral merchant vessels and confiscation of contraband. This aggressive policy and disregard for neutral flags fueled antagonism toward Great Britain in the Baltic countries.

In December 1800 a Treaty of Armed Neutrality was concluded between Sweden and Russia with the adherence of Denmark and Prussia. Thus opposing Great Britain with the combined threat of the Scandinavian and Russian fleets, Napoleon hoped to destroy the foundation of England's strength, her sea power.)

Above: *Napoleon as First Consul.*

Above: *Vice-Admiral Jan de Winter, defeated at Camperdown (Kamperduin).*

Above: *Admiral Adam Duncan receiving the sword of De Winter at Camperdown. What made the victory particularly notable was the fact that Duncan's men had been disaffected during the Nore Mutiny only a short while before. At one stage he had been reduced to only one ship (his own) prepared to put to sea.*

Opposite: *Camperdown, fought on 11 October 1797 marked the extinction of the Dutch as a first-class naval power. In a battle as ferocious as any since the seventeenth century the Royal Navy sustained more casualties than it had in the Seven Years' War.*

Right: *John Cranford, a gallant sailor who nailed the flagship Venerable's colors to the mast after they had been shot away. When Duncan's fleet remained at the Nore during the mutiny he boasted that even if the Venerable were sunk by the Dutch his masthead would still be above water, and his men remembered this during the battle.*

Chapter 14

Copenhagen and Trafalgar

By the peace of Lunéville Great Britain was left alone, and for the moment against all Europe. The ministry met the emergency with vigor and firmness, though possibly with too much reliance upon diplomacy and too little upon the military genius of the great seaman whose services were at their disposal. Upon the Continent nothing could be effected, all resistance to France had been crushed by the genius of Bonaparte; but time had to be gained for the expedition then under way against Egypt and destined to compel its evacuation by the French. The combination in the North also must be quickly dissolved, if the country were to treat on anything like equal terms.

An armed negotiation with the Baltic powers was therefore determined; and a fleet of eighteen sail-of-the-line with thirty-five smaller vessels was assembled at Yarmouth, on the east coast of England. Rapidity of movement was essential to secure the advantage from the ice, which, breaking up in the harbors less rapidly than in the open water, would delay the concentration of the hostile navies; and also to allow the Baltic powers the least possible time to prepare for hostilities which they had scarcely anticipated

The fleet sailed from Yarmouth on the 12th of March, 1801; and on the 19th, although there had been some scattering in a heavy gale, nearly all were collected off the Skaw, the northern

remained to the commander-in-chief to act at once; for the wind was favorable, an advantage which at any moment might be lost.

Having shown the necessity for celerity, Nelson discussed the plan of operations. Copenhagen is on the east side of the island of Zealand, fronting the coast of Sweden, from which it is separated by the passage called the Sound. On the west the island is divided from the other parts of Denmark by the Great Belt. The navigation of the latter being much the more difficult, the preparations of the Danes had been made on the side of the Sound, and chiefly about Copenhagen itself. For half a mile from the shore in front of the city, flats extend, and in the Sound itself at a distance of little over a mile, is a long shoal called the Middle Ground. Between these two bodies of shallow water is a channel, called the King's, through which a fleet of heavy ships could sail, and from whose northern end a deep pocket stretches toward Copenhagen, forming the harbor proper. The natural point of attack therefore appears to be at the north; and there the Danes had erected powerful works, rising on piles out of the shoal water off the harbor's mouth and known as the Three-Crown Batteries. Nelson, however, pointed out that not only was this head of the line exceedingly strong, but that the wind that was fair to attack would be foul to return; therefore a disabled ship would have no escape but by

point of Jutland at the entrance of the Kattegat. The wind being northwest was fair for going to Copenhagen, and Nelson, if in command, would have advanced at once with the ambassador on board. 'While the negotiation is going on,' he said, 'the Dane should see our flag waving every moment he lifted his head.' As it was, the envoy went forward with a frigate alone and the fleet waited. On the 12th it was off Elsinor, where the envoy rejoined, Denmark having rejected the British terms.

This amounted to an acceptance of hostilities, and it only

passing through the King's Channel. Doing so she would have to run the gauntlet of a line of armed hulks, which the Danes had established as floating batteries along the inner edge of the channel—covering the front of Copenhagen—and would also be separated from her fleet. He advised that a sufficiently strong force of the lighter ships-of-the-line should pass outside the Middle Ground, despite the difficulties of navigation, which were not insuperable, and come up in rear of the city. There they would interpose between the Danes and their allies, and be in

Right: *The Battle of Copenhagen,
2 April 1801.*

Opposite left: *The Battle of
Copenhagen was fought on April 1801
to disrupt the armed coalition between
the Northern Powers.*

Opposite right: *Nelson's line of
ships subduing the Danish defenses.
After a heavy bombardment an
armistice was negotiated to spare the
city.*

position to assail the weaker part of the hostile order. He offered himself to lead this detachment.

Nelson asked ten ships-of-the-line and a number of smaller vessels, with which he undertook to destroy the floating batteries covering the front of the city. These being reduced, the bomb vessels could be placed so as to play with effect upon the dockyard, arsenals, and the town, in case further resistance was made.

The nights of the 30th and 31st of March were employed sounding the channel. On the first of April the fleet moved up to the north end of the Middle Ground, about four miles from the city; and that afternoon Nelson's division, to which Parker had assigned two ships-of-the-line more than had been asked—or twelve altogether—got under way, passed through the outer channel and anchored towards sundown off the southeast end of the shoal, two miles from the head of the Danish line. Nelson announced his purpose to attack as soon as the wind served; and the night was passed by him in arranging the order of battle. The enterprise was perilous, not on account of the force

to be engaged, but because of the great difficulties of navigation. The pilots were mostly mates of merchantmen trading with the Baltic; and their experience in vessels of three or four hundred tons did not fit them for the charge of heavy battle-ships.

The next morning the wind came fair at south-southeast, and at eight a.m. the British captains were summoned to the flag-ship for their final instructions. The Danish line to be attacked extended in a northwest and southeast direction for somewhat over a mile. It was composed of hulks and floating batteries, eighteen to twenty in number and mounting 628 guns, of which about 375 would—fighting thus at anchor—be on the engaged side. The southern flank now to be assailed was partly supported by works on shore; but from the intervening shoal water these were too distant for thoroughly efficient fire. At half-past nine signal was made to weigh. The ships were soon under sail; but the difficulties of pilotage, despite careful soundings made during the night by an experienced naval captain, were soon apparent. The *Agamemnon*, of sixty-four guns, was unable to weather the point of the Middle Ground, and had to anchor out of range. She had no share in the battle. The *Bellona* and *Russell*, seventy-fours, the fourth and fifth in the order, entered the Channel; but keeping too far to the eastward they ran ashore on its farther side—upon the Middle Ground. They were not out of action, but beyond the range of the most efficient gunnery under the conditions of that period. Nelson's flag-ship following them passed clear, as did the rest of the heavy ships; but the loss of these three out of the line prevented by so much its extension to the northward. The result was to expose that part of the British order to a weight of fire quite disproportioned to its strength. A body of frigates very gallantly undertook to fill the gap, which they could do but inadequately, and suffered heavy loss in attempting.

The battle was at its height at half-past eleven. There was then no more manoeuvring, but the simple question of efficient gunnery and endurance. At about two p.m. a great part of the Danish line had ceased to fire, and the flag-ship *Dannebrog* was in flames. During the action the Danish crews were frequently

re-enforced from the shore; and the new-comers in several cases, reaching the ships after they had struck, renewed the fight, either through ignorance or indifference to the fact. The land batteries also fired on boats trying to take possession. Nelson seized on this circumstance to bring the affair to a conclusion. He wrote a letter addressed 'To the brothers of Englishmen, the Danes,' and sent it under flag of truce to the Crown Prince, who was in the city. 'Lord Nelson has directions to spare Denmark when no longer resisting; but if the firing is continued on the part of Denmark, Lord Nelson will be obliged to set on fire all the floating batteries he has taken, without having the power of saving the brave Danes who have defended them.' The letter was sent on shore by a British officer who had served in the Russian navy and spoke Danish. The engagement continued until about three p.m., when the whole line of floating defences southeast of the Crown Batteries had either struck or been destroyed.

The fortifications were still unharmed, as were the ships west of them covering the harbor proper; but their fire was stopped by the bearer of a flag of truce who was bringing to Nelson the reply of the Crown Prince. The latter demanded the precise purport of the first message. Nelson took a high hand. He had destroyed the part of the enemy's line which he had attacked; but it was important now to withdraw his crippled ships, and with the existing wind that could only be done by passing the Crown Batteries. Had the three that ran aground been in the line, it is permissible to believe that that work would have been so far injured as to be practically harmless; but this was far from the case. The admiral in his second letter politicly ignored this feature of the situation. He wrote, 'Lord Nelson's object in sending on shore a flag of truce is humanity; he there-fore *consents* that hostilities shall cease till Lord Nelson can take his prisoners out of the prizes, and he consents to land all the wounded Danes and to burn or remove his prizes. Lord Nelson, with humble duty to His Royal Highness, begs leave to say that he will ever esteem it the greatest victory he ever gained, if this flag of truce may be the happy forerunner of a lasting and happy union between my most gracious Sovereign and His

Left: *It was during the bombardment of Copenhagen that Nelson is reputed to have said that he had a right to be blind some times, having only one eye. His superior Sir Hyde Parker was convinced that Nelson's force was being beaten and had hoisted the recall signal, but Nelson merely moved closer inshore and silenced the Danish fire.*

Above: *Napoleon at the height of his power, Emperor of France and ruler of most of Europe. The struggle between France and Great Britain finally resolved itself into a contest between supreme sea power and supreme land power.*

Below: *The Danes capitulated as soon as Nelson's ships subdued the fire of the shore batteries, for his ships were now free to move within range of the city.*

Majesty the King of Denmark.' Having written the letter, he referred the bearer for definite action to Sir Hyde Parker, who lay some four miles off in the *London*; foreseeing that the long pull there and back would give time for the leading ships, which were much crippled, to clear the shoals, though their course for so doing lay close under the Crown Batteries. Thus the exposed part of the British fleet was successfully removed from a dangerous position and rejoined Parker north of the Middle Ground. The advantage obtained by Nelson's presence of mind and promptness in gaining this respite was shown by the difficulties attending the withdrawal. Three out of five ships-of-the-line grounded, two of which remained fast for several hours a mile from the batteries, but protected by the truce.

(Editor's note—*On 17 June 1801 was signed at Saint Petersburg a convention between Russia and Great Britain, settling the points that had been in dispute. Sweden and Denmark necessarily followed the course of Russia and acceded to the terms of the convention between that court and Great Britain; Sweden on 23 October 1801, and Denmark on the 30th of the following March. Thus had fallen resultless, as far as the objects of Napoleon were concerned, the vast combination against Great Britain which he had fostered in the North.*

Preliminaries of a peace between Great Britain and France were signed in London on 1 October 1801. Of all her conquests, Great Britain retained only the islands of Ceylon in the East Indies and Trinidad in the West Indies. France consented to leave to Portugal her entire possessions to withdraw her troops from the Kingdom of Naples and the Roman territory, and to acknowledge the independence of the Republic of the Seven Islands. The capitulation of the French troops in Alexandria was not yet known in England; and the preliminaries merely stipulated the return of Egypt to the Porte. Malta, returned to the Knights of St John, was to be freed from all French or British influence and placed under the guarantee of a third power.

Above: *Vice-Amiral Bourgues-Missiessy conducted a spirited and successful defense of Antwerp in 1809, taking advantage of the indecision shown by Admiral Strachan and General Lord Chatham. As the doggerel verse had it,*
'Sir Richard Strachan stood there with his sword drawn,
Waiting for the Earl of Chatham
To be up and at 'em.'

Right top: *Charles Middleton, later Lord Barham was a superb administrator despite his advanced years. His decisions at the Admiralty were as important as Nelson's tactical genius in bringing the Trafalgar Campaign to a successful conclusion.*

Above: *Captain Edward Rotheram commanded the 1st Rate* Royal Sovereign, *Collingwood's flag-ship at Trafalgar.*

Above: *Nelson's departure from the Sallyport, Portsmouth on his way to Trafalgar, 14 September 1805.*

The definitive treaty was signed on 25 March 1802. The terms did not materially differ from those of the preliminaries, except in the article of Malta. French intrigues on the Continent, as well as British distrust caused the treaty to become little more than an armed truce.

On 26 January 1802 Napoleon was named President of the Cisalpine Republic, soon renamed the Italian Republic. At the same time France continued its interference in Switzerland and other parts of Europe, ignoring the British. These events, in addition to the well-known secret treaty in which Spain ceded Louisiana to France, fueled England's distaste for the peace. On 16 May, Great Britain declared war against France.

On 30 April 1803 Napoleon signed a treaty selling 'the whole of Louisiana as Spain has possessed it' to the United States. Having thus relinquished a position he could not defend and, as far as he could, secured the French possessions beyond the sea. Bonaparte could now give his whole attention to the plans he had for subjugating the British Isles which had long been in his mind. He resolved to strike straight at the vital center of the British power by a direct invasion of the British Islands.

The plan for invasion was marked by the comprehensiveness of view and minute attention to detail which distinguished his campaigns. Consequent to a series of political and military maneuvers between France and Great Britain, Spain declared war on 12 December 1804, against Great Britain.)

The Spanish declaration of war was followed by a new treaty of alliance with France, signed in Paris on the 5th of January, 1805, and confirmed on the 18th of the month at Madrid. Spain undertook to furnish, by March 21, to the common cause, at least twenty-five ships-of-the-line and eleven frigates; but the military direction of the whole allied effort was entrusted to Napoleon.

This accession of Spain could not become immediately operative, owing to the backward state of her armaments caused by the previous demands of Great Britain. The emperor therefore adhered for the time to his existing plans, formulated on the 27th and 29th of September. These proving abortive, he next framed, upon lines equal both in boldness and scope to those of the Marengo and Austerlitz campaigns, the immense combination which resulted in Trafalgar.

In December detailed instructions for executing the plan of September 29 were issued to Admirals Villeneuve and Missiessy. The latter, after leaving Rochefort, was to steer between the Azores and Canaries, so as to avoid the British squadrons off the Biscay coast of Spain, go direct to Martinique, take the British islands Santa Lucia and Dominica, and upon Villeneuve's arrival place himself under his command. In pursuance of these orders Missiessy escaped from Rochefort on January 11. He was seen next day by a lookout vessel belonging to the blockading squadron; but the latter, for whatever reason, was off its post, and Missiessy reached Martinique safely on the 20th of February. On the 24th of that month six British ships-of-the-line, under Rear-Admiral Cochrane, sailed in pursuit from before Ferrol; where their place was taken by a detachment of equal force drawn from before Brest.

Villeneuve's orders were to go from Toulon direct to Cayenne recapture the former Dutch colonies of Guyana, form a junction with Missiessy, re-enforce San Domingo, and start on his return for Europe not later than sixty days after reaching South America. With the combined squadrons he was to appear off Ferrol, release the French ships there blockaded, and bring the whole force, amounting to twenty of the line, to Rochefort. 'The result of your cruise,' wrote Napoleon to him, 'will be to secure our colonies against any attack, and to retake the four Dutch colonies on the Continent, as well as such other British islands as may appear open to the force under your command.' Six thousand troops were embarked on board his squadron for the operations on shore. Both he and Missiessy were expressly forbidden to land their crews for that purpose; a decision of the great emperor worthy to be remembered in these days.

Villeneuve was ready to sail early in January, but his first need was to elude the watchfulness of Nelson. The British admiral was known to move from point to point in his command, between the Maddalena Islands and Cape San Sebastian on the Spanish coast, while he kept before Toulon lookout ships always informed of his whereabouts. Villeneuve therefore thought indispensable to start with a breeze strong enough to carry him a hundred miles the first night. For a fortnight the wind hung at northeast and southeast—fair but very light; but on the 17th of January it shifted to northwest, with signs of an approaching gale. The next morning Villeneuve sent a division to drive off the enemy's lookouts; and when these disappeared the squadron sailed, numbering ten of the line and seven frigates. Nelson with eleven ships-of-the-line was at the moment at anchor in Maddalena Bay.

Following Napoleon's plan for deceiving the British admiral, the French squadron steered for the south end of Sardinia, as though bound eastward. During the night it was dogged by the enemy's frigates, which had retired no further than was necessary to avoid capture. At ten o'clock they were close by; and at two in the morning, satisfied as to the French course, they parted company and hastened to Nelson—the wind then blowing a whole gale from the northwest. Twelve hours later they were seen from the flag-ship with the signal flying that the enemy was at sea, and in two hours more the British fleet was under way. Unable to beat out by the western entrance in the teeth of the storm, it ran in single column through the narrow eastern pass as night fell—Nelson's ship leading, the others steering by the poop lanterns of the vessel next ahead. When clear of the port the fleet hauled up to the southward, and during the night, which was unsettled and squally kept along the east coast of Sardinia. The frigate *Seahorse* was sent ahead to pass round the south end of the island and get touch again of the enemy.

During the night the wind changed to south-southwest, and blew heavily throughout the 21st. On the forenoon of the 22nd the fleet, still struggling against a heavy southwesterly gale, was fifty miles east of the south end of Sardinia. There it was re-joined by the *Seahorse*, which the day before had caught sight of a French frigate standing in toward Cagliari, but had not seen the main body. Not till the 26th did Nelson reach Cagliari, where to his relief he found the French had not been. Nothing even was known of their movements; but the same day the frigate *Phoebe* joined from the westward with news that a French eighty-gun ship, partially dismasted, had put in to Ajaccio. The British fleet then stretched across to Palermo, where it arrived on the 28th. Having now fairly covered the approaches from the westward to Sardinia, Sicily, and Naples, Nelson reasoned that one of two things must have happened; either the French, despite the southerly gale, had succeeded in going east between Sicily and Africa, or they had put back disabled. In the latter

Above: *Sir William Cornwallis, known as 'Billy Blue,' succeeded Jervis in command of the Channel Fleet in 1801. Under his guidance the close blockade of Brest was brought to a pitch of perfection never seen before.*

Above: *Admiral Sir Hyde Parker, Nelson's superior at Copenhagen. In spite of his reputed timidity on that occasion he had distinguished himself in the Revolutionary War.*

case he could not now overtake them; in the former, he must follow. Accordingly, after sending scouts to scour the seas, and three frigates to resume the watch off Toulon, he shaped his course along the north side of Sicily, and on the 30th of January passed through the straits of Messina on his way to Egypt.

Villeneuve had in fact returned to Toulon. On the first night an eighty-four-gun ship and three frigates separated, and the former put in dismasted to Ajaccio, as Nelson had learned. The following day and in the night, when the wind shifted to southwest, three more ships-of-the-line were crippled. Forced to the eastward by the gale, and aware that two enemy's frigates had marked his course, the admiral feared that he should meet the British at a disadvantage and determined to retreat.

Thus prematurely ended the first movement in Napoleon's naval combination for the invasion of England. The Rochefort squadron had escaped only to become a big detachment, wholly out of reach of support or recall. The Toulon fleet, forced to await a heavy wind in order to effect the evasion by which alone the combination could be formed, was through the inexperience of its seamen crippled by the very advantage it had secured. In truth, however, had it gone on, it would almost infallibly have been driven by the southwest gale into the very spot, between Sardinia and Sicily, where Nelson went to seek it, and which was ransacked by his lookouts. Neither Villeneuve nor Nelson doubted the result of such meeting.

The other factor in this combination, the Brest fleet and army corps of twenty thousand men, had been held in readiness to act, dependent upon the successful evasion of the two others. 'I calculate,' Napoleon had said, 'that the sailing of twenty ships from Rochefort and Toulon will force the enemy to send thirty in pursuit,' a diversion that would very materially increase the chances for the Brest armament. For a moment he spoke of sending to India this powerful body, strongly re-enforced from the French and Spanish ships in Ferrol. This was, however, but a passing thought, rejected by his sound military instinct as an eccentric movement, disseminating his force and weakening the purposed attack upon the heart of the British power. Three months later, when he began to fear failure for the latter attempt, he referred to the East India project in terms which show why he at first laid it aside. 'In case, through any event whatsoever, our expedition have not full success, and I cannot compass *the greatest of all ends, which will cause all the rest to fall,* I think we must calculate the operation in India for September.' India in truth was to the imagination of Napoleon what Egypt was to Nelson, an object which colored all his ideas and constantly misled him. As was shrewdly said by an American citizen to the British government, in this very month of January, 1805, 'The French in general believe that the fountains of British wealth are in India and China. They never appeared to me to understand that the most abundant source is in her agriculture, her manufactures, and the foreign demand.' This impression Napoleon fully shared, and it greatly affected his judgment during the coming campaign.

The return of Villeneuve and the delay necessary to repair his ships, concurring with the expected re-enforcements from Spain, wholly changed the details of Napoleon's plan. In essence it remained the same from first to last; but the large number of ships now soon to be at his command appealed powerfully to his love for great masses and wide combinations. Now, also, Villeneuve could not reach the West Indies before the sickly season.

The contemplated conquests in America, which had formed so important a part of the first plan, were therefore laid aside, and so was also the Irish expedition by Ganteaume's fleet. The concentration of naval forces in the West Indies or at some point exterior to France became now the great aim; and the sally of the various detachments, before intended to favor the crossing of the flotilla by a diversion, was now to be the direct means of covering it, by bringing them to the English Channel and before Boulogne. The operations were to begin in March; and urgent orders were sent to Spain to have the contingents in her several ports ready to move at a moment's notice.

The situations of the squadrons in March, when the great Trafalgar campaign opened, need to be stated. On the extreme right, in the Texel, were nine ships-of-the-line with a due proportion of lighter vessels; and some eighty transports lay ready to embark Marmont's army corps of twenty-five thousand men. The Boulogne flotilla was assembled; the few detachments still absent being so near at hand that their junction could be confidently expected before the appearance of the covering fleet. The army, one hundred and thirty thousand strong, was by frequent practice able to embark in two hours. Two tides were needed for all the boats to clear the ports; but as word of the fleet's approach would precede its arrival, they could haul out betimes and lie in the open sea, under the batteries, ready to start. In Brest, Ganteaume had twenty-one ships-of-the-line. The Rochefort squadron was now in the West Indies with Missiessy; but two more ships were ready in that port and one in Lorient. In Ferrol were five French and ten Spanish; of the latter it was expected that six or eight could sail in March. In Cadiz the treaty called for twelve or fifteen to be ready at the same time, but only six were then actually able to move. There was also in Cadiz one French ship. In Cartagena were six Spaniards, which, however, took no part in the campaign. At Toulon Villeneuve would have eleven ships. All these were ships-of-the-line. The total available at the opening of the campaign was

therefore sixty-seven; but it will be observed that they were disseminated in detachments, and that the strategic problem was, first, to unite them in the face of an enemy that controlled the communications, and, next, to bring them to the strategic centre.

The disposition and strength of the British detachments varied with the movements of the enemy and with the increasing strength of their own navy. Lord Keith, in the Downs with eleven small ships-of-the-line, watched the Texel and the Straits of Dover. The Channel fleet under Cornwallis held Brest under lock and key, with a force varying from eleven, when the year began, to twenty or twenty-four in the following April. This was the centre of the great British naval line. Off Rochefort no squadron was kept after Missiessy's escape. In March that event had simply transferred to the West Indies five French and six British ships. Off Ferrol eight ships were watching the combined fifteen in the port. In October, when the Spanish war was threatening, a division of six was sent to blockade Cadiz. Nelson's command, which had before extended to Cape Finisterre, was now confined to Gibraltar as its western limit, and the Cadiz portion assigned to Sir John Orde—a step particularly invidious to Nelson, depriving him of the most lucrative part of his station, in favor of one who was not only his senior, with power to annoy him, but reputed to be his personal enemy. Nelson had within the Straits twelve of the line, several of which, however, were in bad condition; and one, kept permanently at Naples for political reasons, was useless to him. Two others were on their way to join, but did not arrive before the campaign opened. It may be added that there were in India from eight to ten ships-of-the-line, and in the West Indies four, which Cochrane's arrival would raise to ten.

On the 2nd of March Napoleon issued specific orders for the campaign to Villeneuve and Ganteaume. The latter, who was

Opposite below: *A Napoleonic War cartoon showing flags of truth and lies. The French flag indicates that citizen First Consul Bonaparte offers to make a return visit to England, when his arrangements are ready. John Bull retorts 'He'll be damned if he don't sink him if he does.'*

Left: Lord Elphinstone, formerly Lord Keith, commanded the North Sea Station in 1803–07 and concerned himself with defeating invasion attempts.

Below left: Napoleon shown playing leapfrog with the nations of Europe. John Bull informs him of the English reaction to Napoleon's Imperial plans 'I'll be d . . . .d if you do Master Corsican.'

Below: An English sailor at a French eating-house, a stock situation for jokes at the expense of the 'Jean Crapauds.'

AN ENGLISH SAILOR at a 'French Eating House'.

to command-in-chief after the junction, was directed to sail at the first moment possible with his twenty-one ships, carrying besides their crews thirty-six hundred troops. He was to go first to Ferrol, destroy or drive off the blockading squadron, and be joined by the French and Spanish ships there ready; thence by the shortest route to Martinique, where he was to be met by Villeneuve and, it was hoped, by Missiessy also. If Villeneuve did not at once appear, he was to be awaited at least thirty days. When united, the whole force, amounting to over forty of the line, would, to avoid detection, steer for the Channel by an unusual route and proceed direct to Boulogne, where the emperor expected it between June 10 and July 10. If by Villeneuve's not coming, or other cause, Ganteaume found himself with less than twenty-five ships, he was to go to Ferrol; where it would be the emperor's care to assemble a re-enforcement. He might, however, even with so small a number, move straight on Boulogne if he thought advisable.

Villeneuve's orders were to sail at the earliest date for Cadiz, where he was not to enter but be joined outside by the ships then ready. From Cadiz he was to go to Martinique, and there wait forty days for Ganteaume. If the latter did not then appear he was to call at San Domingo, land some troops and thence go to the Bay of Santiago in the Canary Islands where he would cruise twenty days. This provided a second rendezvous where Ganteaume could join, if unexpectedly delayed in Brest. The emperor, like all French rulers, did not wish to risk his fleet in battle with nearly equal forces. When Ganteaume, at a most critical instant, only six days before Villeneuve got away, reported that he was ready, that there were but fifteen British ships in the offing and success was sure, Napoleon replied: 'A naval victory now would lead to nothing. Have but one aim— to fulfil your mission. Sail without fighting.' So to the old delusion of ulterior objects was sacrificed the one chance for

compassing the junction essential to success. By April 1 the British fleet off Brest was increased to twenty-one sail.

Meanwhile Nelson had returned from his fruitless search at Alexandria, and on the 13th of March again appeared off Toulon. Thence he went to Cape San Sebastian, showing his ships off Barcelona to convince the enemy he was fixed on the coast of Spain; reasoning that if they thought him to the westward they would more readily start for Egypt, which he still believed to be their aim. From Cape San Sebastian the fleet next went to the Gulf of Palmas, a convenient roadstead in the south of Sardinia, to fill with provisions from transports lately arrived. It anchored there on the 26th of March, but was again at sea when, at 8 a.m. of April 4, being then twenty miles west of the Gulf, a frigate brought word of the second sailing of the Toulon fleet. When last seen, in the evening of March 31, it was sixty miles south of Toulon, steering south with a northwest wind. One of the pair of lookouts was then sent to Nelson; and the other, losing sight of the enemy during the night, joined him a few hours after the first. The only clue she could give was that, having herself steered southwest with a wind from west-northwest, the enemy had probably kept on south or borne away to the eastward. Nelson, therefore, took the fleet midway between Sardinia and the African coast, scattering lookout ships along the line between these two points. He was thus centrally placed to cover everything east of Sardinia, with means of speedy information if the French attempted to pass, at any point, the line occupied by him.

Villeneuve had indeed headed as reported by the British frigates, swayed by Nelson's ruse in appearing off Barcelona. Believing the enemy off Cape San Sebastian, he meant to go east of the Balearic Islands. The next day, April 1, a neutral ship informed him that it had seen the British fleet south of Sardinia. The wind fortunately hauling to the eastward, Villeneuve

Above: *Dodd's view of Trafalgar from the rear captures the air of tranquillity as the two British divisions sailed sedately toward the Franco-Spanish line.*

would join him, and with the combined force of fifty-six of the line at once enter the Channel. Magon sailed with these orders early in May, and on June 4 reached Villeneuve just in time to insure the direction given by the latter to his fleet upon its return. To facilitate the junction at Brest very heavy batteries were thrown up, covering the anchorage outside the Goulet; and there, in May, Ganteaume took up his position, covered by one hundred and fifty guns on shore.

It will be recognized that the emperor's plan, while retaining its essential features, had now undergone a most important modification, due to the closeness of the British blockade of Brest. A combination of his squadrons still remained the keystone of the fabric; but the tenacity with which the largest of his detachments was held in check had forced him to accept—what he had rejected as least advantageous—a concentration in

Right: *HMS* Victory, *Nelson's flag-ship was an elderly 100-gun 1st Rate launched at Chatham in 1765, but she was always popular because she was fast and handy. In fact she was alleged to sail like a two-decker, but later copies from the same lines did not reproduce her unique qualities.*

changed his course to pass north of the Balearics; and on the 6th of April, when Nelson was watching for him between Sardinia and Africa, he appeared off Cartagena. The Spanish division there declined to join him, having no instructions from its government; and the French fleet, continuing at once with a fresh easterly wind, passed Gibraltar on the 8th. On the 9th it reached Cadiz, driving away Orde's squadron. Following his orders strictly, Villeneuve anchored outside the port; and was there at once joined by the French seventy-four *l'Aigle*, and six Spanish ships. During the night the combined force of eighteen of the line sailed for Martinique, where it anchored May 14, after a passage of thirty-four days. Some Spanish ships separated the day after sailing; but, having sealed instructions giving the rendezvous, they arrived only two days later than the main body.

As the advancing season gave less and less hope of the blockade relaxing, Napoleon formed a new combination. Two ships-of-the-line, now nearly ready at Rochefort, should sail under Rear-Admiral Magon, carrying modified instructions to Villeneuve. The latter was now commanded to wait thirty-five days after Magon's arrival, and then, if Ganteaume had not appeared, return direct to Ferrol, discarding the alternative rendezvous of Santiago. At Ferrol he would find fifteen French and Spanish ships, making with his own and Magon's a total of thirty-five. With these he was to appear before Brest, where Ganteaume

the Bay of Biscay, the great hive where swarmed the British navy.

The fault of Napoleon's calculations was in over-estimating both the importance and the danger of India, and also in not allowing for the insight and information of the British government. He himself laid down, with his peculiarly sound judgment, the lines it ought to follow: 'If I had been in the British Admiralty, I would have sent a light squadron to the East and West Indies, and formed a strong fleet of twenty of the line which I would not have dispatched until I knew Villeneuve's destination.' This was just what the Admiralty did. A light squadron was on its way to India, and eight ships were ordered to the West Indies under Collingwood; but that able officer, finding Nelson had started, contented himself with sending two to re-enforce him, and took up his own position with six before Cadiz, thus blocking the junction of the Cartagena ships. The strong body of twenty was kept before Brest, much to Napoleon's annoyance.

While the emperor was wildly reckoning on imaginary squadrons hastening to India, and guessing where Nelson was, both the latter and his government knew where Villeneuve had gone, and the British admiral was already in the West Indies. About the beginning of May it was known in England not only that the Toulon fleet had sailed, but whither it was bound; and about the first of June, despite the cautions about secrecy imposed by Bonaparte, the British were informed by a prisoner that 'the combined fleet, of sixty-sail-of-the-line, will fight our fleet (*balayer la Manche*), while the large frigates will come up channel to convoy the flotilla over. The troops are impatiently awaiting the appearance of the ships to set them free.'

The Admiralty therefore understood as well as did Napoleon that the crucial necessity in their dispositions was to prevent the combination of the enemy's squadrons, and that the chief scene of operations would be the Bay of Biscay and the approaches to the Channel. They contented themselves, consequently, with strengthening the force there, and keeping before Cadiz alone a detachment under Collingwood, lest a concentration in that port should compel them to weaken the Biscay squadrons. At the time Villeneuve sailed, an expedition of five thousand troops, whose destination was kept profoundly secret, was ready to

Above: *Nelson's leisurely approach in two columns should in theory have resulted in his annihilation because the French and Spaniards were 'Crossing his T.' However he calculated that the enemy would waste valuable time in trying to disable his ships' rigging, and by the time they changed to shooting low his crews' superb discipline and gunnery would provide a decisive margin of superiority.*

Left: *The other part of Nelson's plan for Trafalgar was to dismember Villeneuve's line, thereby destroying the cohesion of the Combined Fleet.*

start for the Mediterranean. This re-enforcement secured the naval bases of Gibraltar and Malta, and the Mediterranean otherwise was abandoned to frigates, supported by two or three ships-of-the-line.

The secret expedition was met by Nelson just as he started for the West Indies. During his heavy beat down the Mediterranean he too, as carefully as Napoleon, had been studying the field on which he was to act; but while the one planned with all the freedom and certainty of an offensive, which, disposing of large means, moves upon a known object, the other, though in a restricted sphere, underwent the embarrassments of the defensive, ignorant where the blow was to fall. One clear light, however, shone step by step on his path—wherever the French fleet was gone there should he go also.

The west wind which delayed his progress brought swiftly to him, on April 19, a vessel from Gibraltar, with word that, two hours after Villeneuve passed the Straits, a frigate had started for England with the news, and that the French and Spaniards had sailed together from Cadiz. From this circumstance he reasoned, accurately, that the destination was the British Islands; but he did not penetrate the deep design of a concentration in the West Indies. He therefore sent the frigate *Amazon* ahead of the fleet to Lisbon, to gather news and rejoin him off Cape St Vincent; and by her he wrote the Admiralty, and also to the admirals off Brest and in Ireland, that he should

take position fifty leagues west of the Scilly Islands, and thence steer slowly toward them. To any person who will plot this position on a map it will be apparent that, with winds prevailing from the westward, he would there be, as he said, equally well situated to reach Brest or Ireland; in short, in an excellent strategic position known to the authorities at home.

Stopping but four hours at Gibraltar on May 6, on the 9th he was off Cape St Vincent, and there received news that the combined squadrons, to the number of eighteen of the line, had gone to the West Indies. His concern was great, for he fully understood the value of those islands. He had served there, knew them intimately, and had married there. Not a year before he had written, 'If our islands should fall, England would be so clamorous for peace that we should humble ourselves.' Still, with all his anxiety, he kept his head. The convoy of troops was close at hand, he must provide for its safety. On the 11th of May it arrived, Nelson's fleet being then under way. To the two ships-of-the-line guarding it he added a third, the *Royal Sovereign*, whose bad sailing delayed him; and to this circumstance it was owing that that ship, newly coppered, bore Collingwood's flag far in advance of either British column into the fire at Trafalgar. Three hours after the convoy's junction, at seven p.m. of May 11, Nelson with ten ships was on his way to the West Indies, to seek eighteen which had thirty-one days' start.

Left: *A simplified view of Trafalgar, from an engraving by Sutherland after Whitcombe.*

Right: *Clarkson Stanfield's view of the battle at 1430 hours with the* Victory *in the center of the Combined Fleet. She is disengaging herself from the* Redoutable, *which is lashed alongside HMS* Temeraire, *whose men are engaged in boarding and capturing the* Fougeux.

Opposite below: *The moment when Nelson was hit by the musket ball from the* Redoutable's *mizzentop, as seen by Dighton.*

On the 4th of June the British fleet, having gained eight days on the allies, anchored at Barbados, where it found Cochrane with two sail-of-the-line. The same day Magon with his two joined Villeneuve.

On the 4th of June the two hostile fleets were but a hundred miles apart, the distance separating Barbados from Martinique. Most singularly, at the very moment Villeneuve started north to return upon Barbados, false news, too plausible to be slighted, induced Nelson to go south. Positive information was sent by the officer commanding at Santa Lucia that the allies had been seen from there, May 29, steering south. Nelson anchored at Barbados at five p.m. June 4, embarked two thousand troops during the night, and at ten a.m. next day made sail for the southward. On the 6th he passed Tobago, which was reported safe, and on the 7th anchored off Trinidad; where to the astonishment of every one nothing had been heard of the enemy. Cursing the news which had forced him to disregard his own judgment, when only a hundred miles of fair wind severed him from his prey, Nelson turned upon his tracks and steered for Martinique, tortured with fears for Jamaica and every exposed British possession.

On the 8th of June, when Nelson left Trinidad, the combined fleets were nearly four hundred miles from him, off the west side of Antigua. Here they captured fourteen merchant ships which had imprudently left port, and by them were informed that Nelson with fourteen ships (instead of ten) had reached Barbados. To these fourteen, Villeneuve, whose information was poor, added five as the force of Cochrane, making nineteen to his eighteen. Supposing therefore the enemy to be superior, not only in quality, which he conceded, but in numbers also, he decided, in view of so unexpected an event as the arrival on the scene of the greatest British admiral, to return at once to Europe. In this he doubtless met the wishes of Napoleon.

Villeneuve also doubtless hoped to shake off his pursuer by his sudden change of purpose. Transferring troops necessary to garrison the French islands to four frigates, he directed the latter to land them at Guadaloupe and rejoin him off the Azores —a mistaken rendezvous, which materially lengthened his backward voyage. The combined fleet then made sail on the 9th of June to the northward, to reach the westerly winds that favor the passage to Europe.

Three days later Nelson also was off Antigua, and convinced himself that the allies were bound back to Europe. With the tireless energy that brooked no rest when once resolve was formed, the night was passed transferring the troops which but one week before he had embarked at Barbados. But not even a night's delay was allowed in sending news to Europe. At eight p.m. he hurried off the brig *Curieux* with dispatches to the Admiralty, which the captain, Bettesworth, was to deliver in person; a momentous action, and one fraught with decisive consequences to the campaign, although somewhat marred by an overcautious admiral. On the 13th, at noon, the fleet itself, accompanied by one of Cochrane's two ships, the *Spartiate*, sailed for the Straits of Gibraltar; but Nelson, uncertain as to the enemy's destination, also sent word to the officer commanding off Ferrol, lest he might be taken unawares.

Ganteaume was not able to elude Lord Gardner, and on the 8th of May, the emperor, having received in Italy the news of Magon's sailing, gave his final decision. If before midnight of May 20 an opportunity offered, the Brest fleet should start; but from daybreak of the 21st, had it every chance in the world, it should stand fast. A frigate was to be kept ready to sail the instant the latter condition took effect, carrying to Villeneuve orders for his action upon reaching Ferrol. This frigate did sail May 21, but of course did not find the admiral in the West Indies. Duplicate instructions were sent to Ferrol.

Villeneuve was by them informed that he would in Ferrol find ready for sea five French and nine Spanish ships, which, with those already under his orders, would make a force of thirty-four sail-of-the-line. In the roads off Rochefort would be five more. At Brest twenty-one ships were lying outside the Goulet, under the protection of one hundred and fifty cannon, ready to get under way at a moment's notice. The great point was to concentrate these three masses, or as much of them as possible, off Boulogne. Three courses were open to him. If the squadron at Ferrol could not leave the port when he appeared, on account of head winds, he should order it to join him at Rochefort and go there at once himself. Thence with forty ships he should proceed off Brest, join Ganteaume, and at once enter the Channel. If, however, the wind was fair for leaving Ferrol, that is, southerly, he would see in that a reason for hastening to Brest, without stopping for the Rochefort squad-

the fact. For his decision he relied upon his own judgment. In dispatching the *Curieux* the night before he himself sailed, he directed her captain to steer a certain course, by following which he believed he would fall in with the allied fleet. Accordingly the *Curieux* did, on the 19th of June, sight the enemy in latitude 33° 12′ north and longitude 58° west, nine hundred miles north-northeast from Antigua, standing north-northwest. The same day Nelson himself learned from an American schooner that a fleet of about twenty-two large ships of war had been seen by it on the 15th, three hundred and fifty miles south of the position in which Bettesworth saw it four days later.

Bettesworth fully understood the importance of the knowledge thus gained. The precise destination of the enemy did not certainly appear, but there could be no doubt that he was returning to Europe. With that intelligence, and the information concerning Nelson's purposes, it was urgent to reach England speedily. Carrying a press of sail, the *Curieux* anchored at Plymouth on the 7th of July. The captain posted at once to London, arriving the evening of the 8th, at eleven. The head of the Admiralty at that time was Lord Barham, an aged naval officer, who had been unexpectedly called to the office two months before, in consequence of the impeachment of Lord Melville, the successor to St Vincent. It was fortunate for Great Britain that the direction of naval operations at so critical a moment was in the hands of a man, who, though over eighty and long a stranger to active service, understood intuitively, and without need of explanation, the various conditions of weather and service likely to affect the movements of the scattered detachments, British and hostile, upon whose rapid combinations so much now depended.

Barham having gone to bed, Bettesworth's dispatches were

ron; the more so as every delay would increase the British force before Brest. Thirdly, he might possibly, as he drew toward Ushant, find the winds so fair as to give the hope of getting to Boulogne with his thirty-five ships three or four days before the enemy's fleet at Brest could follow. If so, it was left to his discretion to embrace so favorable an opportunity. To these three courses Napoleon added a fourth as a possible alternative. After rallying the Ferrol ships he might pass north of the British Islands, join the Dutch squadron of the Texel with Marmont's corps there embarked, and with these appear off Boulogne. The emperor, however, looked upon this rather as a last resort. A great concentration in the Bay of Biscay was the one aim he now favored.

When Nelson started back for Europe, although convinced the French were thither bound, he had no absolute certainty of

Left: *After the battle a storm blew up, endangering the dismasted ships, both victors and vanquished. Nelson's last orders were to anchor but Collingwood decided to get a good offing from the shoals off Cape Trafalgar. No British ships were lost but only four out of 19 prizes reached port.*

Right: *Nelson described his captains as a 'band of brothers' and meant it. A feature of his Trafalgar plan was an eve-of-battle conference in which he outlined his intentions, making certain that everyone could anticipate what was wanted. Below is a plan of the French and Spanish forces.*

not given him till early next morning. As soon as he got them he exclaimed angrily at the loss of so many precious hours; and, without waiting to dress, at once dictated orders with which, by nine a.m. of the 9th, Admiralty messengers were hurrying to Plymouth and Portsmouth. Cornwallis was directed to raise the blockade at Rochefort, sending the five ships composing it to Sir Robert Calder, then watching off Ferrol with ten; and the latter was ordered, with the fifteen ships thus united under his command, to cruise one hundred miles west of Cape Finisterre, to intercept Villeneuve and forestall his junction with the Ferrol squadron. With Nelson returning toward Cadiz, where he would find Collingwood, and with Cornwallis off Brest, this disposition completed the arrangements necessary to thwart the primary combinations of the emperor, unknown to, but shrewdly surmised by, his opponents.

Fair winds favoring the quick, Cornwallis received his orders on the 11th; and on the 15th, eight days after the *Curieux* anchored in Plymouth, the Rochefort ships joined Calder. The latter proceeded at once to the post assigned him, where on the 19th he received through Lisbon the tidings of Villeneuve's return sent by Nelson from the West Indies. The same day Nelson himself, having outstripped the combined fleets, anchored in Gibraltar. On the 22nd the sudden lifting of a dense fog revealed to each other the hostile squadrons of Calder and Villeneuve; the British fifteen sail-of-the-line, the allies twenty. The numbers of the latter were an unpleasant surprise to Calder, the *Curieux* having reported them as only seventeen.

The length of Villeneuve's passage, which so happily concurred to assure the success of Barham's masterly move, was due not only to the inferior seamanship of the allies, but also to the mistaken rendezvous off the Azores—assigned by the French admiral when leaving the West Indies. The westerly gales, which prevail in the North Atlantic, blow during the summer from the south of west, west of the Azores, and from the north of west when east of them. A fleet bound for a European port north of the islands—as Ferrol is—should therefore so use the southwest winds as to cross their meridian well to the northward. Nelson himself sighted one of the group, though his destination was in a lower latitude. In consequence of his

mistake, Villeneuve was by the northwest winds forced down on the coast of Portugal, where he met the northeasters prevalent at that season, against which he was struggling when encountered by Calder. This delay was therefore caused, not by bad luck, but by bad management.

On the 2nd of August the emperor set out for Boulogne, and there on the 8th received news of Villeneuve's action with Calder and of his subsequent entry into Ferrol. The fleets had fought on the afternoon of July 22, and two Spanish ships-of-the-line had been taken. Night-fall and fog parted the combatants; the obscurity being so great that the allies did not know their loss till next day. One of the British ships lost a foretopmast, and others suffered somewhat in their spars; but these mishaps, though pleaded in Calder's defence, do not seem to have been the chief reasons that deterred him from dogging the enemy till he had brought him again to action. He was preoccupied with the care of the prizes, a secondary matter, and with the thought of what would happen in case the Ferrol and Rochefort squadrons sailed. In short, the British admiral had fallen into the error against which Napoleon used to caution his generals. He had 'made to himself a picture,' and allowed the impression produced by it to blind him to the fact (if indeed he ever saw it) that he had before him the largest and most important of the several detachments of the enemy, that it was imperatively necessary not to permit it to escape unharmed, and that at no future day could he be sure of bringing his own squadron into play with such decisive effect.

Villeneuve had no more wish to renew the action than had Calder. Less even than that admiral could he rise to the height of risking a detachment in order to secure the success of a great design. In the eighteen ships left to him were over twelve hundred men so ill that it was necessary to put them ashore. Constrained by the winds, he put into Vigo on the 28th of July. Calder, on the other hand, having seen his prizes so far north as to insure their safety, returned off Cape Finisterre where he hoped to meet Nelson. Not finding him, he on the 29th resumed the blockade of Ferrol. On the 31st Villeneuve, leaving three of his worst vessels in Vigo, sailed for Ferrol with fifteen ships, of which two only were Spaniards. The fleet, having a

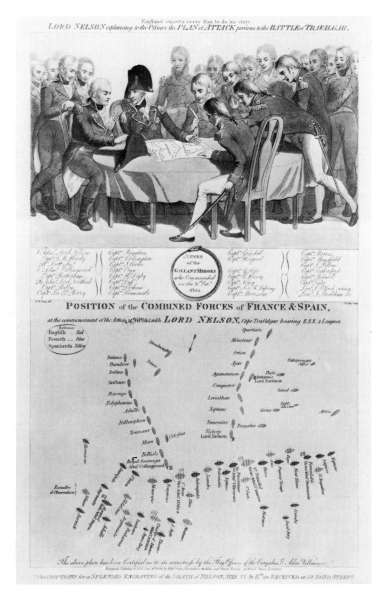

Above: *On the morning of the battle Nelson wrote a prayer in his private diary which has since become part of his country's heritage.*

strong southwest gale, kept close along shore to avoid meeting Calder; but the latter, having been blown off by the storm, was not in sight when Villeneuve reached the harbor's mouth. The allied ships were entering with a fair wind, when the French admiral received dispatches forbidding him to anchor in Ferrol. If, from injuries received in battle, or losses from any causes whatever, he was unable to carry out the plan of entering the Channel, the emperor preferred that, after rallying the Ferrol and Rochefort squadrons, he should go to Cadiz; but, the Brest fleet being ready and the other preparations complete, he hoped everything from the skill, zeal, and courage of Villeneuve. 'Make us masters of the Straits of Dover,' he implored, 'be it but for four or five days.' Napoleon leaned on a broken reed. Forbidden to enter Ferrol, Villeneuve took his ships into the adjacent harbor of Corunna, where he anchored August 1.

The immediate result of the junction in Ferrol was the abandonment of the blockade there. On the 2nd of August Calder sent five ships to resume the watch off Rochefort, whence the French squadron had meantime escaped. Not till August 9 did he know of Villeneuve's entrance into Ferrol. Having with him then but nine ships, he fell back on the main body before Brest, which he joined on the 14th—Cornwallis then having under him seventeen ships, which Calder's junction raised to twenty-six.

The next day, August 15, Nelson also joined the fleet. On the 25th of July, a week after reaching Gibraltar, he had received the *Curieux's* news. Obeying his constant rule to seek the French,

he at once started north with the eleven ships which had accompanied him from the West Indies—intending to go either to Ferrol, Brest, or Ireland, according to the tidings which might reach him on the way. After communicating with Cornwallis, he continued on to England with his own ship, the *Victory*, and one other whose condition required immediate repairs. On the 18th he landed in Portsmouth, after an absence of over two years.

The ships in Cadiz being blocked by Collingwood, and those in Cartagena remaining always inert, the naval situation was now comparatively simple. Cornwallis was superior to either of the enemy's detachments, and he held an interior position. In case Villeneuve approached, it was scarcely possible that the two hostile squadrons, dependent upon the wind, which if fair for one would be foul to the other, could unite before he had effectually crushed one of them. It ought to be equally improbable, with proper lookouts, that Villeneuve could elude the British fleet and gain so far the start of it as to cover the Straits of Dover during the time required by Napoleon. In his concentrated force and his interior position Cornwallis controlled the issue—barring of course those accidents which cannot be foreseen, and which at times derange the best-laid plans.

Such was the situation when, on August 17, Cornwallis was informed that Villeneuve had put to sea with, it was said, twenty-seven or twenty-eight ships-of-the-line. He at once detached toward Ferrol Sir Robert Calder with eighteen sail, keeping with himself sixteen. This division of his fleet, which is condemned by the simplest and most generally admitted

principles of warfare, transferred to Villeneuve all the advantage of central position and superior force, and was stigmatized by Napoleon as a 'glaring blunder.' 'What a chance,' he wrote, upon hearing it when all was over, 'has Villeneuve missed. He might, by coming upon Brest from a wide sweep to sea, have played hide and seek with Calder and fallen upon Cornwallis; or else, with his thirty ships have beaten Calder's twenty and gained a decided preponderance.' This censure of both admirals was just.

On the 13th of August after three fruitless attempts, Villeneuve got to sea with his twenty-nine ships-of-the-line. The frigate *Didon* was sent to seek the Rochefort squadron and direct it also upon Brest. Yet the unfortunate admiral was even then hesitating whether he should go there with his vastly greater force, and the orders were likely seriously to endanger the smaller division. As he sailed, he penned these significant words to the Minister of Marine: 'The enemy's forces, more concentrated than ever, leave me little other resource than to go to Cadiz.'

Shortly after he cleared the harbor the wind shifted to northeast, foul for his purpose. The fleet stood to the northwest; but the ships were badly handled and several received damage. On the morning of the 15th they were two hundred and fifty miles west-northwest from Cape Finisterre; the wind blowing a moderate gale, still from the northeast. Three ships of war were in sight—two British, the third the frigate that had been sent to seek the Rochefort squadron, but which had been captured. A Danish merchantman reported that they were lookouts from a hostile body of twenty-five ships. The story had no foundation, for Cornwallis had not yet divided his fleet; but Villeneuve pictured to himself his inefficient command meeting a force with which it was wholly unable to cope. Losing sight of the great whole of which his own enterprise was but a part, though one of vital importance, his resolution finally broke down. That evening he ordered the fleet to bear up for Cadiz. On the 20th it was sighted from the three ships commanded by Collingwood, who with a small division of varying strength had watched the port since the previous May. With steady judgment, that admiral in retiring kept just out of gun-shot, determined, as he said, not to be driven into the Mediterranean without dragging the enemy too through the Straits. Villeneuve had little heart to pursue. That afternoon he anchored in Cadiz, where were then assembled thirty-five French and Spanish ships-of-the-line. Collingwood at once resumed his station outside. That night one ship-of-the-line joined him, and on the 22nd Sir Richard Bickerton arrived with four from the Mediterranean. On the 30th Calder appeared, bringing with him the eighteen detached by Cornwallis. In compliance with his orders he had been before Ferrol, found the port empty, and, learning that Ville-

neuve had sailed for Cadiz, had hastened to re-enforce the blockade. With twenty-six ships-of-the-line Collingwood held the enemy securely checked, and remained in chief command until the 28th of September, when Nelson arrived from England. Thus ended, and forever, Napoleon's profoundly conceived and laboriously prepared scheme for the invasion of England.

Nelson, having spent at home only twenty-five days, left England for the last time. On the 28th, when he joined the fleet off Cadiz, he found under his command twenty-nine ships-of-the-line, which successive arrivals raised to thirty-three by the day of the battle; but, water running short, it became necessary to send the ships, by divisions of six, to fill up at Gibraltar. To this cause was due that only twenty-seven British vessels were present in the action, an unfortunate circumstance; for, as Nelson said, what the country wanted was not merely a splendid victory, but annihilation; 'numbers only can annihilate.' The force under his command was thus disposed: the main body about fifty miles west-southwest of Cadiz, seven lookout frigates close in with the port, and between these extremes, two small detachments of ships-of-the-line—the one twenty miles from the harbor, the other about thirty-five. 'By this chain,' he wrote, 'I hope to have constant communication with the frigates.'

Napoleon's commands to enter the Mediterranean reached Villeneuve on September 27. The following day, when Nelson was joining his fleet, the admiral acknowledged their receipt, and submissively reported his intention to obey as soon as the wind served. Before he could do so, accurate intelligence was received of the strength of Nelson's force, which the emperor had not known. Villeneuve assembled a council of war to consider the situation, and the general opinion was adverse to sailing; but the commander-in-chief, alleging the orders of Napoleon, announced his determination to follow them. To this all submitted.

On the 19th eight ships got clear of the harbor, and by ten a.m. Nelson, far at sea, knew by signal that the long-expected movement had begun. He at once made sail toward the Straits of Gibraltar to bar the entrance of the Mediterranean to the allies. On the 20th, all the latter, thirty-three ships-of-the-line accompanied by five frigates and two brigs, were at sea, steering with a southwest wind to the northward and westward to gain the offing needed before heading direct for the Straits. That morning Nelson, for whom the wind had been fair, was lying to off Cape Spartel to intercept the enemy; and learning from his frigates that they were north of him, he stood in that direction to meet them.

During the day the wind shifted to west, still fair for the British and allowing the allies, by going about, to head south. It was still very weak, so that the progress of the fleets was slow. During the night both manoeuvred; the allies to gain, the British to retain, the position they wished. At daybreak of the 21st they were in presence, the French and Spaniards steering south in five columns; of which the two to windward, containing together twelve ships, constituted a detached squadron of observation under Admiral Gravina. The remaining twenty-one formed the main body, commanded by Villeneuve. Cape Trafalgar, from which the battle took its name, was on the southeastern horizon, ten or twelve miles from the allies; and the British fleet was at the same distance from them to the westward.

Soon after daylight Villeneuve signalled to form line of battle on the starboard tack, on which they were then sailing, heading south. In performing this evolution Gravina with his twelve ships took post in the van of the allied fleet, his own flag-ship heading the column. It is disputed between the French and

Left: *The* Victory *in the thick of the action. She had suffered 57 killed and 102 men wounded. Her mizzenmast had been shot away and she was making a foot of water an hour through shot-holes below the waterline.*

Right: *The French 74-gun* Achille *ablaze as night fell, shortly before she blew up.*

Spaniards whether this step was taken by Villeneuve's order, or of Gravina's own motion. In either case, these twelve, by abandoning their central and windward position, sacrificed to a great extent their power to re-enforce any threatened part of the order, and also unduly extended a line already too long. In the end, instead of being a reserve well in hand, they became the helpless victims of the British concentration.

At eight a.m. Villeneuve saw that battle could not be shunned. Wishing to have Cadiz under his lee in case of disaster, he ordered the combined fleet to wear together. The signal was clumsily executed; but by ten all had gone round and were heading north in inverse order, Gravina's squadron in the rear. At eleven Villeneuve directed this squadron to keep well to windward, so as to be in position to succor the centre, upon which the enemy seemed about to make his chief attack; a judicious order, but rendered fruitless by the purpose of the British to concentrate on the rear itself. When this signal was made, Cadiz was twenty miles distant in the north-northeast, and the course of the allies was carrying them toward it.

Owing to the lightness of the wind Nelson would lose no time in manoeuvring. He formed his fleet rapidly in two divisions, each in single column, the simplest and most flexible order of attack, and the one whose regularity is most easily preserved. The simple column, however, unflanked, sacrifices during the critical period of closing the support given by the rear ships to the leader, and draws upon the latter the concentrated fire of the enemy's line. The essential feature of his plan was to overpower twelve of the enemy by sixteen British, while the remainder of his force covered this operation. The destruction of the rear was entrusted to the second in command; he himself with a smaller body took charge of the more uncertain duties of the containing force. 'The second in command,' wrote he

Left: *Eyewitnesses reported that the French and Spanish ships bunched together 'like a forest' in a vain attempt to stop the British ships from piercing their line. What little cohesion and discipline they had would melt away as soon as they lost formation.*

in his memorable order, 'will, after my instructions are made known to him, have the entire direction of his line.'

The justification of Nelson's dispositions for battle at Trafalgar rests therefore primarily upon the sluggish breeze, which would so have delayed formations as to risk the loss of the opportunity. It must also be observed that, although a column of ships does not possess the sustained momentum of a column of men, whose depth and mass combine to drive it through the relatively thin resistance of a line, and so cut the latter in twain, the results nevertheless are closely analogous. The leaders in either case are sacrificed—success is won over their prostrate forms; but the continued impact upon one part of the enemy's order is essentially a concentration, the issue of which, if long enough maintained, cannot be doubtful. Penetration, severance, and the enveloping of one of the parted fragments, must be the result.

The two British columns were nearly a mile apart and advanced on parallel courses—heading nearly east, but a little to the northward to allow for the gradual advance in that direction of the hostile fleet. The northern or left-hand column, commonly called the 'weather line' because the wind came rather from that side, contained twelve ships, and was led by Nelson himself in the *Victory*, a ship of one hundred guns. The *Royal Sovereign*, of the same size and carrying Collingwood's flag, headed the right column, of fifteen ships.

To the British advance the allies opposed the traditional order of battle, a long single line, closehauled, in this case heading north, with the wind from west-northwest. The distance from one flank to the other was nearly five miles. Owing partly to the

Below: *Damaged French and Spanish survivors desperately try to reach Cadiz in the great storm after the battle.*

Below: *The Battle of Trafalgar, 21 October 1805. First phase.*

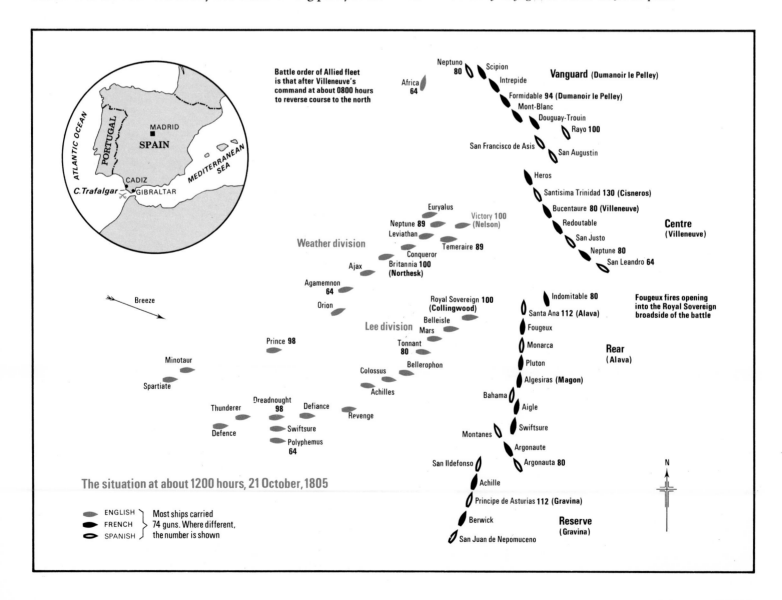

The situation at about 1200 hours, 21 October, 1805

ENGLISH ⎫ Most ships carried
FRENCH ⎬ 74 guns. Where different,
SPANISH ⎭ the number is shown

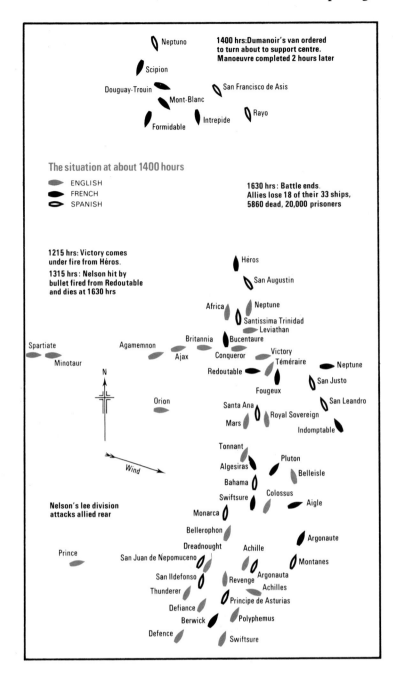

Neptuno

1400 hrs: Dumanoir's van ordered to turn about to support centre. Manoeuvre completed 2 hours later

Scipion

Douguay-Trouin

San Francisco de Asis

Mont-Blanc

Rayo

Formidable Intrepide

The situation at about 1400 hours

- ENGLISH
- FRENCH
- SPANISH

1630 hrs: Battle ends.
Allies lose 18 of their 33 ships,
5860 dead, 20,000 prisoners

1215 hrs: Victory comes
under fire from Héros.
1315 hrs: Nelson hit by
bullet fired from Redoutable
and dies at 1630 hrs

Héros

San Augustin

Africa   Neptune

Santissima Trinidad
Leviathan

Britannia Bucentaure

Spartiate

Agamemnon

Conqueror   Victory

Minotaur   Ajax   Téméraire

Neptune

Redoutable   San Justo

Fougueux

Santa Ana   San Leandro

Orion

Mars   Royal Sovereign

Indomptable

Tonnant

Pluton

Algesiras

Belleisle

Bahama

Swiftsure   Colossus

Monarca   Aigle

Nelson's lee division
attacks allied rear

Bellerophon

Prince   Dreadnought   Achille   Argonaute

San Juan de Nepomuceno   Montanes

San Ildefonso   Revenge   Argonauta

Thunderer   Achilles

Defiance   Principe de Asturias

Berwick   Polyphemus

Defence   Swiftsure

N

Wind

Above: *The Battle of Trafalgar, 21 October 1805. Second phase.*

Above: *A French frigate driven ashore in the storm following Trafalgar, c 22 October 1805, painted by Butterworth.*

lightness of the breeze, partly to the great number of ships, and partly to the inefficiency of many of the units of the fleet, the line was very imperfectly formed. Ships were not in their places, intervals were of irregular width, here vessels were not closed up, there two overlapped, one masking the other's fire. The general result was that, instead of a line, the allied order showed a curve of gradual sweep, convex toward the east. To the British approach from the west, therefore, it presented a disposition resembling a re-entrant angle; and Collingwood, noting with observant eye the advantage of this arrangement for a cross-fire, commented favorably upon it in his report of the battle. It was, however, the result of chance, not of intention, due, not to the talent of the chief, but to the want of skill in his subordinates.

The commander-in-chief of the allies, Villeneuve, was in the *Bucentaure*, an eighty-gun ship, the twelfth in order from the van of the line. Immediately ahead of him was the huge Spanish four-decker, the *Santisima Trinidad*, a Goliath among ships, which had now come forth to her last battle. Sixth behind the *Bucentaure*, and therefore eighteenth in the order, came a Spanish three-decker, the *Santa Ana*, flying the flag of Vice-Admiral Alava. These two admirals marked the right and left of the allied centre, and upon them, therefore, the British leaders respectively directed their course—Nelson upon the *Bucentaure*, Collingwood upon the *Santa Ana*.

The *Royal Sovereign* had recently been refitted, and with clean new copper easily outsailed her more worn followers. Thus it happened that, as Collingwood came within range, his ship, outstripping the others by three quarters of a mile, entered alone, and for twenty minutes endured, unsupported, the fire of all the hostile ships that could reach her. A proud deed, surely, but surely also not a deed to be commended as a pattern. The first shot of the battle was fired at her by the *Fougueux*, the next astern of the *Santa Ana*. This was just at noon, and with the opening guns the ships of both fleets hoisted their ensigns; the Spaniards also hanging large wooden crosses from their spanker booms.

The *Royal Sovereign* advanced in silence until, ten minutes later, she passed close under the stern of the *Santa Ana*. Then she fired a double-shotted broadside which struck down four hundred of the enemy's crew, and, luffing rapidly, took her position close alongside, the muzzles of the hostile guns nearly touching. Here the *Royal Sovereign* underwent the fire not only of her chief antagonist, but of four other ships; three of which belonged to the division of five that ought closely to have knit the *Santa Ana* to the *Bucentaure*, and so fixed an impassable barrier to the enemy seeking to pierce the centre. The fact shows strikingly the looseness of the allied order, these three being all in rear and to leeward of their proper stations.

For fifteen minutes the *Royal Sovereign* was the only British ship in close action. Then her next astern entered the battle, followed successively by the rest of the column. In rear of the *Santa Ana* were fifteen ships. Among these, Collingwood's vessels penetrated in various directions; chiefly, however, at first near the spot where his flag had led the way, enveloping and destroying in detail the enemy's centre and leading rear ships, and then passing on to subdue the rest. Much doubtless was determined by chance in such confusion and obscurity; but the original tactical plan insured an overwhelming concentration upon a limited portion of the enemy's order. This being subdued with the less loss, because so outnumbered, the intelligence and skill of the various British captains readily compassed the destruction of the dwindling remnant. Of the sixteen ships, including the *Santa Ana*, which composed the allied rear, twelve were taken or destroyed.

Above: *The death of Nelson as seen by A W Devis. The spot can be seen to this day on HMS* Victory.

Not till one o'clock, or nearly half an hour after the vessels next following Collingwood came into action, did the *Victory* reach the *Bucentaure*. The latter was raked with the same dire results that befell the *Santa Ana*; but a ship close to leeward blocked the way, and Nelson was not able to grapple with the enemy's commander-in-chief. The *Victory*, prevented from going through the line, fell on board the *Redoutable*, a French seventy-four, between which and herself a furious action followed—the two lying in close contact. At half-past one Nelson fell mortally wounded, the battle still raging fiercely.

The ship immediately following Nelson's came also into collision with the *Redoutable*, which thus found herself in combat with two antagonists. The next three of the British weather column each in succession raked the *Bucentaure*, complying thus with Nelson's order that every effort must be made to capture the enemy's commander-in-chief. Passing on, these three concentrated their efforts, first upon the *Bucentaure*, and next upon the *Santisima Trinidad*. Thus it happened that upon the allied commander-in-chief, upon his next ahead, and upon the ship which, though not his natural supporter astern, had sought and filled that honorable post—upon the key, in short, of the allied order—were combined under the most advantageous conditions the fires of five hostile vessels, three of them first-rates. Consequently, not only were the three added to the prizes, but also a great breach was made between the van and rear of the combined fleets. This breach became yet wider by the singular conduct of Villeneuve's proper next astern. Soon after the *Victory* came into action, that ship bore up out of the line, wore round, and stood toward the rear, followed by three others. This movement is attributed to a wish to succor the rear. If so, it was at best an indiscreet and ill-timed act, which finds little palliation in the fact that not one of these ships was taken.

Thus, two hours after the battle began, the allied fleet was cut in two, the rear enveloped and in process of being destroyed in detail, the *Bucentaure*, *Santisima Trinidad*, and *Redoutable* practically reduced, though not yet surrendered. Ahead of the *Santisima Trinidad* were ten ships, which as yet had not been engaged. The inaction of the van, though partly accounted for by the slackness of the wind, has given just cause for censure. To it, at ten minutes before two, Villeneuve made signal to get into action and to wear together. This was accomplished with

difficulty, owing to the heavy swell and want of wind. At three, however, all the ships were about, but by an extraordinary fatality they did not keep together. Five with Admiral Dumanoir stood along to windward of the battle, three passed to leeward of it, and two, keeping away, left the field entirely. Of the whole number, three were intercepted, raising the loss of the allies to eighteen ships-of-the-line taken, one of which caught fire and was burned. The approach of Admiral Dumanoir, if made an hour earlier, might have conduced to save Villeneuve; it was now too late. Exchanging a few distant broadsides with enemy's ships, he stood off to the southwest with four vessels; one of those at first with him having been cut off.

At quarter before five Admiral Gravina, whose ship had been the rear of the order during the battle and had lost heavily, retreated toward Cadiz, making signal to the vessels which had not struck to form around his flag. Five other Spanish ships and five French followed him. As he was withdrawing, the last two to resist of the allied fleet struck their colors.

During the night of the 21st these eleven ships anchored at the mouth of Cadiz harbor, which they could not then enter, on account of a land wind from southeast. At the same time the British and their prizes were being carried shoreward by the heavy swell which had prevailed during the battle; the light air blowing from the sea not enabling them to haul off. The situation was one of imminent peril. At midnight the wind freshened much, but fortunately hauled to the southward, whence it blew a gale all the 22nd. The ships got their heads to the westward and drew off shore, with thirteen of the prizes; the other four having had to anchor off Cape Trafalgar. That morning the *Bucentaure*, Villeneuve's late flag-ship was wrecked on some rocks off the entrance to Cadiz; and toward evening the *Redoutable*, that had so nobly supported her, was found to be sinking astern of the British ship that had her in tow. During the night of the 22nd she went down, with a hundred and fifty of her people still on board. On the 24th the same fate befell the great *Santisima Trinidad*, which had been the French admiral's next ahead. Thus his own ship and his two supports vanished from the seas.

For several days the wind continued violent from northwest and southwest. On the 23rd five of the ships that had escaped with Gravina put out, to cut off some of the prizes that were near the coast. They succeeded in taking two; but as these were battered to pieces, while three of the five rescuers were carried on the beach and wrecked with great loss of life, little advantage resulted from this well-meant and gallant sortie. Two other prizes were given up to their own crews by the British prize-masters, because the latter were not able with their scanty force to save them. These got into Cadiz. Of the remaining British prizes, all but four either went ashore or were destroyed by the orders of Collingwood, who despaired of saving them. No British ship was lost.

Of thirty-three combined French and Spanish ships which sailed out of Cadiz on the 20th of October, eleven, five French and six Spanish, mostly now disabled hulks, lay there at anchor on the last day of the month. The four that escaped to sea under Dumanoir fell in with a British squadron of the same size near Cape Ortegal, on the 4th of November, and were all taken. This raised the allied loss to twenty-two, two more than the twenty for which Nelson, in his dying hour, declared that he had bargained.

No attempt to move from Cadiz was again made by the shattered relics of the fight. On the 25th of October Rosily arrived and took up his now blasted command. Nearly three years later, when the Spanish monarchy, so long the sub-missive tool of the Directory and of Napoleon, had been overthrown by the latter, and the Spanish people had risen against the usurper, the five French ships were still in the port. Surprised between the British blockade and the now hostile batteries of the coast, Rosily, after an engagement of two days with the latter, surrendered his squadron, with the four thousand seamen then on board. This event occurred on the 14th of June, 1808. It was the last echo of Trafalgar.

Such, in its leading outlines and direct consequences, was the famous battle of Trafalgar. Its lasting significance and far-reaching results have been well stated by a recent historian, more keenly alive than most of his fellows to the paramount, though silent, influence of Sea Power upon the course of events: 'Trafalgar was not only the greatest naval victory, it was the greatest and most momentous victory won either by land or by sea during the whole of the Revolutionary War. No victory, and no series of victories, of Napoleon produced the same effect upon Europe. . . . A generation passed after Trafalgar before France again seriously threatened England at sea. The prospect of crushing the British navy, so long as England had the means to equip the navy, vanished. Napoleon henceforth set his hopes on exhausting England's resources, by compelling every state on the Continent to exclude her commerce. Trafalgar forced him to impose his yoke upon *all* Europe, or to abandon the hope of conquering Great Britain. . . . Nelson's last triumph left England in such a position that no means remained to injure her but those which *must result in the ultimate deliverance of the Continent.*'

These words may be accepted with very slight modification. Napoleon's scheme for the invasion of Great Britain, thwarted once and again by the strategic difficulties attendant upon its execution, was finally frustrated when Villeneuve gave up the attempt to reach Brest and headed for Cadiz. On the part of the allies Trafalgar was, in itself, a useless holocaust, precipitated in the end by the despair of the unfortunate admiral, upon whose irresolution Napoleon not unjustly visited the anger caused by the wreck of his plans. Villeneuve was perfectly clear-sighted and right in his appreciation of the deficiencies of his command— of the many chances against success. Where he wretchedly failed was in not recognizing the simple duty of obedience—the obligation to persist at all hazards in the part of a great scheme as-signed to him, even though it led to the destruction of his whole

Above: *Greenwich pensioners celebrating the news of Trafalgar on Observatory Hill. Public rejoicing was tempered by genuine grief at the loss of Nelson, who had a remarkable way of endearing himself to everyone, despite his faults.*

force. Had he, upon leaving Ferrol, been visited by a little of the desperation which brought him to Trafalgar, the invasion of England might possibly—not probably—have been effected.

An event so striking as the battle of Trafalgar becomes, however, to mankind the symbol of all the circumstances— more important, perhaps, but less obvious—which culminate in it. In this sense it may be said that Trafalgar was the cause—as it certainly marked the period—of Napoleon's resolution to crush Great Britain by excluding her commerce from the Continent. Here, therefore, the story of the influence of Sea Power upon this great conflict ceases to follow the strictly naval events, and becomes concerned simply with commerce-destroying, ordin-arily a secondary operation of maritime war, but exalted in the later years of Napoleon's reign to be the principal, if not the sole, means of action.

Right: *Pocock's view of the final phase of the battle, just before 1630 hours. Firing then died away and it was noted in the Victory's log that Nelson died of his wound. The most momentous naval victory in the history of the world was over, guaranteeing Great Britain another century of peace and unparalleled prosperity.*

Index

Numbers in italics refer to illustrations

Acknowledgments

The publisher would like to thank the following organizations and individuals for supplying pictures. The National Maritime Museum, Greenwich, provided all the pictures, except:

BBC Hulton Picture Library: 204, 227 (top right), 239 (bottom right), 242, 247.

J E Bulloz: 115 (top left), 162, 184, 190, 200 (bottom right), 216 (left), 236 (top left).

Cooper-Bridgeman Library: 2-3 (The Guildhall), 32 (National Maritime Museum), 113 (British Museum), 116 (top) (British Museum), 193 (top) (National Maritime Museum), 196-97 (bottom) (The Guildhall), 201 (bottom) (Portsmouth City Art Gallery), 205 (top right) (National Maritime Museum), 205 (bottom) (Bristol City Art Gallery), 216 (right) (National Maritime Museum).

Costa Fotografo: 25, 28-29, 80, 95, 104-105, 175.

Mary Evans Picture Library: 14, 15, 17, 35 (right), 36, 39, 50, 51 (left), 54 (top), 55 (bottom), 57 (right), 69, 94 (top), 101 (top), 112 (top), 116 (top right), 127, 128 (top right), 134 (top), 136-37 (main), 143 (middle left and bottom), 146 (top left), 147 (left), 153 (top), 154 (top right and left), 160 (bottom), 165 (top), 166 (top), 167, 180 (right), 189, 195, 199, 207, 221 (top right), 226 (top), 227 (top left), 231 (top left), 236 (top center), 238 (bottom), 239 (bottom left).

Mansell Collection: 12, 54 (bottom), 55 (top), 221 (bottom).

Musée de la Marine: 46-47, 100 (top), 112 (bottom), 125 (top left).

Peter Newark's Western Americana: 62-63, 65, 159 (top right), 169, 171 (bottom), 200 (bottom left), 205 (top left), 140 (right).

Parker Gallery: 23 (top), 24 (bottom), 40, 48 (left), 61 (right), 75, 88, 96, 107, 108 (top), 114 (top), 115 (top right), 116 (bottom), 117 (bottom), 119 (bottom left), 121 (top), 122 (top), 126 (bottom), 128 (bottom), 132, 139 (top left), 141 (bottom), 143 (top), 146 (top right and bottom), 147 (right), 148, 149 (bottom), 156, 160 (top left and center), 164 (top), 174 (bottom), 176 (bottom), 177, 179 (bottom), 188 (right), 191 (top), 203 (right), 210 (bottom), 211 (center and bottom), 213 (top right), 214-15, 218 (bottom), 219, 223 (bottom left and right), 225 (top), 227 (bottom right), 228, 231 (bottom left), 240 (top left), 241 (top right), 248, 249.

Scala: 42 (bottom).

Science Museum, London: 4-5, 16, 18, 19, 23 (bottom), 26, 27, 37 (top and center), 44-45, 52 (left), 60, 61 (left), 73 (top), 74, 124, 125 (top right and bottom), 152, 153 (bottom), 202, 206.

US Navy: 7, 9, 141 (top), 158-59 (except top right), 163, 172.